THE AMERICAN ALPINE JOURNAL

2016

[Front Cover] Link Sar West, Pakistan, with K6 in the background (see p.303). *Andy Houseman*
[This page] Billy Brown climbs a gargoyle on pitch 13 (5.12b) of Time is the Master, Acopán Tepui, Venezuela (see p.194). *Eric Bissell*

2016   VOLUME 58 ISSUE 90

CONTENTS

RECON

[Photo] **Will Sim** enduring a cold night and destroyed camp below the northwest face of Mt. Deborah, Hayes Range, Alaska (see p.153). *Jonathan Griffith*

CLIMBS & EXPEDITIONS

The American Alpine Journal, 710 Tenth St. Suite 100, Golden, Colorado 80401
Telephone: (303) 384-0110 Fax: (303) 384-0111
E-mail: aaj@americanalpineclub.org
www.publications.americanalpineclub.org

ISSN: 0065-6925
ISBN: 978-1-933056-91-3
ISBN: (hardcover edition): 978-1-933056-92-0

[Photo] The Titan as seen from the Netherworld, between the Fisher Towers and the Mystery Towers (see p.124). *Joe Forrester*

Photo: Jon Glassberg of Louder Than Eleven

THE EVOLUTION OF ULTRALIGHT

Black Diamond Ambassador Tommy Caldwell climbs with the all-new Camalot™ Ultralight, now 25% lighter.

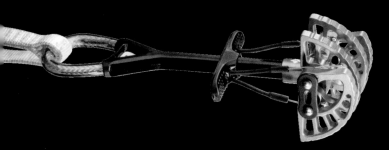

◆ **Black Diamond**®

BlackDiamondEquipment.com

FRIENDS OF THE AAJ

[Photo] Skiy DeTray revels in his position atop a precarious snow mushroom on the east face of the Mooses Tooth, Alaska (see p.147). *Alik Berg*

GREAT RANGES FELLOWSHIP

[EIGER]

Nicole Alger & Zachary Karabell
Malinda & Yvon Chouinard
Wes Edens
Timothy Forbes
Clark Gerhardt
Todd Hoffman

Lou Kasischke
Craig McKibben
Allen Miner
Mark & Teresa Richey
Carey Roberts
Jim Simons

Cody J Smith
The Spitzer Family Foundation
Doug & Maggie Walker
Anonymous (2)

[ALPAMAYO]

Patti Casey
Jeffrey R. Cohen
Maryclaire & Jim Collis
Kit & Rob DesLauriers
Philip Duff
Charles & Lisa Fleischman
Gerald E. Gallwas
Eric Green

Rocky & Laura Henderson
Stephen Hindy
Bradley Hoffman
Phil Lakin Jr.
David Landman
George Lowe III
Shelly Malkin
Peter Metcalf

James Morrissey
Vanessa O'Brien
Steve Schwartz
William Sheil
Barbara & Bill Straka
Geoff Unger
Finn Wentworth

[ROBSON]

Warren Adelman
Penn Burris
Bruce Carroll
John Catto
Eric Christu
Christopher Croft
James Crosslin
William Davis
James & Cheryl Duckworth
Kevin Duncan
Alexander Eaton
Jim & Michelle Edwards
Greg Engelman
Philip Erard
Gary Evans
Jim Frush

Chris Gay
Marilyn Geninatti
Neil Gleichman
David Goeddel
Jeffrey Hall
Robert B. Hall
Roger Hartl
Sandy Hill
Richard Hoffman
Denny Hogan
Robert Horton
Robert Hyman & Deborah Atwood
Thomas Janson
Paul Morrow
Karla Pifer

Paul Rose
Charles Sassara
Stewart Sayah
Ulrika & Mark Schumacher
Stephen Scofield
A.C. Sherpa
Theodore Streibert
Robert Strode
Lewis Surdam
Joshua Swidler
David Thoenen
Pete Thompson
Jack & Sasha Tracy
Lawrence True & Linda Brown
Robert Wilson

[TEEWINOT]

Lisa Abbott
Robert Anderson
Jon Anderson
Melissa Arnot
Joseph Ashkar
James Balog
Gail Bates
Vaclav Benes
Brook Bennett
Tanya Bradby & Martin Slovacek
Wesley Brown
Deanne Buck
William Burd
David Burton
Betsy Cabot
Dan Cohen
Kevin Cooney
Matt & Charlotte Culberson
Rupert Dance
John Davidge III
Joseph Davidson
Scott Davis
Ed Diffendal

Jesse Dwyer
Bill Egger
Ken Ehrhart
Lee Elman
Dan Emmett
Terrence English
Marc Evankow
Todd Fairbairn
Chas Fisher
Chris Flowers
Charlotte Fox
James Frank
Ellen Gallant
James & Franziska Garrett
Frank Gould
Wayne & Cynthia Griffin
John Hebert
Christopher Heintz
Peter Helmetag
Michael Hodges
Marley Hodgson
Thomas Hornbein M.D.
Michael Hornsby
Tony Horton

Bradford Johnston
Rodney Korich
Misha Logvinov
Chris Lynch
Garrett Madison
Brent Manning
George McCown
Gary McElvany
Garry Menzel
Doris & Charlie Michaels
Hacksaw Morris
David Morton
Bob Palais
Alan Peterson
Louis Reichardt
John Reppy
Wolf Riehle
Michael Riley
Joel Robinson
Darren Rogers
Jeb Sanford
Janet Schlindwein
Stephen Scofield
George Shaw

John Sheu
Fred Simmons
Jay Smith
De Snook
Vincent Starzinger
John Stauffer
Oliver Stauffer
Robert & Jennifer Stephenson
Duncan Stuart
Steven Swenson
Thomas Taplin
John Townsend
Ronald Ulrich
Dieter Von Hennig
Roger Walker
Mark Wilford
Warren Wilhide
Todd Winzenried
Steve Wunsch
Rob Ziegler
Anonymous (2)

THE AMERICAN ALPINE JOURNAL

EXECUTIVE EDITOR
Dougald MacDonald

SENIOR EDITOR
Lindsay Griffin

ASSISTANT EDITOR
Erik Rieger

ART DIRECTOR
Erik Rieger

CONTRIBUTING EDITORS
James Benoit, *In Memoriam*
David Stevenson, *Book Reviews*

ILLUSTRATIONS AND MAPS
Glen Boles, Emilie Lee

PROOFREADERS
Rolando Garibotti, Clark Gerhardt, Damien Gildea, Bruce Normand, Joel Peach, Katie Sauter

INDEXERS
Ralph Ferrara, Eve Tallman

TRANSLATORS
Vittorio Bedogni, Elena Dmitrenko, Anna Piunova, Todd Miller, Alexander von Ungern

REGIONAL CONTACTS
Steve Gruhn, Mark Westman, *Alaska*; Sevi Bohorquez, Sergio Ramirez Carrascal, *Peru*; Luis Pardo, *Colombia*, Damien Gildea, *Antarctica*; Rolando Garibotti, Marcelo Scanu, *Argentina-Chile*; Alex von Ungern, *Bolivia*; Geoff Hornby, *Middle East*; Harish Kapadia, Nandini Purandare, *India*; Rodolphe Popier, Richard Salisbury, *Nepal*; Tamotsu Nakamura, Hiroshi Hagiwara, *Japan*; Peter Jensen-Choi, Oh Young-hoon, *Korea*; Elena Dmitrenko, Anna Piunova, *Russia, Tajikistan, and Kyrgyzstan*; Xia Zhongming, *China*

ADVISORY BOARD
Andrew Bisharat, Kelly Cordes, Damien Gildea, Colin Haley, Mark Richey, Freddie Wilkinson, Emily Stifler Wolfe

WITH HEARTFELT THANKS TO...
Fred Beckey, Megan Bond, Eddie Espinosa, Claude Gardien, Steve Gruhn, Dave O'Leske, Jonathan Thesenga, Keegan Young, and all of our generous donors, authors, and photographers

THE AMERICAN ALPINE CLUB

OFFICIALS FOR THE YEAR 2016

EXECUTIVE DIRECTOR/CEO
Phil Powers

EXECUTIVE COMMITTEE

Honorary President
James P. McCarthy

Honorary Treasurer
Theodore (Sam) Streibert

President
Matt Culberson

Vice President
Clark Gerhardt

Secretary
Deanne Buck

Treasurer
Phil Lakin

[DIRECTORS]

Term Ending 2017
Janet Wilkinson
Kit DesLauriers

Term Ending 2018
Mia Axon
Stacy Bare
Brad Brooks
Mark Butler
Ken Ehrhart
Chas Fisher
John Heilprin
Lauren Sigman

Term Ending 2019
Philip Duff
Kevin Duncan
Chuck Fleischman
Peter Metcalf
Carey Roberts
Vik Sahney

PREFACE

LOCAL HEROES

IN RECENT YEARS we have noticed an exciting trend in the *AAJ*: a steady increase in the number of significant new routes by climbers native to developing countries. For generations, most cutting-edge climbs in developing countries have been completed by visitors from Europe, North America, Japan, or other well-off areas with long mountaineering traditions. Local climbers often partnered with these visiting mountaineers—one only has to mention Tenzing Norgay—but usually these were employer/employee relationships.

There are precedents for "locals" climbing big routes in their own countries, of course, including a long history of Indian mountaineering and the brilliant second ascent of Fitz Roy, by a new route, in 1965, by Argentines Carlos Comesaña and José Luis Fonrouge. But the growing number and scope of recent climbs is unprecedented.

In this year's *AAJ* you will find many reports of excellent climbs by all-local teams: a bold high traverse in Bolivia, numerous first ascents in Colombia, several high peaks in Nepal by all-Sherpa teams, exploratory mountaineering in Argentina and Chile, a solo big wall in China, and the list goes on. We also have reports of native alpinists doing significant climbs with visiting climbers—but as equal partners, not as porters or rope-fixers. One reason for this: The ranks of internationally certified guides in developing countries such as Bolivia, Peru, and Nepal now number in the dozens, and Ecuador and Kyrgyzstan are on their way to full IFMGA membership. Increasingly, these guides are using days off to explore their own mountains for new routes.

We've also witnessed some tragic deaths and near misses among ambitious climbers in developing countries. One hopes such mountaineers will be patient with the long apprenticeship necessary to survive and flourish in the alpine environment. As these climbers gain experience, their desire to push their limits, along with access to better equipment and the opportunity to respond quickly when a climb is in good condition—especially as climate change alters traditional climbing seasons—should lead to many marvelous ascents in the coming years. We look forward to reporting them.

THIS YEAR WE HAVE STOPPED publishing the Club Activities section of the *AAJ*, which reported on the climbs and other activities of regional mountaineering clubs and the AAC's local sections. These activities are now much more thoroughly and promptly covered by other online and print publications. Since the beginning, Club Activities has been edited by our longest-servicing volunteer, Frederick O. Johnson, a California climber who was recruited to manage this section of the *AAJ* by then-editor Francis Farquhar, way back in 1956. Six decades later, Johnson said, "It's been a rewarding, long run for me, with the chance to do a small part for the Club, of which I've been a minor but enthusiastic member since 1950." Thank you, Fred!

— DOUGALD MACDONALD, *EXECUTIVE EDITOR*

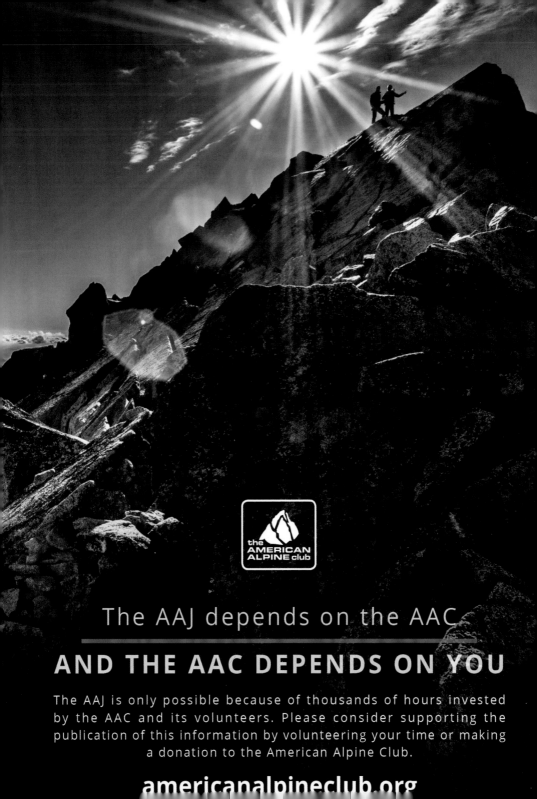

HIGHER POWERED

THE FIRST ASCENT OF TALUNG'S COVETED NORTHERN PILLAR

NIKITA BALABANOV & MIKHAIL FOMIN

Ever since we first saw photos of Talung's north wall, this mountain had been very much on our minds. There is no doubt the north-northwest pillar of Talung (7,349 meters) was one of the most aesthetic and logical unclimbed lines anywhere in the Himalaya. The spur's pure beauty, technical difficulty, and relatively safe appearance inspired every climber who saw it. But despite several attempts, starting in 2002, no one had climbed the direct route.

After completing a difficult new line on the northwest face of Langshisa Ri (6,412 meters) in Nepal, in the fall of 2014, both of us felt confident we could climb more technical terrain at a higher altitude. We hoped to return to Nepal in the following post-monsoon season. After the earthquakes in April, we decided to look for an objective in the Indian Himalaya instead. We soon realized, however, that we didn't have enough time to navigate the Indian bureaucracy and get a permit, and so our attention switched back to Nepal. Quick research showed the Kangchenjunga region hadn't been impacted much by the earthquakes. Now there was no doubt which mountain we would try to climb.

Once in Nepal, our motivation for Talung only grew—in part because we had to spend so many days without climbing! After we'd finally prepared everything in Kathmandu, our bus was blocked by strikes for 24 hours on the way to Taplejung, where our trek would begin. During the approach, we were bogged down in the late-monsoon rains and we fed numerous leeches. Finally, on September 28, we established base camp at Oktang, above Ramche, and began two weeks of acclimatization. We climbed Boktoh and slept on its 6,114-meter summit. Then we headed up the western slopes of Talung (our planned descent route), but it took a long time to find a safe and non-technical route above 7,000 meters. Eventually we reached 7,100 meters and bivouacked there.

During these first two weeks in the area, we made three round trips up the 15-kilometer length of the Yalung Glacier. Each way required a day and a half of trekking through wild moraine and rough ice in high-altitude boots. (The nine days of glacier trekking nearly destroyed our boots.) When we were ready at last to climb, a month after our departure from Ukraine, it was like a New Year's gift for the kids.

Advanced base was right under Talung's north-northwest spur. We had already checked out the line at the start of our acclimatization phase, and it looked impressive—like mixed climbing in Chamonix, but mostly above 6,000 meters, and we would have heavy packs. We planned to carry food for seven days and fuel for nine.

The very first pitch above the bergschrund, at 5,600 meters, is one of the cruxes of the

[Counterclockwise from top left] **Nikita Balabanov and Mikhail Fomin after the climb. The route starts with a bang: VI+ A3 M6 straight off the bergschrund.** *Balabanov-Fomin Collection*

route. It is really impressive: You begin climbing a thin snow and ice pillar that stands like a stalagmite above the 'schrund. From this you step onto the face and climb hard, vertical mixed terrain (M6). This leads to a rock overhang dripping with icicles. You have to switch to tough aid climbing (about 10 meters of A3) using beaks and thin pitons—the only crack is so thin you can't fit the picks of your ice tools into it. Above the overhang you have to climb about eight meters on thin ice over rock slabs without any chance of protection, until you reach a hanging belay on beaks in thin cracks on the right wall of the chimney.

After such a start, we understood the mountain wouldn't be giving us a rest anywhere on the lower buttress.

The next three days were full of hard mixed and ice climbing, mainly M5 but with some pitches up to M6 and AI6. Often we had thin, super-delicate ice with long runouts. Some pitches were rock slabs covered with steep, unconsolidated snow, which sometimes took more time than the hard mixed terrain. Although the granite on the route was nearly always good, it was very compact with few cracks for protection. Beaks and Peckers (three or four per pitch)

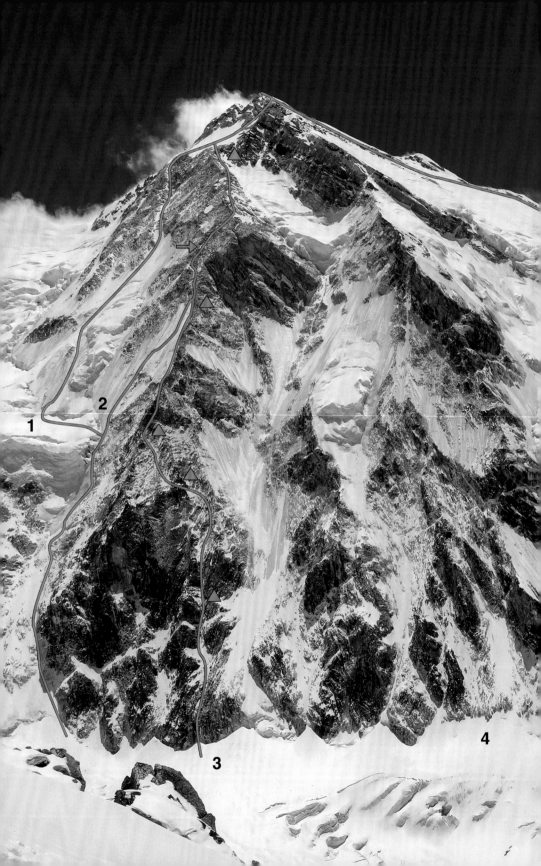

[Photo] Talung from the northwest. (1) Holecek-Hruby (2013). (2) Italian attempt (2014, arrow marks high point. (3) Balabanov-Fomin (2015). (4) Unclimbed northwest buttress. (5) Linder-Nindra (1964, first ascent and standard descent route). Photo taken in spring 2014. The face had more snow coverage during the successful post-monsoon ascents in 2013 and 2015. *Giampaolo Corona*

5

TALUNG (7,349M) CLIMBING HISTORY

1920 — 1963	British reconnaissance and attempts, reaching as high as 7,120m
1963	Japanese attempt
1964	First ascent of Talung by west-southwest face. Franz Linder (Austria) and Tenzing Nindra (Nepal)
1991	New route on west face. Marko Prezelj and Andrej Stremfelj (who stopped below south ridge), both from Slovenia
2002	First attempt on north-northwest pillar, reaching 5,900m. Alena Cepelkova and Petr Kolouch (Czech)
2004	Attempt on north-northwest pillar, reaching 5,900m. Marek Holecek and Tomas Rinn (Czech)
2013	First ascent of northwest face. Marek Holecek and Zdenek Hruby (Czech)
2014	Pre-monsoon attempt on north-northwest pillar, reaching over 6,600m. Daniele Bernasconi, Giampaolo Corona, and Mario Panzeri (Italy). *See Climbs & Expeditions.*
2015	First ascent of north-northwest pillar. Nikita Balabanov and Mikhail Fomin (Ukraine).

Steep ice on the lower buttress, headed for the first bivy on the face. *Balabanov-Fomin Collection*

were our primary pro. We were the only climbers in the area that autumn, and knowing that we were completely alone made all our actions more deliberate and all our emotions much more memorable.

Yet despite the technical and psychological difficulties, each of us got great pleasure from the climbing. We changed leaders each day, and the one seconding with the heavy pack was always looking forward to his turn to lead. The unexpected pleasure of high-quality technical climbing overshadowed our anxieties.

We ended each day in darkness, building a site for our small Firstlight tent. It took us nearly two hours every evening to chop a ledge big enough to get in the tent without a chance of slipping off during the night.

On the third day we reached the crest of the north-northwest spur. We had hoped to outflank a huge gendarme on its left side, but that was not possible, and therefore we were forced to climb two more pitches on the right side of the spur. Horrible vertical, unconsolidated snow led up rock slabs to a totally dry corner. Here we found another crux, with 10 to 15 meters of aid climbing (A3) and hard mixed. The middle of the corner was full of loose blocks, and the top was overhanging.

The corner continued with another pitch of hard mixed. We didn't have big enough cams to protect the wide crack in the back of the corner, so sometimes we had to stretch far to either side to find pro. The upper corner was covered with unconsolidated powder snow, also without good protection. At the top of this 100-meter corner, the door was open to the upper spur.

Now the angle was easier, but protection remained difficult to find in the unconsolidated snow. We simul-climbed several ice and névé pitches, and we found several more mixed sections with quite demanding climbing (mainly M4 but also one pitch up to M6), thankfully with good cracks.

On the fifth day we climbed the upper rock band, which had been the main question mark of the whole route—from the glacier it's impossible to see what waits for you there. What awaited was quite difficult mixed climbing and more thin ice on rocky slabs. But anticipating the end of the technical climbing gave us new power and speed, and in the evening we finally reached the ice ramp leading up and right to the summit ridge. Here we chopped a ledge for our fifth night on the wall.

On October 23 we climbed the ramp and simul-climbed up the ridge, and at 2 p.m. we were standing on the summit of Talung. We had climbed to the top in thick fog, but after 10 minutes on the summit a strong wind blew it all away, and the views were like a dream—the east face of Jannu and the south side of Kangchenjunga were close at hand. We made some photos and a video panorama, ate some traditional summit chocolate (and non-traditional ice creams of totally frozen energy gels), and in half an hour started our descent. That day we went down the western slopes to 6,700 meters and bivied there, and on the seventh day we descended all the way to the glacier.

For both of us, this route showed not only how much we still have to learn in the Himalaya but also how much we can do. Each of us lost 10 to 15 kilograms during the ascent, but the experience and huge motivational charge at the end were totally worth it. We named our route Daddy Higher Power [Папа Высшая Сила, also translated as Daddy Magnum Force]. Every time we ran into trouble on our way to base camp and during acclimatization, we recalled a favorite phrase of one of our friends: "Guys, Daddy Higher Power always takes care of his Jedis—this is just a little test to see whether you are persistent enough for the main objective." On the summit we felt like we'd earned a reward from Daddy Higher Power. We had definitely been quite persistent.

SUMMARY: First ascent of the north-northwest spur of Talung (7,349 meters) by Nikita Balabanov and Mikhail Fomin (Ukraine), October 18–24, 2015. The 1,700-meter route was graded ED2 AI6 M6 A3. The two men spent five and a half days on the route and a day and a half descending the western slopes.

ABOUT THE AUTHORS: *Nikita Balabanov, 26, works in an outdoor shop, and Mikhail Fomin, 34, works in information technology, both in Kiev, Ukraine. The two men did their first Himalayan climb in 2014, completing a new route on Langshisha Ri with Viacheslav Polezhaiko (AAJ 2015).*

Translated from Russian by Anna Piunova / Mountain.ru.

Pitch 21, at 6,200 meters, above the third bivy site: A3 and hard mixed. *Balabanov-Fomin Collection*

THE SPARROW AND THE PIGEON

TWO NEW ROUTES IN EASTERN KISHTWAR, INDIA

URBAN NOVAK

The 1,200-meter east face of Cerro Kishtwar is bathed in morning sun and plastered with ice and snow. As we approach the base, the wall grows and grows. It looks steep. It looks hard. Even though we had all agreed to try an inspiring line through the middle of the face, it's hard to keep our focus. Just to the left, another line appears to offer a higher probability of success. In Slovenia we have a saying: "It's better to have a sparrow in the hands than a pigeon on the roof." It's hard not to think of the sparrow to our left.

Marko senses our hesitation. He knows this is a turning point. He understands the pressure of potential failure—but what kind of failure are we hoping to avoid? Choosing the alternate route might increase our chances standing on the summit we've dreamed about for more than a year. But it also might mean we'd failed to give the mountain our best. Marko steps to the front and starts breaking trail directly toward the face. Straight toward the pigeon. The rest of us follow in his tracks.

IN THE FALL OF 2014, during an ascent of Hagshu in eastern Kishtwar, Marko Prezelj looked to the southeast and took a picture of an exceptional group of mountains. Among them, the black pyramid of Cerro Kishtwar (6,173 meters) stood out: a stunning fang of icy granite.

Before Kashmir was officially closed to foreigners, in 1993, British mountaineers were most active in the area. Before they gathered the courage and tried to climb Cerro Kishtwar, they summited the nearby peaks. In 1983, Stephen Venables and Dick Renshaw climbed the north face of Kishtwar Shivling (5,935 meters) in pure alpine style. In 1988, Roger Everett and Simon Richardson made the first ascent of Chomochior (6,278 meters) along the west ridge.

The first to stand below the northwest face of Cerro Kishtwar were Mick Fowler and Mike Morrison. In 1989, however, they could only inspect possible routes of ascent. The first real attempt to climb this mountain was made in 1991 by Brendan Murphy and Andy Perkins. They chose a visionary route up the middle of the northwest face and managed to climb to within 100

Photo) The author greets the dawn at the summit of Cerro Kishtwar after three long days of climbing. Behind is Kishtwar Kailash (6,451m), first climbed in 2013. *Marko Prezelj*

[Above] Cerro Kishtwar (6,173m, left) and Chomochior (6,278m), showing the 2015 climbs. *Mick Fowler*
[Below] Eastern Kishtwar mountains. (A) Arjuna. (B) Spear. (C) Maha Dev Phobrang. (D) Tupendeo. (E) Kishtwar Shivling. (F) Hagshu. (G) Shiepra. (H). Lahara. (I) Chomochior. (J) Cerro Kishtwar. (K) White Sapphire. (BC) Base camp. (L) Manasuna. (M) Kishtwar Kailash. (N) Gupta. *© Mapbox, © OpenStreetMap*

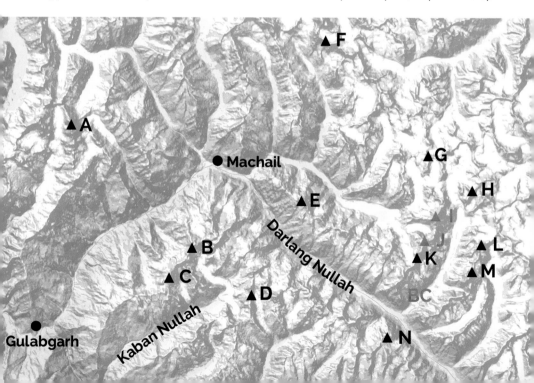

meters of the summit. They were climbing in capsule style and spent 17 days on the wall.

In 1993, Fowler returned to the mountain with Stephen Sustad. They chose a system of ice runnels in the left part of the northwest face. Their route leads to a notch on the north ridge, and from there the British continued along the northeast face to the north peak. The neighboring south peak appeared to higher, and so of course they traversed to that summit as well.

No other climbers obtained a permit to visit eastern Kashmir until 2011. That year, the Swiss Denis Burdet and Stephan Siegrist, the Austrian David Lama, and the American Robert Frost climbed a new mixed route on the right side of the northwest face of Cerro Kishtwar, leading to the south peak.

All of these ascents and attempts on Cerro Kishtwar were made from the Haptal Glacier, on the west side of the mountain. The eastern sides of these peaks have not seen a lot of visits from alpinists. However, in 2013, Fowler and Paul Ramsden entered the Chomochior Valley and did the first ascent of Kishtwar Kailash (6,451m) by its southwest face. Mick's striking photo of Cerro Kishtwar and the neighboring Chomochior, taken from high on Kishtwar Kailash, added to Marko's enthusiasm about the region, and convinced four of us to meet in Delhi on October 10: Marko and I from Slovenia, Hayden Kennedy from the USA, and Manu Pellissier from France.

[Top] The scary drive to Gulabgarh, start of the approach trek. [Bottom] Base camp at 3,900m. *Urban Novak (both)*

STARTING IN MANALI, we spend two days driving along a picturesque but extremely exposed road to the town of Gulabgarh, where we start a four-day trek to base camp. The first two days follow a quite populated trail toward the village of Machail, where a famous Hindu temple stands. The rest of the hike to base camp leads through the exceptionally colorful Darlang Nullah valley, where there are no permanent settlements, only occasional huts used by shepherds during the summer months. In addition to outstanding natural scenery, the eastern Kishtwar region is also interesting from a cultural point of view, since three religions interweave here: Buddhism from the north, Hinduism from the east, and Muslim culture from the west.

We put base camp at 3,900 meters, at the mouth of the Chomochior Valley, directly below a beautiful granite crag. Unfortunately our mules—or more precisely their guides—cannot find a way over the last moraine. Thus our first acclimatization effort is doing the work of mules and carrying equipment for the final half an hour to base camp.

After a day of rest we begin to explore access through the eastern foothills of Cerro Kishtwar and Chomochior. A three-hour, fairly unpleasant hike up the valley brings us to a site for ABC on a small sand dune in the middle of a rock-covered glacier. Before an expected deterioration in the weather, we examine the possible lines on Chomochior and Cerro Kishtwar. There is very little snow and ice on the faces, especially the lower halves, which are completely dry. In anticipation of an improvement in snow conditions after the predicted storm, we return to camp, where it rains and snows for three days. The deluge floods our camp, and Manu is soon homeless. We dig drains and build dikes to protect the rest of our camp from the worst of the flooding.

By September 26 the situation in the mountains and in our heads has stabilized to the extent that we are ready to attempt Chomochior. We head back up to ABC, where we are greeted by a broken tent and wet equipment. With a little improvisation, following the example of MacGyver, the idol from my youth, we manage to reconstruct the tent's broken poles and dry our wet equipment. Unfortunately, due to chest pain, Manu decides to descend to base camp, accompanied by our guide Bagwal and cook's assistant Betoo, who had helped to carry the equipment to the ABC that day.

Our ascent of Chomochior will not be merely for acclimatization. In addition to acquiring a sufficient number of red blood cells, we aim to prepare psychologically for the greater difficulties we anticipate on Cerro Kishtwar. The mind that is prepared to deal with the current circumstances and environment will—when this is significant and necessary—push a tired body forward. Anxiously awaiting what the next day would bring, we go to bed that evening under a gentle snowfall and wake to a quiet, clear morning.

From ABC we break trail through deep snow, moving slower than expected, and establish our first bivouac after excavating a flat spot on the broad saddle between Cerro Kishtwar and Chomochior. Once again we go to sleep in falling snow and wake to a cold, lovely sunrise—some photography from this impressive vantage delays our departure. From the saddle we move together along the south ridge of Chomochior. Higher, the ridge becomes exposed and in places technically demanding, requiring occasional belays and three short abseils to bypass sharp gendarmes.

By evening we have climbed to the end of the snow-covered rocky ridge, and we set up a second bivouac at a height of about 5,900 meters. The next morning we set off toward the peak without any bivy equipment, reaching the top around 11 a.m. Throughout the climb, we excitedly admire the outstanding views of nearby peaks, dominated by nearby Cerro Kishtwar. The mountain's spectacular shape ripens our powerful desire to climb it.

DURING OUR DAYS ON CHOMOCHIOR, we all wondered how our friend Manu was doing, and we are extremely happy when he hikes out from base camp to meet us. His chest pain had disappeared after two days, and while we were climbing Manu did not just sit in camp; together with Bagwal and Betoo, he made acclimatization ascents on two 5,000ers above base

[Above] Traversing the south ridge of Chomochior during the second day of the ascent. *Urban Novak*
[Below] Approaching the awe-inspiring east face of Cerro Kishtwar. Near the foot of the 1,200-meter wall the team vacillated, wondering whether to try an easier-looking line to the left, but eventually they forged directly up the rock wall. *Urban Novak*

camp. Now, he too is ready for our main goal—in fact, since he had been deprived of climbing Chomochior, his motivation is even greater. He describes himself as a bullet eager to be shot.

Initially, we had quite seriously examined the northeast face of Cerro Kishtwar, which appeared to offer a number of possible lines. But the view from Chomochior had revealed fresh deep snow covering this shadowy face. The alternative was the east face, steeper and sunnier than its neighbor.

Following three days of rest, on October 4 we head back to ABC, where we prepare our equipment. In the afternoon we continue the approach under the east face of Cerro Kishtwar in cloudy weather and a light whirl of snowflakes. We set up two small tents under the face, and during the night the snowfall subsides.

In the morning we begin the two-hour final approach to the face. The days of uncertainty ahead and the technically challenging wall above weigh upon us—at least on the somewhat younger and less experienced members of the team. We start to shift our gaze toward the left, where a prominent couloir suggests a more feasible route—the sparrow in our hands. In these moments of doubt and hesitation, Marko showcases why he is what he is in alpinism. Some positive provocation and motivational insults are enough to erase our doubts, and we redirect our attention solely on our intended route, the fat pigeon on the roof.

The first day is mainly rock climbing. The difficult terrain and evening snowfall do not allow us to progress quickly, but we are not concerned with speed. We climb one pitch at a time, unburdened by the final result. In the evening, a couple of us complete another two rocky pitches while the others dig a narrow ledge in the snow for our two little tents. The night is "comfortable" and the sky is clear.

After warming up by ascending the two ropes we'd fixed the previous evening, we begin

Hayden Kennedy leads steep rock during the first day on Cerro Kishtwar. "We climb one pitch at a time, unburdened by the final result." *Urban Novak*

Morning at the open bivouac on the third day of the climb. The climbers didn't get into their sleeping bags until 2 a.m. the previous night. *Marko Prezelj*

the most uncertain part of the route. Steep ice softened and corroded by sun brings us to a four-pitch ramp of hard ice. The ramp runs into a branched system of corners. About halfway up these, amid steep ice and mixed terrain, we are caught by nightfall. In the darkness we were utterly unable to find a suitable place for a bivouac, so we keep climbing long into the night. At 2 a.m., after gaining about 600 meters of elevation, we crawl into our sleeping bags on a small ledge chopped into steep snow. It's impossible to set up the tents, so this night is a little less comfortable, but at least it is short. Manu is the happiest when the day dawns clear, because he has brought only a super-light sleeping bag, best suited for summer camping by the seashore.

A wide crack and a chimney with steep ice bring us to a point where the route becomes less clear. The exit chimney on the left is not what we'd hoped: It appears to involve two difficult pitches, where we probably would need to employ some aid. We are not thrilled by this possibility. A diagonal traverse toward the right would lead onto the northeast face, where we know there is a lot of unpacked snow. In the end it's Hayden's call—he is in the lead at the time. Soon he is building an anchor on the snow-covered northeast face. When we climb into view, he shrugs and says, "I don't know if this goes."

"Give me the gear!" Marko responds. After 30 meters of complex slabs, covered with piles of fresh snow, Marko looks back and gives us a thumbs-up. We just laugh. The way ahead is still not easy—powder snow covers the steep rock at the top of the face, ensuring the climbing will continue far into the night. But at least there is a way. Our last anchor is in rock just below the cornice, about 20 meters from the summit of Cerro Kishtwar. Manu and Marko set up their tent on the very top, and Hayden and I sleep just a meter below.

We descend along a couloir to the left of the east face—the same line we had considered attempting. In the upper section we are surprised to find no snow or ice after three days of clear weather. In the lower part it is like canyoning. In 1,200 meters, we can find only one Abalakov and one screw anchor; all of the others are placed in rock. "We would have fucked ourselves if we had pooped our pants and chosen this line," someone says. There's no doubt the sparrow would have been a hollow prize. When we reach the bottom of the east face, we see the ice we'd climbed there has disappeared as well. We caught the wall at the perfect time.

Two days later we start a rapid descent into the "synthetic" world. Over two days we walk 60 kilometers to the road in Gulabgarh, and the next night, after 18 hours of driving, we arrive in Manali, and soon Delhi and then home. We leave the mountains so quickly that it seems our thoughts and feelings are still there.

SUMMARY: First ascent of the south ridge (1,400m, D+) of 6,278-meter Chomochior in eastern Kishtwar, India, by Hayden Kennedy (USA), Urban Novak, and Marko Prezelj (Slovenia), September 27–29, 2015. The same three men and Manu Pellissier (France) then made the first ascent of the east face of Cerro Kishtwar (6,173 meters): Light Before Wisdom (1,200m, ED+ 5.11 A2 WI6 M6), October 5–8, 2015, descending the southern slopes to the eastern couloir. Summit heights were measured by GPS.

ABOUT THE AUTHOR: *Urban Novak, 30, lives in Prikrnica, Slovenia. When he's not working on his Ph.D. at the National Institute of Chemistry, he helps his dad on their small family farm.*

[Left] Steep ice on day three. *Urban Novak* [Right] A traverse onto the snowier northeast face led into uncertainty on day three. "Give me the gear," commanded Prezelj, who led the way across the snowy slabs. *Urban Novak*

LET THE PROGRESSION CONTINUE!

FREEING THE TOM EGAN MEMORIAL ROUTE IN THE BUGABOOS

WILL STANHOPE

I first visited the Bugaboos in 2008 with under-the-radar alpine legend Chris Brazeau. Braz, a low-key, wide-smiling local, knew all the tricks to help an alpine climbing neophyte like myself. After driving up the bumpy logging road for about an hour, he wrapped his car in chicken wire to protect it from porcupines and stashed a few barley beverages to chill in the creek while we were in the mountains. I was giddy with excitement. I'd heard about the fabled Bugaboos since I was a kid. And now, at age 21, I was finally going to hike into the cirque of mint granite spires.

After a few hours of trudging, the humid Kootenay forest gave way to a rocky moraine, and the east face of Snowpatch Spire came into view. I was blown away. The beautiful, sheer pane of granite was laced with corner systems, and a creamy dollop of snow—its namesake— perched on the left side of the face. Once we got a bit closer to the face, a striking, barely perceptible thin crack splitting the diamond-shaped headwall on the right side of the face caught my eye.

"What's that!?" I exclaimed.

"The Tom Egan Memorial Route," Braz replied. "Old Daryl Hatten FA."

Squamish, my home climbing area, is rife with Daryl Hatten legends. He was an aid-climbing master and could party harder than anyone else, according to local lore. The Pan Wall on the Chief is home to a handful of bold, incipient Hatten testpieces. He had established the Tom Egan Memorial Route with John Simpson in 1978. Tom Egan was a friend of theirs that had passed away in a small-plane crash. Braz and I climbed a few stellar lines on that trip and cemented the idea of one day attempting the Tom Egan.

[Photo] Will Stanhope climbs the Blood on the Crack pitch (5.14-) while Matt Segal belays from the portaledge below. *Tim Kemple*

I got my chance to see the route up close two years later, with visiting Brit climber Hazel Findlay. Hazel and I climbed the Power of Lard, a classic 5.12, and then pendulumed into the Tom Egan Memorial Route. We rappelled down the line with mouths agape. A laser-cut splitter ran the entire length of the face, barely big enough for fingers.

Two years later, in 2012, I returned to attempt the line in earnest with my longtime pal Matt Segal. It soon became apparent that the first 30 feet of the splitter would not go free. Matt and I spent the first month of that summer swinging around the face, looking for a feasible line into the crack. Near the end of the trip, Matt found what we were looking for: a crescent line of crimpers, the smallest we could possibly hold, leading into the Tom Egan from the neighboring route Sweet Sylvia to the left. After slamming in six bolts on the 40-foot traverse, and beefing up the old aid belays, it became apparent that we had a mega-hard project to sink our teeth into. The work had only begun.

The next two summers—2013 and 2014—Matt and I essentially wrote off July and August as Tom Egan time. We'd hike in with giant packs and set up at Applebee Campground for the duration. The first splitter crack pitch—though perhaps as hard as the Cobra Crack (5.14) in Squamish— wasn't the most difficult lead. It was the face traverse, by then dubbed the Drunken Dawn Wall pitch (5.14), that gave us the most trouble. Never before had we both been so rudely and unpredictably chucked off a wall. This was cryptic, subtle, gently overhanging granite trickery at its finest. Those were trying summers. By the end of August we'd shoulder our toppling packs and trudge down the trail

The east face of Snowpatch Spire. The free Tom Egan Memorial Route approximately follows the white line shown, up the steep wall on the right side of the face for 13 pitches, with two pitches of 5.13 and two pitches of 5.14 climbing. *Artwork by Glen Boles*

[Above] Matt Segal bears down on the small crimps of the Drunken Dawn Wall pitch (5.14), a face climbing variation that made the free route possible. *Tim Kemple* [Below] Will Stanhope ascends a sustained, flaring 5.13 crack high on the route. *Tim Kemple*

with sliced fingers, utterly burnt out and empty-handed.

In the summer of 2015, things started to come together. I got a job helping a wild, charismatic tree trimmer in West Vancouver named Steeno. I'd spend the days heaving rounds of wood, then exile myself to a dusty corner of the climbing gym and dangle with weights strapped to my harness. This combination actually duplicated big-wall free climbing quite well: a huge amount of manual labor interspersed with intense bits of climbing.

As soon as Matt and I arrived in the Bugaboos we quickly matched the previous year's high point. I managed to free the Blood on the Crack pitch (5.14-), and both of us were consistently one-falling the Drunken Dawn Wall pitch—a big improvement. Hiking across the glacier toward Snowpatch for the umpteenth time, I had Bob Dylan queued up on my iPod: "Any day now, any day now, I shall be released."

In mid-August I got very lucky and barely managed to free the Drunken Dawn Wall, putting Matt in an uncomfortable, unenviable position. He now had to climb it as well. As he is a few inches shorter than me, a few of the moves on the pitch were savagely hard for him. Watching Matt, I was almost in tears, witnessing him put in some of the most fierce, gritty efforts I've ever seen. When he came up short, the tension that evening on the portaledge was palpable.

Over the next few days I climbed the remaining difficult crack pitches—5.14-, 5.13, and 5.13- R—and rappelled each evening to the portaledge, fingers crossed that Matt would send the Drunken Dawn Wall pitch. Alas, it was not to be. With a storm threatening, we rocketed up the fixed lines, intent on finishing the route before the rains began. Above the final headwall pitch, I led leftward, up very wandering, choose-your-own-advenure style alpine rock climbing to gain the Yellow Tower and the ridgeline of Snowpatch Spire, not the true summit itself. This is where Daryl and John had finished their climb, and given the dark clouds enveloping the Howser Towers in the distance, this is where we chose to descend as well. We rigged the rappels and threw our ropes down the Sunshine Route raps, just as the storm began in earnest.

On the descent we got hit with savage hail and terrifying thunder. We arrived back at camp soaked and frazzled, but otherwise safe, thanking the Bugaboo spirits profusely for allowing us safe passage. Our friend Ian Welsted had left us a bottle of Ballantine's Scotch. After a few swigs I passed out, unable to comprehend the long saga that was now complete.

Looking toward the future, perhaps someone, someday, will link all the pitches on the Tom Egan headwall, ledge to ledge, in one 80-meter, 5.15 pitch. We broke up our climb using the old aid belays, none of which could remotely be called no-hands stances. As always, the style can be improved upon. Let the progression continue!

SUMMARY: The first free ascent of the Tom Egan Memorial Route (Hatten-Simpson, 1978) on the east face of Snowpatch Spire (13 pitches, V 5.14) in the Bugaboos, Purcell Mountains of British Columbia, Canada, August 11–14, 2015, by Matt Segal and Will Stanhope. Stanhope freed the entire climb in a ground-up push, with Segal free climbing all but the crux section of 5.14 face climbing.

ABOUT THE AUTHOR: *Will Stanhope is based out of Squamish, British Columbia. He notes that, "For the last few years my main focus has been free climbing big walls. Trying your absolute best, thousands of feet off the ground, surrounded by beauty, is as good as it gets." He plans to support Matt Segal in 2016 on an attempt to complete his own free climb of the Tom Egan Memorial Route.*

HASTA LAS WEBAS!

THE SECOND ASCENT OF
CERRO RISO PATRÓN IN PATAGONIA

JERÔME SULLIVAN

I n El Chaltén's Hostal Del Lago, the wall of the common room is pasted with maps of the vast Southern Patagonian Ice Field, and it is quite normal to observe climbers staring at the wall and daydreaming of windless days on a rime-capped summit, while outside the treetops are bent almost to the ground by gales. Four years ago, Diego Simari, an Argentine climber and friend, pointed out Cerro Riso Patrón on one of these maps. The contours revealed steep features that seemed to plunge directly into the fjords of western Chile. When I tried to pry more information out of Diego—the size of the faces, the history of climbs, how to get there—he told me it was quite a mystery, that very little was known.

With much help from Rolando Garibotti and Carlos Comensaña, I was able to learn more. Cerro Riso Patrón is an island of rock and rime pinned between the edge of the ice cap and the Chilean fjords. Although it is just 50 kilometers southwest of Cerro Torre, that short distance makes a colossal difference. The arid desert that borders the east side of the ice cap contrasts forcefully with the humid forests and swamplands framing the west side. Pacific storms crash into the bordering mountains, and hellish weather is the norm. Although the combination of complex terrain, poor climate, and isolation makes these mountains terribly complicated to climb, paradoxically it also makes them extremely attractive. When an alpinist sets eyes upon the gravity-defying rime coating these beautiful peaks, an inexplicable chemical transformation occurs in the brain. Against all common sense, and with the collapse of one's natural instinct of self-preservation, there comes an unwavering desire to scale them.

Riso Patrón Central was first climbed by Casimiro Ferrari, Bruno Lombardini, and Egidio Spreafico, all from Italy, in August 1988, via the southeast face. No one had been to the summit since. Riso Patrón South was still unclimbed, and we set our sights on its great west face. The project took three years to materialize. By the end of the summer of 2014, we had a team of four, ready and motivated. We knew our chances of success were minimal, but we all felt that exploring this wild and hostile region would make the experience worthwhile.

NOVEMBER 2014 — THE FIRST ATTEMPT

OUR TEAM WAS COMPOSED of Lise Billon, my companion on many Patagonian escapades; Martín Elías, a Spanish climber of numerous first ascents and corrosive humor; Antoine Moineville, our filmmaker and a member of the Flying Frenchies high-lining team; and me.

[Facing page] **The author searches for safe passage through a "sea of frost" on Riso Patrón.** *Lise Billon*

Our hope was to hire a boat to take us to the end of Fiordo Falcón, where we would wait for good weather to attempt Riso Patrón South. The logistics proved complicated. Weeks passed in Puerto Natales as the alcoholic sailor who was supposed to manage our trip to Fiordo Falcón bailed time after time. I will skip the details, but it was an emotionally complicated moment.

Eventually we resigned ourselves to taking a ferry, the Navimag, to an isolated island of fishermen called Puerto Edén, in hopes of finding a boat there for the rest of our journey. Halfway between Puerto Natales and Puerto Mont, Puerto Edén is 400 kilometers from any other civilization, almost completely cut off from the rest of the world. This outpost is home to a couple of hundred people who mostly make a living diving for seafood and fishing, living in a very basic way. When we arrived we were pleased to hire Rigoberto, the proud captain of a small motorboat, the Principe, to transport us to Fiordo Falcón. May Santo Pedro bless our journey!

Three long weeks passed between our landing in Puerto Natales and our arrival at the end of the fiord. At the inlet we called Bahía Fonrouge, we landed on a beautiful beach of fine, white sand, littered with icebergs abandoned by the falling tide. This gave way to a long, deep valley, the Valle Comensaña, which in turn led through dense clouds to unseen Riso Patrón. We felt like the occupants of the Mayflower, arriving in a new land.

We had decided that one of the keys to success would be to stay as dry as possible while we waited and scouted out the approach in the steady rain. If we were to spend three weeks in a tent, unable to dry our clothes, we would be miserable and worn out whenever a weather window finally arrived. So we worked for three days to build a small cabin and install the little homemade woodstove we had bought in Puerto Natales. A meter and a half of humid moss covered the ground, making it complicated to find a place to build, but eventually we had the stove smoking and hot in our little home in the forgotten fjords of Patagonia.

After a week in our shack we still hadn't glimpsed the mountain. On day ten, our weatherman announced (by satellite phone) three to four hours of blue skies in late afternoon of the next day. We immediately set off to stash some gear and inspect the approach. It took us a long day to reach the glacier, walking under pouring rain across marshlands where we'd sink up to the knees, overtopping our plastic wading boots. Eventually we traded the wading boots and fisherman-style foul-weather gear for mountaineering boots and Gore-tex—like Clark Kent transforming into Superman, we hoped. The clouds slowly parted and we finally set foot on the ice.

Approach to Cerro Riso Patrón. Red line: route of the Navimag ferry. Yellow line: route of the Principe from Puerto Edén into Fiordo Falcón. (1) 2014 base camp. (2) 2015 base camp. *Google Earth. Data SIO, NOAA, U.S. Navy, NGA, GEBCO. Image Landsat.*

[Top] The Principe moored in Fiordo Falcón. *Lise Billon* [Bottom left] Anticipating weeks of bad weather, the team built a small but well-stocked shack above the fjord. *Martin Elias* [Bottom right] Approaching Riso Patrón South, moments before the crevasse fall that ended the 2014 attempt. *Lise Billon*

As the mist ebbed, a gigantic white throne, plastered with rime and smoking white with the wind, slowly emerged. The vision left us in a state of euphoria! And then, literally and emotionally, I went from top floor to bottom in an instant: One second I was ogling one of the most entrancing mountains I had ever seen, and the next I was dangling at the end of the rope with terrible pain in my right shoulder. A snow bridge had fallen away beneath my feet. I immediately understood this meant the end of the expedition.

The rescue was complicated. Inside the crevasse, I had pendulumed beneath a few meters of compact snow, which now separated me from freedom. My shoulder was dislocated, and the wind made it nearly impossible for my friends and me to hear each other. After 40 minutes I was able to dig through the lip and, with the help of my partners, climb out of the dark trench. I was close to hypothermia and my shoulder was impossible to reset. The return to our hut was long and painful, hiking down through dense jungle, and I admit the morphine tablets helped a lot. The icebergs had shifted with the tide and we were in danger of being trapped in the fiord. I was miserable and in pain, but even more I felt shattered by the abrupt ending to our expedition.

There was no chance of a helicopter. We called the fishermen on our satellite phone, and eventually they arrived, slowly picking a route through the icebergs clogging the bay. By the time I reached the hospital and got my dislocated arm back into its socket, it had been seven days since the accident.

We had been well aware of the rules of this game. I had only popped a shoulder, nothing fatal, and the worst-case scenario was going to be nerve damage in my shoulder. But it was easy to imagine a worse outcome. The commitment of climbing remote mountains in Patagonia seemed much more real now.

SEPTEMBER 2015 — THE SECOND ATTEMPT

MY OBSESSION with the mountain only grew. But my friends hesitated, considering the low chances of success. Martin bailed and went to China. It took a bit of convincing, but Antoine decided to give it another go. Lise stayed motivated, as always. Our experience had shown us that a big team would give us a better chance of evacuating someone if anything happened. Diego Simari, who had first pointed to Cerro Riso Patrón on the map in El Chaltén four years earlier, now joined our group. And so we were four again. This time we decided to go in September, two months earlier, in hope of better ice conditions and because the weather often seems slightly better at the end of the southern winter.

Just as we all arrived in Puerto Natales, the forecast announced a high-pressure system headed our way in only eight days, which left us very little time to get to Fiordo Falcón. With experience on our side, this time the logistics in Natales went quite smoothly. Only five days later we were in Puerto Edén, meeting up with our fishermen friends. We embarked on the Principe and took off for the fiords, our hearts full of hope and desire. But when we reached the entrance to Fiordo Falcón, we discovered the waters were still choked with ice. We had known this was a possibility in late winter, but had refused to acknowledge its consequences.

The fishermen, seeing our despair, tried to force their way through the ice. We cut down two big trees and lashed them to the front of the boat, turning Principe into a fragile icebreaker. Slowly we gained headway. We were close to Bahía Fonrouge, maybe a kilometer away, when a big chunk of ice passed beneath the vessel and crippled the rudder. Could it be that this time we would fail without even disembarking from the boat? Surely this was a bad joke!

The fjord walls, covered with loose rock and dense vegetation, wouldn't let us land, and we were forced to spend the night anchored in a rocky creek. Juan, one of the fishermen, pulled on an ancient wetsuit, a mask, and a breathing tube running from an air compressor and plunged into the ice-filled waters to attempt a provisional repair. As he dropped into the cold darkness, he yelled, "*Estamos hasta las webas!*" Webas was Chilean slang for *huevos*, which in turn is slang for "balls"—the phrase is roughly equivalent to "we're in neck-deep." This turned out to be a good motto for the rest of the journey.

In the morning we weighed our options. Our one and possibly unique weather window was hurtling toward us. We decided the only way to make something of it was to give up our original objective, the west face of Riso Patrón South, because we couldn't even start the approach up the Valle Comensaña. The east face of Riso Patrón Central, another unclimbed line, offered our only chance. This approach would be longer, and we weren't even sure how to begin. Twenty-seven years earlier, Ferrari and his team had approached Riso Patrón from Fiordo Falcón, but we didn't know where. A few miles back was another bay where we could reach shore and, we hoped, hike up to the ice cap. As the fishermen dropped us off and we

[Clockwise from bottom right] Scenes from the approach in 2015: A Chilean sailor prepares to get *hasta las webas* to fix the Principe's rudder. Hacking a path away from the fjord. Above the forest and in the clear, en route to Riso Patrón, with ice-choked Fiordo Falcón in the distance. *Lise Billon*

unloaded our gear, we crossed a mental barrier. We had no time to build a cabin, scout out the access, or stash gear. It was to be all or nothing.

The high pressure arrived as forecast, and on September 20 we set off with huge packs, hiking toward the mountains. The weight was terrible, and in poor weather we might have given up. But the view of those giants of rock and snow sucked us in, full of motivation. We crossed a flat marsh where our boots left knee-deep holes in a colorful slush of fungus and algae, then climbed through a nearly vertical forest, using ice axe and crampons to make progress. Eventually we reached an open ridge and put on snowshoes. The ice cap extended in front of us, its flat surface a blessing after the jungle hills we'd climbed. Mountains of enormous proportions surged from the glacier, every rock protrusion capped with outrageous white rime. After two and a half days of struggle, the east face of Riso Patrón Central filled the skies overhead. We happily swapped our snowshoes for crampons. Our backs and legs ached, but our minds were set on the wall in front of us.

Our only photograph of the face had been taken in summer, and what we saw now barely resembled the dry, rocky peak in that photo. The spur we hoped to climb separates the

north and east faces. Its lower half was painted in smears of ice, and the upper half plastered in rime. The pillar eventually gave way to a snowy arête and a huge summit mushroom. Our bet on the early season had paid off, as the air was cold and everything on the mountain seemed well glued together. We decided to start climbing immediately, even though we were tired and it was already 4 p.m. Conditions on the wall were great. Three pitches of ice up to 90° brought us to a bivy atop a snowy spur beneath a promising mixed wall. It was only the second day of spring, and the night was chilly, but the air was clear and still, allowing us to see Volcán Lautaro to the north and Cerro Murallón to the south. The immense ice cap, the Hielo Continental, glowed in the light of a full moon.

The next day we drifted upward over vertical rock and streaks of ice, soaking up the morning sun. The protection was almost nonexistent, but

Brilliant mixed climbing early on day two. *Lise Billon*

the quality of the ice and the moderate grade (AI 5 M5) left us confident. Rapidly we climbed the first 400 meters of the spur, switching leads, until we reached a large amphitheater. To our left, the line we had planned to follow was plugged with snow over black overhangs, and we quickly dismissed it. A low-angle gully led to our right and into the sea of frost.

We switched the lead again and I headed upward, with no idea exactly where to go. A vague feature called for my attention, but after 30 meters I had to downclimb as the rime

Cerro Riso Patrón Central and Hasta las Webas (1,000m, 2015) from the east. The 1988 route is farther left, beyond the rock butress. Unclimbed Riso Patrón South on the left. *Robert Koschitzki*

beneath my picks turned to froth. I needed to escape to the other side of the spur—this wall was unclimbable. A slight depression to the right seemed to lead to the edge of the pillar. I felt the tension in our team as I started for this option. If it didn't work we would have to rappel and look for another way, but the good weather wasn't eternal and we were losing time!

The rope beneath my feet arced loosely toward my partners below. Occasionally I heard an encouraging *Allez, Jerôme!*, reminding me that a world existed outside the arm's length bubble of rime surrounding me. This pitch was one-way: The pro was purely psychological, and downclimbing would be impossible. Fleeing forward, I plunged my feet deep into the rime and swung my tools furiously. The sun was low. The vague groove allowed me to keep my weight on my feet, but then one of them would unexpectedly drop a few centimeters and send my heart into spasms. *Hasta las webas!* The trick was not to think about it. Little by little I approached the arête, and when I finally hammered a pin into solid rock, I whooped with joy at being alive. My partners had put on their headlamps. The ice cap blushed pink and fiery red as the sun sank beneath the fjords. My friends quickly seconded the pitch—*Are you kidding me?*—with little difficulty.

The east side of the spur looked significantly easier. We rappelled to a vague ledge for what was left of the night. As we melted snow and ate, Diego scalded himself with the stove and, startled, dropped his sleeping bag, which tumbled to the glacier below. He let loose a string of curses I wouldn't dare repeat in a journal like this. We loaned him our big jackets as the temperatures dropped to -20°C, fortunately for only a few hours, as the rising sun soon started to warm his bones.

A beautifully sculpted arête of snow, with crazy cornices and tunnels created by the wind, led us upward until we bumped against the summit mushroom. As we approached this last crux, I really thought we might fail to make the summit. Classic Patagonian rime led to a

10-meter overhang, a boiling ring of inconsistent snow that barred our way. But maybe there was a way around? We rappelled 10 meters and began traversing to the right. Streaks of blue appeared beneath the sparkling white crystals. After a game of rock , paper, and scissors (which I won), I set off for the last pitch. I happily buried screws in ice and climbed through the wild rime. On the backside of the mushroom was easy snow, and we unroped and climbed to the top. We screamed and chanted as the sun dropped below the dark waters of the fjords.

That night we left deadman after deadman, bouncing from one mushroom to the next, as we rappelled the north arête and meandered downward through white meringue, looking for paths of weakness. The wind became stronger and clouds engulfed the mountain. We eventually left the ridge and dropped along the eastern flank, hoping to reach our approach tracks. Seemingly forever we descended, shivering and exhausted, until suddenly we were in the bergschrund. We had made it.

Two days later we returned to the bay where the fishermen had left us. We had been gone for a week, most of which had seen good weather. A mix of luck and audacity and friendship had been the recipe for our success. We had tasted the salty flavor of wild lands. We had seen so many unclimbed, unnamed summits, ridges, and faces hidden behind the swamps, forest, and lakes. These mysteries remain—for those willing to go *hasta las webas*.

[Previous page] **Good but poorly protected ice in the middle of the face.** [Above] **A stunning sunset view to the northeast, over the icecap to Cerro Buracchio and the Cordón Riso Patrón.** *Lise Billon (both)*

SUMMARY: First ascent of the east spur of Cerro Riso Patrón Central (ca 2,550 meters), and second ascent of the peak, by Lise Billon, Antoine Moineville, Diego Simari, and Jerôme Sullivan, September 22–24, 2015. The team descended by the north ridge and eastern slopes and returned to base camp seven days after leaving. Hasta las Webas: 1,000 meters, ED-.

ABOUT THE AUTHOR: *Jerôme Sullivan is best described as a nomadic climber, as his home is wherever he pitches his tent. He guides in Chamonix for a few months a year. After two accidents in three years, Patagonia has marked his body and mind, yet the magnetic attraction continues.*

RETURN TO THE KARAKORAM

FIRST ASCENTS ON CHANGI TOWER AND K6 WEST

STEVE SWENSON & GRAHAM ZIMMERMAN

S TEVE: My dear friend and longtime cook and guide Ghulam Rasool sat next to me as our jeep rolled into the village of Hushe. It had been eight years since we had last seen each other, and I was happy to be reunited for another adventure. This would be our 10th expedition together and my 11th trip to the Pakistan-administered side of the Karakoram.

A deteriorating security situation since my last trip, in 2007, combined with opportunities for first ascents in the eastern Karakoram, had caused me to shift my interest to the Indian side of the Line of Control, where I did two expeditions. Before returning to Pakistan's mountains, I was waiting to see how the government—the Army and their intelligence services, in particular—would handle the growing threat from Islamic militant groups in the tribal areas near the border with Afghanistan. Many of these groups had been supported by the Pakistani security forces for years, serving as proxies in the conflicts in Afghanistan and India-administered Kashmir, but they had now turned on their benefactors. After several high-profile militant attacks, the Pakistan security forces and the public were sufficiently outraged for the military to launch full-scale offensives in the tribal areas. Security began to improve, and I felt it was time to climb in Pakistan again, visit my friends, and assess the security situation for myself.

Over the years, territorial disputes between China, India, and Pakistan have restricted access to parts of the Karakoram, and the resulting "political wilderness" contains one of the largest collections of unclimbed 6,000- and 7,000-meter peaks in the world. After 15 expeditions to the Karakoram spread over the past 35 years, I'd become familiar with many areas of the range. Armed with this knowledge and additional research, I tried to find a politically accessible, technically challenging unclimbed mountain that had minimal hazards from rockfall or snow and ice avalanches.

I focused my attention on the K6 group, which contains three separate summits, all above 7,000 meters. K6 Main (7,282 meters) was first climbed by Austrians in 1970. K6 West

[Photo] Balti guide Ghulam Rasool, happy to rejoin author Steve Swenson for another expedition after an eight-year hiatus. *Scott Bennett*

Changi Tower (6,500m) from ABC. The climbers ascended the icefall to the Polish Col, left of the peak, and then generally followed the left skyline to the top. *Steve Swenson*

(7,040 meters) had been climbed by Canadians in 2013. But K6 Central (7,100 meters) was still unclimbed. I'd seen the central summit from the Charakusa Valley, to the north, and that side comprised a very steep, technical wall threatened from above by hanging ice cliffs. However, I had never been to the Nangmah Valley on the south side of the massif, from which the Austrians had approached K6 Main.

Reviewing maps, photos, and satellite imagery, I could see that a rock and ice buttress extended down from the summit on the south face of K6 Central, perhaps protruding enough to be protected from avalanches on either side. The approach would follow the 1970 approach over the "Austrian Col" from the upper Nangmah Valley to the upper Lachit Glacier.

With this objective in mind, I continued my research to find a smaller peak in the area for acclimatization—and in case K6 Central was not feasible. I found a photo in the 1970 Austrian account showing a beautiful granite tower with the caption, "Changi (6500m) from the east – a fine peak south-east of K6." Further research turned up an unsuccessful Polish attempt in 2010 on this same peak, which was located just across the Lachit Glacier from the south face of K6 Central, and which the Poles called Changi Tower. The peak's remote, hidden location, along with the confusion caused by a similarly named tower in the upper Nangmah Valley, had kept Changi Tower off the radar of most climbers looking for appealing first ascents.

I asked Graham Zimmerman to join me on the proposed expedition, and he invited Scott Bennett to fill out the team. Both of my partners were 29 years old—32 years younger than me. I thought they could benefit from my expedition planning experience, and I figured their youthful enthusiasm and strength would help get us up the peaks—my challenge would be trying to keep up with them. Our permit was issued by the Gilgit-Baltistan Council on June 18, just 15 days before we left the United States. Fortunately, our visas were issued within a week.

Before leaving the U.S., we promised our friends and family that we would fly from Islamabad to Skardu as a security precaution and not allow ourselves to go overland by the Karakoram Highway. After arriving in Islamabad we were pleased to find that Pakistan International Airlines was flying an A320 jet to Skardu on the weekends; this was a much larger plane than the usual turboprop and would eliminate any backlog. The weather was good on Sunday, July 5, and soon after takeoff our plane circled to a landing in Skardu in peaceful Baltistan. We drove to Hushe and then made the two-day approach hike to base camp at 4,300 meters in the upper Nangmah Valley.

Our objectives were far from base camp, and I knew from previous trips with similar circumstances that establishing a well-stocked advanced base camp (ABC) would prevent us from getting overextended. We agreed to establish an ABC on the far side of the divide between the Nangmah and the Lachit. Launching our alpine-style attempts from a comfortable place to sleep, eat, and wait out bad weather meant we would be stronger—both physically and mentally—when we started up the peaks we came to climb.

GRAHAM: By the 21st of July, with the help of our friends Nadim and Ibrahim, we had established an ABC. We chose to reach the Lachit by crossing Hidden Col (the same saddle used by the 2010 Polish expedition), which was lower and more direct than the less steep but heavily melted-out Austrian Col. We fixed three ropes over the col to ease load carrying.

From ABC we could see the entirety of the south pillar of K6 Central, pointing directly toward the summit. We were disappointed to discover this feature did not continue all the way down the wall, but instead tapered into a broad snow slope that covered the lower third of the face. Here we would be exposed to avalanches falling from the large seracs perched high above. Our concerns were confirmed a few days later when a massive release from one of the seracs scoured the lower third of the face and heavily dusted our camp, over a kilometer from the wall. We also could clearly see Changi Tower from our ABC. Reaching this summit had been our acclimatization strategy, but with the south face of K6 Central now off the menu, Changi became our primary goal.

On July 24 we reached the basin directly below the 250-meter slope leading to the "Polish Col" at 5,900 meters. The 2010 team had reached this col and climbed three pitches up the north side of Changi Tower before retreating. It took us two days to navigate a complex icefall leading to this point. Not being fully acclimatized, and with a storm approaching, we cached some food and equipment in the basin and descended to base camp.

In the first week of August, we received a forecast of four consecutive days of good weather. We packed our bags and headed for ABC, and early on the morning of August 8 we made our way back up the icefall under partially clear skies. With a track in place and crisp snow conditions, the icefall took only three hours to navigate. At our cache below the Polish Col, we reorganized our gear and packed supplies to spend three and a half days on the route.

We climbed unroped up 50° snow and ice to reach the col and immediately started up the north face of the tower. We planned to split the

Steve Swenson arrives at the Polish Col, with the Lachit Glacier behind. Graham Zimmerman

climbing into two blocks—day one would be mine to lead, and the second day was up to Scott. We climbed in "caterpillar style," with the leader carrying a light pack and fixing his rope for the second, who would jug quickly with a medium-size pack. This second would trail another rope to fix for the third, who would jug with the heaviest pack. I climbed the 60° ice above the Polish Col as quickly as I could. This eventually led into a series of mixed pitches made challenging by deteriorating ice conditions in the heat of the day. I was very happy when I finally placed a solid rock anchor after six pitches.

We decided to bivy at the base of a rock wall about 200 meters above the col. While Scott and I climbed the cliff above, Steve stayed behind to work on the tent platform. We had carried an ice hammock developed by Steve's longtime climbing partner Mark Richey, which made the job of building a ledge in the 60° ice much easier. Scott and I fixed our two ropes and rappelled to help Steve finish the platform, put up our tent, and start melting snow.

As we settled in for the night and ate, we discussed our strategy for the following day. Steve felt we needed to carry bivy kit with us, but Scott thought we could move fast enough to reach the summit if we went light and left our bivy gear behind. The unknown nature of the terrain above loomed heavily as we discussed how we should proceed. In the end, we decided to try to reach the summit and return to our tent in a single push, but we would carry a single sleeping bag and stove to make it possible to spend the night out and continue to the summit the next day if we didn't reach the top before dark.

From the top of our two fixed ropes, the climbing began with moderate snow and ice involving short vertical sections. Above us, around a corner on the northwest face, loomed a steep corner system we called the Great Dihedral, which seemed to offer a promising route through the formidable final headwall. As Scott led into this giant corner, he switched between rock shoes and crampons, short-fixing above each belay anchor to increase our speed. An overhang capped the top of the Great Dihedral, and I wondered if this obstacle would force us to climb into the night. But Scott cut left below the roof on face holds and quickly moved out of sight, calling off belay a few minutes later. Steve looked over at me and smiled: "He is climbing very well!"

Two pitches later, Scott was standing just below the summit, with the final rays of the sun peeking over the horizon. We each made the last few moves to the final rocky wedge of a summit, whooped and high-fived, and then I started leading the descent in pitch black. Scott

had been right: We had been able make it to the summit from our bivy in one day—mostly because of his efforts. After many hours of rappels, we arrived back at our bivy tent at 3:30 a.m., exhausted but happy. We slept late the following day before starting the rappels to the Polish Col and the basin below.

GRAHAM: On the 12th of August we moved all of our equipment from the Lachit Glacier back over to the western

Swenson (left) and Scott Bennett, fresh as daisies after descending Changi Tower.
Graham Zimmerman

Graham Zimmerman midway across the key traverse on K6 West's southwest buttress. *Scott Bennett*

side of Hidden Col. In the past weeks, Scott and I had spied a possible alternative way up the southern ramparts of K6: the southwest ridge of K6 West. It weaved over and through a series of towers that represented major question marks, but through our spotting scope it seemed we should be able to find a way. From the summit of K6 West it looked like an easy traverse along a snow ridge to the summit of unclimbed K6 Central. The western summit had been climbed only once, by our friends Raphael Slawinski and Ian Welsted in 2013, via the northeast face, on the other side of the mountain.

Steve made the challenging decision that he would sit out the attempt on K6 due to the short turnaround time after Changi Tower and a recurring sinus problem. Instead, he gave us advice on how best to prepare for the route, and he offered, along with help from Nadim and Hadim, to bring down the remaining gear we had cached from our Changi Tower climb and to take care of our exit logistics. Scott and I felt conflicted about leaving our partner, who had offered so much help, but we were also very excited at the opportunity to attempt another route.

We departed camp at 10 p.m. on August 17. Throughout the expedition we had been receiving forecasts from Jim Woodmencey at Mountainweather.com, and his latest prediction was for a large storm to arrive on the 21st, so we needed to move fast. Our hope was to climb the lower snow slopes at night while they were frozen. Unfortunately, when we reached the gear cache we had left on the upper Nangmah, it was snowing hard and visibility was poor. We pitched our tent, planning to start moving once the weather cleared.

The skies finally cleared as the sun rose, and our late start placed us on the steepening snow slopes below the southwest ridge just as the heat of the sun began to bear down upon us. We peeled off layers and swore at the deteriorating conditions, but kept moving forward. By early afternoon we had reached a bivy, and we slept through the remaining heat of the day.

The following morning we were moving by 2:30 a.m., simul-climbing in the dark toward the looming buttresses we knew would constitute the crux of the route. As the sun rose we

The K6 massif from the south, showing the new route up the southwest buttress of K6 West (7,040 meters), with the unclimbed central peak in the middle. In 1969, an Italian team reached ca 6,900 meters on K6 West by the snow and ice ramps right of the buttress. *Scott Bennnett*

came across signs of an earlier attempt on the route—pitons and bail cord that looked to be from the 1960s or '70s, just below the first difficulties. Later, Steve would discover that these were most likely from an Italian attempt on K6 Main in 1969. (Like us, the Italians hoped to climb over K6 West and Central. They first attempted the southwest buttress, reaching around 6,000 meters, and then climbed ice ramps to the right to about 6,900 meters on K6 West.) In the morning light we traversed alongside the buttresses on moderate benches of snow and ice, with short mixed pitches (up to M6) that led to more snow ramps. The crux showed up in midmorning at an overhanging chimney and short icicle. A sequence of good sticks and wide stems brought us to yet another snow bench.

As the day wore on, we moved onto the ice sheet that gave access to the ridge crest far above. The sun came around and once again we stripped layers, moving together up the 60° to 70° slope. Our calves burned while kicking into hard ice under a thin layer of rotten snow, and we started to feel the effects of climbing for over 18 hours. Just as darkness began to settle over the range, we reached the ridgeline and stumbled onto a perfect tent platform. In the fading light we spied our line to the summit: a series of low-angle snow ramps through an icefall. As we set up the tent and dove in, I quietly hoped the snow ahead would be firm.

These hopes were quickly dashed in knee- to hip-deep snow when we moved away from the tent at 7 a.m. The summit was only 400 meters above us over moderate terrain. But it proved to be an ordeal plowing through the deep snow, until finally we reached the top of K6 West at 1 p.m. Under stunningly blue skies, the breadth of the Karakoram was spread before us.

It was a powerful moment, staring out to the 8,000-meter peaks to the northwest and the lesser-known mountains along the front line between India and Pakistan to the east. A moment filled with inspiration and beauty. But my eyes wandered back south toward our descent. We had hoped to continue along the technically easy traverse to unclimbed K6 Central, but the round trip would have taken another whole day of climbing, and our forecast still predicted a major storm for the next day. We turned and started back down.

At our tent we slept for a few hours before waking at 8 p.m. to finish the descent at night, when the temperatures would be cooler. During the climb we had spotted a potential descent route that avoided the rock buttresses we had traversed. It involved rappelling the west face to reach the West Nangmah Glacier, from which we could traverse back up and over the southwest ridge before descending the snow slopes we had climbed on our first day.

After 29 rappels, we were back on the glacier by midmorning on the 20th. Cirrus clouds spun across the blue sky, indicating a storm was in fact on its way. As we walked back to base camp, Scott and I chatted happily about how well the climbs had gone, and our conversation consistently came back to Steve and how, in many ways, his guidance had made these climbs possible. We were both grateful and extremely psyched.

STEVE: On August 25 we left base camp with 27 porters and reached the road in the Hushe Valley that afternoon. Four days later we boarded the weekend A320 flight from Skardu to Islamabad. It was the first time I'd ever flown both in and out of Skardu on the scheduled days.

Flying to and from Skardu eliminated traveling along the Karakoram Highway, the main security risk faced by climbers going to Baltistan. Rasool had said, "The people in Baltistan are peaceful Shia Muslims who welcome foreign tourists," and I found this to be true. The mountains' natural barrier, along with a strong military presence near the frontier with India, makes it very difficult for militant Sunni groups to travel to this region. In addition, the recent military crackdown in the tribal areas has resulted in the lowest level of terrorist violence in Pakistan since 2008. A Skardu policeman seemed to reflect the feelings of many local people when he said to me, "We are supportive of these military operations and want the country to be rid of these miscreants."

It remains to be seen whether the Pakistan intelligence service or senior army officials will stop supporting all militant Islamic groups. For now, we found that taking certain travel precautions minimized our security risks, and we enjoyed a safe, friendly, and successful expedition to the Pakistan Karakoram.

SUMMARY: First ascent of Changi Tower (6,500 meters) by the north face and northwest face (850m, 5.10 A2 M6), August 8–10, 2015, by Scott Bennett, Steve Swenson, and Graham Zimmerman. Second ascent of K6 West (7,040m) by a new route, the southwest ridge (1,800m, M6 90°), August 18–21, by Bennett and Zimmerman.

ABOUT THE AUTHORS: *Steve Swenson, 62, is a retired civil engineer based in Seattle and Canmore, Alberta. He is finishing a book on his expeditions to the Karakoram, to be published in the spring of 2017. Graham Zimmerman, 30, based in Bend, Oregon, is an alpinist and filmmaker. The climbers wish to thank the American Alpine Club, Mugs Stump Award, New Zealand Alpine Club, and Mount Everest Foundation for support of this expedition.*

View from K6 West to the spectacular upper north side of K6 Main (7,282 meters). *Scott Bennett*

PATAGONIA TODAY

THE TORRE TRAVERSE AND THE WAVE EFFECT IN ONE DAY EACH

COLIN HALEY

Torre Traverse in a Day: Alex Honnold and I had only one sure goal for the season: the Torre Traverse in less than 24 hours. We had nearly succeeded on this awesome objective the year before, retreating two pitches below the top of Cerro Torre—the final summit. With a good forecast and good conditions, we hiked into the Torre Valley on January 29.

Alex likened our Torre Traverse to El Cap speed climbing. We knew exactly who would lead what, where we would simul-climb, and where we would short-fix. We knew that Alex would lower me on the first 30-meter rappel while being pulled up on counter-balance. We knew the order in which we would tag each summit. For one of the belays, on Torre Egger, I was even able to tell Alex exactly which three cams to place, in order, having soloed the route less than two weeks earlier. For all but one rappel we planned to simul-rappel. Approaching our first bivy at Niponino, we reviewed our strategy out loud.

On January 30, we hiked from Niponino to a second bivy below the east pillar of Aguja Standhardt. We started the timer at 1:42 the next morning. Carrying four liters of water each, we headed up to the Standhardt Col. I started up the first pitch above the col at 3:20 a.m., and we continued simul-climbing and short-fixing up the Exocet route with only seven total ice screws.

From the top of Standhardt we made excellent time to the base of Spigolo dei Bimbi on Punta Herron. We changed into rock shoes: Alex's turn to lead. We simul-climbed all the rock of Spigolo dei Bimbi in two pitches. At the top of the rock we snacked, sucked water out of a puddle, and switched back into crampons. I led one pitch of simul-climbing to Punta Herron's summit and down the other side to our rappel anchor.

We made a double-rope rappel, and while Alex pulled down the lead line I tied into it and led up to the base of the Huber-Schnarf on Torre Egger. In rock shoes again, Alex led off. We simul-climbed all the rock in one pitch, and soon we were dangling from an overlap, awkwardly changing back into crampons at a hanging stance, where I kept reminding us how fucked up it would be to drop a boot. I then led the summit mushrooms of Torre Egger in one pitch.

Rappelling the south face of Torre Egger felt full-on as usual but went fast with simul-rappelling. After the final rappel into the Col de la Mentira (the Torre Egger–Cerro Torre col), while Alex pulled the ropes, I tied into one end and led a mixed pitch to reach Cerro Torre's north face. We took a fairly relaxed break here before Alex started up the first pitch of Directa de la Mentira. Many of the cracks now were gushing torrents of water, and the ice mushrooms above were raining rime chunks. We were now getting the full experience that the Torres

CERRO TORRE
20:40

[Routes]
(1) Exocet. (2) Spigolo dei Bimbi.
(3) Huber-Schnarf. (4) Directa de la
Mentira and the upper Ragni Route.
(5) Final descent down southeast
ridge. *Photo by Rolando Garibotti*

TORRE EGGER
09:28

PUNTA HERRON
07:21

3

AGUJA STANDHARDT
04:10

4

5

2

1

Standhardt
Col
00:00

Glacier Bivy
30:39

usually deliver. Alex did a predictably amazing job of leading the pitches quickly, taking huge runouts and going monstrous distances between belays.

At the belay below the last rock pitch on the north face, which usually is plastered in rime but now was less covered, I asked Alex if he wanted to keep leading. "Fuck that, I'm done," he replied. At this point we stopped speed climbing and simply suffered our way up in classic fashion. Alex jugged up to the belay at the top of the rock, we both put on crampons, wrung water out of our clothes, and prepared ourselves to battle hypothermia en route to the summit. I led one last pitch of rime on the north face, Alex jugged off my belay loop, and then I lowered him 20m down the other side to join the Ragni Route (west face of Cerro Torre). I downclimbed behind and short-fixed up to the base of the last pitch.

The last pitch of the Ragni was a steep, slushy mess, so Alex got comfortable at the belay. There was no protection for the first half. Higher, I was relieved to get several decent ice screws before a traverse on vertical rime. The last crux was thankfully on good ice, but was slightly overhanging and desperate after so much climbing. Alex jugged up and we climbed to the summit, arriving at exactly midnight, 20 hours and 40 minutes after leaving the Standhardt Col.

We spent the rest of the night and the first part of the morning rappelling Cerro Torre's southeast ridge. Like many nocturnal rappelling sessions in Patagonia, the memory is a blur of anchors and dehydration and shivering. We reached our tent on the glacier a little more than 30 hours from the Standhardt Col. By the time we arrived in town we had done an enormous amount of exercise and been awake for about 45 hours.

I feel that the Torre Traverse in a day was a beautiful "redpoint" of alpine climbing. Alex and I made a great partnership, a very efficient symbiosis of alpinist and rock climber, as neither he nor I would have climbed the Torre Traverse in a day without the other.

WAVE EFFECT IN A DAY: Alex and I arrived back in El Chaltén late on February 1. Not surprisingly, Alex insisted we climb a multi-pitch 5.12 sport route on one of our two rest days. On February 4—though we had wavered about trying another big traverse because we were both tired—we began hiking back to Niponino. Although not as famous as the Torre Traverse, the Wave Effect (Magro-Opp-Wharton, 2011) is also a badass enchainment of towers. It links the southern aspects of Aguja Desmochada, Aguja de la Silla, and Fitz Roy.

Exercise rejuvenated us. After a night at Niponino, we scrambled to the base of Desmochada at a leisurely pace, in effect a half rest-day. While the Torre Traverse had been

FITZ ROY
17:07

[Routes]
(1) Golden Eagle. (2) Il Bastardo. (3) California Route. *Photo by Damian Llabres*

AGUJA DE LA SILLA
11:12

AGUJA DESMOCHADA
05:14

Start
00:00

about half rock climbing and half crampon climbing, the Wave Effect is a pure rock climb, and there was no doubt that it would be Alex getting us up Aguja Desmochada and Aguja de la Silla, while I would lead the more moderate California Route on Fitz Roy. Of course we would simul-climb as much as possible.

On February 6 we started up Golden Eagle shortly before 5 a.m. We simul-climbed 5.10–5.11 often with only two pieces between us, which set the tone for the day. We arrived on the summit of Desmochada five and a quarter hours after starting and immediately started our descent to the col between Desmochada and Aguja de la Silla. For this next spire, we chose on the spot to climb the unrepeated Il Bastardo (Huber-Huber-Walder) instead of Vertical Current, as the Wave Effect's first climbers had. Alex Huber's topo showed several pitches of 6c A0, and Alex figured that it wouldn't be too hard to free climb the whole thing. I was more skeptical, but since we had both freed all of Aguja Desmochada, I decided to give it a shot.

Il Bastardo got intense quickly. Sometimes on the verge of falling, I was thankful we had brought two Micro Traxions to help protect the simul-climbing and that Alex put me on a real belay above a sustained wide crack. On our second simul pitch, fortunately not as difficult, Alex linked seven topo pitches into one. The terrain got progressively snowier and icier as we climbed. Our time from the base of Il Bastardo to the summit was 4:11, and we made the first free ascent of the route. Considering the runouts and heavy packs, Alex's lead up this route was the most badass block of rock climbing I've ever witnessed. Freeing all of it, while simul-climbing, was a huge challenge for me as well. No one forces you to rise to the occasion quite like Alex does!

We descended to Col de los Americanos (the col between Aguja de la Silla and Fitz Roy) to reach the California Route. It was my lead and I took us to the end of the fifth-class rock in three moderate but long pitches of simul-climbing, where we unroped and started scrambling to the summit. We arrived on the summit of Fitz Roy just past 10 p.m. (17:07 from the base of Desmochada), right at dusk, and promptly started down.

Our descent of the French Route went quickly. Once at La Brecha (the col between Fitz Roy and Aguja Poincenot) we descended west, over a serac and down a couloir, the most dangerous portion of our climb, making rappels on terrain that one could easily downclimb in steel crampons but not with aluminum crampons on tennis shoes. It was a relief to make the last rappel and scramble back toward our bivy, reaching it after a 25:17 round trip.

The whole hike out was windy and rainy. The door was closing on what had been a truly incredible week of climbing.

SUMMARY: The first one-day ascent of the Torre Traverse (crossing Aguja Standhardt, Punta Herron, Torre Egger, and Cerro Torre), completed by Colin Haley and Alex Honnold in 20:40 (Standhardt Col to summit of Cerro Torre), January 31, 2016. The only previous ascent was made over four days in January 2008, by Haley and Rolando Garibotti. The first one-day ascent, all free by both climbers, of the Wave Effect (crossing Aguja Desmochada, Aguja de la Silla, and Fitz Roy), completed by Haley and Honnold in 17:07 (base of Desmochada to summit of Fitz Roy), February 6, 2016. The only previous ascent was made over three days in 2011.

ABOUT THE AUTHOR: *Colin Haley (31) has made 13 trips to the Chaltén Massif, totaling a bit less than three years of his life. He considers most of his best climbing achievements to be those done in the Chaltén area, and the one of which he is proudest is the first solo ascent of Torre Egger, made only 12 days before the one-day Torre Traverse described in this article.*

POSITIVE VIBES

THE FIRST ASCENT OF GAVE DING IN WESTERN NEPAL

PAUL RAMSDEN

No matter how many times the Kathmandu baggage carousel went around, I knew my bags were not going to turn up. It's funny: You often joke about bags going missing at the start of an expedition, but now that it was happening for real I realized it could mean the end of the trip before it had really begun. On top of that came the minibus driver's comment that, due to India's blockade of fuel for Nepal, there might not be enough petrol in his tank to get us to Nepalgunj, and that the plane from there might not have enough fuel to fly us into Simikot. All this meant things were off to a bad start for the British 2015 West Nepal Expedition.

Mick Fowler is one of the most positive people I have ever met. We had traveled to Kathmandu separately—Mick from England, along with Steve Burns and Ian Cartwright, and me directly from work in Saudi Arabia, both planes amazingly landing within minutes of each other. Mick now stood next to the carousel, grinning and assuring me the bags would arrive on the next flight, and that fuel for the minibus would be available on the black market, and that aviation fuel must be stockpiled in Nepalgunj.

Mick's positive vibes obviously worked, as my bags did turn up on a flight later that day, petrol was available—at a premium—and the Nepalgunj airfield was indeed well supplied with aviation fuel. In the end we made it to the mountains more smoothly than usual. It's amazing how things just tend to work out if you persevere, especially in Asia, where the transition from chaos to smooth progress is totally unpredictable but nearly always around the corner, if you wait long enough.

We came upon this year's objective, Gave Ding (6,571 meters), by the typical contorted search for a suitable route. A British team, led by Julian Freeman-Attwood, had attempted the south side of the peak in 2011. Although they were unable to see the north face, they told Mick it had potential. We got our hands on a short video clip from a helicopter, taken by another team that was retreating from a valley to the northwest after heavy snow cut them off. From the video it was clear the mountain had a striking profile.

Mick suggested I spend some satellite time cruising the Tibetan border west of Gojung (a.k.a. Mugu Chuli, 6,310m), a peak he had climbed with Dave Turnbull in the autumn of 2011. Google Earth is a genuine revolution in exploratory mountaineering. While the images vary in quality to a huge degree, they do give a really good indication whether a particular

[Previous page] Mick Fowler low on Gave Ding, with the daunting north wall overhead. It would take Fowler and the author five days to climb the 1,600-meter face. *Paul Ramsden*

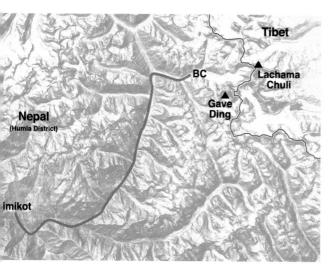

After flying to Simikot, the team trekked four days up the Dojam Khola and Lachama Khola valleys. A British team attempted Gave Ding's south side in 2011, but no climbers had tried the peak from the north. © Mapbox, © OpenStreetMap

valley is worth a visit. (Though, it can be misleading! In 2012 I climbed a peak in India with Mick called Shiva, which looks like a hill walk on Google Earth, but very definitely wasn't.) Once I got my eye in, it seemed that Mick was indeed correct about Gave Ding's potential, with one particular face producing an impressive shadow across the glacier below—a very good sign. Mick's definitely got a feel for these things.

I first met Mick in a rainy car park below Millstone Edge in England's Peak District in 1999. Our climbing partners had decided not to show up, due to the steady rain. After staring at each other from our respective cars for a while, introductions were made and we discovered a mutual enthusiasm for climbing in the wet. Bond Street and Great North Road were climbed in challenging but memorable conditions. It felt slightly odd, having read about Mick as a teenager and even going to one of his slide shows, to be enjoying foul conditions with the man himself.

From Millstone we moved onto new winter routes on Skye and our first Himalayan expedition, which was a miserable failure. Stood at the bottom of that particular route, we decided, simultaneously, that it was too dangerous, and we simply turned around and went home. It's good to know that your climbing partner will try very hard but also knows when to retreat.

Fourteen years and eight expeditions to the Greater Ranges later, Gave Ding stood breathtaking above the end of a beautiful valley. The last village had been left behind after just one ridiculously hot day's walk from Simikot; beyond lay nothing but summer grazing in the occasional flat valley bottom between steep rock walls. On the fourth day we turned a corner into the Lachama Khola and got our first full view of the mountain, but we still couldn't see our intended face. Unfortunately, conditions under foot got worse and the mule men said this was as far as they were prepared to go, a day short of our intended base camp. We made camp there, at about 4,500 meters. We later learned that a Japanese team had attempted Lachama Chuli (6,721 meters) from this valley in 1983, but no one else had ever climbed here.

MICK AND I RARELY SPEND more than a few days in base camp on any expedition. Our plan was to explore the approach to the north face before heading up a nearby, less challenging peak to acclimatize. Progress from base camp was relatively straightforward up an ablation valley to the side of the glacier, and once there you couldn't deny that the north face of Gave Ding dominated the area. As we studied the face through the binoculars, it was clear the choice of line was going to be trickier than expected. From the satellite images I had gained the impression that the left side of the north face held some impressive ice lines, which it did—however, most led into large snow basins and looked like really bad places to be should the weather turn. To the right, seracs threatened all the lines to varying degrees. The only really safe line was the center of the north buttress, but smooth granite bands promised very hard climbing, unless we could find a sneaky way through.

Ruminating on how best to climb the mountain, we headed northwest up a side valley, hoping to find a nice peak around 5,800 meters on which to acclimatize. Despite the fact that the north side of Gave Ding was very icy, we soon discovered that everywhere else was totally devoid of snow, making a high camp very difficult to sustain—if you wanted to drink water, that is.

After the acclimatization had been deemed suitably long (that is, we got bored) we headed back down to base camp for a few days' rest and relaxation before the main event. This is always a pleasurable phase of any expedition for me—eating, sleeping, and fiddling with kit as the anticipation builds for the route. It's at this stage, after seeing the face and realizing just how much food and gas we will have to carry, that the rack tends to get seriously pared back. Wires get thinned, pegs and cams are set aside, and the number of screws to take is earnestly debated. In reality, less rack just makes for potentially shorter pitches, but that is no bad thing at altitude, as it's a good excuse for a rest. Luckily, Mick and I have compatible runout tolerances. The biggest worry at this stage is that the binge eating might result in stomach upsets, which would potentially jeopardize the whole trip. Fortunately, our cook was scrupulous about his food hygiene, with nobody getting any dodgy guts until we hit civilization again at the end of the trip.

Steve and Ian had accompanied us on the acclimatization outing and decided to go for a peak just to the south of Gave Ding that offered an interesting north face. They planned to set off the day after us. On our expeditions, time constraints due to home and work commitments effectively mean there is only enough time for one attempt on a route. It either would go this time or not at all. It's a committing feeling but certainly increases motivation to the maximum, and this might be a key reason why Mick and I, as a team, have achieved a higher than normal success rate in the Himalaya.

We packed seven days of food and four gas canisters. The plan for the first day was to reach a position below the main difficulties of the first rock bands. Studying the face in the evening sunlight had indicated that a small pillar stood proud from the wall, with the possibility of a bivy on the little col behind it. Reasonably amenable climbing and occasional exhausting, bottomless powder in a shallow gully system brought us to the foot of the rock barrier. Here, a very exposed and poorly protected

Mick Fowler (left) and Paul Ramsden: a 14-year Greater Ranges partnership.
Ramsden Collection

traverse led left in several pitches to our home for the night.

The small col provided the only real bivy option, but it wasn't going to be comfortable. The snow was soft and weak, collapsing constantly as we tried to chop a ledge. Mick's idea of pissing on the snow to add to its stability once it froze seemed questionable. It's times like this, preparing a difficult bivouac for the night, that I'm grateful for how long we've been climbing

[Above] **The author at the precarious first bivy site, which Fowler attempted to improve by urinating on the snow and letting it freeze.** *Mick Fowler* [Next page] Fowler starts a difficult lead on day two. *Paul Ramsden*

together. Both of us knows what needs doing, and each gets on with it without much discussion. Once in our sleeping bags, the discomfort is just accepted—any moaning is usually meant as a joke. After all, what can you do about it?

Things started to get interesting the next day. From below we had identified the best line and several alternatives, but now that we were in position it was clear there was no Plan B—it would be Plan A or nothing. A complicated line led across smooth, snow-covered slabs before turning the overhangs up steep mixed grooves.

Swinging leads, we slowly made our way diagonally across the smooth rock walls. Mick led a suitably challenging steep groove. Squeaky blobs of perfect névé, clearly produced by a monsoon's worth of spindrift falling down the face, showed the way. However difficult, the climbing was exhilarating, with increasing and occasionally disturbing exposure. Mick led another particularly fine pitch up a vertical groove, climbing without a rucksack, and even heel-hooking in places. Unusually, he was heard to shout out with pleasure at how good the climbing was. Seconding with a big sack was pretty much impossible for the puny Ramsden body. Much pulling ensued from Mick. The second bivy emerged from a snow bank below an overhang. Surprisingly, we ended up with a perfectly pitched tent, good anchors, and a beautiful sunset as well—bliss.

More ice appeared during our third day on the wall, but more route choices led to an outbreak of dithering. In the end we plumped to continue the rising diagonal traverse, which led again across steep, thinly iced walls and one very run-out pitch, requiring me to ditch my rucksack on an ice screw. It was one of those steep groove lines with good but thin ice that just draws you upward, until the ice turns to crud and you realize just how far above the gear you are, and just how hard it would be to reverse the last few moves. This scary lead broke onto an icefield approximately halfway up the route.

As the technical difficulties eased we scampered toward the side of a serac band that offered the chance for another good tent pitch inside a crevasse. Comfortable, yes, but very distressing when a loud crack shook the tent in the middle of the night. Nearly continuous

The 1,600-meter north buttress of Gave Ding, climbed with four bivouacs on the ascent and two on the way down. *Paul Ramsden*

spindrift buried us nicely by morning. But what can you expect if you camp in a crevasse?

A long fourth day saw us progressing nicely up the upper buttress, which consisted mostly of a sharp ice ridge, like the Peuterey on Mont Blanc. Hard blue ice and patches of powder snow made for difficult work, but at least we were moving, and for the first time in four days we were in the sun, though it continued to be very cold. The end of the ridge brought us to another serac band that had looked challenging from below, as it ran across the ridge and appeared to overhang alarmingly. Fortunately, a fin of vertical ice in a wildly exposed position, right on the crest of the buttress, allowed us to reach another perfectly flat camping spot in the ocean of powder snow filling the basin directly below the summit.

That night it snowed heavily, and though the summit looked close, it wasn't going to be easy to reach. Plowing a trench across the hanging basin was one of the most exhausting things I have ever done, with the snow chest-deep in places. A steep bergschrund and several pitches of bulletproof ice, climbed with very blunt ice tools, gave access to the summit ridge. Then a short traverse brought us to the top. Any first ascent is a privilege, but to climb a virgin summit from a little-known valley via a demanding route, up a steep north face, was a real joy.

After a very cold night near the summit, we descended the southwest ridge, which was quite broad and glaciated on its southern aspect, allowing us to weave an almost pleasant route through benign-looking seracs. By late morning we had arrived at the col on the ridge from which we planned to descend to the north. However, it was a nice flat spot and it was sunny, so we decided to stop for the day, though it was only late morning.

I have noticed that as we get older Mick and I take longer to descend. It's not that we are moving slowly, but if the weather is nice and the camping good, we seem to find any excuse not to go down. After all, it's far nicer on the mountain than it is at base camp, and we both understand that it will be at least another year before we could find ourselves in a similar position. As the afternoon wore on, we relaxed with endless brew-making and idle chatter. (Mind you, when a tax inspector and a health and safety consultant are sharing a tent, you can't expect the most thrilling of conversations.) In the morning we continued down a prominent couloir, which initially was very steep. I have developed a certain degree of skill with Abalakov anchors, so we have fallen into a routine of me setting up the anchors and Mick following behind. It's quicker for one person to carry all the rack and gear than changing over all the time. I also think Mick likes the snooze while waiting. About 25 threads later, we crossed the bergschrund, having only left one nut.

Several hours later we stumbled into base camp. Steve and Ian had not been quite so lucky with their objective, but we all agreed it had been a very fine trip as we walked back out to Simikot. Now back at work in Saudi Arabia, it feels like a long time ago and an awful lot warmer! Time to focus on next year, I think.

SUMMARY: First ascent of Gave Ding (6,571 meters) in the Changla Himal of western Nepal, via the north buttress (1,600 meters, ED+). Mick Fowler and Paul Ramsden (both U.K.) left base camp on October 17, started climbing the next day, and spent five days on the route. They bivied once near the summit and once on the way down, and returned to base camp on October 24.

ABOUT THE AUTHOR: *Paul Ramsden, 46, calls Nottingham, England, home. Between work and family, he says, "I hardly ever go climbing, sometimes not wearing crampons between expeditions."*

BECKEY AND THE AAJ

A LOOK BACK AT FRED BECKEY'S
UNRIVALED, UNREPEATABLE LEGACY

DOUGALD MACDONALD

No climber in the 88-year history of the *AAJ* has written more reports or had more climbs cited in these pages than Fred Beckey. No one even comes close. Reflecting his extraordinarily long climbing career, the *AAJ* database holds more than 700 articles by or about Beckey (plus nine reports where his surname was misspelled as Becky). These include hundreds of first-person stories and 22 feature articles, documenting now-classic climbs as well as obscure first ascents that may never have been repeated.

Friedrich Wolfgang Beckey did his very first first ascent at age 16, in 1939, in Washington's North Cascades. His first appearance in the *AAJ* came three years later, when he wrote a feature article about the second ascent of Mt. Waddington in British Columbia, with his brother Helmy. (Helmy Beckey actually appeared in the *AAJ* a year before Fred did, as part of the team that made the first ascent of South Howser Tower in the Bugaboos.) After World War II, Fred's new-route production and the significance of his climbs accelerated rapidly, and from the late 1940s through the 1960s he was like a force of nature, completing a dozen or more major new routes nearly every summer. Though he didn't get everywhere—Beckey never did a new route on El Capitan, for example—elsewhere he was prolific, often returning again and again to favorite areas, from Alaska to the Canadian Rockies, the Sierra to the Wind Rivers, the hit list growing ever longer. The volume didn't tail off until the 1980s, when Beckey was in his mid-60s.

More recently, citations *of* Beckey routes have been more common than new climbs by the man himself. But his life in the mountains has continued, including the first ascent of a remote peak in Alaska in the mid-1990s that was subsequently named for him. He has continued to plan and inspire new routes well into this decade.

In the following pages we recall Beckey's nearly seven decades of contributions to this journal. His reports reflect his skills not only as a climber but also as a geographer, historian, amateur geologist, and evocative and often playful writer. No climber will ever leave a greater mark on the *AAJ*—or on American climbing.

"Fred Beckey," original oil painting on wood panel, after a photo by Kris Stanton. *Emilie Lee*

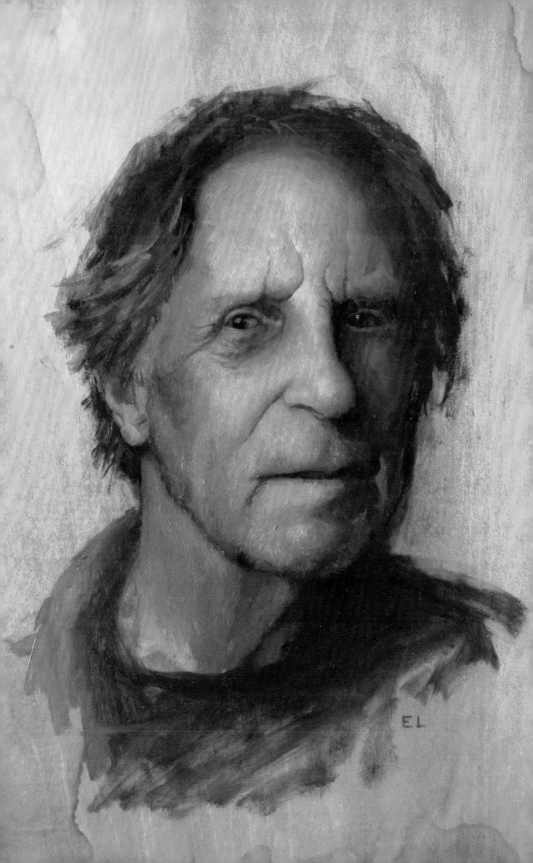

FRED BECKEY: SELECTED CLIMBS

Notable first ascents from a lifetime of climbing are outlined in the timeline above and the AAJ excerpts that follow. All excerpts are by Fred Beckey and have been lightly edited for modern style.

"CLIMBING AND SKIING IN THE WADDINGTON AREA" — *AAJ 1943*

BY 4 O'CLOCK I had changed to tennis shoes with felt pullovers, and we rapidly mounted the slabs of the upper face. The pullovers adhered well to the rock when wet and could be removed quickly for more friction on dry rock. Rock climbing was a pleasant relief from the ice work below.

In two hours the base of the final 500-foot rock wall was reached, Helmy leading across two steep snowpatches. Ice axes and one pair of boots were left behind here. Crampons had been cached lower down. I decided to attempt a face route slightly to the right of the chimney climbed by Wiessner and House. [*Fritz Wiessner and Bill House did the first ascent of Mt. Waddington in 1936.*] Difficulties immediately increased as we started up the nearly vertical wall. For 300 feet wet slabs and difficult pitches, with a few overhangs mixed in, were climbed. Many pitons were used for safety on this wall, which was no place for one who suffered from acrophobia.

The most difficult pitch was a traverse on a vertical face with very delicate holds, followed by a wet, high-angled slab with few useful holds. I had luckily noticed the wet slab from below and redonned my felt pullovers, for one couldn't hope to stick on the wet slab in tennis shoes.... A short traverse brought us to a vertical chimney, the same one climbed by Wiessner, that led to the narrow, snow-covered summit ridge. At 8:30 p.m. the second ascent of Waddington was made. A wonderful view rewarded us, but little time could be had for rest. The match-can register in the cairn was found, and then we hurriedly left the summit at sunset.

Editor's note: The author, although but 19 years old, is a mountaineer of experience, and writes of training for the Mt. Waddington expedition, as follows: "Between June 16th and 21st, 1942, Helmy Beckey, Walt Varney, and I made first ascents of seven rock spires on Kangaroo Ridge, in the N.E. part of the Cascade Mtns. in Washington. Four of these, Big Kangaroo, the Temple, Half Moon Peak, and Mushroom Tower, were technical climbs. To reach the summit of the latter (8,300 ft.), we had to overcome a pitch a good deal more difficult than anything encountered on Mt. Waddington."

[Photo] A teenager in the mid-1930s, already at home in the mountains. *Fred Beckey Collection*

1945
Mt. Shuksan, Price Glacier; Mt. Adams, Adams Glacier, Cascades

1946
Liberty Bell and Nooksack Tower, North Cascades; Kates Needle and Devils Thumb, Coast Mountains, Alaska

1947
Hozomeen, South Peak, North Cascades; Mt. Asperity, British Columbia

1948
Mt. Baker, north ridge, Prusik Peak, Cascades; Pigeon Spire, northeast face, Bugaboos, Canada

1949
Big Baron Spire, Red Finger, and Fishhook Spire, Sawtooths, Idaho; Michael's Sword, Juneau Icefield, Alaska

Burgundy Spire, Mt. Goode, west tower and northwest face, North Cascades

Denali, northwest buttress; first ascents of Mt. Deborah and Mt. Hunter, Alaska; Mt. Goode, northeast face, North Cascades

Mt. Rainier, Mowich Face; Prusik Peak, west ridge, and Mt. Maude, north face, North Cascades

Liberty Bell, west face, Inspiration Peak, east ridge, Golden Horn, north face, Argonaut, north face, North Cascades

Mt. Hood, Yocum Ridge; Snowpatch Spire, east face, Bugaboos; Mt. Owen, Crescent Arête, Tetons; Squamish Buttress

Into dirty clothes

[Above, left] Beckey, at far right, and the team for Mt. Hozomeen's South Peak, 1947. [Right] Leo Scheiblehner on the first ascent of Mt. Hood's Yokum (now Yocum) Ridge in 1959. *Fred Beckey Collection*

"MT. DEBORAH AND MT. HUNTER: FIRST ASCENTS" — *AAJ 1955*

SOON THE CREST SHOWED ITS METTLE. [Heinrich] Harrer hacked his way over some fantastically steep pinnacles, some of them completely overhanging the eastern edge. In what seemed like hours, we exchanged leads; I found slightly better going along the left edge of the ridge, and it was possible to climb safely with the 12-point crampons and good belays. As the ridge steepened again, we had to cut steps. This was a team climb; if anyone slipped, the others would have to leap over the opposite side of the ridge.

How to get up three vertical ice steps near the summit was a provocative question. The steep slope of ice on the left would require hours of chopping and the use of many ice pitons. I was prepared to do battle, but welcomed [Henry] Meybohm's suggestion that he try to cut a channel directly up the steps. At least we could belay safely. Chopping vertically upward to remove masses of rotten ice so that a ladder of clean steps could be made, he worked his way up the narrow pillar-like wall. It was hard work, but success was near.

As we stepped onto the summit at 9:45 p.m., it was our unanimous conclusion that Deborah was the most sensational ice climb anyone of us had ever undertaken....

The setting sun, barely above the horizon, made everything terrestrial seem to fade into insignificance. The biting cold began to take its effect as we lingered to admire the grand view—it was time to descend. Even with the steps carved and aided by a few rappels, it took over four hours of fast climbing to get off the ridge. The climb had been a delicate one, and we felt years younger once on the the relative safety of the glacier.

"MT. HOOD, YOKUM RIDGE" — *AAJ 1960*

As we swung the car up the last few switchbacks to Timberline, Mt. Hood stood crystalline clear against the blue sky. There had not been many clear days like this during the present season.... The Austrian, Leopold Scheiblehner, and I had some ski mountaineering in mind, but after scanning the upper slopes of the mountain, we could not resist the idea of something more complex. At the time we did not know that the entire [Yokum, or Yocum, Ridge, on the west side] had never been climbed. Since the mock-up in the lodge did not show a dotted route, it aroused our curiosity.

...It is not hard to oversleep, and we managed this well.... Putting the crampons on, we roped immediately and crossed the saddle to the Reid Glacier. Here we descended and traversed to the lower flanks of Yokum Ridge. The knife-like blades of ice seemed like a nightmare of ice problems instead of a route to the summit. With a covering of ice feathers, not a single rock was visible. Getting onto the crest was a toe and ice-pick workout—a strenuous one for the first cramponing of the season.... Because of the frost and rime formations, the whole surface was often a buildup of frost feathers. An axe belay was often useless, and ice pitons could not be placed....We continued flanking the worst towers just under the crest, being careful to work into tiny belay spots on the ridge or behind towers. Once I chimneyed my way up a 30-foot section of vertical ice, grasping long columns of ice feathers and pulling outwards to keep my balance while kicking and cutting footholds. This required great care, for the wrong slash of the ice axe might have brought the whole chimney wall down. It was a difficult and dangerous place—sometimes I could see daylight through the frost feathers two feet under the veneer surface. At one point Leo cut some huge holds over his head and somehow swarmed up a 12-foot overhang.

...About one o'clock we stood on the top, facing a strong, biting wind. Our descent down the normal route led us into camp again. Skiing wide open, we raced for the lodge in the afternoon sun.

[Below, left] Yvon Chouinard, Beckey, and Dan Doody (left to right) below Mt. Edith Cavell in 1961. [Right] Celebrating atop Mt. Hunter after the first ascent in 1954. *Fred Beckey Collection*

Mt. Ratz, Stikine
Icecap, British
Columbia; Glacier
Peak, north face,
Beartooths,
Montana

Mt. Robson, Canadian
Rockies, first winter
ascent; Squamish,
Northwest Passage;
Stiletto, southwest
face, Coast
Mountains, Canada

Echo Tower, Utah, Mt.
Alverstone, northeast
face, Yukon; Mt.
Seattle, St. Elias
Mountains; Squamish
Chief, Tantalus Wall

Great White Throne,
Zion National Park;
Middle Sister,
Monument Valley;
El Matador, Devils
Tower; Whitney Portal
Buttress, California

South Early
Winter Spire, east
buttress, Cascades;
Premiere Buttress,
Whitney Portal,
and Carillon Peak,
east face, Sierra

"TEHIPITE DOME" — *AAJ 1964*

IF TEHIPITE DOME were in YOSEMITE VALLEY, it would come close to rivaling El Capitan in height and grandeur. But it is located in the wilderness of the Middle Fork of the Kings River, and here it has no rival. Its 7,700-foot summit towers 3,600 feet above the glaciated valley floor.... Standing next to an abandoned prospector's cabin, after a 21-mile hike from the North Fork of the Kings, Ken Weeks and I just shook our heads in despair. Not only were we cut off from our projected assault of the immense south face by a torrent called Crown Creek, but the majesty and size of the Dome was simply overwhelming....

[*Beckey and Weeks recruited two more climbers, John Ahern and Herb Swedlund, and a week later began an "expeditionary rock climb" of the 17-pitch south face.*]

...During the night the cloud cover vanished, and the morning, June 2, was brilliant. We planned to push the lead ropes up the face another day, and then make a final push with bivouac gear after another trek out for more food. While Weeks and Ahern were hauling supplies up the deep chimney, Swedlund and I prusiked up to our high mark and continued up the dihedral system that became our route line. I worked up an overhanging layback that was difficult but went free to the end of a lead. Swedlund then spent several hours nailing up a pitch that was a slanting overhang.... It was still early afternoon; we decided to make one more lead and then leave all ropes hanging for the finale. The dihedral flared out badly, forcing me to do a great deal of hand-jamming and awkward pressure work with the right shoulder. It was slow going. Fortunately the protection opportunities were adequate, and once past a really hard

[Below, left] **Beckey scoping Moses tower in Canyonlands National Park.** [Right] **Working the pay phones to line up partners and check the weather.** *Eric Bjørnstad Collection*

1969	**1970**	**1971**	**1972**	**1973**
Ellingwood, north face, Fremont, west face, Sacajawea, west face, Arrowhead, south face, Wind River Range	Warlock Needle, south face, Charlotte Dome, south face, Lone Pine Peak, direct south face, Sierra Nevada	El Segundo, Whitney Portal; Fresno Dome and Balloon Dome; Bastille Buttress, Lone Pine Peak, California	Moses, Canyonlands, Utah; Chinle Spire, Arizona; Mt. Hickman and the Tusk, Alaska	Jacobs Ladder, Monument Valley; early climbs in Cochise Stronghold, Arizona

[Above, left] Beckey gearing up for the first ascent of Mt. Seattle. *Don Liska* [Above, center] On the glacier below Mt. Beckey in Alaska. *John Middendorf* [Above, right] Wind Rivers, 1998. *Cameron Burns*

crux move, I saw that the angle of the wall began to decrease. Also, knobs and solution holds were beginning to appear. After Herb arrived, we held a war council and decided to risk a lead further.

Sensing a victory that day, because of the lessening angle and the appearance of knobs, we took only a selection of iron, some slings, and with the one rope began to climb like demons. After a pitch Herb yelled that it looked even better, so we continued up on several pitches of marvellous, exposed face climbing, always with just sufficient knobs.... At a crucial smooth slab, the dihedral suddenly reappeared, much to our relief. Swedlund made a fine direct-aid maneuver around a corner, on a slanting overhang, and then swung left from a piton to a bush. "Climb like mad," was the shout, "I think we'll make it."

"MOSES, CANYONLANDS NATIONAL PARK" — *AAJ 1973*

ONE OF THE LAST GREAT DESERT TOWERS, this one discreetly hidden in remote Taylor Canyon east of the Green River, was climbed October 26. Lin Ottinger, Moab tour guide, had long known of it under the name "Moses," its curious shape resembling the image of the desert leader of history. Eric Bjørnstad and I had examined the 500-plus-foot tower in 1970 during the climb of "Zeus," then climbed the overhanging first pitch a year later, only to become stalled by a heat wave. With a solid base camp resembling a safari, with the jeep, VW bus, tents, assorted friends, and a kennel of three hungry dogs, the climb had to be a success this time. Our timing was perfect, for downpours preceded and followed the climb. The climbing was largely careful aid on Wingate sandstone, with three "super-solid" hanging belays.

"CATHEDRAL MOUNTAINS" — *AAJ 1997*

IN JUNE, John Middendorf, Calvin Hebert, and I visited a small, isolated cluster of granitic peaks with small glaciers to the west of Mt. Foraker, at the edge of the high tundra. The peaks are bordered by Cathedral Creek on the west; one wonders if they were originally intended to be the Cathedral Spires (now the Kichatna Spires) to the southwest. The "Cathedral Mountains" are in fact a Kichatna miniature, with an inferior quality of rock.

After an airdrop on the Cathedral Creek glacier, we hiked into our base camp from the roadway of the Purkypile Mine. The ascent of the highest summit of the peaks (just over 8,500 feet) had an interesting glacial sweep, then a narrow summit snow ridge. The crux was a really loose section of flaky rock (5.5). Most of the climb was done with light snow falling, so the views we expected were limited. The area has some wall climbing potential, but much smaller than the Kichatnas. It seems certain that we were the first climbers to visit these peaks.

Editor's note: This report was one of three Beckey accounts of new routes published in AAJ *1997. The Alaskan mountain was subsequently named Mt. Beckey.*

THE FRED BECKEY FILM

Dirtbag: The Legend of Fred Beckey is a feature documentary premiering in 2017. Director Dave O'Leske spent a decade filming with Beckey in the mountains of North America and China, getting to know the man whose prolific alpine accomplishments inspired generations of climbers. As a nonprofit sponsor of the project, the AAC is accepting tax-deductible donations to help fund the film. More info is available at *www.dirtbagmovie.com.*

Kedemath, south
face, attempt, India;
Heartstone Peak,
north buttress,
Canada; Caliban
Peak, south
buttress, Alaska

Cathedral Mountains,
Alaska, first ascent
of Peak 8,500, later
named Mt. Beckey

Bomber Lake Arete in
the Wind Rivers—the
Cameron Burns *AAJ*
report was the last
to document a new
route climbed by
Beckey

Snowcap Mountain,
Alaska—the 2010 *AAJ*
account was the last
report Beckey has
submitted (he did not
attempt to summit)

The 2014 *AAJ*
reported the
first ascent of
Joey Shan in
China, during an
expedition led by
Beckey

Below Mt. Edith Cavell, Canadian Rockies,
2007. *Alain Denis*

THE NEACOLA MOUNTAINS

A BRIEF HISTORY, NEW CLIMBS, AND MUCH LEFT TO EXPLORE

ERIK RIEGER

Many climbers have never heard of Alaska's Neacola Mountains. In half a century, only a handful of climbing expeditions have gone there—and even fewer successful ones. Lower-elevation peaks (for Alaska), a remote location, harsh weather, and unnamed mountains and glaciers likely play a large part in the range's obscurity. Moreover, the first significant climbs in the area, in 1965, were never widely reported, and Fred Beckey, who made the second known trip into the central Neacolas, in the early 1970s, thought the area fine enough to keep it secret for upwards of two decades.

However, as with the recently "rediscovered" Revelation Mountains, to the northwest of the Neacolas, it would seem this range is finally getting more climbers' attention, with two separate European parties climbing new routes in 2015. But there's still plenty to do. Alaskan climbing historian Steve Gruhn suggests that more than 90 percent of the peaks in the range remain unclimbed.

GEOGRAPHY

THE NEACOLA MOUNTAINS rise where the southwest tip of the Alaska Range meets the northeast end of the Aleutian Range. The Neacolas are bound to the southeast by the Tlikakila River; to the northeast lie the Tordrillo Mountains; just north are the Hidden Mountains; to the northwest, the Revelations.

This article will focus on the central Neacola Mountains, bound by Turquoise Glacier to the west, the main North Fork Glacier to the south, Neacola, Tuning Fork, and Slingshot glaciers to the north, and the main Pitchfork Glacier on the east side. This area, which lies entirely within the Lake Clark National Park Wilderness Area, holds a dense array of ice-covered peaks. The

[Next page] **Looking southeast across the Pitchfork Glacier area. Citadel is the pointy, sunlit summit in back left, with the distant Redoubt Volcano visible over its left shoulder. In the back right are unclimbed Peak 8,505' (the blocky summit with the squared-off top) and to its right unclimbed Peak 8,908'; just down and left is Mt. Reaper. The central summits form the ridgeline north of the Pitchfork Glacier's north fork. The photo was taken in October.** *Dan Bailey*

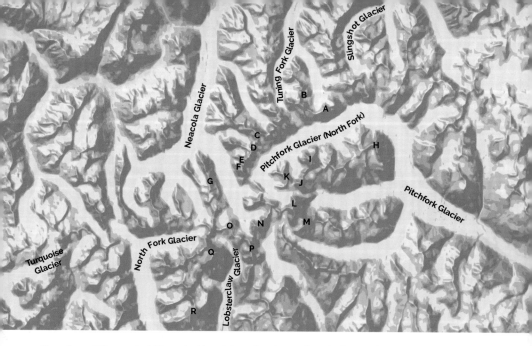

Overview of the central Neacola Mountains, showing major glaciers and selected peaks. (A) Knox Peak. (B) Anvil Tower. (C) Peak 7,235 and Dogtooth Spire. (D) Peak 6,710. (E) Triangle Peak. (F) Peak 6,950 and Aguja Ulysses. (G) Peak 6,310. (H) Peak 7,105. (I) Citadel. (J) Mt. Reaper. (K) Mystery Mountain. (L) Peak 8,908. (M) Peak 8,505. (N) Peak 7,230. (O) Mt. Anklyosaur. (P) Bernese Girl. (Q) Mt. Neacola. (R) Peak 8,250. Peak elevations (in feet) cited in this article are quoted from USGS 7.5-minute quadrangles or estimated from contour lines (+/- 50 feet). *Base map by © Mapbox, © OpenStreetMap*

glaciers hover around 4,000 feet, with maximum peak elevations of just over 9,000 feet. Most of the peaks are not officially named.

Some of the peaks in the Neacolas are comprised of Bugaboo-like granite, with soaring, crack-laden walls. Others have extensive black basalt or diorite layers, which, when covered in snow and ice, add great complexity to this unassuming range. A short season, poor coastal weather, and intricate glaciers compound the difficulty of planning a trip. At least one climber has described the range in a relatable and desirable context: "A heavily glaciated version of the North Cascades." Let's go with that.

HISTORY

THE CLIMBING HISTORY in the central Neacola Mountains began in 1965 when Joe and Joan Firey and Frances and George Whitmore (who made the first ascent of the Nose of El Capitan) completed the first known expedition into the range. After climbing two smaller peaks and attempting a couple of others, they made the first ascent of Citadel (8,305'), a hallmark peak of the area. In the early 1970s, Hooman Aprin and Fred Beckey attempted Mt. Neacola, the highest summit in the range, at approximately 9,350 feet, but were unsuccessful.

In 1979, Peri Chickering, Todd Denman, Jon Stevens, and Michael Witz, believing they were the first climbers to enter the range, planned an attempt on Mt. Neacola. Their warm-up was the west ridge of a peak they reported as 6,820 feet but was likely Peak 6,920', now known as Mt. Anklyosaur. During the descent, Denman fell about 35 feet, badly bruising his tailbone. He and Stevens decided to attempt the 25-mile ski out to Telaquana Lake and try to find a

Joan and Joe Firey climb and name Citadel (8,305'). The Fireys and Frances and George Whitmore also climb Peak 6,310' and Peak 6,920' (now called Mt. Anklyosaur).

Fred Beckey and Hooman Aprin attempt the north side of Mt. Neacola (ca 9,350').

Peri Chickering and Michael Witz attempt the north face of Mt. Neacola and climb the north face and north ridge of Peak 7,230' at the head of the east fork of the Neacola Glacier, as well as "Peak 6,959" (possibly Peak 6,950').

Fred Beckey, James Garrett, Lorne Glick, and Kennan Harvey visit the area, and Garrett, Glick, and Harvey make the first ascent of Mt. Neacola from the west. Garrett climbs Peak 7,020', naming it Bernese Girl, across the Lobsterclaw Glacier from Mt. Neacola.

Topher Donahue and Kennan Harvey climb a direct route up the north face of Mt. Neacola but do not reach the summit. The pair also climb and name 6,920-foot Mt. Anklyosaur.

Joe Stock, Dylan Taylor, and Andrew Wexler make a full-length ski traverse of the Neacola Mountains from Ch'akajabena Lake to Little Lake Clark.

Daron Huck and Dustin Schaad climb and ski several couloirs near the big bend in the north fork of the Pitchfork Glacier, mostly off the east side of Peak 7,105' and the northwest side of Peak 6,005'.

Aaron Fetter, Dan Oberlatz, and Joe Stock lead a 12-day ski mountaineering trip in the area. Oberlatz attempts Citadel, and five team members climbed Peak 6,710' on the northwest side of the north fork of Pitchfork Glacier.

Curro González and Gerard van den Berg climb a subpeak of Peak 6,950', near the head of the Pitchfork Glacier, which they call Aguja Ulysses. They then move down the Pitchfork Glacier and climb several subpeaks in a cirque north of the glacier's bend.

Ben Chriswell, Sam Johnson, and Aaron Thrasher climb the northeast ridge of Peak 7,035', near the head of the north arm of Pitchfork, calling it Mystery Mountain. They also attempt a 7,210-foot peak they call Triangle and climb a 14-pitch, east-facing route up a formation they call Dog Tooth (7,150'), a subpeak of Peak 7,235' on the north side of Pitchfork's north arm.

Jake Gaventa, Patrick Graham, and Chris Marshall climb off the Tuning Fork Glacier, to the north of the Pitchfork, making the first ascent of Knox Peak (6,950') and skiing the Two Towers Couloir between a pair of stunning granite spires.

Hansjörg Auer and Much Mayr climb the north face of Mt. Reaper (7,425').

Jon Bracey and Matt Helliker attempt the northwest ridge of Citadel, then climb the north ridge to the summit. [Photo at right] Matt Helliker on day one of the northwest ridge attempt. *Alastair Lee*

THE CITADEL, 1965

BY JOE FIREY

The "Clarkachamna Peaks" are a very remote group of mountains, west of Cook Inlet and the Aleutian volcanic peaks, and lying about halfway between Lake Clark, to the south, and Lake Chakachamna, to the north, hence my joking unofficial name. [*Today these are known as the Neacola Mountains, and Ch'akajabena is the recognized name of the lake.*] Very little mountaineering has been done in this area, probably because these are low-altitude peaks. When climbers go to Alaska they usually have the big peaks in their sights.

George and Frances Whitmore, my wife, Joan Firey, and I flew from Kenai to the north fork of a pitchfork-shaped glacier, located in the center of the Lake Clark D-1 USGS map. This Pitchfork Glacier is the origin of the Glacier Fork of the Tlikakila River, which flows southwest out of Lake Clark Pass and into Little Lake Clark. Most of the peaks in this area appeared to be granite, but two of the highest peaks were of a steep-sided, jet-black rock, perhaps intrusive gabbro.

We climbed a prominent 8,300-foot peak on the south side of this north fork of the glacier and named it Citadel [now given 8,305'], due to its fortress-like appearance. We also ascended two peaks at the head of the north glacier fork. An attempt on a 7,800-foot peak on the north side of the glacier was turned back by snow avalanche conditions. All of these climbs appeared to be first ascents.

The two prize peaks in this area eluded us: an 8,900-foot black tower at the head of the middle fork of the glacier [*Peak 8,908'*], and a 9,400-foot black block of a peak [*Mt. Neacola, 9,350'*], just a bit south of the head of the Neacola Glacier, which feeds the Neacola River. The weather in this area was not cooperative, and during a stay of over two weeks we only had four

The return flight to Kenai was challenging. The Piper Cub, with ski wheels, needed to be rocked back and forth to keep the plane mostly on one ski at a time, since the double-ski drag prevented picking up flying speed. The pilot took us one at a time off the glacier, so there was always someone available to rock the plane while running along outside. On the last flight, I ran alongside, rocking the plane, and then, at the last minute, jumped into the plane. This was all very exciting, and my adrenaline content didn't taper off until after we landed at Kenai.

EDITOR'S NOTES: *The late Joe and Joan Firey, whose first ascents in the Cascades and Coast Mountains appeared frequently in the AAJ throughout the 1960s and 1970s, never reported this pioneering trip to the Neacolas. Joe Firey provided this account to Lowell Skoog (alpenglow.org) in a hand-written note in 2006.*

Alaska mountaineering historian Steve Gruhn and Carla Firey, daughter of the Fireys, have clarified details of this previously unreported 1965 trip after reviewing various notes and correspondence, including letters between the team members and Vin Hoeman collected at the University of Alaska Anchorage.

The four-person party flew to the north branch of the Pitchfork Glacier on June 15, 1965, placing a base camp at around 4,200 feet. The climbers first attempted the east face of the south ridge of the Citadel, climbing within 50 feet of the ridge crest before retreating in the face of fog and overhanging rime. The Fireys then attempted Peak 7,850' (60°53'N, 153°18'W), from a col north of the summit, getting about 300 feet above the col.

After moving camp to the Neacola Glacier's eastern fork (4,300'), the four climbers summited Peak 6,310' from the southeast, via third-class snow and mixed rock. On June 26, the Fireys and George Whitmore attempted another mountain, east of the Neacola Glacier headwall, but the precise elevation and location are not certain. On June 27, all four climbed Peak 6,920', now called Mt. Anklyosaur, a snow climb via the east slope.

After returning to the Pitchfork Glacier, the Fireys went for the Citadel again on July 3. Deviating from their earlier attempt, they angled across the upper east face to gain the south ridge higher up. The climb was mostly snow, with a short rock pitch, and they summited after eight hours. The second known ascent did not come for another 50 years.

Joe Firey and George and Frances Whitmore take in the view from Peak 6,310', above the west side of the east fork of the Neacola Glacier. The view is to the southeast, toward Peak 6,925' and Peak 7,230' at the head of the glacier. *Joan Firey*

[Above] **Fred Beckey at camp on the Lobsterclaw Glacier below Mt. Neacola (left peak) during the 1991 trip. The rocky subsummit to the right is likely unclimbed.** *Kennan Harvey* [Below] **Mt. Neacola from the west. The 1991 route ascended the prominent couloir to the saddle and then traversed to the summit.** *Dan Bailey*

plane. After two days they reached the lake, and, with food running out, they discovered a rowboat, rigged a sail out of their tent fly, and sailed 10 miles across the whitecapped lake to an old village marked on their map. The village was deserted. Luckily, they were able to flag down a plane and leave the mountains. Chickering and Witz were unsuccessful on the big north face of Neacola but did make the first ascent of Peak 7,230', at the head of the east arm of the Neacola Glacier, via the "fantastic" north face and ridge, and also the west face of "Peak 6,959" (likely Peak 6,950').

Fred Beckey eventually spilled out photos and enthusiasm for the area to longtime exploratory climber James Garrett, and the two, along with Lorne Glick and Kennan Harvey, traveled there in spring of 1991. Beckey stayed in camp, assuming his role as "spiritual leader," while the three made the first ascent of proud Mt. Neacola by a steep, icy ramp on its west face.

Garrett wrote in *AAJ 1992* that they underestimated the route from photos: "The hard ice provided secure belays, although it was a wrenching effort to get the anchors in. Rock placements yielded little protection in rock unlike so much of the beautiful granite on surrounding peaks. The angle steepened to 65° as evening neared.... Ice clogged many of the screws and they became difficult to place; long runouts followed. Kennan led the last pitch through the ice bulges below the saddle. Three hundred feet, two ice screws! Lorne and I cheered him on. He was in his own private Hell."

Considering the timeline of Alaskan climbing, it's incredible to consider that only two of this range's great peaks—Citadel and Neacola—had been climbed by the early 1990s.

THE CITADEL, 2015

BY MATT HELLIKER

On May 2, Jon Bracey and I set off to attempt the unclimbed northwest ridge of the Citadel (8,305') in the Neacola Mountains. Unfortunately, a few days before our arrival, a heavy snowfall buried the ridge under powder, making for slow going. On the first day of climbing there was hard mixed, free, and aid on very good rock. We bivied after 2,300' of climbing and a huge day.

We woke the following morning to snow showers but continued up to the base of a large tower with a snow crest above. The cracks had been good to this point, but the rock now blanked out—smooth, steep granite without a crack or seam in sight, for aid climbing or otherwise. We spent much time looking for an alternative route, off the ridgeline to the left or right, but found only featureless granite in these snowy conditions. We descended from there. It was clear that we could have drilled, bolted, and bat-hooked our way up the tower. But that's not our style. Maybe we missed something, or maybe in drier summer conditions, with rock shoes, it would be possible.

Following a day of recovery in base camp, Jon and I set off again, but this time to attempt the unclimbed north ridge. After a steep glacial approach, we reached the base of the ridge and quickly climbed up snowy ramps, open faces, and a few mixed steps to reach a large tower, which we aided in cold and windy conditions. This led us to a typical Alaskan corniced ridge, which eventually led us to snow slopes and to the summit, completing what is likely the second ascent of the peak. We descended our line on the north ridge.

SUMMARY: *New route on the Citadel (8,305') via its north ridge (3,700'), by Jon Bracey and Matt Helliker (both U.K.), May 5, 2015.*

[Photo] **Citadel's north ridge (left) and northwest ridge (right).** *Alastair Lee*

SUGAR MAN

BY HANSJÖRG AUER

The summits of the Neacola Mountains are not as high as in the nearby Revelation Mountains or Central Alaska Range, but the glaciers are much lower, meaning the walls still reach heights of 1,000m or more. With three different projects in mind in the Neacolas, Much Mayr and I headed to Alaska at the beginning of May. We had some pretty unstable weather—this range is well known for that—and only during the first day of our trip did we enjoy blue sky.

We first attempted a warm-up on a rock pillar next to our base camp, on the Pitchfork Glacier, but conditions were pretty bad and we were forced to retreat after around 400m of climbing. Then we got struck by an intense storm. We spent over three days in a whiteout, constantly freeing the tent from snow. I'd begun to think this wouldn't be the luckiest trip. Living on the glacier, hundreds of kilometers away from civilization, demands strong belief and a great friendship to keep high spirits and good vibes.

The 750m north face of Mt. Reaper (Peak 7,425'), showing the route Sugar Man. *Hansjörg Auer*

We focused on the north face of Peak 7,425', which rises from the massive Pitchfork Glacier with a stunning 750m north face. However, the temperatures were warmer than we expected, so our objective was kind of tricky. After a day of checking out the approach, we decided to give it a go. I knew that we needed to be super-light and that we had to try and climb in less than ideal weather, in order to avoid higher temperatures on the face.

On May 17 we climbed the north face in a 12-hour push from camp to summit and back, staying on top for less than five minutes because heavy clouds were coming in. We experienced lots of spindrift due to strong winds higher up, and some really challenging steep pitches with bad protection. While I was leading the crux, where a fall was out of the question, I recognized for the first time that this route might belong under the class of "knife edge." Some of the belays were made only with ice axes, and the ice, mainly just plastered to blank granite, really couldn't have been any thinner, otherwise our alpine-style climb would have ground to a halt.

SUMMARY: *The first ascent of Mt. Reaper (Peak 7,425') by its north face, via the route Sugar Man (750m, M7 85° A1), by Hansjörg Auer and Much Mayr (both Austria), May 17, 2015.*

[Left] Topher Donahue during the near-miss attempt on Mt. Neacola's north face—the Medusa Face. He and Kennan Harvey topped out the face but then retreated in a storm. [Right] The complex north face of Mt. Neacola. The 1995 attempt followed weaknesses up the sunlit prow. Donahue said, "Take knifeblade pitons for the compact rock. We had 15 and used all of them, leaving most of them in anchors on the descent." *Kennan Harvey (both)*

In 1995, Harvey returned with the young and talented Topher Donahue. Their focus was on difficulty, and they aimed for the massive north face of Mt. Neacola—what Donahue calls the "Medusa Face," about 4,500 feet tall. Using a portaledge and completing much intricate ice, mixed, and aid climbing (up to 5.10 and A3), they reached the top of the face at midnight, "about 800 feet" of easier climbing below the summit. "We spent the night doing the dance of life on a tiny ledge chopped into the ice," Donahue wrote in *AAJ 1996*. "Morning brought no improvement, and clouds poured off the ocean to the east. Opting for descent while we still could, we rappelled through the storm." The face hasn't been attempted since.

Until recently, much of the activity in the central area of the Neacolas has been skiing. One high point came in 2006, when Joe Stock, Dylan Taylor, and Andrew Wexler made the first ski traverse of the entire range, traveling over 100 miles from end to end. In the same year, Daron Huck and Dustin Schaad reported climbing and skiing a number of 3,000-foot couloirs in the northern sector of the Pitchfork Glacier.

Climbing activity has gradually increased. In 2009, European climbers Curro González and Gerard van den Berg visited the Pitchfork Glacier, making several ascents of small peaks by mixed routes and gullies. A couple of years later, in 2011, Ben Chriswell, Sam Johnson, and Aaron Thrasher also visited the Pitchfork Glacier, making the probable first ascent of a

[Above] Looking toward the southwest sides of unclimbed Peak 8,908' (left) and Peak 8,505' (right) from the north face of Mt. Neacola. The sunlit Citadel can be seen in the background to the left. *Kennan Harvey* [Below, left] The east side of Dog Tooth (7,150'), a subpeak of Peak 7,235'. The 2011 route generally followed the right skyline. *Joe Stock* [Below, right] The main peaks in the photo above, now seen from the opposite side, looking west toward the head of the Pitchfork Glacier's middle prong: Peak 8,505' (left) and Peak 8,908' (right). Part of Mt. Neacola can be seen through the notch in the background. *Joe Stock*

snowy peak they dubbed Mystery Mountain and a fine granite spire they called the Dog Tooth—the latter resembles the east face of Pigeon Spire in the Bugaboos, both in shape and rock quality. In 2013, a three-man party climbed Knox Peak above the Tuning Fork Glacier.

The spring of 2015 saw two impressive ascents off the Pitchfork Glacier by visiting European teams: Hansjörg Auer and Much Mayr made the first ascent of Peak 7,425', which they called Mt. Reaper, by its steep north face, and Jon Bracey and Matt Helliker climbed the 3,700-foot north ridge of Citadel for the peak's second ascent, after first attempting the striking northwest ridge.

The northwest face of unclimbed Peak 8,250, south of Mt. Neacola, above the North Fork Glacier. *Dan Bailey*

POTENTIAL

THE HIGHEST CONCENTRATIONS of interesting peaks in the central area are located off the Pitchfork Glacier, the head of the Neacola Glacier, and the North Fork and Lobsterclaw glaciers. The huge north face of Neacola remains unclimbed to the summit. Topher Donahue commented, "There's a rad, El Cap–size ice line to be done on the right side of the face, but it was threatened with an active serac when we were there [in 1995]. Maybe with climate change the serac is less active now, or gone entirely, in which case one of the sickest ice lines in North America is waiting."

At the head of the central arm of the Pitchfork is a pair of stunning unclimbed summits, steep on all sides: Peak 8,908' and Peak 8,505'. On the west flank of "Triangle Peak" (Peak 7,210') and its neighbors is a group of complex granite spires reminiscent of the Waddington area. Many impressive peaks west and north of the Pitchfork and west and south of Mt. Neacola are unclimbed. Undoubtedly, other objectives will reveal themselves as more climbers visit.

LOGISTICS

MOST CLIMBING EXPEDITIONS have flown in by ski plane with Doug Brewer (Alaska West Air), based outside of Kenai. No commercial helicopters are allowed to land in Lake Clark National Park, which means teams must rely on ski-plane landings in this lower-elevation area. Because of this, the best time to visit is likely to be from April to early June.

Special thanks to Dan Bailey, Topher Donahue, Carla Firey, Steve Gruhn, Kennan Harvey, Dan Oberlatz, and Joe Stock for assistance with this article.

CLIMBS & EXPEDITIONS

2016

CLIMBS & EXPEDITIONS reports generally are arranged geographically, from north to south, and from west to east, within a country or region. Unless noted, all reports are from the 2015 calendar year. We encourage climbers to submit notable ascents for future editions (email us at *aaj@americanalpineclub.org* or use the submission form at *publications.americanalpineclub. org*). The complete *AAJ* database, from 1929 to present, can be searched at *publications. americanalpineclub.org*. Online reports frequently contain additional text, photos, maps, and topos—look for these symbols indicating additional resources at the website:

FULL-LENGTH REPORT	ADDITIONAL PHOTOS	MAPS OR TOPOS	VIDEO OR MULTIMEDIA

[Photo] Matt Pickles pulls the crux roof of Reflections (E6 6b), a new route on the Mirror Wall in Renland, East Greenland (see p.180). *Matt Pycroft / Coldhouse Collective / Berghaus*

UNITED STATES

COLFAX PEAK, NORTH FACE, KIMCHI SUICIDE VOLCANO

AT THE END of the 2015 winter and into spring, I had a little obsession with Colfax Peak, the prominent subsummit on the western side of Mt. Baker (a.k.a. Kulshan). Ever since simulsoloing the Cosley-Houston with Roger Strong back in 2007, I knew that Colfax Peak held some of the highest-quality alpine climbing in the Cascades.

In March, Sarah Hart and I made a repeat ascent of the Polish Route, which was a spectacular ice climb. Following this, we went back twice in early April. On April 5, Sarah and I climbed the classic Cosley-Houston with skis on our backs, hoping to ski from the summit of Mt. Baker. We returned four days later, on April 9, and this time got serious, heading up a line I had scoped on earlier forays.

The route we climbed takes an independent line to the left of the Polish Route. It is, I believe, the first route on the face that is more of a mixed climb than a pure ice climb. The rock on Colfax is amazingly well featured, with tons of face holds everywhere. Protection isn't always easy, of course. We named our route Kimchi Suicide Volcano (300m, AI4+ M5 R). It is definitely one of the highest-quality alpine climbs I've ever done in the Cascades (along with the Cosley-Houston and the Polish Route). 📷

– COLIN HALEY

COLFAX PEAK, NORTH FACE, FORD'S THEATRE

ON APRIL 20, Andrew Fabian and I put up a fourth route on the north face of Colfax Peak. Most of the route is hidden during the standard approach to the face due its location in a cleft around the right side of a buttress. We climbed three pitches of steep ice before mellowing out

The north face of Colfax Peak. (1) Kimchi Suicide Volcano. (2) Polish Route. (3) Cosley-Houston. (4) Ford's Theatre. *Dana Bellows*

Tim Halder leading a steep flake on the fourth pitch of Stonehenge. *Jason Schilling*

on steep snow gullies and climbing the final 100' of the Cosley-Houston toward the summit. It's a spectacular setting, and the climbing is fun and sustained but without many belay options after the first pitch. We called the route Ford's Theatre (500', AI4+).

— DANA BELLOWS

HIMMELHORN, SOUTH FACE, STONEHENGE

"WE WERE BORN TOO LATE. Roper's already been here. We're just picking up his scraps," Tim Halder mused as we gazed up at the unclimbed south face of the Himmelhorn (7,880'). Our adventure had started on July 3, as we lugged monster packs up the Goodell Creek jungle and then camped below the Chopping Block above Crescent Creek. On July 4 we set our sights on the easternmost tower of the Rake (7,840'), believing it to be unclimbed. The short climb went quickly and we found no evidence of an ascent. However, John Roper has since informed us that he climbed this tower in 1984, calling it the Turret. We were indeed picking up his scraps.

We spent the next day resting at our camp and scoping lines on the Himmelhorn, whose south face towers above the wildflower meadows of Crescent Creek basin. [*Himmelhorn is part of the Crescent Creek Spires, the westernmost extension of the southern Picket Range. The peak is also referred to as the Himmelgeisterhorn.*] It probably sees an ascent every other year or so—by either its standard route (Cooper-Denny-Firey-Firey-Whitmore, *AAJ 1962*) or the highly regarded Wild Hair Crack (Kroeker-Roper-Wild, 1981), both on the northwest aspect. The south face looked complex but presented several options.

We left camp on July 6 at 4 a.m. By 5 a.m. we'd reached the snow slope below the wall and then climbed up easy rock ramps and ledges for approximately 600'. This took us to a grassy col where we pulled out the rope and rack. Tim led the first pitch up blocky terrain (5.8). I took the second up a dead-end dihedral, eventually traversing left onto the face and up another hand crack (5.10-). The third pitch was quite easy. And on the fourth pitch, Tim led up a steep, quality flake (5.8). The rock went from solid to excellent as we moved higher. On the fifth pitch we traversed right to the base of the summit tower and I lobbied for going straight up, thinking it would be two pitches or less. On the sixth pitch I led up a steep and run-out face, which took us two-thirds of the way up the tower (5.10-). From here, Tim opted for a moderate but wild rightward traverse on solid but unprotected climbing. This gained a notch between the summit tower and a pinnacle, marking the end of the difficulties.

From the notch we climbed one easy, loose pitch to the summit. On top we were amazed to find the original summit log from 1961 in a film canister. The rest of the trip was all downhill, more or less. Back at camp we watched Spinal Tap's "Stonehenge," inciting our route name: Stonehenge (8 pitches, 5.10-). 📷

– JASON SCHILLING

MT. TRIUMPH, EAST FACE, MEMENTO MORI

ROLF LARSON AND I finally got our stuff together this summer and enjoyed discovering a new line up Mt. Triumph on August 12. The route climbs directly up the east face and is characterized by a ton of juggy and often steep 5.8-ish climbing, with many passages of 5.9. After eight pitches we joined the northeast ridge for its final couple of hundred feet of scrambling to the summit. We spent about 10 hours on the route and then descended the south ridge for the complete alpine experience. Night befell us while still above the glacier, so we endured—I mean enjoyed—a shiver bivy on an exposed ridge. We left fresh tat on this descent.

We called the route Memento Mori (a.k.a. the Tom Thomas Memorial Route, 8 pitches, 5.9+), after Tom Thomas, who died attempting to solo this wall in 1988. His frayed rope hovered above the belay atop our fourth pitch, which was affecting and sobering, even for crusty, salty types. As with all mountain routes, there's some loose rock, but it's primarily solid gneiss. The route deserves more traffic, as it offers solid adventure and aesthetic pulling. I'd recommend a rack up to four inches, with some pitons, glacier gear, and double ropes. 📷

– ERIC WEHRLY

GOLDEN HORN, EAST FACE

ON A FRIDAY EVENING in June, Jason Schilling and I hiked in to explore the unclimbed east face of Golden Horn (8,366'), just north of Washington Pass on the eastern slope of the North Cascades. Fred Beckey and company made the first ascent of Golden Horn via the Southwest Route in 1946, then returned in 1958 to ascend the north face. Around the corner, Gordy Skoog and Jim Walseth climbed the Northeast Arête (III 5.8) in 1979. Gordy and his brothers, Carl and Lowell, returned with a film crew a year later to create an episode for KOMO-TV's Exploration Northwest, called "The Goldenhorn Pinnacle." Despite this colorful history, the peak's 1,000' east face had never seen an ascent, in part because it was rumored to be chossy. Eight years ago, I scrambled the Southwest Route with my wife, Arun, to sneak a peek for myself.

Jason and I approached up Swamp Creek to reach Snowy Lakes, a popular camp spot off the Pacific Crest Trail. The next day we scrambled up the ridge and dropped east via a snow couloir, a straightforward descent with crampons and axe. We hit our stride en route, and I enjoyed leading the route's technical 5.10+ third pitch, the crux, on good rock. The heat of the day hit us as Jason led the fourth pitch, which quickly turned into the day's true crux, an expanding crack with poor protection and disintegrating holds (5.10 R). We rationed our remaining water and navigated up intermittent cracks (5.8–5.10). We encountered one more loose section on pitch seven, and I worked hard to keep the rock together and sneak in some pro.

[Left] The east face of Mt. Triumph, showing Memento Mori. *Eric Wehrly* [Right] View of the east face of Golden Horn from the ridgeline at sunrise. *Joe Sambataro*

All in all, we free climbed the 11 pitches in 11 hours, onsight and without bolts or fixed protection. If, for some reason, other climbers are drawn to the golden morning glow of Golden Horn's east face, they should expect to encounter bands of both good rock and kitty litter. We dubbed the route Fuck the Pain Away (IV 5.10+ R), after a hilariously bad Peaches song. 🔘

— JOE SAMBATARO

BUCK MOUNTAIN, NORTH FACE, WILD GAME

AROUND MIDDAY on February 21, Braden Downey and I drove to Fish Lake and the start of Chiwawa River Road, only to find it closed more than 20 miles from the trailhead. In hindsight, we probably should've checked on this minor detail before loading up the truck and driving out there. After asking around, we discovered there were snowmobiles available for rent right where the road was closed. Problem solved. We strapped our climbing and bivy gear to the back of two rented sleds and rode them to the end of the road, where we spent the night.

The next day we started at 4 a.m. from our trailhead bivy (ca 2,800'), walking on three to five feet of well-consolidated snow beside the Chiwawa River and then along Buck Creek to access the north face of Buck Mountain. With hard snow the whole way, it took us about five hours to arrive at the small glacier at the base of the face. Before the trip, I had read in Fred Beckey's guidebook that the north face "...was climbed by Cal Folsom and Mark Moore in September 1976. The climb proved to be extremely loose and dangerous—the party warned others to avoid this climb."

We started up steep ice to the left of the ice/mixed route Buckshot (Cappellini-Larson,

AAJ 2009) and then continued by simul-climbing through less-sustained terrain. As the face got steeper, we pitched out two mixed sections. Braden took the crux lead, which involved wandering, tenuous dry-tooling to connect patchy snow and ice, with limited protection opportunities and some mandatory simul-climbing due to a lack of suitable anchors. After this we simul-climbed up snow and easy mixed terrain before leading two more mixed pitches. We gained the upper ridge around 6 p.m. In all, we climbed eight pitches with quite a bit of simul-climbing (about 1,800' of vertical gain) to the summit (8,528').

To descend, we traversed the summit plateau and went down the southeast face into the Alpine Creek drainage, ending up next to the Chiwawa River about a mile from our bivy. This descent was straightforward, with the only problem being we were now on the wrong side of the Chiwawa River. We searched for a place to cross but couldn't find one, so in the dark we waded the river, holding on to each other to stay upright. After more than 17 hours on the move, the cold water felt refreshing on our feet and legs.

My head hit the pillow at home the same time I had woken up that morning, the ending to a memorable Cascade adventure—Wild Game (IV WI5 M6 R/X). 📷

The initial ice pitch of Wild Game. *William Hinckley*

— **WILLIAM HINCKLEY**

MORNING STAR PEAK, VEGAN TOWER, MILE HIGH CLUB

ON SEPTEMBER 12, Darin Berdinka and I completed the first ascent of the Mile High Club (700', III 5.10a) on a striking 5,280' subsummit of Morning Star Peak in the Headlee Pass area. The route offers seven pitches of excellent face climbing and exposure on the crest of a southwest-facing buttress, which we believe was previously unclimbed and have dubbed Vegan Tower. We cleaned and bolted the route from the top down. The route is fully bolted, but be prepared for a steep snow approach in spring, rappels on the descent, and some loose rock. 📷

— **RAD ROBERTS**

ARGONAUT PEAK, NORTH FACE, CHAD KELLOGG MEMORIAL ROUTE

VERN NELSON JR. and I climbed a new route on Argonaut Peak (8,451'), just east of Mt. Stuart, on April 26. Our route starts in a major left-facing corner system on the sheer north-facing wall between the northeast buttress and northwest arête. It was the culmination of several failed attempts, as the long approach and ephemeral nature of the route made for a challenging project. In all we climbed 800' of new terrain on the Chad Kellogg Memorial Route (1,250', AI4 M6 R A1). Chad was killed while descending Fitz Roy with me in 2014. We miss him every day. 📄 📷

— JENS HOLSTEN

DRAGONTAIL PEAK, NORTH FACE, LEFT HAND FREEZE

CRAIG POPE AND I teamed up for a new route on Dragontail Peak, following the thickest ribbon of water ice above and left of Triple Couloirs' initial ice step. On April 25 we bivied on the far side of Colchuck Lake. I'd never tried a new route and was intimidated though excited. Next morning, we reached the base of the wall by 5 a.m. We soloed up the first pitch of Triple Couloirs and then wallowed up snow about 60m to the start of our route. I took the first pitch (WI4/5), and Craig led the second, which was steeper and thinner than the first (WI5/5+). Above this, a short pitch of WI3 brought us to a sheltered hanging belay. It was during this transition, while Craig took an awkward hanging shit, that I dropped a glove; however, we decided to continue. Craig took the fourth lead—mostly bare rock and rather cruxy. He took a 15' fall while traversing under a roof, but he nailed it on the second try. Some thin, rotten ice up a narrow gully capped the 50m pitch (WI5 M6+). The fifth pitch involved less-severe ice as we continued up the narrow gully. Eventually we popped over a ridge to our right to gain low-angle ice and snow slopes.

All things considered, we had made decent time to this point, but it was 2:30 p.m. and the headwall above looked pretty daunting. At a semi-hanging belay we opted to traverse right toward easy couloirs, simul-climbing about two pitches. We eventually gained the Triple Couloirs about 50m below that route's final ice step. From here we unroped and continued to the summit, reaching the top around 4:30 p.m. We called our route Left Hand Freeze (360m, WI5 M6+), with about seven pitches of new terrain. We hope to complete a direct line through the headwall when the ice comes in again. 📄 📷

— KIRSTEN GARDNER

PRUSIK PEAK, SOUTH FACE, ENERGIZER BUNNY

SEVERAL YEARS AGO, Jon Pobst spotted a continuous link-up of cracks on the left side of Prusik Peak's south face, just left of Solid Gold. Approaching the route on a Sunday evening, after a full day of climbing, neither of us had any expectations. It seemed farfetched to knock out a new five-pitch route in the four hours of remaining daylight. But four hours later, we were on the west ridge. Although it seemed possible the route had been climbed previously, we saw no signs of passage and other local climbers knew of no prior ascents. Either way, the thrill of the unknown was there and that's what counts.

We decided to call our route Energizer Bunny (450', 5.10+ A0) after the bunny ear–like appearance of the cracks at the end of the fourth pitch, where the route joins Solid Gold, and

Jon Probst attempting to free the crux pitch of Energizer Bunny, Prusik Peak. *Steph Abegg*

from our decision to climb the route at the end of a tiring day. The first pitch is a bit burly and dirty, but the cracks above are cleaner, and there are some excellent splitter crack sections. It was all free climbable at 5.8–5.10+ except for a 15' section of 5.11+/5.12- terrain, where we pulled on gear. What an adventure! 📷 🔍

– STEPH ABEGG

PRUSIK PEAK, SOUTH FACE, DER MILKMAN

IN LATE JULY, Gaelen Engler and I climbed a probable new route up Prusik Peak's south face, finding crack systems that led to the top. Our route started far right of other recorded routes, and we were pleasantly surprised by the quality of the climbing. Most of the cracks had a fair to significant amount of lichen in them, and we saw no obvious signs of previous passage. We finished on the final short pitch of the Beckey-Davis Route to the summit. We called it Der Milkman (650', 5.9). It could be a near classic with some cleaning. 📷

– MATT HARTMAN

CALIFORNIA / SONORA PASS

ATLANTIS WALL, THE ODYSSEY

INSPIRED, IN PART, by the new wave of Grade V big-wall climbs in Yosemite Valley featured in recent *AAJ*s, Tim Tuomey and I established a new route on Atlantis Wall this summer. The south-facing, ca 1,000' wall is located on Broad Dome, along the Sonora Pass highway corridor, in the Stanislaus National Forest. [*Atlantis Wall has four other reported Grade IV–V routes. See "Broad Dome" on www.summitpost.org for more information.*] This region hosts solitude and wildness typically unavailable in the Valley. Logistics involved a 4WD, canoes, PFDs, paddles, and a mountain of gear and ropes. As working stiffs, and without the abilities of guys like McNeely or Caldwell, we primarily toiled on weekends. Objective challenges included 12 miles of dirt road, humping loads and canoes to the water line, and paddling full loads across Donnell Reservoir in windy class 2 whitewater conditions—on a lake! There's no cell service in this remote area.

Our line climbs a buttress on the right side of the formation. Most of the existing lines on Atlantis start directly out of a boat. Fortunately, we were able to use the beach below, which we called Talus Island. An oak tree at the base kept us from sweltering at the low elevation of 4,700' while preparing gear.

Once we had fixed pitches above the Lifeguard Station ledge, we started to feel the route was possible. Using telephoto images, we were able to piece together a series of cracks up high. We just had to overcome a steep headwall. With some deep-soul wide climbing, using mixed free and aid, Tim got us past the first part of the Sea of Despair pitch. The next day I was able to get us past the second half of this hollow section, which rang like a Japanese funeral bell. The psychological crux was now behind us.

Weeks later our canoe was stolen. It took four days to bring in a new canoe, finish the remaining pitches, and strip our gear. Tim got the upper crux, a crystalline crack system covered in dirt and filth. Above this, a final technical pitch brought us to lower-angled territory, from which we descended and paddled back with our loads. Given the unknowns, trials, and the inherent water factor, we named our route the Odyssey (V 5.9 C2+). "By hook or by crook this peril too shall be something that we remember."—Homer

— ROBERT BEHRENS   Paddling to the Atlantis Wall. *Robert Behrens*

MT. BRODERICK, UNEMPLOYMENT LINE, FIRST FREE ASCENT

LIFE IS ALL ABOUT BALANCE—at least that's what you call it when you sacrifice work, relationships, and life maintenance to pursue a silly climbing goal. So when Scotty Nelson and I (two average climbers) eagerly agreed to a hefty training program with Cedar Wright and the North Face in exchange for a free trip to Yosemite, where we would attempt to free an old aid route (Unemployment Line, V 5.9 A3, Bartlett-Gerberding, May 1981) on the southwest face of Mt. Broderick, it seemed like a win-win.

The hard work had been done. In fall 2013 we had knocked off the death blocks, bolted a short free variation around a rivet ladder and pendulum, and even worked out most of the hard moves. With two months of arduous training with Rob Shaul at Mountain Athlete and "whipper homework" from Cedar, we expected to be able to complete our relatively short eight-pitch climb.

I met Scotty in Yosemite in June, glad to finally be done with step-ups, and we spent two days adding a harder, more direct two-pitch start to the old aid climb. Scotty started us off on our third day, leading both pitches of the direct start. (We had added three bolts to the second pitch from fixed lines.) I took the next four pitches. The meat of the third pitch involves a magnificent 50' undercling utilizing a finger-size crack (5.11+). The fourth pitch involves some awkward underclings and thin laybacking up a flake (5.11+), and the fifth is a short pitch of 5.11. The sixth pitch is a long and hard one. It starts off a big ledge with wild laybacking, followed by big hands up a thin flake and a gorgeous dihedral that the first ascensionists proposed at 5.10++ and didn't free climb. All this leads to a good stance and a small roof traverse, a delicate section and the technical crux of the route (5.12-).

The southwest face of Mt. Broderick, showing the free Unemployment Line (solid line) and original aid route (dashed line). *Shaun Reed*

I had worked the sixth pitch the day before and got it clean top-roping, so I knew I could do it. This time, though, I was tired from all the prior pitches. I fell once…twice…three times! Each time I fell, I lowered back to a no-hands rest so Cedar (who was filming) could remove the cams I'd placed on the crux. On my fourth go, I eased into the small pinky jams and crimps and got my feat to stick, then reached up and grabbed the finishing jug. Scotty led us up the last two pitches on some easier terrain to finish it off: Unemployment Line (IV 5.12-). 📷 🔍

— SHAUN REED

MT. BRODERICK, SOUTH FACE, NEW ROUTES

THE SOUTH FACE of Mt. Broderick saw a number of new routes in 2015. Alec Zachreson and I established Thugz Mansion (V 5.10 A2) in the spring. Thugz Mansion is a varied line that ascends from the valley between Liberty Cap and Mt. Broderick. The route reaches Gangsta's Paradise, a deluxe bivouac ledge at the halfway mark. Above the ledge is a headwall comprised of stellar rock, with mostly clean aid and some incredible, moderate free climbing. This has to be one of the great, moderate Grade V routes in Yosemite.

Shortly after finishing this route, Alec and I established a variation to the topout that we called Arch Nemesis (C2). It ascends a long and arching offwidth crack to the summit. We climbed with aid; however, it would make for a tremendous offwidth project for the free climbing afficianado. In May, Tito Krull and I climbed yet another variation to Thugz Mansion, a five-pitch variation to the upper part that we called Voodoo Child (C2).

Next up, Adam Ramsey and I climbed Runaway Train (V 5.9 A3+). This route begins further east, up the valley between Mt. Broderick and Liberty Cap. The route ascends splitter cracks of all sizes on glacier-polished stone. This line had been scoped for several decades and has now finally been realized. I would note that the first four pitches are particularly classic. For all of these routes, installed hardware is three-eighths inch and stainless steel.

– BRANDON ADAMS

RIBBON FALLS AMPHITHEATER, SPAGHETTI WESTERN

The team en route on Spaghetti Western, Ribbon Falls. *Tom Evans*

OVER THE SUMMER, Steve Bosque and I walked up to Ribbon Falls to start a new line in the back left corner of the amphitheater (approximately 100' left of the start of Sky People). It was a true wilderness experience, with bright green frogs unfazed by the falls and no noise from the bustle of the valley floor. Over the next few weekends, we made quick work of the first three pitches, nailing a contrived beak line (A1) to link easier free climbing.

After we had reached the top of the third pitch, Josh Mucci was able to join us. We'd promised him a "perfect easy crack on vertical rock" on the fourth pitch, but this turned out to be closed off, marking the beginning of more difficult climbing. Armed with beak tips and copperheads, we slowly worked our way up the Fistful of Copper pitch. Above, the route continued to push back, with more difficult and circuitous aiding, until we reached a bivy at Karmac Ledge. This ledge became the site of what we believe to be the first magic show ever performed on a big-wall first ascent, with Steve Bosque doing magic acts that honored the work of Jean Eugène Robert-Houdin.

After a bit of mungy free climbing off our bivy ledge, another pitch of vertical aiding past an array of horizontal dikes brought us to the start of the obvious beige corner clearly visible from the floor of the amphitheater. Happily, this feature, which looked like a roof from the ground, turned out to be a less-then-vertical corner that offered spectacular climbing back out to the edge of the buttress. A final pitch of easy mixed free and aid, with a sketchy aid traverse (rivets interspersed with beak tips and hooks), brought us to the top just as the sun was setting. Another long pitch of circuitous free climbing (5.8) will bring a climber to the true summit of the formation and an obvious tree that can be used to return to the ledge at the top of our route. The route is equipped to rap back to the ground without the need to leave any ropes fixed: Spaghetti Western (V 5.6 A3).

– KEVIN DEWEESE

FIFI BUTTRESS, CENTER OF THE UNIVERSE

FIFI BUTTRESS is the impressive formation just right of Leaning Tower, first climbed in 1960 by Steve Roper and Richard McCracken. In 1980, Chick Holtkamp and Randy Russell climbed Vortex, which Russell freed with Eric Zschiesche in 1982 (IV 5.12). (This route was finally repeated by Alex Honnold in 2015, on his second effort, the first known repeat, to my knowledge.) After about 20 years without activity, I came in and soloed Romulan Warbird in 1999 as an aid route. A few other aid routes were established around this time. [See www.yosemitebigwall.com for more routes.]

After trying to free Romulan Warbird for years, I asked the talented Lucho Rivera to head up with me, and in 2013 he freed the route, calling it Romulan Freebird (*AAJ 2013*). This is when word started to get out about Fifi Buttress. James Lucas soon asked if another route I had aided in 1999, Final Frontier, would go free. I said yes, and he and Nik Berry went on to free this spectacular 5.13 (*AAJ 2014*). I aided Backburner (V 5.7 A3) around this time, and though it didn't quite connect as a free route, there was plenty of reward in finding and free climbing the nearby Voyager (IV 5.11+).

Pitch seven of Center of the Universe, with Leaning Tower and El Cap in the background. *Dan McDevitt*

I spent the following seasons putting up quality shorter routes in the Fifi Amphitheater, which I've dubbed the Coliseum because of the great view of all the gladiators working the big routes above. These short pitches are some of the best I will ever climb. However, 2015 found me wanting more adventure. Casey Jones and I had just finished a great three-pitch 5.11a in the Coliseum we called Torpedo. From below, I couldn't help but wonder if there might be another route to do left of Voyager.

It was scary walking out the final bit of the exposed approach ledge past Voyager to a crack I had not been able to view before. Thankfully, it turned out to be a beautiful overhanging crack (5.11a). After this, I spent time scouting the lower wall, below the Voyager approach ledge, finding four great 5.10+ pitches, one of which I had established years earlier. Higher on the wall, pitch seven was the real question mark. It turned out to be a long, leaning splitter ending in knobs on an arête (5.11a). Above that, a couple of easy pitches led up to a 5.10b squeeze chimney. This pitch lands you atop Fifi Buttress: Center of the Universe (IV 5.11a). And now that you've done 10 pitches, you can choose whether to complete the "Beyond" finish up a separate wall above, which has three more good 5.10+ pitches of adventure. You can walk off or rap the route with one 70m rope. 📷 🔍

— DAN MCDEVITT

FREE HEART ROUTE

BY MASON EARLE

While free climbing El Capitan's Golden Gate (VI 5.13b, Huber-Huber, *AAJ 2001*) in 2009, I spotted a system of beautiful cracks and corners leading out the left side of the massive, heart-shaped recess in the middle of El Cap's southwest face. This system belonged to the Heart Route (VI 5.9 A4, *AAJ 1971*), a natural line first climbed in 1970 by Scott Davis and Chuck Kroger. The upper part of the Heart Route went free when Alex and Thomas Huber climbed Golden Gate, a link-up that started on the Salathé Wall. The lower route remained a mostly forgotten aid climb.

Exploring and establishing first ascents has always been the most intriguing part of climbing for me. After a few solo missions on the route, I enlisted Brad Gobright. It wasn't long before we were completely consumed by the project. Brad and I put a lot of time and effort into adding bolts to variations, cleaning out cracks, scrubbing holds, and of course climbing. The route boasted some mind-blowing terrain—like the exposed roof pitch exiting the heart feature in the middle of the wall and the wildly technical slab getting to Heart Ledges, a few pitches lower. We knew we had something special.

After a couple of seasons of attempts, the first free ascent still eluded us. Eventually we put the entire project on the back burner as Brad and I focused on other things. I began to wonder if I still possessed the skill, and mad determination, required to free El Cap. Then the Dawn Wall went free and something clicked. Kevin Jorgeson asked the world, "What's your Dawn Wall?" I was reminded that *my* Dawn Wall was just a few routes left of *the* Dawn Wall. The Heart Route was still waiting for us, all equipped and ready to go.

Brad and I met up in spring 2015 and got straight to work. The first seven pitches of the

Mason Earle mid-flight on the Dub Step pitch (V10). *Ben Ditto*

route (what we called the Heart Blast) feel almost like a route in themselves. Pitch six, the Dub Step, has the hardest moves of the route: a difficult slab downclimb to an outrageous, sideways dyno (approximately a V10 move). The next pitch, a slab getting to Heart Ledges, appears impossible to climb—and, indeed, some of the holds are no bigger than the edge of a nickel (5.13a). The biggest question marks on the route were these pitches, and it was an exhilarating process to find the way through these variations.

While the hardest climbing is down low, the steepest climbing is in the middle of the wall, starting with the Heart Roof. Here, the route climbs through classic El Cap terrain, with exposed, sweeping granite and unbelievable climbing (two long pitches of 5.13 as well a bouldery 5.13 arête.) Above this one must head up a spooky flake (5.11 R/X) before the angle eases. Another wild pitch of crack climbing marks the end of our newly free climbed terrain (16 pitches for us), and the route then joins Golden Gate to the top (10 pitches for us).

Brad and I spent six days on the wall for our final push, starting June 12. We had previously stashed bivy gear right below Heart Roof and made our main camp there. This spot spared us from the intense heat and sun that plagued the wall every afternoon. Although the hardest single moves were on the Dub Step (which I free climbed but Brad could not, due to him being shorter), the biggest challenge was completing the steep and sustained climbing above our

camp. I had injured my shoulder on the dyno a week before setting off, and it worsened with each pitch. Even in full battle mode, I was doubtful I could even follow the 5.13 arête. But by the skin of my teeth I was able to climb the final cruxes to reach Golden Gate.

On our final day we jugged several hundred feet to our high point and completed the final eight pitches to the top. The final pitch of any El Cap route is a special thing. Totally exposed above the valley floor, worked to the core, and slaying a dragon that had haunted us for five years, it was truly a profound time and place.

SUMMARY: *First free ascent of the Heart Route, El Capitan, Southwest Face, June 2015. Aside from 10' of climbing that Gobright was unable to free climb on pitch six, both climbers led or followed each pitch of the entire wall free. In all, the free Heart Route has five 5.13 pitches and many of 5.11 or 5.12. The pair also climbed all three 5.13 pitches on the upper part of Golden Gate; however, Earle believes the Golden Desert and A5 Traverse pitches are 5.12+ for tall climbers.* 📷

[Previous page] **Mason Earle works out of the Heart Roof.** [Right] **Brad Gobright ascends a 5.13 crack above Heart Roof.** *Ben Ditto (both)*

FAIRVIEW DOME, RUMOUR HAS IT

I ALWAYS KNEW that my wife, Heather Baer, and I would do a classic, signature new route in the Sierra Nevada, somewhere. But if somebody told me that route would be within spitting distance of the Regular Route on Fairview Dome, I would have called them nuts. But that's where it is.

Our climb started out as a variation to a variation (Crowd Pleaser, 2004), and from there it blossomed into a full-blown route of its own. Starting on the same initial belay ledge as the Regular Route, our route surfs left and up. It crosses the Regular Route a pitch above Crescent Ledge and climbs directly to the tree located at the end of the difficulties on the Regular Route. Of the eight pitches, there are three pitches of 5.11, with the first pitch (5.11b) being the crux.

Due to the climb's proximity to the Regular Route, I used tactics that were new to me in Yosemite. I would top-rope a section first, making sure it was worthy, and then mark bolt placements. Later I drilled the holes and placed the bolts on lead, according to my staunch Yosemite trad ethics. Back in the day, I never would have rehearsed a section like this.

We redpointed the route on August 1, 2014, finishing a four-year vigil. I placed all 31 bolts by hand, belayed by Heather. All the pitches are PG, and you've got to really work for the bolts. We called the route Rumour Has It (IV 5.11b). It is a great route, and despite pumping out a bunch of public topos, it still remains to be repeated, as far as I know.

– STEVE SCHNEIDER

DRUG DOME, HIGH TIMES

IN 2012 I SPOTTED the steep, northeast side of Drug Dome. The black streaks and seemingly blank rock took root in my subconscious; I dropped a pin on the location on my mental map of possibilities. In July 2015, I talked Katie Lambert and Brittany Griffith into checking out some of the existing single-pitch routes on the northeast side. The prospects were exciting. A few days later I walked to the top of the dome with Eric Bissell, loaded down with gear and uncertainty. Rappelling down, I began to scour the wall for signs of a climbable line, not quite finding what I was looking for. On another mission I found signs that some climber had tried to piece together a climb, but the project seemed abandoned. This section of wall is steep, and the small, knobby holds easily become inadequate for upward progress.

My perceptions changed on my second and third days of trying the old project. On the fourth pitch, a line of knobs links a crack to horizontal

Ben Ditto leads the fourth pitch of High Times. *Owen Bissell* holds, and then tiny knobs climb through a roof to the top of the wall. I had found the line. After splitting left from Spinner (established by Dave Bengston) at 25', I could forge a way through cracks and steep face to finish up the top bulge of the wall. On my fourth day on the route I was joined by Ian Nielsen and Ryan Alonzo.

The seventh day on the route was hard. Ian and I spent the day hand-drilling protection bolts and anchors. A few days later (day eight) was Labor Day (literally), and Ian and Steele Taylor helped me put the finishing touches on the route. After nine days of work, the climb was ready for a ground-up attempt.

On day ten the first pitch went without a hitch. The second pitch requires a bit more skill to surpass the crackless dihedral, with palming, stemming, and micro-knob edging. Pitch three is a joy, with moderate, knobby arête climbing and steep cracks. Pitch four begins at a cramped belay ledge below a steep crack. There's a loose block (caveat emptor) to get things started and then some pumpy moves up the crack, leading to high-quality, knobby,

The west side of the Incredulous Bulk, showing the approximate location of the Davis-Sibald Route from the 1990s on the left and Causative Striations on the right. *Josh Finkelstein*

bouldering-like moves. Leading this pitch took a bit more energy than the top-roped rehearsal I'd done. A few lock-offs, edges, heel hooks, and knobs later and I was on top.

The journey was complete, but the destination had been reached weeks before. I watched gleefully as Katie Lambert worked out the crux—High Times (350', 4 pitches, 5.13b).

— BEN DITTO

INCREDULOUS BULK, WEST FACE, CAUSATIVE STRIATIONS

THE SIERRA was unseasonably warm in early October. With a few days at our disposal, Pete Fasoldt and I hiked up to the Incredible Hulk to find the usually crowded cliff, and indeed all of Little Slide Canyon, totally empty. On our second day we wandered a half-mile down the canyon to check out an intriguing wall and splitter crack below the Hulk, located on the same (east) side of Little Slide Canyon. The next morning we hiked down to the junction of the main trail and marsh outlet, ditched our packs and bivy gear, and 15 minutes later we reached the base of the wall. I managed to free the splitter crack start at around 5.11-. Seven varied pitches led to the

The Cleaver's south face. (1) Bloody Cleaver (Othemr-Weiss, 2010). (2) Possible start of the original south face route (Condon-Killian, 1961). (3) Cleavage Dreamer (Ricklin-Stamatiou, 2008). (4) Chronic Harmonic (Reed-Ricklin, 2014). (5) Southeast arête. *Nate Ricklin*

summit. After downclimbing the 5.8 summit block, we rappelled 100' down the northeast face from a short piece of red cord that we threaded under a block just north of the summit proper. Once at the notch northeast of the summit, we traversed east over two gendarmes to reach a plateau. From the plateau, we easily skied game trails down the broad scree slope just south of the second gendarme to get back to our packs.

We saw no sign of previous passage. However, Hulk aficionado Dave Nettle reported this formation had been climbed at least once before, in the early to mid-'90s, when Mike Davis and Hunter Sibald mistook it for the Hulk and climbed the large, right-facing corner system on the left side of the west face. Davis and Sibald jokingly named it the "Hunk" or the "Bulk" after their accidental ascent. Although the shimmering white granite of the Hulk will always dominate Little Slide Canyon, we enjoyed our route Causative Striations (900', III 5.11-).

— JOSH FINKELSTEIN

BASIN MOUNTAIN, EAST FACE

IN FEBRUARY, I soloed a couloir that zigzags up the central east face of Basin Mountain (13,240'). The route is comprised of steep snow, short rock bands, and alpine ice (1,800', AI2).

— JOE REIDHEAD

CLEAVER, SOUTH FACE, CHRONIC HARMONIC

NATE RICKLIN: Since first seeing the Cleaver (ca 13,000') from the northeast ridge of Lone Pine Peak, I was drawn to it—a wide, 850' tall, white granite wall. I climbed two new routes on the cliff in 2008 along with others from the Pullharder Alpine Club (*AAJ 2009*). Prior to our adventures, it had only one known route (Condon-Killian, 1961). The amazing thing about the

Cleaver is its location only two miles from Whitney Portal; however, it's hidden from view on the approach to Mt. Whitney or Mt. Russell. I was left mesmerized by the upper dihedrals in the center of the wall, directly below the summit. Long and perfect, they looked tricky to reach, as the wall is concave, blank, and steep directly below.

In May 2010, Konstantin Stoletov and I made our first recon, aiming straight up the center. We made it up nearly two pitches, placing seven bolts on the second pitch, a hard water groove. We placed our last bolt at a stance out in space on an arête and vowed to come back when it was warmer. We returned in September 2010, finished the second pitch, and placed a bolt at the start of the third pitch before snow forced us down. From that high point I had no idea where to go, but it looked like 50 more feet would probably connect the dots into the upper wall.

In 2014, I told Shaun Reed I'd take a week off and scope new lines in the Wind River Range with him. However, the forecast was awful. On a whim I checked the weather in Lone Pine—sun! We made a last-minute, 18-hour drive from Colorado to the Whitney Portal.

SHAUN REED: With a completely clear forecast in the Sierra we didn't even bring a tent. Carrying 30 bolts, a 300' static line, and giant cams, it took us four hours to reach the Cleaver. On our first morning we decided to climb up to the previous high point and see if we could push it a bit further. Nate fired the initial 5.10 pitch, and I attempted the 5.11+ second pitch. Nate took the 5.11- third pitch up an innocuous flake through a couple of small roofs. The rock quality on this pitch was amazing—the best on the route. On the fourth pitch we headed up a corner to a delicate flake and then through an easy roof to reach another fun corner. We called it for the day, planning to come back the next day and go for a complete free ascent.

The following day, we sent the first four pitches, the second being the crux of the route. The fifth pitch gained the upper dihedrals that Nate had been dreaming about by an unlikely, right-trending foot traverse to reach a nice 5.10 corner. A final easy pitch brought us to the top. Once topping out, we found the inobvious descent gully with cairns to climber's left of the Cleaver. Our new route is called Chronic Harmonic (IV 5.11+). 📷 🔍

— NATE RICKLIN *AND* SHAUN REED

CALIFORNIA / KINGS CANYON NATIONAL PARK

KETTLE DOME, SOUTHWEST FACE

JON SCHUTZ, JULIE TRAN, AND I climbed a new line on the southwest side of Kettle Dome (9,451') in Kings Canyon: Two Bucks in the Truck (approx. 1,000', 5.10). As far as we could tell, nobody had climbed this wall since the mid-1970s, by the west face (II 5.7, Beckey-Vennum-Warrender, *AAJ 1976*). 📄

— MATTHEW SCHUTZ

TOMBSTONE RIDGE, NEW ROUTES

BETWEEN OCTOBER 30 AND NOVEMBER 1, Daniel Jeffcoach, Brian Prince, and I completed three new routes on Tombstone Ridge (ca 9,000'), along the western boundary of Kings Canyon National Park. On our first day, Daniel and I climbed the southeast face of a formation 1.5 miles east of Obelisk. We dubbed this complex wall Tombstone Towers and our route

Tephra (1,000', 5.11-). Brian joined us on our second day to climb the Knobelisk, one-third mile southeast of the Obelisk. First, we climbed the lower southeast face by a route we called Improbable Overhangs (500', 5.10c). After lunch on the terrace separating the upper and lower walls, we established Trust Issues (500', 5.9) on the upper east face. For all three climbs, the crux is definitely the approaches! 📄 📷

— DANIEL MOOR

BUBBS CREEK WALL, THE EMPEROR, FIRST FREE ASCENT

THE BUBBS CREEK WALL is one many excellent formations found along the popular Rae Lakes Loop near Kings Canyon. After completing the first ascent of the Emperor in 2014 (*AAJ 2015*), this route became my own "mini Dawn Wall." While not pushing the global limits of what is possible, this route gave me big motivation to advance my own skills. With sustained technical pitches, the exposure of a Yosemite big wall, and views of gorgeous waterfalls and peaks of the High Sierra, free climbing the Emperor was a journey to remember.

I spent 20 days focused on this route over two years, hiking over 230 miles, gaining approximately 90,000' of elevation, and driving too far from San Francisco. The route was sustained, with all but one of the first 15 pitches containing at least one 5.11 crux. To my relief, there were only two or three sections of 5.12a climbing. Freeing this climb led to some 40' whippers and brought a complete mix of experiences and emotions. It was especially nice to finally complete the first free ascent with Caitlin Taylor, the partner with whom I initially started the route in 2014. The Emperor (2,200', V 5.12a) is not a scary route but could be exciting in places, which should not scare anyone off. 📄 🔍

— VITALIY MUSIYENKO

ERICSSON CRAG NUMBER 3, NORTHWEST ARÊTE

In *100 Favorite North American Climbs*, Fred Beckey describes Vinland, a line he and Alan Bartlett climbed on the north aspect of Ericsson Crag, as "one of my finest in the Sierra" (*AAJ 1988*). While working on the Emperor, on Bubbs Creek Wall, I noticed a jagged arête splitting Ericsson Crag Number 3 straight down the middle, left of Vinland. This feature was not among the three technical routes known on the formation. I convinced Maxim Belyakov to join me for an adventure.

On the first day we hiked to Charlotte Creek camp and climbed the first eight pitches of the Emperor. The following day we hiked eight or nine miles to the base of Ericsson Crag Number 3 and climbed the line I had my eye on. From the base it looked steep. There was an obvious spire halfway up and a clean headwall guarding the easier terrain to the summit. The rock was "alpine" but solid.

I started left of the arête, aiming for an obvious hand crack, after which I climbed over a bulging overhang (crux) and up easier terrain. Pitch two traversed right and up to a roof, which is directly on the arête. Throughout the day I mostly kept to the arête, and two-thirds of the way up we finally hit the white, protruding, fang-like spire. I was psyched to find a few moves of overhanging hand jamming on the right side of it. This led directly to the notch between the spire and a short headwall of featured red rock of lesser quality. Before moving on to the headwall above, I stood atop the spire.

An obvious splitter crack snaked up the upper fourth of the headwall. Incut black knobs, with intermittent cracks, brought me to this final splitter. After the headwall, easier climbing brought us to the crest of the ridge. The summit was nearby to the east. On top, I noted original entries by prominent climbers who have done a lot of the exploratory climbing in the Sierra Nevada. The views from here were well-summarized by Fred Beckey: "Getting to the summit was like a taste of ambrosia, for it was possible to sight picturesque lake chains, lush meadows, and rugged peaks where glaciers once flowed."

To descend, we scrambled about 300' of fourth-class terrain to the east, where we found a prominent gully; it led north and was simple to follow. Several steep drop-offs were avoided on the skier's left (west). After picking up our stashed gear, we hiked back to the Charlotte Creek camp and hiked out the following day—The Northwest Arête (IV 5.10c).

— VITALIY MUSIYENKO

The Northwest Arête of Ericsson Crag Number 3 climbs the prominent rib forming the left skyline. Vinland climbs the foreground rib. *Vitaliy Musiyenko*

THE PRISM, SOUTH FACE, MONKEYS IN THE CLOUDS

WHEN I FIRST SAW a route overlay for the Prism in *AAJ 2011*, I wondered: Why had the obvious wide cracks snaking up the middle of the wall been ignored?

As I dug out bushes and pounds of dirt from the beginning of a giant crack, I realized the other guys knew better. After the digging was done, however, the route unfolded like a dream. My partner, Luke Stefurak, and I climbed a full rope length of featured offwidth climbing, protected by small to medium cams. The following pitches included awesome face climbing on stellar rock. The only crux was feeding slack quickly enough to the excited leader, as we raced against the possibility of rain. The face climbing was moderately run-out but very featured. An occasional crack or flake kept things reasonably safe.

We kept to a direct line, mostly up the middle, and after approximately 1,200' of climbing, reached the upper apex of the wall. Several hundred feet of simul-climbing up the ridge took us to the summit proper, where we recovered a Nalgene with a register. Our route was the fifth recorded on the formation. [*Editor's note: The routes, from left to right, are Left Facet (13 pitches, 5.10a R, Harder-LaBounty-Thau, 2007); Monkeys In The Clouds (IV 5.10*

PG13, Musiyenko-Stefurak, 2015); South Face (III 5.10, Croft-Grant-Grant-Schwartz, 2014); Pig with Lipstick (11 pitches, 5.9 R, LaBounty-Thau, 2010); Right Facet (11 pitches, 5.9, Harder-LaBounty, 2009).]

To descend, we made two rappels from high on the ridge—one to the north and one to the east. We climbed in June and felt the route would likely be warm enough to climb in late or early season, as long as snow did not affect the approach. Oh, and check the forecast or end up like us: Monkeys in the Clouds (IV 5.10 PG13). 📷

– VITALIY MUSIYENKO

The Globe is the larger dome on the right, with the line of Standing Ovation shown. The other, smaller dome is likely unclimbed. *Vitaliy Musiyenko*

THE GLOBE, SOUTH FACE, STANDING OVATION

WHILE CLIMBING THE PRISM and Saber Ridge earlier in the summer I noticed two attractive, unclimbed domes to the west on the same ridgeline, above Tamarack Lake. Local climbers had dubbed these the Choss Boobs. The larger of the two domes was quite impressive and at least 1,000' tall. Other climbs in this area are composed of solid, white granite; however, the rock on the domes looked unlike anything I have seen in the High Sierra, with much of it composed of different shades of red. Brian Prince and I were puzzled by the mystery and excited to check it out for ourselves in September.

From the High Sierra Trail, we took the Lone Pine cutoff and continued toward Elizabeth Pass. Once we were slightly above the domes, we cut beneath the smaller of the two, on its west side. Up close, both looked steep and complex. We decided to take a direct line up the middle of the south face of the bigger formation. Go big or go home. Hopefully both.

The day went better than expected, with fun climbing, adequate protection, and awesome views to all sides. The red rock was covered with features, which allowed us to pull several of the roofs on large jugs—hero climbing at a very moderate grade. Even though the climbing was never too hard, it was never too easy. Terrain we covered had no sign of previous passage, and neither did the summit.

During our weeklong September outing we read Shakespeare. Since many of his plays were originally performed in a theater named the Globe, that's what we called the formation, and the route is called Standing Ovation (1,000', III 5.10). We did not attempt the other, likely unclimbed dome. 📷

– VITALIY MUSIYENKO

ANGEL WINGS, SOUTHWEST BUTTRESS, KILLING IN THE NAME

THE SOUTHWEST BUTTRESS (far left side) of Angel Wings was completed by Fred Beckey, Bill Lahr, Craig Martinson, and Alan North in 1977. It took four days spread over a few years to finish the route Wings Over Sequioa.(*See Fred Beckey's* 100 Favorite North American Climbs *and AAJ 2014 for details and route lines.*) They climbed the southern aspect of the pillar, steering right into a notch about four-fifths of the way up the wall. After the climb, they tossed their haul bags, which exploded at the base. The event evolved into an untrue legend about Beckey's "black book" being lost and later recovered by another climber.

I was attracted to Angel Wings by its fascinating geometry and beautiful but discontinuous cracks. When Luke Stefurak and I scoped out the wall from the base, we had trouble putting the puzzle together for an obvious route. Both of us were interested in a natural weakness, something that would allow us to climb mostly free. We saw two attractive crack systems left of the Beckey route. About 600' up, the cracks were separated by a 150' band of dark rock. Could we connect them?

Without wasting much time, we started the climb with a short pitch that included a wet, spicy 5.10 boulder problem. From there, the climb evolved into steep, clean, high-quality cracks. The second pitch (5.11b/c) and the third (5.10+/11-) mostly climb awesome

The southwest buttress of Angel Wings, showing the approximate location of Wings Over Sequoia (Beckey-Lahr-Martinson-North, 1977) at right and Killing in the Name at left. *Vitaliy Musiyenko*

hand cracks in a right-facing corner. The fourth pitch includes cruxy face climbing (5.11). As we hoped, the dark rock band (which we dubbed the A5 Traverse) went free, at 5.11+, but only with four bolts added for protection. Above this we regained a weakness and found three great pitches of varied, sustained, and quality 5.10 and 5.11 cracks. At this point we reached a blank wall, and both of us were worn out by the sustained climbing. We wouldn't accept a bolt ladder as a legit method to advance the route, so we decided to pull the plug, plenty happy with the quality of the climbing we had done up to our high point.

The following day, I opted out of a needed rest day and hiked up to view our line again. In order to spy a way to connect the crack system, and avoid the need for a bolt ladder, I took multiple close-up photos of the wall, hoping to find a weakness.

Unfortunately, Luke could not join me for a rematch, as he lives in Seattle, but it did not take me long to find the right partner. "I don't care if we fail," said Adam Ferro in a phone conversation. A few weeks after discussing the logistics, Adam and I made the 17-mile trek to the campground at Hamilton Lakes.

The following day we approached the base of the southwest buttress and started climbing just after first light. To my surprise, I was able to lead or follow free to the previous high point. There, I managed to do some thin, clean aid up a hollow flake, including one hook move; I placed a single bolt to pendulum to another crack. This took us to a giant ledge. A 100-foot traverse left and then back right put us at the base of a giant chimney system. It was very intimidating and jammed with massive flakes. Adam took the first pitch in the chimney (5.11), and we swapped the next two pitches (5.10 C1), pulling on gear in a few spots for efficiency. We lost the race against the sun and climbed the final two pitches in the dark. At 9:42 p.m. on July 24 we stood atop the southwest buttress and let out a few celebratory roars. With 1,700' of quality free climbing and less than 30' of direct aid, we couldn't have asked for a better line. We reached camp again at midnight. Our route is called Killing in the Name (V 5.11+ C2). 📷

– VITALIY MUSIYENKO

Cherubim Dome, showing the three known routes: (1) Archangel. (2) What Dreams May Come. (3) Dark Angels Have More Fun. *Vitaliy Musiyenko*

CHERUBIM DOME, SOUTH FACE, NEW ROUTES

CHERUBIM DOME (10,440') is a beautiful rock face towering above the Valhalla and Hamilton lakes, just east of Angel Wings. I was able to find only one recorded rock climb, up the south-southwest face: Archangel (IV 5.10+ A0, Joe-Leversee, *AAJ 1986*). Of this route, E.C. Joe wrote, "Avoiding drilling as much as possible, we took a line up a series of flakes and cracks on the nearly featureless south face. Eight long pitches on superb golden granite." The south face, to the right of Archangel, seemed low-angle enough for another free route; however, I did not want to get on a featureless slab requiring dozens of bolts. The dome is around 1,200' tall, and only eight bolts were placed on Archangel. I decided—not for all the right reasons—that I didn't want to place more than that.

The original line I proposed to Adam Ferro in August was an obvious white streak up the center of the south face—it screamed to be climbed. But as we hiked up and examined the dome, it was obviously lacking crack systems. We opted for a line to the right, which seemed to have several connectable systems. We found perfect granite and fun climbing up featureless slabs, corners, knobs, and even laser-cut splitters that appeared from nowhere and ended just as abruptly. The line was as enjoyable as the south face of Charlotte Dome, but with less choss and scrambling. We climbed many 60m pitches to the right edge of the summit headwall. A brief third-class scramble to the west took us to the top: Dark Angels Have More Fun (IV 5.9+ R). Climbing the entire route without placing a single bolt was a big confidence booster; it made me believe a line up the central white streak would be possible.

A month later, I took a week off work and returned with Brian Prince. After a day hiking in, we went for the central white streak. Bulletproof granite with unique features allowed for several awesome pitches before we reached an obvious bulge. After delicate climbing up to the bulge, I found sloping jugs just right of the white streak that

The west face of Hamilton Dome with Subliminal Verses on the left and Hamlet Buttress on the right. *Vitaliy Musiyenko*

provided manageable climbing. On the following pitch, Brian climbed straight up the streak, gaining a thin crack with orange jugs to its right. After about 850' of climbing up the streak it morphed into an easy groove, so we traversed left and climbed straight up the middle of the summit headwall, which was very steep and intimidating. As with the rest of the route, things managed to work out better than expected. Awesome crack climbing over a few roofs took us straight to the summit proper. We called the route What Dreams May Come (IV 5.10 R). We placed eight bolts, with six for protection and two for a belay anchor.

The variety of climbing styles, immaculate rock, and views make these routes some of the best in the High Sierra. If you're going out to climb Angel Wings, add one to your list. 📷

– VITALIY MUSIYENKO

HAMILTON DOME, WEST FACE, NEW ROUTES

BRIAN PRINCE AND I visited the west face of Hamilton Dome in September as part of a weeklong trip to the area. We found it had incredible rock, many possibilities, and the best moderate route I have climbed in the High Sierra. The west face is almost as wide as it is tall—about 1,700'.

On the first day of climbing we started up the center-right side of the wall via a left-facing dihedral. This led to mostly moderate face climbing with a few cracks here and there. Two-thirds of the way up the formation, we had lunch on a ledge large enough for a battalion to bivy. Above this a chicken head–covered, near-vertical fin took us to the top. The upper feature itself was about 400' tall. Slinging knobs allowed for adequate protection on this otherwise crackless monolith, and a wild jump-across was required below the summit. The route was no worse than the mega-classic south face of Charlotte Dome—Hamlet Buttress (IV 5.9+)

Our route the next day was even better—we picked a steeper line on the center-left side of the wall, traveling through a couple of roofs. We found a cool splitter crack initially, and above, thankfully, we found a hidden crack that led up to and through a 5.10 roof. As we gained elevation up three pitches of fun cracks, our smiles grew bigger. We soon reached the second prominent roof, which we climbed via monkey bar–like jugs. Some face climbing above this required a couple of bolts to keep the climbing adequately protected. More chicken heads, dihedral climbing, slabs, and several more cracks took us to the top of the difficulties. Four hundred feet of scrambling, with an amazing view, brought us to the top once again—Subliminal Verses (IV 5.10a/b).

The 360° views from this summit are some of the best in the whole range, with Castle Rocks to the west, Eagle Scout Peak, Kaweahs, and the Hamilton Spires to the east, many rock spires to the south, and Angel Wings, Prism, Cherubim Dome, Mt. Stewart, the Globe, and the Saber to the north. To descend the formation on both climbs, we scrambled east toward a notch. A short, fourth-class downclimb gained the first rap off a slung horn, and three more rappels reached a notch. One 60m rope works well.

The lengthy approach, without a trail to the base of the formation, is a blessing in disguise. For those who plan to venture out and repeat either of these climbs, a true adventure is in store. The camping in the upper Eagle Scout Creek drainage is spectacular, and there is plenty of rock around for new-routing, scenic photo-ops, and even fishing. 📷

— VITALIY MUSIYENKO

An overview of the Hamilton Lakes area, where California-based Vitaliy Musiyenko and various partners established many new routes spread across multiple trips during the summer and fall of 2015. [See reports on pages 107–115.] Select formations are labled: (A) Hamilton Dome. (B) Rowell Tower. (C) Serpent's Tooth. (D) Eagle Scout Creek Dome. (E) Eagle Scout Peak. (F) Angel Wings. (G) Cherubim Dome. (H) Mt. Stewart. (BC) The standard base camp at Hamilton Lakes used for climbing Angel Wings, etc. (ABC) The approach and high camp used by Musiyenko and Brian Prince to climb Hamilton Dome, Rowell Tower, and the Serpent's Tooth. Map layer © Mapbox, © OpenStreetMap

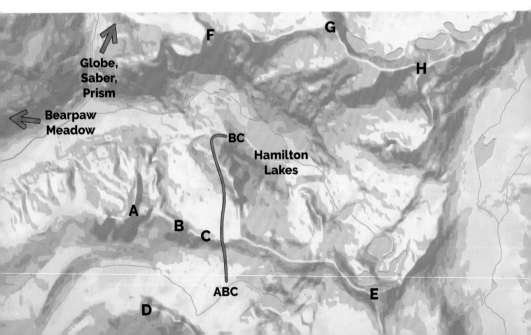

ROWELL TOWER, FULL NELSON

DURING AN EARLIER OUTING in the Eagle Scout Creek area [*see page 115*], Brian Prince and I found heinous bushwhacking while approaching the Hamilton Towers via Granite Creek. On a weeklong trip later in the summer, we decided on a different approach. We set up a base camp at Hamilton Lake, which would allow us to attempt several peaks in the surrounding area, and on the third day of our trip, after climbing a new route up Cherubim Dome [*see page 110*], we hiked over to the south side of the long ridge extending from Eagle Scout Peak to Hamilton Dome, between the Hamilton Creek and Eagle Scout Creek drainages. We gained about 2,000' and crossed the ridge at the notch east of the spire dubbed the Serpent's Tooth [*see next report*]. We brought four days of food and set up camp next to a stream, 15 minutes west of a beautiful lake.

Our goal was the largest of the Hamilton Towers. I suspect its north face was climbed by Greg Henzie, Chris Jones, and Galen Rowell in 1970. We chose the left-leaning weakness on the west (left) end of the south face. After soloing a 5.8 approach pitch, three more long pitches took us to a large ledge on the western flanks of the tower. By this point we were

Brian Prince on the initial pitches of the south face of Rowell Tower. *Vitaliy Musiyenko*

fairly worked by the approach from Hamilton Lake and the burly, run-out climbing. The continuous, steep crack systems above had a blank, vertical section that would likely involve a bolt ladder. Thus, we made a 30m rappel, traversing further left, until we found a system that allowed us to continue bailing upward. We climbed another five pitches (simul-climbing about 400' on one pitch). The final pitch negotiated stacked flakes that could have killed Brian if I looked at them too hard—Full Nelson (1,200', IV 5.10+ R)

The top of the formation was spectacular, with exposed twin summits and a sharp knife-edge that led to the high point. From the summit, we rappelled east with a 60m rope. On one of the rappels we slung a chicken head and easily recovered the sling with a flick of a rope. The next rappel we came up short. Fortunately, we were able to downclimb 5th-class vegetation to reach a ledge. From there we scrambled toward the notch and the base of the tower.

To honor one of the first ascensionists, we suggest the name Rowell Tower. His spirit is well alive here in the Sierra, where unclimbed faces and untraveled canyons still allow a lifetime of exploration. 🖸

– VITALIY MUSIYENKO

Looking north from the summit of Eagle Scout Creek Dome toward the Hamilton Towers and other formations. (A) Prism. (B) Saber. (C) Rowell Tower, with the 2015 route shown. (D) Serpent's Tooth, with the 2015 route shown. (E) Mt. Stewart. *Vitaliy Musiyenko*

THE SERPENT'S TOOTH, WILD WEST CRACK

FOR A CLIMBER, finding a direct line from the bottom of the peak to a spire-like summit is equivalent to winning a lottery. Emilio Comici's most famous quote is, "I wish some day to make a route, and from the summit let fall a drop of water, and this is where my route will have gone." While hiking toward Eagle Scout Creek from Hamilton Lake on a weeklong trip (*see approach description on previous page*), Brian Prince and I daydreamed of finding awesome crack systems. We did not expect to find a 700' direct line to a spire-like pinnacle.

After fourth-classing for a bit, Brian and I roped up below a long crack system on the south side of the Serpent's Tooth. A long, somewhat run-out pitch with a wild 5.10 crux got us to an exposed stance below an intimidating flare. Brian solved a 5.11 boulder problem to get into it. The flare evolved into a squeeze, then a section of slabby face climbing. We continued swinging leads up the continuously challenging corner above, with Brian onsighting difficult 5.11 jamming. Higher up, a chimney reminiscent of the notorious Harding Slot guarded the path to the summit. After an overhanging offwidth, which evolved into a squeeze, I was spit out to the base of the final obstacle: 40' of unprotected face climbing to the smooth summit pinnacle.

In the notch, I saw an ancient rappel anchor that likely belonged to members of the Rock Climbing Section of the Sierra Club. They claimed an ascent of the Serpent's Tooth from the north in 1953. I expected the top to have an anchor as well. But when I climbed up the smooth, unprotected 5.8 face, the top was featureless. I drilled a single bolt and belayed Brian up. In Yosemite, crowds would line up for this climb. Knowing it is deep in the backcountry, I would be surprised to hear about the second ascent happening in the next few years. However, if someone is looking for a direttissima with Astroman-like climbing, on a needle-like spire, with High Sierra views, the Wild West Crack (800', IV 5.11+) is waiting—a five-star route! 📷

– VITALIY MUSIYENKO

DARTH VADER TOWER; EAGLE SCOUT CREEK DOME, WEST FACE

CLIMBERS LIKE TO ARGUE about which is the most difficult summit in the High Sierra. Some claim Castle Rock Spire, others note Clarence King, Devil's Crag, or other challenging peaks in remote parts of the range. After climbing most of these aforementioned peaks, I would plead that Darth Vader Tower is the one.

Brian Prince and I hiked over Timber Gap along Cliff Creek and set up camp near Granite Creek, with Darth Vader Tower and nearby Eagle Scout Creek Dome on our agenda. The morning after completing this 12-mile approach, we made a hellish bushwhack up the south fork of Granite Creek to reach Darth Vader Tower. Boulder-hopping from one slippery rock to another, I questioned my motivations for such outings.

When we finally arrived at the base of the tower's south face, we decided to scramble up a lower-angle dihedral. For the second pitch we roped up, and then we unroped for another 300' of scrambling. Above this initial section we roped up for five pitches. A final knife-edge ridge led us to the summit block, which is overhanging on all sides and gave Darth Vader Tower its name. Fortunately, I was able to grab a chicken head and heel-hook another feature, which allowed me to mantel and reach a perfect tabletop summit. Even the smoke from a nearby wildfire could now be appreciated, adding a mystical touch to the first ascent of this tower (III 5.9). We walked all around the summit block and found no opportunity for a natural anchor and no sign of previous passage. After drilling a bolt—the first of the day—we rappelled to a notch with a single 60m rope. Another roped pitch of downclimbing and we were down.

The following day we approached Eagle Scout Creek Dome via the north fork of Granite Creek, which was easier to travel than the south fork. We picked the most prominent system in the middle of the west face. It includes pumpy jam cracks from thin to offwidth, awesome stemming, and burly boulder problems. The rock quality was mostly good to great. We free climbed everything 5.11 and easier but gave into gear-pulling in a few spots for speed. On top of the fourth pitch we drilled a bolt and made a pendulum left. From there we continued taking the most direct line to the top. All eight pitches were at least 5.10, but usually harder—the Direct West Face (IV 5.11 C1). It could be done free by someone willing to put in the effort. To descend, we scrambled east with a few steps of fifth-class climbing. 📷

— VITALIY MUSIYENKO

PANTHER PEAK, SOUTH FACE, NEW ROUTES

IN THE SPRING, Adam Burch, Daniel Jeffcoach, Adam Sheppard, and Alaina Robertson, and I climbed two new 600–700' routes and one shorter variation up the south aspect of Panther Peak (9,006') in Sequoia National Park. *Find a full report at the AAJ website.* 📄 📷 🔍

— VITALIY MUSIYENKO

MT. SILLIMAN, NORTH CHIMNEY

MT. SILLIMAN (11,188') is a popular summit for peak baggers in Sequoia National Park. In addition to its easier scrambles, the peak's featured orange rock has two routes on its 800' west face, one up its northwest ridge, and a short route up its northeast shoulder. [*R.J. Secor's guidebook details these.*] The steep north face, however, had no reported routes.

Bryan Lang and I set off for the north face in mid-June, planning for a long day. [*The approach alone covers 16 miles and nearly 6,000' of elevation gain.*] Once there we completed an enjoyable, direct route up the right side of the north face. The wall was very steep, and we had a light rack with no bolt kit, so we focused on a chimney system with several roofs. This was fun and straightforward, and it ended directly on the summit: North Chimney (600', 5.9).

— DANIEL JEFFCOACH

LOWER TOKOPAH DOME, MANGO LASSI LULZ MACHINE

IN MID-APRIL, Adam Burch and I finished a route I'd started on Lower Tokopah Dome in 2014. The climb starts between Boardwalk Chimney and Welcome to Walmart on the southwest face (*AAJ 2015*). We clalled it Mango Lassi LULZ Machine (620', III 5.10+). We descended west between Lower Tokopah Dome and Santa Cruz Dome.

— VITALIY MUSIYENKO

CASTLE ROCK SPIRE, EAST FACE, FIRST FREE ASCENT

THE EAST FACE of Castle Rock Spire was first attempted in 1949 by John Salathé and Jim Wilson; the direct crack system is obvious. However, it took 64 years for the route to see a complete ascent (*AAJ 2013*), at 5.9 C1. When Daniel Jeffcoach mentioned that a strong crack climber could potentially free the line, I was excited to try. In 2014, I was shut down by the second pitch. While bailing, though, I saw a good-looking hand crack 40 feet to the left of the thin crack I had tried.

This year I returned with Maxim Belyakov. The alternative second pitch went at an enjoyable 5.10a. The third and fourth pitches were the crux, with the most demanding sections going at solid 5.11+. Even though I was able to onsight all the pitches, I felt the two crux sections required all the skill and strength that I had. In all, the route is 600', III 5.11+.

This ascent was special to me, as this spire has rich history and is considered to be the hardest summit to reach in the Sierra. To date, fewer than 50 people have stood on top, a short list that includes some of the most accomplished climbers in North America. With good climbing and an easy descent with a 70m rope, the east face may now be the preferred way to reach this elusive summit.

— VITALIY MUSIYENKO

SPRING LAKE WALL, NEW ROUTES AND OTHER CLIMBS

LAST SUMMER I worked as a backcountry ranger in Sequoia National Park, stationed about 15 miles south of Valhalla along Little Five Lakes. From here it was easy to hike three to ten miles in any direction and get to nice granite walls along the Great Western Divide—some climbed, some not. The following descriptions are of new routes I climbed, in chronological order. [*Route lengths are based on total climbing distance rather than vertical gain.*]

In June, Austin Siadak and I climbed The One That Got Away (1,500', 5.11b C1) on Spring Lake Wall, up a prominent sun-shadow arête left of the previously established routes (*the north face, III F6, Beckey-Dellinger-Winters, AAJ 1976, and That's a Sheer Cliff, IV F9, Clevenger-Rowell, AAJ 1976*). Later, we climbed a formation just east of Sawtooth Peak, above Columbine Lake. We followed a beautiful ridge of Tuolumne-esque rock (5.8) to a fourth-class traverse onto a face. It's not clear if the peak had been climbed or named previously. We named the route For Want of a Sheer Salamander.

[Left] The Spring Lake Wall, showing The One That Got Away (yellow) and Standard Deviation (red). That's a Sheer Cliff and the original north face route ascend the clean wall to the right. [Right] The tower climbed by Cody Cavill and Chris Kalman in Lost Canyon. *Chris Kalman*

On July 14, I climbed my best route of the season with Cody Cavill, up a previously unclimbed pinnacle in Lost Canyon. The route consisted almost entirely of perfect hand and finger cracks. We named the formation Lost Pinnacle and our route A Fine and Pleasant Romp (III 5.11+), because that's exactly what it was. I know of only two routes in Lost Canyon: ours and the northwest buttress of Needham Mountain (IV 5.7, Hallet-Kirk, 1968).

My girlfriend, Megan Kelly and I then added a three-pitch sit start to Sawtooth Peak's north face, which included run-out 5.10+ knob climbing on excellent rock. I cannot find any account of the face having been freed before, but it certainly could have been.

My next visitors were Drew Smith and Miranda Oakley, whom I met July 19 at the Spring Lake Wall. The following day we climbed a new nine-pitch route (though three pitches are shared with my earlier route) that we called Standard Deviation (1,260', 5.11+ C1).

After Drew and Miranda left, I soloed three new routes, each of them between 800' and 1,000' long. The first two I soloed in the same day, using a Pakistani Death Loop (a long loop of slack tied through an anchor for minimal protection) on some pitches. Starting from the Big Arroyo, I soloed an unnamed cliff, calling the route PDL (800', 5.11). After finishing this route, I scrambled a third- and fourth-class ridge over to Mt. Lipincott's north face. I climbed a new line here that was about equal in quality with Cathedral Peak, but longer and harder. I called this route Me and My Arrow (800', 5.10). For my final route, I went back to Lost Canyon and rope-soloed a beautiful 1,000' east-facing wall on the north side of Needham Mountain. After a lot of 5.9 and a perfect 5.10 hand crack, I got into some rotten granite. I aided this poor rock with a lot of cursing and praying. I finished the route, Paradise Lost, on some heads-up free climbing (5.11-).

Later, I visited Tamarack Lake with another ranger, Matt Zussman, and attempted a Dave Nettle route on Mt. Stewart's north face. I couldn't follow the questionable topo, and we climbed through wild layback flakes (5.11- R). I don't know if this was a new route. Nettle, et al, were very active on this face and probably climbed it. It was quite good. ▤ ▣

– CHRIS KALMAN

WINDY PEAK, NORTH FACE, DREAM WITHIN A DREAM

IN APRIL, Larry DeAngelo, Chad Mueler, Bill Thiry, and I climbed a new route on the north face of Windy Peak: Dream Within a Dream (800', 5.8). It joins Big Sleep (5.9) for three pitches to reach the summit. We descended via a nontechnical hike. ▤ ▢

– SAM TAGGART

ZOROASTER, SOUTHEAST FACE, FIRST FREE ASCENT

IN APRIL I convinced Jeff Snyder and Blake McCord to visit Zoroaster Temple and try to free the southeast face with me. This had been a "serious" project of mine ever since Mathieu Brown and I established the route in 2012 (*AAJ 2013*).

I was able to link and free pitches one and two first try, combining roof liebacking and face climbing (5.11 R). I knew the third pitch was going to be the crux of the route, requiring desperate friction in a corner, but after falling twice I was able to free the pitch (5.11+). The fourth lead starts with a thin fingers crux (5.11+) and stays challenging the whole way. The view on this pitch was truly memorable: As the late afternoon light richened, the rainbow of colors and shadows evolved into an explosion of inspiration. The location and the quality of the climbing make for a very memorable route (520', III 5.11+ R). ▤

– ZACH HARRISON

TEMPLE OF SINEWAVA, LATENT CORE

IN THE EARLY 1990s—back when I was running around in romper suits—Conrad Anker tried a big-wall climb on the Temple of Sinewava, just left of the wall's large waterfall. He and Doug Heinrich climbed five pitches before retreating. While rappelling, one of their ropes got stuck. Conrad and I made plans to complete the route and remove that old rope.

Sitting on a ledge, high above the valley floor, Conrad said, "We've done the first five pitches now. Will you lead the next one?" I nodded. Hanging gear onto my harness, I prepared to start up virgin terrain. With a mix of free climbing and all kinds of aid trickery, we made our way upward. On pitch seven, the crack we had been following disappeared for a few meters. Conrad was forced to toil away, placing bolts by hand, for several hours until we could reach the crack system again. With rainy and cold weather, the final three pitches took two full days. However, the joy of doing a first ascent together prevailed.

We named our route Latent Core (IV 5.11 A1), a pun that refers to the rope left behind long ago but also to the legendary Layton Kor. ▢

– DAVID LAMA, *AUSTRIA*

Photo] David Lama leads while Conrad Anker belays on Latent Core (IV 5.11 A1). *James Q Martin*

TUCUPIT POINT, NEW CLIMBS

The west face of Tucupit Point showing (1) Forrest-March and (2) Tucupit Occidentalis. *Brandon Gottung*

In November 2014, Cullen Kirk, Karl Kvashay, and I climbed the first of many new routes on Tucupit Point. Astrolizard (IV 5.11) climbs a clean, mostly wide crack system on Tucupit's south face and is comprised of mostly Indian Creek–quality cracks.

In June 2015, Karl and I established Tucupit occidentalis (800', IV 5.10+) on the west face, in Kolob Canyon. The west face was first climbed by Bill Forrest and Bill March (V 5.8 A2, *AAJ 1982*), and our route shares the first two pitches with the obvious crack system of that route. [*Editor's note: Tucupit was incorrectly spelled "Tucapit" in the original 1982 report. Tucupit is Paiute for "wildcat."*] After that, our route branches left into crisp, clean cracks and corners, linked with spectacular face climbing, to the top of the wall. I'd say the route represents one of the best of its length and grade in Zion. Expect great morning shade in a spectacular setting, exciting positions, consistent quality, and great rock. As a bonus, climbing in Kolob has a magical backcountry feel that the main canyon does not offer.

Karl and I continued to have a busy year following our ascents of Astrolizard and Tucupit occidentalis. Just left of Astrolizard, we climbed a two-pitch route we called Lead-Free Gut Pile (II 5.11). We also climbed a variation to pitch three of Tucupit occidentalis, which we called Red Morph (5.11+).

[*Editor's note: The remainder of the routes described here were established with free climbing in mind but have not yet been redpointed.*] After this, we climbed Tucupit nova (IV 5.11+), which follows the obvious pillar on the left side of the west face for two pitches before traversing further right into the next pillar feature for another two pitches. The fourth pitch is the crux, which we led with one fall and then followed clean. After this we joined the final three pitches of Tucupit occidentalis to the top of the wall.

Next up was the Stone Age. This climb starts via one pitch of aid (A2 beaks and hooks) to access the obvious splitter crack system on the northwest buttress. The fifth pitch is the crux (proposed 5.12+) and has a difficult traverse right into a right-facing corner, ending at a beautiful bivy ledge. Six more pitches of excellent free climbing top off the route.

Finally, we climbed two shorter routes. Skeleton Key starts on an obvious weakness below a giant corner system on the north face (proposed 5.12+). The Pain Chamber is equal parts strenuous free climbing and wild caving. We accessed the climb by moving left under the west face and then rappelling off a tree to a lower ledge system and traversing left behind a flake. The follower freed every pitch, but it has not yet been freed on lead (proposed 5.11+). ▤ ◙

– BRANDON GOTTUNG

PEAK 6,925'–PEAK 6,991' TRAVERSE; PEAK 6,760', NORTHEAST ARÊTE

In April, Owen Lunz and I made a five-day journey through the Great West Canyon—what you might call ultralight backpacking with a big-wall rack. Along the way we made the first ascents of three technical summits surrounding Stevenson Canyon, a prominent tributary of the Right Fork of North Creek.

After a day's travel to access the high country on April 17, we spent April 18 making a north-to-south traverse of Peak 6,925' and Peak 6,991' (these have been nicknamed Stevenson Peak and Great White Dome by local peakbaggers). This was classic Zion chossaneering, with lots of 4th-class travel on loose terrain and the occasional 5th-class step (up to 5.7).

The following day, April 19, we made the probable second descent of Stevenson Canyon to reach the aesthetic northeast buttress of a large and beautiful sandstone dome: Peak 6,760'. Striated in red and white bands and surrounded by deep faults, the dome looks like a Jovian planet erupting through the crust of the earth. The dome's northeast arête provided a surprisingly enjoyable route. After six pitches of climbing to 5.9, we climbed 1,000' of easier but exposed terrain to the summit rim. The descent was adventurous. We first traversed rotten rock to a neighboring 6,840' peak. We then rappelled to the northeast and traversed beautiful slickrock terrain before descending the canyon wall due north of the start of our route. We dubbed the peak Iron Lion, and our route is the Kingdom (III/IV 5.9). We left nine drilled angles in situ.

On April 20 we exited Stevenson Canyon and managed to bypass deep potholes by staying high on the canyoneer's left side. We made one rappel near the mouth and spent a final night in the Grand Alcove before a glorious trek out the Right Fork. Future climbers should note that the flat-topped summits in this area of North Creek and the Great West Canyons (including Great White Dome, Ivins Mountain, and Inclined Temple) are technically off limits, as they are designated Research Natural Areas (RNA) by the park; however, climbing their walls to the summit rim is not prohibited. We only became aware of this after our climb of Great White Dome.

— DARIN BERDINKA

Owen Lunz on the Kingdom, on the dome the climbers named Iron Lion. Ivins Mountain can be seen in the background. *Darin Berdinka*

IVINS MOUNTAIN, WEST FACE

Over four days at the beginning of April, Matthew Mower and I completed the first ascent of Ivins Mountain (7,049') by its west face. This peak is located on the west side of the park, and is considered one of the most remote mountains in Zion. To reach the base of the route, we had

The west sides of Inclined Temple (left) and Ivins Mountain (right), as seen from the West Rim Trail. The new route on Ivins climbs the steep slab below the peak to a vegetated ledge and then up the prominent corner system in the center of the wall. Approximately two-thirds of the way up the corner system, the climbers traversed right and climbed the face right of the corner to the summit. The 2013 route on Inclined Temple climbs the unseen south side. Comparing Inclined Temple to Ivins Mountain, Dan Stih notes that, "Ivins is much, much harder." *Matthew Mower*

to navigate miles of slot canyons and difficult 5th-class climbing with very heavy loads. I had first attempted to solo the peak, in April 2014. My next attempt was with Mower in October 2014. On our second trip, we took a different approach than I'd tried previously, scrambling around the back of Inclined Temple. (Michael Schash and I made the first ascent of this peak, by its south face, in November 2013.) There is a semi-technical shelf that runs along the west side of the Inclined Temple, which provides more reasonable access to Ivins if carrying heavy loads.

Our route on Ivins required moderately difficult nailing. The first pitch required a combination of 16 tied-off knifeblades and beaks in addition to other pins and cams. From the top of the first pitch, a pendulum and some slippery, sandy free climbing reached an obvious ledge with a tree. From there we found enjoyable free climbing up a prominent crack and corner system. Typical for these kinds of routes in Zion, we made use of tied-off bushes. Toward the top we traversed right onto the main face before climbing straight up to the summit. We left no trace except for a two-piton rappel anchor, and when we used trees or bushes to rappel we left no slings. We did not drill. We climbed a total of 12 pitches (5.9+ A2+). Six of these pitches climbed a steep slab (5.9+) from the bottom of the canyon to the base of the peak, and the next six climbed from the base of the wall to the summit. 📷

— DAN STIH

CASTLE DOME, SOUTH FACE; MAGIC RABBIT PEAK, PORK GREEN CHILE; RED TOOTH, SOUTH FACE

ON OCTOBER 30, Matt Mower and I made what is likely the first ascent of Castle Dome. From the West Rim, we rappelled into the saddle between the West Rim and Castle Dome. We eventually reached the southeast corner, where one can look down onto Zion Lodge. From there, we climbed around the corner and up to the summit. The level of difficulty is similar to the south face on Twin Brothers (up to 5.5). Mostly it's a scramble on loose, sandy, white sandstone. We rappelled north from the summit cap, downclimbed a bit, and then made three double raps to the saddle.

On November 12, Courtney Purcell (author of *Zion National Park: Summit Routes*), Aron Ralston, and I reclimbed the south face on Castle Dome, this time approaching by descending Behunin Canyon. From the canyon we scrambled up cliffs to the south from just before the first rappel point in the canyon. From there one can hike across to the ramp that hugs the blank east face of Castle Dome and the start of our south face route. This probably will become the normal approach and has since been repeated. We downclimbed back to Behunin Canyon.

On November 13, Purcell, Ralston, and I did the first ascent of a formation in the Court of the Patriarchs. This is the highest in a cluster of peaks that make up the tail end of the southeast side of the Court, east of the Sentinel. The last pitch, the crux, is similar to the Mace in Sedona: There is a chasm between you and the summit peak (5.8+ or 5.9 R). The R rating is given because the only protection is a tied-off, downward-facing piton in bad sandstone, where a fall would send you tumbling into the chasm. The summit is similar to Ancient Art in the Fisher Towers: Only one person can stand on it at a time. The views are spectacular. We called this summit Magic Rabbit Peak and the route Pork Green Chile.

On November 30, Purcell and I did the first ascent of a peak that Courtney calls Red Tooth. This peak is northeast of Bridge Mountain, on the edge of the cliffs above the east entry tunnel road. Access is the same as Bridge Mountain. We climbed four roped pitches with two cruxes of 5.8+ to 5.9 R. We used tied-off knifeblades for protection on delicate face climbing. There are four summits. Our route climbs the face on the south side to the first summit. The highest summit is then reached by traversing north across the top in the direction of East Temple as the crow flies.

— DAN STIH

NEW ICE ROUTES

In early November, Nathan Smith, Matt Tuttle, and Angela VanWiemeersch climbed a new ice route in Henry's Fork Basin, below King's Peak (13,528'), on the north slope of the Uinta Mountains. The climb, Trivium (100', WI4), is significant for its 10-mile approach, starting elevation of 12,050', and for the recent ice exploration in the Uinta high country. Later in November, Smith and Chris Thomas climbed a longer ice and mixed route on Hellgate Cliffs in Little Cottonwood Canyon. The Bone Collector (595', WI5 M5) ascends five pitches of ephemeral ice to a point at two-thirds height on the wall.

— ERIK RIEGER, *WITH INFORMATION FROM* NATHAN SMITH

BRIDGER JACK BUTTE, OUT FROM THE SHADOWS

Mary Harlan and I started this climb when we climbed and cleaned the first two pitches of Sucker Punch (*AAJ 2014*) and this route, located just right of Sucker Punch on the northwest face, over two days. I added the remaining hardware over several other missions with various partners. Two years later, my wife, Lisa, finished the route with me. This is a fun and varied adventure with great crack climbing on pitches two and three. I named the route Out from the Shadows (5 pitches, 5.11), as it is in the shade for most of the day and, more importantly, it was Lisa's first big adventure after a difficult fight with Lyme disease for the past two years.

— JASON NELSON

THE NETHERWORLD

BY JOE FORRESTER

I first climbed in the Fisher Towers during my freshman year of college. During the next three years, I gradually climbed one tower after the other, learning from each success and failure, until I had done them all.

My most profound failure was on Sundevil Chimney on the Titan. Without funds to buy pitons, my partner and I purchased aluminum tent stakes at an Army surplus store. Unwilling to spend money on food, we purchased cans of wet dog food. Naive about how hot the desert could be, we hiked in only two gallons of water. And too proud to admit we didn't know where the start of Finger of Fate was, we chose Sundevil because "it was a better line." At the end of the first day, beaten, we watched the sun set on a wall behind the Titan. As the orange glow turned to dark red, a buttress stood out. I would start calling this untrodden zone—between the Titan, at the east end of the Fishers, and the Hydra, forming the west end of the Mystery Towers—the Netherworld.

Years later, I obsessed about the logistics of climbing in the Netherworld, and what I would do when faced with my own fears, in a far-out valley, high up on red Cutler sandstone.

HELL HOUND (V 5.8 A3): Over Labor Day 2013, Jeremy Aslaksen and Hilary Bagshaw helped me hump loads behind the Titan to reach Cerebus Gendarme. With temperatures in the 90s, we could only climb two pitches over the three-day weekend.

A month and a half later, Jeremy and I were back. This time, we recruited Dave Hoven, another glutton for punishment. We were faced with freezing temperatures. After Jeremy led a short pitch, I led up a 200' section of overhanging Cutler. As I led the crux pitch over seven hours, Jeremy and Dave suffered in the cold as they were pelted with a steady stream of dirt and rock. Loose beaks in terrible rock led to a thin seam. Move by move, I dug into that spot where I had kept my prior failures and used it to fuel myself upward. Eventually the seam ended. Standing on a beak, with one small cam between me and the anchor, I finally broke down. As the wind and cold ate into my confidence, I yelled for the drill. After placing two bolts, I reached another beak-size crack and the end of the pitch. We rapped in the dark.

In November, Jeremy and I were back. Our focus was sharp, and our eyes were on the summit. Jeremy finished leading up to the caprock, and the next day I led two pitches with a finale of unprotected 5.9 offwidth moves through a roof. Pulling onto the mesa top, looking out over the Mystery Towers, the Fishers, and Castle Valley, I yelled with joy. But one climb was not enough in the Netherworld—there were other lines to explore.

DURIN'S BANE (V 5.8 A2+): In the winter 2013, Jeremy and I hiked back out to the Netherworld. We had spotted a series of roofs on a south-facing, yellow-orange wall. Below the main crack system were blank bulges. I felt strongly that the continuous upper crack system merited a bolt ladder to get there. Jeremy did not. So, solo, I worked upward, bolting and beaking to the crack system. A lot of bolts were required: 23 including anchors. But looking up from my high point, I knew the climbing would be incredible, all the way to the summit.

Over two additional weekends, we went back to complete the route. The route required

Joe Forrester and Jeremy Aslaksen work across the complex gendarmes of Hydraform Ridge, a massive route located between the Fisher and Mystery towers. *Joe Forrester Collection*

only three additional lead bolts. The crack system was excellent, one of the best I have climbed in the Fishers. The larger of two roofs overhangs about 15 feet, and is likely the most overhanging pitch in the Fisher or Mystery towers.

HYDRAFORM RIDGE (VI 5.8 A3): Durin's Bane and Hell Hound were just the warmups. The ridge rising from the summit of the Hydra, which we would come to call the Hydraform Ridge, was the prize. Like a bizarre, giant fence of Cutler sandstone, this ridge separates the Netherworld from the Mystery Towers. The Hydra, originally climbed in 1994 by Duane Raleigh and Tony Wilson, represented a small but fierce testpiece of Cutler climbing trickery. Our route up the ridge leading from the top of the Hydra to the Moenkopi caprock took it to a whole new level, with another 900 feet of gargoyle climbing.

Each weekend in the Netherworld left us beaten and bruised, but we persisted. With the periods of absence lasting a month or more, our desire to complete the ridge only grew.

The first pitch of our climb starts out with a lasso and takes an independent line along the prow before it meets up with the 1994 route. On the last of the Hydra's four original pitches, after a short beak seam, the ridge became blank—this was obviously where the first ascent team had famously thrown an ice axe as a grappling hook. We'd come prepared: Jeremy whipped our axe around his head and let go. The axe caught 20 feet above us. We didn't know how long it would hold. Jeremy attached his ascenders to the 7mm cord and started jugging. The axe had hooked over a small indent of sandstone. Hydra had let down her hair and let us past.

Crossing the spectacular fin of the Hydra required unnerving acrobatics, running and jumping from one hoodoo to the next. Being on untrodden ground, we were unsure if these formations would support body weight. As ravens sailed in the dry breeze, we topped out to the upper plateau wth thunderclouds rolling in. With lighting flashing and thunder booming, we made the long rappels down the face, now flowing in mud. Covered in grime and fear-sweat, we collapsed at the base. After 10 months, we had finally completed the Hydraform Ridge.

A PEAK AND BLACKWELL GLACIER AREA, NEW ICE & MIXED CLIMBS

In February and March, Scott Coldiron and partners climbed two long new routes in the Cabinet Mountains. On February 22, Coldiron and Christian Thompson climbed Blackwell Falls (900', WI5 M4), a mostly ice route below the northeast side of A Peak (8,634'), fed by the Blackwell Glacier. They descended the route. On March 7, Beu Carrilo, Coldiron, Benjamin Erdmann, and Jonah Job climbed Unprotected Four-Play (2,000', AI4+ M6 R) on the left side of the northeast face of A Peak. The route ends a few hundred feet below the summit, where the ice ends, and the group walked off to descend. Coldiron, Joe Lind, and Jeff Zickler have developed other four- to five-pitch ice climbs in a drainage adjacent to Blackwell Glacier; however, details are lacking.

– ERIK RIEGER, WITH INFORMATION FROM SCOTT COLDIRON AND ALPINIST.COM

STORM POINT, HIGHWAY TO HEAVEN

In July, Pete Walka and I completed Highway to Heaven (11 pitches, 5.8) on Storm Point in the Tetons. As reported in *AAJ 2015*, the route ended at a high point I dubbed Tranquility Point. Upon returning in 2015, we found a free route to reach the true summit of Storm Point, with two pitches of outstanding 5.10 climbing on flawless granite, along with fourth-class scrambling, and one short 5.8 pitch.

– RON WATTERS

FREMONT PEAK, WEST FACE, THEY LIVE

Our time was running out. Mark Evans, Oli Shaw, and I had already bailed from high on Fremont Peak's west face—twice. On our first magnificent failure, in September 2014, we nearly froze to the wall (*AAJ 2015*).

The second retreat had been a week before now, from the last technical pitch, below the start of easy ground to the summit. Reluctantly, we rapped the entire face in a whiteout. With the end of July approaching, and with only a few days left before our pack horses arrived, it was evident that our decision not to blast for the top was agonizing. Cozy in our bags, under a boulder above Mistake Lake, I grew paranoid: Had we blown our final chance?

We descended to our base camp, and, after we'd recovered sufficiently from our midday whiskey rounds, decided to have another go at the wall. We hiked up at dusk to our boulder bivouac, hopeful the morning would dawn clear and still.

July 26 was by far the best single day of stable climbing weather we'd seen in our nearly six weeks here, spread across two seasons. That morning, we hastily retraced our way by headlamp up the loose, steep approach to the base of Fremont's west face. Anxious to avoid being caught just shy of the top again, we soloed the initial 500' of fourth- and easy fifth-class climbing and dispatched the familiar lower pitches with renewed urgency. Oli handily sent the crux at 5.10+, pulling us out of the shaded gully forming the left margin of the face and unveiling the vast, red upper headwall.

Less than four hours after launch, we were a pitch below our high point. Kissed by sun, Mark re-led a brilliant, exposed pitch, gaining the right edge of the west pillar. Above this, Oli and I followed perfect cracks in red-patina rock up the huge, steep corner of the upper West Face Dihedral (*AAJ 2015*). Oli's bold final lead (5.10 R) put us on low-angle terrain above the corner. Ten minutes later we were unroped atop the Continental Divide. We'd turned a yearlong haunting into a frenzied half-day ascent. We named our route after John Carpenter's 1988 cult, sci-fi classic: They Live (1,500', 5.10+ R).

– SHINGO OHKAWA

MT. HOOKER, NORTHEAST FACE, GAMBLING IN THE WINDS

I CRACKED OPEN A PBR TALLBOY. Before me was a massive pile of food, climbing gear, camping equipment, four bottles of whiskey, herbal assistance, and a 40-pound Costco freezer bag full of baby-back ribs, steaks, and bacon. "This should be an enjoyable camping experience," I thought, smirking. It was August 8, and Jesse Huey, Whit Magro, Mike Pennings, and I were about to spend ten days climbing on Mt. Hooker.

Oli Shaw leading the crux of They Live, west face of Fremont Peak. *Mark Evans*

Jesse and Mike had an incredible trip, completing a free ascent of the Jaded Lady and the second free ascent of Hook, Line, and Sinker (*AAJ 2015*), while Whit and I put our efforts into climbing a new line. We spent six days climbing ground-up to establish our line, employing the use of fixed ropes. On the seventh day, we climbed the route in a single push to the summit, completely free. Nothing like a 9-to-5 workweek in the backcountry! The climbing was truly stunning and incredibly varied. Some sections seemed like they would be 5.13 but ended up only being 5.11 or easy 5.12.

Our route starts on the obvious "ski track" cracks that trend right toward two large, green, marbled slabs on the northeast face, left of the Hook, Line, and Sinker route. From the top of the first marbled slab, we climbed a wild 5.12 roof pitch that we dubbed the Rifle Pitch. This ends at a good ledge, and the crux 5.12 pitch is next, the Good Hand Pitch. A third 5.12 pitch leads though the second marbled slab to another nice ledge. Two more 5.11-ish pitches led us to Der Minor Ledge, at which point we traversed right and then finished on the top section of the Boissoneault-Larson (VI 5.11 A4, 1979).

We called our new route Gambling in the Winds (10 pitches, VI 5.12). A direct finish would be a spectacular way to end the route and would probably add at least one more 5.12 pitch. All the belays are bolted, and it's possible to rappel from the top of the sixth pitch with two 70m ropes. A 70m rope is mandatory on this route due to the length of several pitches.

The Wind Rivers have the feel of a wild, untamed place in a faraway land, only heard in whispers. Let's try our best to keep it that way—respect.

– HAYDEN KENNEDY

Mandy Fabel in the fifth-pitch chimney of Lady and the Tramps. *Sam Lightner Jr.*

DOG TOOTH PEAK, SOUTH FACE, LADY AND THE TRAMPS

IT IS IMPOSSIBLE to shiver through a belay on the north face of the Monolith and not notice the sunny, warm south face of Dog Tooth Peak across the canyon. It is also impossible to ignore the line that splits the middle of Dog Tooth Peak's southernmost spire. In September, Mandy Fabel, Mike Lilygren, and I spent a day establishing a great route up this south-facing wall.

Dog Tooth Peak is located in the cirque above Papoose Lake, about two miles east of the Cirque of the Towers, accessed via the North Fork Trail. It takes a little over an hour from Papoose Lake to reach the base of this face. Our route, Lady and the Tramps (6 pitches, 5.11-PG13), begins in the middle of the wall, below a chimney system. [*Editor's note: See* Climbing and Hiking in the Wind River Mountains, *by Joe Kelsey, for additional routes on Dog Tooth Peak. Most of the longer, previously established routes climb the east aspect of the mountain.*]

The first pitch is an easy slab that trends right and then follows a ledge left. Pitch two goes out a bulge to a ledge with about 40m of solid 5.10 climbing. Pitch three is the crux and ascends a layback seam to an overhanging bombay chimney at easy 5.11; the pitch is 50m long and slightly overhanging, making it quite physical. Pitch four climbs a series of cracks via face moves on solid rock at easy 5.10. At the end of this pitch, we belayed about 10m up a big chimney. Pitch five is a rope-stretcher and the mental crux; it is 5.10, but there are very big runouts, and one side of the chimney has a lot of loose stone. Above this, we belayed on an exposed ledge. The final pitch follows the chimney for nearly 60m, going under an obvious chockstone, to reach the summit ridge. We followed the ridge to the summit and then descended east to Lizard Head Meadows. 📷

– SAM LIGHTNER JR.

GUARANTEED PERFECT ADVENTURE

BY JOHN HARLIN III

Can one guarantee a perfect adventure? It seems an oxymoron, at least by Tilman's edict that if the outcome is certain there's no point in starting a journey. Adventure requires uncertainty; uncertainty requires un-guarantee-ability. And yet, mix the cocktail just right—a little of this, more of that, just enough of everything else—and there you are: the perfect trip, every time.

For the last decade, expedition wizard Mark Jenkins has been inviting me to join him on one of his annual perfect little outings in Wyoming. No matter how many grueling multi-week and multi-month expeditions he does, every year Mark drives from Laramie to an obscure cirque in the Wind Rivers or Bighorns. He packs in, puts up a bunch of new routes on 1,000' walls, and emerges a week later, grinning. He seems to have discovered a magic formula.

This year the stars aligned and I finally drank from Mark's potion. Months later the grin is still etched on my face. So what's the formula? For us, it begins with friendship. Mark's and mine goes back three decades and up never-enough mountains on multiple continents. Dougald MacDonald's and mine, well, pretty much the same. Ditto theirs. Just being together is enough to guarantee a good time. But we crave more than talk in a bar.

The next ingredient is that the trip has to actually happen. Organizing a month together?

[Above] **Dougald MacDonald on the third pitch of Grand Delusion, east face, Hallelujah.** *John Harlin III*

[Top, left] Mark Jenkins atop Rabbit Ears Spire, Mt. Woolsey. [Top, right] The 1,300' direct east face of Mt. Woolsey, showing the route Woolsey When We Get There to twin-topped Rabbit Ears Spire. [Bottom, left] The 850'east face of Buffalo Back showing Buffalo Girls. [Bottom, right] The Grand Delusion on the 900' east face of Hallelujah. *Dougald MacDonald (all photos)*

Impossible. A week away? Bring it on. Then there's money. There are times in one's life when every C-note is accounted for. Distant shores become distant dreams. Pooling gas money? Never a problem.

A proper expedition should be exotic, a far cry from day-to-day life. We met our horse packer in a bar in Buffalo. Above our table were the stuffed heads of every animal known to inhabit Wyoming. Next to us was the same desk that territorial judges sat behind when sentencing six-gun-toting horse thieves in the '80s. 1880s, that is. Our buffalo was served by a Stetson- and jeans-wearing college student from Moldavia. I could go on, but this report has a word limit. Let's just say that no teahouse in Tibet is more exotic than our saloon in the Occidental Hotel. And then entered Wes Smiley, who had just packed in our climbing gear and food as far a horse could carry it. His weather-worn cowboy hat never left his head. His hands were as broad and hard as the butt of a hunting rifle. Wes pulled out a Google Earth satellite image and pointed out a dead tree. "Sight along this log to the tree it points to. Your stuff is under that tree."

The next day Dougald's little 4WD nearly floated over the ford across Little Goose Creek before crawling up a ridiculous "road" to the edge of the Cloud Peak Wilderness Area. We walked eight miles of trail through pine forests and across an alpine pass until we spotted the dead tree in the Google Earth photo. We sighted along its bleached trunk and, bang, the gear. Another two much-sweatier miles without trail took us into the nameless cirque surrounding Sawtooth Lakes, where we stopped at a grassy meadow trapped by boulders far above timberline.

Mark and Dougald had been drawn to the Sawtooth Lakes valley after spotting a 12,590' fin called Hallelujah leaping above the neighboring ridges during a climbing trip to Cloud Peak (two valleys to the south) in 2014. We weren't the first climbers to stare at these walls. Guess who beat us to it by nearly half a century? Fred Beckey, of course. He and two partners climbed the biggest face in the area, the northeast side of the Innominate, in 1967. The Iowa and Chicago Mountaineers sent huge teams of good climbers, including Pete Cleveland, Paul Stettner, and Harvey Carter, in the 1950s and 1970s. Long before them a remarkable expedition of Easterners climbed and named the most significant peaks of the Sawtooth Lakes and Spear Lake drainages, including Innominate, Hallelujah, and Woolsey, all of which W.B. Wilcox described in "An American Tyrol," a splendid feature article in *AAJ 1934*. Yet, surprisingly, as far as we could determine, many of the biggest cliffs remained virgin. Every line we laid eyes on had never been touched—or at least never reported. The granite was solid and stable, except where it wasn't. Cracks split the faces from bottom to top, except where they didn't.

This being Mark's backyard, we honored his mantra: no bolts, no pins, no hammer. Two lead-worthy ropes in case one gets cut. Climb all day, every day. Love every minute, no matter what. And so it went: Devious lines connected by head-scratching, finger-pumping, toe-sticking adventure climbing. Splitter fingers. Run-out slabs. Dikes and chicken heads. Mossy wet hand cracks. Rock as solid as the best of Tuolumne. Footholds that popped off without warning. In the end, both ropes were chopped by stones we'd not been smart enough to avoid dislodging.

We summited two unclimbed (best we could tell) spire tops on three virgin (best we could tell) walls. Each route was about 10 pitches and went at low 5.10: Buffalo Gals on the east face of Buffalo Back (ca 12,280'); Grand Delusion on the east face of Hallelujah (12,590'); and Woolsey When We Get There on the southeast face of Mt. Woolsey (12,978'), via the "Rabbit Ears Spire" (you'll see when you get there).

Then we hiked out, better friends than ever and already planning the next guaranteed perfect adventure. 🖭

GUARDIAN, NORTH AND NORTHEAST FACES, POSSIBLE NEW ROUTES

ON JULY 3, Jay Bachhuber, Michael Crouch, Jeff Woodward, and I approached the Guardian (13,617'). The next day we split into two parties. Michael and Jay climbed a new route on the northeast buttress of the peak, ascending a natural line visible from the Guardian-Silex cirque. They called it Theory of the Leisure Class (1,600', IV 5.8). Jeff Woodward and I continued up the snow and scree to a corner system at the base of the north face, slightly downslope from the couloir that splits the face. From here we climbed the steep lower section of the Guardian's north face in five pitches and then simul-climbed the remaining fourth- and fifth-class terrain. We called the route A Prayer to Earl and Valerie: The John Joline Memorial Route (1,400', IV 5.9). Both routes top out on the Guardian's eastern apex. This point is separated from the true summit by a narrow chasm that cleaves the peak, so we skipped the summit. We descended the east face.

[Editor's note: The four known technical routes on the northeast and north faces are as follows, from left to right: Theory of the Leisure Class, Weather Window Waltz (AAJ 2012), Serpentine Son Rise (2013), and John Joline Memorial Route. It's likely that other climbs have occurred on Guardian's northern aspects and gone unreported.]

– BEN CHAPMAN

AMES WALL, BELLY OF THE BEAST

IN DECEMBER 2014, Gary Newmeyer and I made two attempts on the major chimney system right of the Ames Ice Hose on the Ames Wall. We were shut down both times on the third pitch due to smooth rock, little protection, and a large chockstone. We made a third and successful attempt in January 2015. Our route, Belly of the Beast (III WI5+ M6+ C1 X), is six pitches long. I wouldn't call it a classic route, but it's an excellent adventure on par with routes on Camp Bird Road near Ouray. We descended the climber's trail above the Ice Hose.

– NIK MIRHASHEMI

ROCKY MOUNTAIN NATIONAL PARK, SUMMARY OF NEW CLIMBS

IN SEPTEMBER AND OCTOBER 2014, Ben Collett and Rob Smith climbed two moderate new ice/mixed routes in the Longs Peak area. Smith's Route (III M5) ascends the gully left of Zumie's Thumb in the east cirque of Longs Peak. Duncan Did It First (800', WI3 M5) begins from a terrace a couple of hundred feet above Columbine Lake, below Mt. Meeker, and ascends a broken-looking, north-facing wall.

In March 2015, Chris Sheridan and Doug Shepherd climbed Analysis Paralysis (900', M6) on Hallett Peak's third buttress. The route ascends three pitches of what is likely new terrain before joining the Kor–Van Tongeren rock climb (1962) for two pitches in an obvious chimney.

In July, Michael Goodhue and Tim Davis climbed Victory Garden (800', 5.9) on the west face of Aiguille de Fleur.

In August, Maximilian Barlerin and Quinn Brett climbed Geronimo (7 pitches, 5.12 R) on the left side of Chiefshead's northeast face. Adam Baxter and Josh Gross climbed Raise the Roof (III 5.8 R) on Thatchtop's northwest face, in the vicinity of the ice/mixed route Upper Wall, to the right of the Necrophilia gully.

In September 2015, Ben Collett and Will Mayo climbed Taylor Made (700' 5.10) on the lower, south-facing rock tier of Taylor Peak.

– ERIK RIEGER

OTIS PEAK, SOUTH FACE SPIRES, MANY NEW ROUTES

OTIS PEAK (12,486') in RMNP has a broad south face that hosts a plethora of spires along its east to west axis. After climbing Zowie, a tower at the eastern end of Otis Peak, I spotted some uncharted terrain to the left of the standard routes. In 2006, my wife, Liz Donley, our friend Chris Ferguson, and I completed the first ascent of Green Chili (4 pitches, 5.10) on Zowie. But it was not until a few years later that I discovered Otis Peak's full potential. Spire after spire came into view, little gems amid the rubble-strewn south flank.

In 2009, Andy Morgan and I went to the west end, making the first ascent of Otis Flower Tower. Fallen Hero (4 pitches, 5.10+ R) is a route dedicated to our late friend Jonny Copp.

The next year I completed four new routes on four unclimbed spires. We never found any gear or cairns along the way or on the summits. The first route that season was Piton d'Or (4 pitches, 5.9) on Piton Spire, with Jason Maurer and Aaron Miller. I had spray-painted a knifeblade piton metallic gold while getting our gear together in my garage. This piton ended up protecting the traverse over a very dangerous fall at the start of the route. The route is moderate and on good stone, which made for a wonderful day in the mountains.

Next up, I completed Smoky Birthday Climb (4 pitches, 5.10 R) on the Otis Power Tower. Eric Malmgren and I share the same birthday; usually we would go solo together, but this seemed like an equally good adventure. We found good stone and fine cracks. Then there was the Fire Tower and the route I Thought You Had It (4 pitches, 5.10- R). The names derive from a wildfire we could see in the distance and from my partner Thom Engelbach: When I didn't see the climbing rack, I asked him if he had it. "I thought you had it," he said.

After naming my dog Zowie, after the Otis tower, I had to do something for his brother, Cosmo. Later that summer, my wife and I climbed a broad spire basically beside Zowie. The Path (4 pitches, 5.6) is a lovely route up the south face of Cosmo tower.

In 2015 there were still a few more unnamed formations to surmount. Jason Maurer and I ascended Thrill Tower. We named our route The Thrill's Not Gone (3 pitches, 5.8+) in honor of our friend Wayne Crill (a.k.a. Dr. Thrill), who suffered a bad climbing accident in 2014. The next week I returned with Andy Downin to complete the two final obvious towers in a one-day push. As you get to the western end of Otis the routes get a bit shorter, offering only two to three pitches. Hidden Spire's Trundle Bunny Warehouse (3 pitches, 5.8+) and Forgotten Spire's Clean Up Crew (3 pitches, 5.10- R) made a fun link-up for the day.

In total, I climbed nine first ascents and named five of the formations—hard to believe in this Front Range mecca. Many more adventures are possible on these formations. We never took bolts, just a few pitons, a hammer, extra stoppers, and cord. We just hoped for the best and it always worked out well on the perfectly featured granite high up in Rocky Mountain National Park. 📷 🔍

– CORY FLEAGLE

JD Merritt follows the pitch three finger crack (5.11-) on Three Dragons, Pikes Peak. *Phil Wortmann*

MT. EVANS MASSIF, BLACK WALL, SINNERS ON SUNDAY

IN JULY 2014, Dan Godshall, Greg German, Jackie Kuusinen, and I finished a new route on the right side of the Black Wall: Sinners On Sunday (700', 5.12 C0). The seven-pitch route takes a line between Rainbow Highway (*AAJ 2013*) and High Variance (*AAJ 2014*) and ends at the final anchor on Rainbow Highway.

– SCOTT SINOR

PIKES PEAK, CORINTHIAN COLUMN, NEW ROUTES

DURING THE PAST few winters of climbing in the Bottomless Pit on Pikes Peak's north side, I spotted a few crack systems on the Corinthian Column (ca 13,500') that looked interesting for potential summer rock routes. Upon closer inspection, I found they were full of dirt, moss, and loose rock, which would make free climbing them a challenging and unenjoyable affair.

In late 2014 (early winter conditions), Noah McKelvin, Jack Rodat, and I climbed one of these crack systems, which ascends the center of the Corinthian Column. We climbed with ice tools and crampons, treating it as a mixed route, in hopes of clearing out the cracks. We called the route Three Dragons (400', M7). It's possible that someone climbed the first pitch of this route earlier, but most locals were doubtful of a prior ascent.

In June 2015, I returned to Three Dragons, rappelled in, and continued cleaning out the cracks. On June 30, after a prior attempt, JJ Calhoun and I redpointed all four pitches. The route begins on a hand crack, climbing through two roofs with good gear. From there a long pitch of ledgy climbing leads to the crux finger crack (5.11-), and then broken terrain takes you to the top. During this summer outing on Three Dragons, I spotted another thin crack system to the right. I returned a few days later and cleaned it from top to bottom on rappel. On July 25, JJ Calhoun, Noah McKelvin, and I climbed Sunnyvale (400', 5.11). The first pitch is a short 5.9. The crux second pitch (5.11) works up a featured arête and is protected by a thin crack.

The third pitch climbs a 5.10 crack to a brilliantly exposed stance on the arête. More run-out 5.9 terrain gains the top. We left pitons in situ on the crux pitch, as it is hard to protect. 🖼

— PHIL WORTMANN

GREAT POTATO, EAST RIDGE

YEARS AGO I stumbled upon some entertaining written history about a large, unclimbed, freestanding tower called the Great Potato (8,510') in the San Mateo Mountains, southwest of Socorro. The formation was named due to its location in upper Potato Canyon. I eventually mentioned the tower to Walt Whetham, who was extremely interested in an excursion.

In late March we made it into the area. A few miles of hiking from a snowy dirt road (ca 9,200') gave us a good view of the tower, and from there we descended about 1,200' into the canyon. Though only about 200' tall, it is still an impressive formation.

Over two days (due to hand-drilling some anchor and protection bolts on lead) we established the first route up the tower by its airy east ridge (2 pitches, 5.6 R/X). The rock is comprised of poor quality tuff and andesite and presents almost no natural protection opportunities. Despite the runouts, this was an extremely awesome and rewarding adventure. We left a summit register and drilled a two-bolt anchor on top to descend. 📄 🖼

— JASON HALLADAY

CANNON CLIFF, GHOSTRIDER

OVER TWO DAYS in September 2014, Ryan Brooks and I free climbed a new route on the big-wall sector of Cannon Cliff in Franconia Notch. The route ascends seven pitches over roughly 800' and contains some of the best and worst Cannon has to offer. As this is a link-up of three old aid routes (The Ghost, Ghost Roof, and Hierophant Tower), no new protection bolts were added, but three decaying anchors were updated. It is a very direct and natural line that avoids the bolt ladders on the Ghost.

On our first attempt, we sussed out the lower pitches and rapped from below pitch five, the Ghost Roof. We returned a week later and free climbed from the ground to the summit. The crux comes early on the third pitch in the form of a viciously thin face (5.12) and continues for another 80' up fun, bouldery, and spicy 5.10. However, the real crux may have been freeing the Ghost Roof (A4, Ellms-Middleton-Tuthill, 1978). Though probably only 5.10 or 5.11, the lead involved run-out climbing on loose, wet rock over a blindly placed Pecker. Having shared countless memorable days on New England's most adventurous crag, Ryan and I were proud to unlock Ghostrider (800', 5.12, mandatory 5.10 R) from Cannon's fractured flanks.

[*Editor's note: In August 2015, Michael Larson and Will Carey free climbed the Ghost (800', 5.12+), first climbed by Bragg-Peloquin-Ross in 1971, in its entirety, adding bolts to the second and third pitches to protect free climbing.*]

— JEFF PREVITE

ALASKA

WEST MAIDEN, SOUTHWEST FACE, AND OTHER CLIMBS

ON JULY 8, Brooks Range Aviation set us down at Circle Lake under a heavy gale, with 230 pounds of gear, 110 pounds of food, and 310 pounds of human. We cached kayaking gear and a week's worth of food at the lake and then began our trek to the Aiyagomahala Valley via Arrigetch-Aiyagomahala Pass. The weather during our trip was exceptionally mild by reported Arrigetch standards. We camped near the base of Battleship and moved camp once to disperse our impact. We saw no other people or megafauna in the valley, charismatic or otherwise.

On July 14 we warmed up by climbing Citadel via its west ridge (class 4) in terrific weather. We next set out to attempt a new route on the south face of Battleship. However, we found it littered with loose scree and retreated after one roped pitch in the middle of a hailstorm. It appears that clean rock routes up Battleship exist, but we did not take time to explore them. On July 20 we established a new route on West Maiden, following a long, right-angling crack system that splits the southwest face and is clearly visible from the valley below. From the base of the apron, seven pitches of terrific crack climbing delivered us to the ridge just below the top. Our route, Misty Maiden (800', III 5.8+), was excellent and the summit of West Maiden magnificent. We rappelled the east ridge.

Looking west from Citadel. (A) Wichmann Tower. (B) Unnamed. (C) Badile. (D) Disneyland. (E) Camel. (F) East Maiden. (G) West Maiden. (H) Melting Tower. *Johan Ugander*

On July 22 we climbed a variation to the unrepeated 1974 Krakauer-Bullard Route (IV 5.5 AI3) on Arthur Emmons. We ascended the glacier between Pyramid and Arthur Emmons, using only crampons. From the col between these peaks we scrambled up talus toward Arthur Emmons, briefly descending the south face to skirt a sizable gendarme (sometimes called "Holiday" on early maps). We reached the rock portion of the Krakauer-Bullard Route five hours after leaving camp and topped the ridge's final headwall at 11 p.m., after sitting out two rainstorms. The downpours forced us to retreat 100' short of the true summit. We retraced our steps for the long descent and reached camp roughly 26 hours after we set out.

The southwest face of West Maiden, in the Arrigetch Peaks, showing Misty Maiden (800', III 5.8+). *Johan Ugander*

On July 25 we climbed Camel via a prominent 200' dihedral on the southeast face, joining the east ridge. We found a summit register consisting of a vintage chocolate bar wrapper hidden inside a rusted tin can. The register noted Robley Williams Jr. and Michael Westmacott's 1964 first ascent of the east ridge, as well as a variation climbed that same day by Sally Westmacott and Chuck Loucks up the south face to join the east ridge. These routes were only briefly noted in *AAJ 1965*. This was a fine treat, as Robley is a longtime friend. Also on the summit, we found a newer rappel sling, suggesting at least one other ascent. We dubbed our route the Dromedary Dihedral (500', II 5.8).

As the weather remained unstable, we spent the afternoon of the following day exploring a collection of crags just a few hundred feet up the north slope of the Aiyagomahala Valley. These crags offer short but high-quality cracks, just enough for a playful afternoon. When the weather improved the next day, we attempted to climb the 1,000' north face of "Sundial," our name for the low but prominent fin east of Battleship. We found the lower climbing loose and grassy, and we bailed before reaching the attractive upper wall.

On the morning of our last day in the valley, we scrambled up the south ridge of Sundial, finding a cairn on top. Seth Adams later told us that he'd scrambled up the same fin in 2014, via the same route. On the afternoon of July 28, we said farewell to our valley home, returning in two days to our cache at Circle Lake. We portaged to the Alatna River and spent our final week in the wild floating roughly 137 miles down to the Athabascan village of Allakaket in an inflatable kayak, catching grayling and pike along the way. On August 6 we caught a commercial flight from Allakaket to Fairbanks after 30 days in the wilderness. 📖 📷

– STEPHANIE SAFDI & JOHAN UGANDER

SERAPH, EAST FACE, MANDARIN MOUNTY

CHRIS THOMAS AND I completed the first ascent of Seraph (8,540') on April 14. The peak is northeast of and adjacent to the Angel (9,265') and was named by David Roberts during the first climbing expedition to the Revelations (*AAJ 1968*). According to Clint Helander, Roberts and team attempted the peak but did not summit.

Chris and I flew to Anchorage on April 4. The forecast was poor and we heard rumors of other teams being pinned down for up to two weeks in terrible weather. We were finally able to fly into the range on the 10th. We did some recon on the way in and settled on the Revelation Glacier for our base camp due to poor landing options near our other targets. Once on the glacier we found dry climbing conditions, with many of the ice smears we'd seen in photos nonexistent. It then snowed until April 12, relegating us to the occasional scouting mission.

On the 13th we attempted Seraph, climbing one pitch and then descending in snow and spindrift. The skies cleared that afternoon, however, so we went back up and completed the climb the following day. Our route ascends an obvious weakness on the east face of Seraph. We approached by crossing an icefall and hanging glacier below the Angel. The crux came low on the route (WI5+ A2). This was followed by several pitches of sustained 5.10 rock with snow mushrooms. We climbed somewhere in the neighborhood of 15 full-length pitches (there was a lot of simul-climbing in the middle portion), with a significant amount of snow/ridge climbing on either side of these pitches. Overall the route went pretty quickly, due to having the approach dialed, and we were camp-to-camp around 17 hours.

We spent April 15 resting in base camp, eating bacon and reindeer sausage, and drinking a cocktail that Chris concocted of warm Tang and Canadian whiskey. We have decided to name

The Angel (left) and Seraph (right). Mandarin Mounty (2,300', 5.10 A2 WI5+) follows the main weakness visible on the center-left side of Seraph's east face. *Rick Vance*

[Left] Chris Thomas on the crux pitch of Mandarin Mounty on the east face of Seraph. *Rick Vance*
[Right] The east side of Jezebel showing the route Hoar of Babylon (1,200m, WI6 M6 A0). The route climbs to the east summit (9,450'); the main summit (9,650') is just west. *Peter Graham*

the route in honor of this stroke of genius: Mandarin Mounty (2,300', 5.10 A2 WI5+). The Mandarin Mounties were integral to our survival in the coming days.

On April 16 intense winds quickly destroyed our snow walls, cook tent, and nearly our sleeping tent. We sat through the worst of it holding up our sleep tent's internal poles, ready to be thrown out at any moment, jackets and boots on, with the sat phone in my pocket. Eventually things calmed down, but with our weather window gone we departed on the 19th, deciding to ski and walk the 20-plus miles down the glacier, north to Big River, and finally back to the R&R Hunting Lodge, where we waited for our pilot Rob Jones. 📷

– RICK VANCE

JEZEBEL (EAST SUMMIT), EAST FACE, HOAR OF BABYLON

BEN SILVESTRE AND I spent March 25–April 13 in the Revelation Mountains. Our initial objective was the central couloir on Pyramid Peak. However, landing on the melted-out Revelation Glacier was out of the question. We re-routed to try the unclimbed north face of Jezebel (9,650') from the Fish Creek Glacier. Once we'd arrived at base camp and checked out the north face, we focused our efforts on Jezebel's more easily accessed east face.

On March 29 we made our first attempt on the face but were forced down by a difficult step of steep, thin ice on the third pitch. After bailing we spent the remainder of the day reconnoitering the rest of the face. After some poor weather we set out again on April 2, planning for a two-day climb. We chose the same prominent gash/couloir in the center of the east face, but this time we came prepared with 14 ice screws instead of eight. The thin ice pitch was still difficult and proved to be the crux of the route (WI6). The fourth lead had another steep section of thin ice, and the fifth took on a steep, snow-filled chimney (M6 A0). Above these initial difficulties we gained the couloir feature and climbed a few hundred meters up a straightforward gully. We found a good bivy spot on the right side of the couloir that evening.

The next day a couple of easy pitches up a snow ramp led us to the base of an excellent, steep ice chimney we nicknamed the Ice Pencil. This was maybe the best pitch of the route, reminiscent of Exocet on Aguja Standhardt. A few more pitches up mixed ground led us to the top of a tower we jokingly named the Tower of Commitment. To continue from the tower we had to rappel, and we left one of our ropes to re-ascend on our way back. A straightforward snow gully led us to the unclimbed east summit (9,450') of Jezebel just before dark. We descended a few pitches that evening and chopped a sitting bivy.

In the morning we ascended our rope back up the Tower of Commitment and then downclimbed and rappelled the remainder of our route, arriving just before dark on the third day. We called our route Hoar of Babylon (1,200m, WI6 M6 A0). Though we hoped to climb another route, a large snowstorm kept us tent-bound. We thought the granite on the east face was of the highest quality and, if accessed via helicopter in the summer months, would offer countless rock objectives. 📷

— PETER GRAHAM, *U.K.*

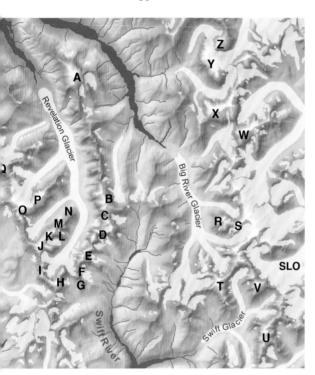

Map of the Revelation Mountains, showing the approximate locations of peaks. A. Hesperus B. Apocalypse C. Dike Peak D. Pyramid Peak E. Four Horsemen F. Century G. Sentry H. Golgotha I. Hydra J. The Angel K. Seraph L. Vanishing Pinnacle M. Sylph N. Cherub O. South Buttress P. Patmos Q. Babel Tower (8,365') R. Exodus S. Medusa T. Ice Pyramid U. Mausolus V. Pirate Peak W. Obelisk X. Jezebel Y. Titanic Z. Peak 9,076' SLO: Area explored by Slovenian expedition (*AAJ 2013*). Anna Riling

OBELISK, SOUTHWEST FACE, EMOTIONAL ATROPHY

THERE WOULD BE NO SLEEPING. The wind moaned a slow, agonizing cry among the summits and the lenticular clouds. My partner, Tad McCrea, was also awake, and we just lay in our base camp tent, listening in silent fear. Despite our snow walls, the wind seemed to blow right through us. As the ferocious storm roared in, our four-season tent flattened, with the fabric

[Left] The southwest face of the Obelisk (Peak 9,304'), showing the route Emotional Atrophy (1,000m, WI5 M6 A0). *Clint Helander* [Right] Clint Helander leads the crux pitch of the Obelisk during the first ascent. *John Giraldo*

stretching and poles creaking. "We're not going to make it through the night," I thought. Like a captain talking to his battered ship amid a tempest, I begged the tent to survive. "Hold strong," I pleaded. Tad and I weren't expecting a windstorm when we landed under halcyon skies a day earlier. Now, in the northern heart of the Revelation Mountains, we felt alone and adrift. "Should I put my boots on?" I wondered.

Early March's morning twilight eked through our sagging tent walls. Now the winds were only gusting to 80mph, but our snow walls were defeated and the glacier was scoured. We spent all day digging to excavate a snow cave under the flat glacier. We couldn't survive another night of wind without it. By that night, the brunt of the storm had passed, but ceaseless wind followed for another five days. We resigned ourselves mostly to the tent and the snow cave, barely escaping long enough to catch a glimpse of our distant prize, the unclimbed monolith of Peak 9,304'.

Tad was running out of time and the wind had yet to subside. We called for a weather update: It would calm the next day. We woke at 4 a.m., but the incessant wind persisted. We rolled over and tried to sleep. By 11 a.m. the winds had subsided and only a quiet aura remained. Our pilot had to pick Tad up in less than 24 hours, but we skied away from camp in rapid procession anyway. The south side of Peak 9,304', a mountain I had long called the "Obelisk," held its triangular form as we approached.

Now on the face, a snow-filled chimney held my picks but threatened to spit me out. After a rope length, a grainy crack offered a decent spot for an anchor. Above this, Tad led a long block of simul-climbing to the base of an ice-streaked headwall. The summit was still many thousands of feet above us. We retreated, and Tad reluctantly flew out the next day as John Giraldo arrived and took his place, fresh and unbeaten by the storms.

John and I quickly reached the previous high point on the Obelisk, and I searched for courage to confront the looming ice above. A bad ice screw penetrated snow and aerated ice, then a few feet higher I found a good, small cam placement. "Watch me, John," I muttered, "this is really hard and scary." My tool shuddered and reverberated as it penetrated nominal ice and struck the granite slab underneath. Another swing and a wide stem and I was still moving upward. I swung again, only this time the tool broke through the ice and into air. A two-inch crack! Hanging there, teetering on my pick, I excavated the crack and placed a dreamy cam. The crack extended for another 15 feet. Difficult climbing continued, and I searched for an anchor as the rope came tight. As John followed the crux, I studied my anchor of small cams and pins in bottoming cracks.

Above the crux, we continued in long blocks of simul-climbing. The absence of the wind seemed so strange, and the sun burned our faces. We approached the summit in the afternoon (March 22), high above most of the surrounding peaks. On top, I thought back to the stress of the previous week, and I pushed the pain of a failing relationship from my mind. I thought silently of two words: Emotional Atrophy (1,000m, WI5 M6 A0). Now on the summit, I found a brief moment of long-desired tranquility. 📷

– CLINT HELANDER

UYURAQ, NORTH RIDGE, AND EXPLORATION

THIS EXPEDITION HAD its beginnings in 2013, when I completed a trip in the Tordrillo Mountains. During an initial recon flight and subsequent ground travel in this area, I became increasingly aware of its rock climbing potential as we walked past beautiful orange granite.

It wasn't until June 2015 that I got the chance to do another recon flight; this time I had an eagle eye for the big rock walls. Flying low and slow, we circled and soared around numerous pinnacles, close enough to the rock to feel like we were climbing. In doing so, we scoped an incredible amount of terrain; however, rapid snowmelt alongside crevasse-riddled landing zones and approaches discouraged us. We continued our flight, looking for a less glaciated area. Our search brought us into the neighboring Hidden Mountains, and what we found was absolutely stunning: a set of gorgeous granite pyramids that upon further investigation proved to be unnamed, unclimbed, and little explored.

The Hidden Mountains are a small group of peaks bounded by the Tordrillo Mountains to the east, the Revelation Mountains to the west, and the Neacola Mountains to the south. They have only seen a handful of expeditions, mostly unsuccessful, and it was very apparent why: The rugged and remote nature of these peaks seems to repel any sort of serious effort. Fred Beckey once lined up a trip here that cost a fortune in flying logistics alone. [*Editor's note: In 2005, Beckey, Ray Borbon, and Aaron Clifford attempted Igitna Peak, about three miles north of Uyuraq.*] This year, with summer temperatures a month advanced, a ski plane–accessed, base camp–style expedition was out of the question. We had to find somewhere free of snow. These mystery peaks were perfect for the occasion.

Our pilot, Doug Brewer, and I took off in a Super Cub, using that as a recon/shuttle

The two granite pyramids of the Talliktok cirque, with Uyuraq on the left and Talliktok on the right. The team made the first ascent of Uyuraq by its north ridge (left skyline) and made multiple, unsuccessful attempts on the prominent west face of Talliktok. *Zach Clanton*

aircraft, while my partners, James Gustafson and Tim Plotke, followed behind in a Beaver floatplane flown by Tom Thibodeau. On Ch'akajabena Lake, we struggled to find an LZ appropriate for both the floatplane and Super Cub, so Doug and I continued toward our objective. After extensive searching and multiple bear sightings, the closest we could land was 12 miles from our destination, on the muddy west bank of Ch'akajabena Lake. The terrain we had to travel looked like serious bush-bashing along the Another River, but we were very committed at this point. Doug shuttled in James, Tim, and the rest of our gear, and then it took us five days to travel those 12 miles. Incessant mosquitoes and alders blocked our path, and a machete was required to cut our way through the denser areas. Some bears were indifferent to our passing, but others showed signs of curiosity and aggressiveness. On one occasion our only option was to spray buckshot from our 12-gauge to deter them.

Eventually, we made it into the rocky cirque that we had begun calling Talliktok (Alaskan native word for "Hidden"). The cirque is located directly east of Merrill Pass. In the weeks that followed, we made the first ascent of Uyuraq (6,625', Alaskan native word for "Brother"), via its north ridge (Silver Linings, 4 pitches, 5.7). We also made multiple attempts at a direct line up the west face of Talliktok (6,850'), climbing corner systems up to 5.10, which ended in dangerously loose rock and very questionable belays. After 24 days, retracing our path out, we arrived back in civilization for glorious burgers and beers after the wildest adventure of our lives. The peak we've called Talliktok is still out there, lurking in the clouds of the Hidden Mountains, awaiting its first ascent. Who will be up for it? 📷 🔍 📄

– ZACH CLANTON

NO COUNTRY FOR OLD MEN

BY TIM BLAKEMORE

Alaska is a land of superlatives. It's big, wild, and hairy—and, as the old joke goes, so are the girls of Talkeetna. I'd heard so much about Alaska that I knew sooner or later I'd end up there. And I did, after Twid Turner and I hatched a plan to climb something in the Kichatna Mountains. [*Editor's note: Mike "Twid" Turner has done more new routes in the Kichatna Mountains in the 2000s than any other individual. See past AAJs for more stories.*]

We arrived in Talkeetna in early May. Paul Roderick met us a day later. He was enthused by our "little" expedition and told us it was to be "just like the good old days." We shoved all our kit into a single-engine Cessna and set forth. The flight was a vomit-inducing, bumpy affair, and at one point my foot hit the roof—all before descending in a violent spiral toward the Tatina Glacier.

On the ground we soaked up the atmosphere of this wild place. The first day or two were spent battening down the hatches, scoping the immediate area with binoculars, and going for a recce to Monolith Pass. After climbing over the pass to Monolith Glacier, we discovered that our primary objective simply hadn't formed this year. However, we glanced alternative possibilities on North Triple Peak.

Wanting to do a route and actually getting up out of bed each day are two very different

North Triple Peak:. The northwest couloir is the prominent, steep gully on the right, and the new route No Country for Old Men (800m, 17 pitches, ED AI6) climbs the ice smear and gully indicated by the arrow. *Tim Blakemore*

things. With unsettled wind and snow, days turned into a week as we ate like champions in the tent. Finally, we got a weather break and ferried a load of kit up to Monolith Pass. Back at camp, the weather was awful and it looked like we might just have an expensive camping trip. Thankfully, the next dawn was clear and we set off for our gear cache on May 18.

Not expecting a bivouac, we packed pretty light and headed up the northwest couloir (Ellsworth-Sennauser, *AAJ 1979*) to reach weeping ice smears on the wall above and left. The couloir proved technically straightforward, but annoyingly insecure and slow (we roped up for its first six pitches). From below, much of our route seemed there, though eventually we would find a few ominous steep and blank bits, and the climbing would become vague near the top.

Twid set off into the maelstrom on what seemed to be pretty good, thin ice. These initial pitches were around AI4+/5—fun and technical, without being too desperate. As we approached the obvious crux, though, it looked trickier: An overlap in the rock was barely iced and had vertical ice leading up to it. I took the lead here. The vertical section was classic AI5+, with good ice and protection. At the overlap I encountered rotten ice and spent an age trying to fiddle in protection. Eventually, I placed a screw in an ice patch,

Twid Turner pulls onto the initial ice smear of No Country for Old Men (800m, 17 pitches, ED AI6) after climbing six pitches up the northwest couloir. *Tim Blakemore*

breathed deeply, shouted "watch me," and pulled through to the end of the 70m pitch (AI6).

The rest of the climbing was a blur. We climbed pitch after pitch of good ice up a gully-like feature to the final snow gullies. The temptation to finish just below the top was strong, as the cornices resembled grotesque meringues and had the consistency of sugar. However, after spotting a crevasse-like crack, I entered it and then back-and-footed upward. With a bit of heavy breathing and levitation, I found myself with no more up. My first Alaskan summit, by a new route. I buried my ice axe and gave Twid a body belay to the top.

On the summit we used our satellite phone to call for a pickup and set a bollard to begin our descent. All that was left was a familiar routine of abseils, threads, and checking anchors. I can't remember exactly the timing of the descent, but we were probably quite tired by the time we reached Monolith Pass again on May 19. Our rack was certainly lighter.

SUMMARY: *New route on the northwest face of North Triple Peak: No Country for Old Men (800m, 17 pitches, ED AI6), by Tim Blakemore and Twid Turner (U.K.), Kichatna Mountains, May 18-19, 2015.* 📷

MT. SILVERTHRONE TO MT. BROOKS TRAVERSE

FROM JULY 6 TO JULY 12, Gabe Messercola and I completed the first known traverse from Mt. Silverthrone to Mt. Brooks, including the three Pyramid peaks (a.k.a. Tripyramid). We climbed the chain of peaks from south to north, and the traverse included the first ascent of East Pyramid's southwest ridge (from the col between Central Pyramid and East Pyramid). [*Editor's note: This group of peaks is approximately 10 miles northeast of Denali. Though individual sections of the ridgeline had been completed before, as well as attempts of the traverse, a complete traverse is not known to have been done before 2015. Wichelns and Messercola accessed the peaks by the Muldrow and Brooks glaciers, but the peaks can be accessed via the Ruth Glacier.*]

– RYAN WICHELNS, *WITH ADDITIONAL INFORMATION FROM* MARK WESTMAN

DENALI DIAMOND, ALL-FEMALE ASCENT

FROM JUNE 15–19, Chantel Astorga and Jewell Lund completed the Denali Diamond (7,800', WI5+ 5.9 A3 or M6 A1/ M7) on the southwest face of Denali. This was the seventh reported ascent of the route and the first time it had been climbed by an all-female team. Mark Westman, Denali National Park mountaineering ranger, noted that, "Without question, Jewell and Chantel's ascent is, by far, the most significant done by an all-female team in the Alaska Range."

For information on other significant repeats, new routes or variations, and climbing statistics in Denali National Park during the 2015 season, see the "2015 Annual Mountaineering Summary" at *http://www.nps.gov/dena/planyourvisit/ams2015.htm*.

– ERIK RIEGER

PEAK 11,300', WEST FACE; REALITY PEAK, WEST FACE

WILLIS BROWN, SAM HENNESSEY, AND I climbed two sustained ice and mixed routes in the West Fork of the Ruth Glacier between May 11 and 21.

From May 13–14 we climbed the longest line available on the west face of Peak 11,300', beginning with a three-pitch "sit start" (M4, M5, M4). Above this, a few hundred feet of snow brought us to three pitches of ice-filled gullies (85°). Another long stretch of steep snow put us below the upper headwall. We climbed this section in three rope lengths, with ice to 90°. On the final 400' to the summit ridge, the angle eased (70°). We climbed three rope lengths through extensive cornices on the ridge and turned around below the summit, around 11,100'. We rappelled through the night with much spindrift (about 20 double-rope rappels). It should be noted that we found an oval carabiner on a fixed nut at two-thirds height.

[*Previously unreported, Thomas Kimbrell and Jeep Gaskin climbed the above-mentioned route in April 1983 and called it Right Couloir. Kimbrell notes that John Bauman and Jim Howe climbed a route just right of theirs soon afterward, which is noted in AAJ 1984, and that both teams had harrowing experiences on their respective routes.*]

After a few days of rest, we skied up the pocket glacier that separates Peak 13,100' ("Reality Peak") from Denali's Isis Face. We found a great-looking line on the west face of Reality Peak and returned to camp to pack. Starting on May 18, we crossed the bergschrund around 8,900' and then climbed 500' of perfect névé. This brought us to the first ice pitch. From

Skiy DeTray heads into one of the A4 cruxes on the headwall portion of Illusions of the Raven, east face of the Mooses Tooth. *Alik Berg*

here we climbed steep, continuous ice for ten rope lengths, two of which had vertical ice. Once out of these steeper gullies, the angle eased slightly for the final 600', until we joined the heavily corniced Reality Ridge (ca 12,000'). Steep snow tunneling and ice traversing got us to the same comfortable bivy I had used during the first ascent of Reality Face (*AAJ 2013*). At 10 p.m. we all crammed into our two-man tent for some rest.

The next day had poor weather, but we hung tight, and the following morning things cleared up. Steep snow and some funky ice along the ridge took about six hours. We topped out Peak 13,100', reversed the ridge, brewed up in our tent, and then started the descent of the face. It was possible to rappel most of the route, with the exception of the ridge above and below our bivy (about 18 double-rope rappels from V-threads and some downclimbing). This is an exceptional route: Devil's Advocate (4,200', AI5 M4). 📷 🔍

– SETH TIMPANO

MOOSES TOOTH, EAST FACE, ILLUSIONS OF THE RAVEN

FROM MAY 2–7, ALIK BERG (Canada) and I established a new route on the east face of the Mooses Tooth (10,335'). Our route starts on the ramps of Arctic Rage (Gilmore-Mahoney, *AAJ 2005*) and then takes a steep and direct line up the massive upper headwall. At the start of the headwall, our line breaks right from Bird of Prey (Arnold-Lama, *AAJ 2014*), climbing terrain approximately 500' to the right before joining that route again on the upper snow slopes.

Alik and I flew in to the Buckskin Glacier on April 23. The east face appeared ominous and intimidating, a formidable feature that caused my stomach to do somersaults. After four days at camp we packed up five days of food and fuel.

In 12 hours we were 2,000' up the lower slopes of Arctic Rage—a fabulous mix of committing snow, rock, and ice. Our first bivy was at Beak Camp, named for its structural integrity, with our tent secured by a single beak! The next morning we awoke to a grim-looking low-pressure system. Six inches of wet snow fell overnight. We pulled the plug and rappelled.

On May 2 at 3:30 a.m. I woke to the horrible sound of my watch alarm. A three-mile flat ski brought us to the lower snow slopes at 6:30 a.m., and we were back in Beak Camp by 8 p.m. The next day I set out on new ground, branching left from Bird of Prey. The first pitch was cerebral and challenging A3 climbing. This took us to within a pitch of Arnold and Lama's bivouac site on Bird of Prey, halfway up the face at the base of the headwall—a spot precariously perched atop a giant snow mushroom. Before making camp, Alik was excited to make more progress. After fixing two pitches (now branching right of Bird of Prey) we returned to the bivy spot, which was luxurious and safe feeling.

We awoke at 3:30 a.m. and squeezed the lactic acid from our bodies by drinking instant coffee and relishing a dehydrated breakfast. The 300–400m headwall loomed above, often overhanging. We'd hoped the climbing would be mostly free drytooling, but the rock quality forced us to aid climb. The climbing hovered right around A3/A4 for the entire headwall, with the rock reminiscent of shark's teeth. With patience the puzzle was revealed. At 1 a.m., 19 hours after starting from the mushroom bivy, we were perched at a hanging belay, where I lobbied for a quick bivy in the lightweight bat hammocks we'd brought along. The two-hour "bat nap" left us fairly rested, and we topped out the headwall 33 hours after leaving the mushroom bivy. Amazingly, the crack system connected and we didn't drill a single hole for the entire route.

It was now 4 p.m. on May 5 and snowing lightly. From atop the headwall, engaging ice and snow led us to the summit by 4 a.m. Rappelling and downclimbing from the summit, we rested our battered, sleep-deprived bodies atop the headwall for a few hours. We then made 26 rappels over the next 27 hours. We were hallucinating something fierce. *What is the limit?* I wondered. By the time we made it back to base camp we'd been on the move for 80 hours. As casual conversations transpired the following day, we realized we were both hallucinating ravens throughout our descent—Illusions of the Raven (1,500m, 5.9 A4 WI4 R [*approximately 400m new terrain*]). 📄 📷

– SKIY DETRAY

MT. DICKEY, NORTHEAST FACE, BLUE COLLAR BEATDOWN

FROM MARCH 20–22, Chad Diesinger, Jason Stuckey, and I made the first ascent of Blue Collar Beatdown (V WI4 M4 65°) on the northeast face (right shoulder) of Mt. Dickey. The route is located to the left of the Byrch-McNeill ice flow (*AAJ 2004*).

On March 19, Jason, Chad, and I departed Talkeetna. Paul Roderick "flew slow" on our way in so we could scope objectives, and we decided on the northeast face of Dickey. After establishing camp, we skied over to glass the face in not exactly confidence-inspiring conditions. The following morning we departed camp at 4:45 a.m. and made the short ski to Dickey. We cached the skis and reached the face proper around 7 a.m. To start we climbed two full pitches of steep sn'ice with solid climbing but little protection. This put us on the prominent snow ramp that slashes up and right across the face. We immediately started leading in blocks, simul-climbing when the terrain allowed for it. We encountered bottomless sugar snow, mixed climbing, and everything in between. I led the final block, starting at dusk and ending past dark.

Our hope had been to exit the face before sunset and descend in the darkness, or worst case sit it out on the summit plateau until first light. However, when we encountered complex

Jason Stuckey starts up the initial sn'ice climbing on Blue Collar Beatdown, on the lower northeast face of Mt. Dickey. *John Frieh*

route-finding up the shoulder, well below the summit, we resigned ourselves to digging a snow cave. Without bivy gear, we kept the stove lit and none of us slept for fear of losing fingers or toes. At first light, after four hours of sitting and suffering, we continued upward by two dead-end routes and finally reached the summit around 5 p.m. We descended to 747 Pass, reaching that around 8 p.m. Here we consumed coffee, Perpetuem, and what little we had left to eat before our final eight-hour trudge to the tent. All told we were awake for about 48 hours. 🖹 📷

– JOHN FRIEH

PEAK 7,400', SOUTHWEST FACE; PEAK 5,850', SOUTHWEST FACE

IN MAY, CARTER STRITCH AND I climbed a pair of possible new routes in the Ruth Gorge. On May 1 we climbed the southwest face of Peak 7,400' (a.k.a. Mt. Hemo) by a couloir that splits the right side of this face. Although the whole feature is certainly climbable, we chose a less committing rock variation due to lack of ice. Pastime Paradise (3,000', III 5.8 50°) is named after fond memories shared with Eitan Green, who climbed a new route on this peak before his death (*AAJ 2014*). [*Editor's note: Cramer and Stritch's initial approach up a broad couloir to gain Pastime Paradise is shared with the south ridge route (AAJ 2007).*]

On May 11 we aimed for a weakness on an unnamed peak (5,850') immediately south of Hut Tower. Understandably, this junky-looking pile had been ignored in favor of the impressive walls surrounding it. However, the path we chose surprised us with the most engaging climbing of our entire trip. Our route followed the couloir dividing the southwest face. At half height we took the right-hand fork and followed this as it zigzagged to the summit ridge and the western summit. Triple Wannabe Cooloirs (1,800', 5.7 WI4) references our social aspirations and a climb of similar character, the Triple Couloirs on Washington's Dragontail Peak. 📷 🖹

– JACK CRAMER

Jack Cramer leading on the southwest face of Peak 7,400' (see previous page). *Carter Stritch*

TROLLS TRAVERSE

AT THE END OF JUNE, Pedro Binfa, Pachi Ibarra, and Drew Seitz made the first reported traverse of the Trolls, located off the Pika Glacier in the Little Switzerland area. They generally climbed from south to north, mostly on the ridgeline, beginning on South Troll and finishing atop a rocky summit just north of North Troll. 📷 ▤

— ERIK RIEGER

TALKEETNA MOUNTAINS

MINT PEAKS TRAVERSE

WHILE THE ROCK QUALITY OF SOUTH-CENTRAL ALASKA leaves much to be desired, there are other redeeming factors: for instance, the endless and striking granite ridgelines of the Talkeetna Mountains. The Mint Valley is home to some of the taller and more rugged peaks in the area. To me, a continuous traverse of the Mint Valley peaks felt like an obvious objective. The line stands out both from the valley floor and on a map.

A perfect forecast appeared over the July 4 weekend, and when I proposed the idea to Clint Helander he was quite excited. Clint and I departed the Gold Cord trailhead at approximately 4 a.m. on July 3. We packed a light rope and rack, a 100' rappel cord, and food and fuel for three days. We decided to leave crampons and ice tools in Anchorage. The weight of our packs was quite reasonable for the seven-mile approach, and we biked the initial four miles.

To begin the traverse, we picked an obvious ramp and chimney line up the southeastern flank of Triplemint Spire. The rest of the day passed quickly—after Triplemint, we climbed up and over Peppermint Peak, Doublemint Peak, Sentry Spire, and Troublemint Spire. We roped up for a few pitches and found difficulties to 5.8. We rappelled often but mainly kept the rope in the pack. After descending the north side of Troublemint, we dug out a snow ledge. It was about midnight, and the sun was just disappearing behind the ridgeline we hoped to hit on day three.

We awoke early on July 4, descended a snow and ice gully onto the Mint Glacier, and then made our way up the southern aspect of Spearmint Spire. We descended straight back to the Mint Glacier and then made our way to Montana Peak, the tallest and most seldom-summited peak of the group. We ascended a broad scree gully on the southern ramparts, but gendarmes blocked the summit ridgeline, so we traversed to the west face and reached the summit by 5.7 climbing. We topped out in zero visibility and then rappelled the west face to gain a series of hanging glaciers below the western aspect of the ridgeline between Montana Peak and Three Bell Spires. Clint and I roped up to navigate monster crevasses in dense fog and rain. It was about midnight by this time, and we were soaked to the bone but still thoroughly enjoying ourselves. Once gaining the ridgeline we bivied in a snow cave covered by a homemade nylon tarp.

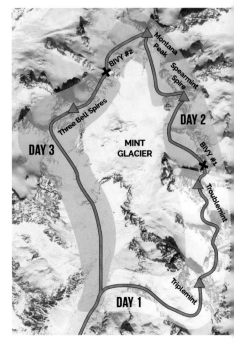

Luckily, the weather cleared early on the morning of July 5. We rappelled directly from the bivy site to another hanging glacier. As our third day progressed we covered more horizontal than vertical terrain, making short rappels and pitching out steep steps on the sharp ridgeline. This part of ridge was characterized by ice and snow to the west and steep granite walls and gullies to the east. We were certainly pushing the limits of possibility for approach shoes as we negotiated steep and icy traverses. Eventually we scrambled to the top of Three Bell Spire, signed the summit register, crossed another pocket glacier, and descended near the area of Back Door Gap. Back in the valley, we sauntered toward Mint Hut and back toward the bicycles—our Mint Peak Traverse covered about 9.5 miles, 8,100' of climbing, and difficulties to 5.8.

– AARON THRASHER

WRANGELL MOUNTAINS

PEAK 11,191', PEAK 8,615'

IN JUNE, Scott Peters and Kristin Arnold of St. Elias Alpine Guides, Ben Iwrey, and I climbed two peaks, one of which might have been a first ascent, in the Wrangell Mountains near Mt. Blackburn. The first climb required two back-to-back attempts due to whiteout conditions. This was Peak 11,191', located at 61°48'31"N, 143°31'55"W, with a summit cornice resembling a dorsal fin. [*Editor's note: Peak 11,191' is believed to have been climbed before 2014 by a NOLS group. The peak is known as Turton Peak on Bivouac.com.*] The second climb was of Peak 8,615' (61°50'45"N, 143°31'46"W), which we called Finacle Pinnacle. It involved glacial ice, steep snow, rock and mixed climbing, a gendarmed ridgeline, and a corniced summit cone. Both routes are approximately Alaska Grade II+.

– ED MCCORD

BAD TO THE BONE

BY WILL SIM

On April 18, Jon Griffith and I were dropped by helicopter on the upper Gillam Glacier in the Hayes Range. This beautifully harsh set of mountains is less conducive to climbing than the granite ranges farther west—ultimately that is their charm.

Upon landing we were immediately met by foul weather, which over the next 24 hours escalated to gale-force winds. All of our tent poles snapped and our base camp was destroyed. We managed to escape into a half-dug snow hole to sit out the next two days of extremely harsh weather. Once the weather passed, we excavated our gear, food, and destroyed tent from under newly drifted snow. By day four we finally had base camp in good shape, with a spacious snow hole to live in. It was also the first day we saw Mt. Deborah (12,339').

We hoped to climb a new route up one of the huge faces on Deborah's north side. A diamond-shaped face on the northwest aspect had caught our attention while scouring the mountain with Google Earth. After a quick recce of the face on skis, we were pleased to discover this face seemed relatively safe from objective hazards and had an obvious line from the 'schrund to the northwest ridge (Cady-Nash-Nolting-Watts, *AAJ 1977*). [*Editor's note: Mt. Deborah has seen various new routes on its west and north aspects since the 1970s but never an ascent by this steep northwest face.*]

We started climbing on the sixth or seventh day after arriving in base camp. Two avalanches, likely caused by cross loading from the storm, had us very nearly turning around at the base. However, we persevered and climbed 1,000m or more on steep and sometimes nearly vertical névé, snow slopes, and some thin ice smears through rotten rock to a point on the upper northwest ridge. We were forced to make a long traverse about two-thirds of the way up

[Previous page] **Will Sim approaching the daunting northwest face of Mt. Deborah. He and Jon Griffith climbed a direct line to about two-thirds height, where avalanches forced a rightward traverse to gain the northwest ridge, just below the prominent black step. They followed the ridge to the summit.** *Jon Griffith* [Above] **The team's destroyed base camp and the entrance to their hastily dug snow cave.** *Jon Griffith*

Will Sim climbs below the corniced northwest ridge of Mt. Deborah. *Jon Griffith*

the face due to large avalanches releasing down our intended exit (a few hundred meters higher than our actual exit); we were very lucky to have a traverse option at that point. This took us about 16–18 hours.

A very windy night on the ridge, inside our bivy tent, was followed by a beautiful dawn and another 1,000m of gain to the summit of Deborah. From our bivy, this involved several hundred meters of easy ground, then traversing for several cold and thought-provoking hours along a knife-edge ridge reminiscent of a reptilian spine. The summit itself is a house-size cornice. "Let's call this the summit," I said to Jon, as I reached his belay a safe distance from Deborah's dorsal-like crest. [*Editor's note: At least one climber has broken the summit cornice while standing on it. See AAJ 2000.*]

From the summit, we descended the south face. Twelve inventive raps off threads and bollards and some downclimbing deposited us on the Yanert Glacier. We descended this glacier for approximately 1km before ascending the south side of the northwest ridge to reach our bivy from the previous night. Here we spent another night before traversing down the lower northwest ridge for approximately 1.5km the next day. Upon reaching a notch in the ridge we had previously identified from base camp, we made about 15 abseils under threatening cornices to the upper Gillam Glacier and our camp. The fuzzy high of whiskey overtook our beaten bodies as George Thorogood's "Bad to the Bone" found its way out of our speakers. It seemed to fit.

SUMMARY: *New route up Mt. Deborah's northwest face to northwest ridge: Bad to the Bone (ca 2,000m of climbing to summit), by Jon Griffith and Will Sim (U.K.), Hayes Range, April 2015.* 🖸

KOOSHDAKHAA SPIRE, NORTH FACE; POINT 2,320M, SOUTHWEST FACE

DURING A SPELL OF EXCELLENT WEATHER from May 18 to May 31, Max Fisher and I returned to the Upper Chilkat area of the Coast Mountains, where we'd climbed a year prior (*AAJ 2015*). The area is located about seven miles southwest of Mt. Foster and spans the border of southeast Alaska and northern British Columbia. On this trip, we succeeded on our previously attempted line up the granite face of what we call Kooshdakhaa Spire, which rises some 2,000' above a hanging tributary of the Chilkat Glacier.

A day after stepping out of Drake Olson's ski plane, we quickly ascended to our previous high point on the north face of the spire. There, we turned an offwidth roof to gain steeper crack systems above. From here, we made our way up sustained 5.10 and 5.11- climbing with three sections of aid to reach the summit. This included a stop to shiver out the night on a diving board ledge, a tactic that was certainly lighter, but not at all faster, than if we'd opted to bring headlamps. After 33 hours on the wall (bergschrund to summit), we honored our friend Cory Hall on the summit by spreading some of his ashes. We descended easier terrain to the south and east, arriving in camp 37 hours after leaving. We called the route Otter Water Boogie Man

(2,000', V 5.11- A1)—a rough translation of the Kooshdakhaa legend of a Tlingit and Tsimshian mythological creature.

After a few days chilling in camp under perfect skies we loaded our backpacks and packraft-sleds and trudged into northern British Columbia in search of another climbing objective. We found it: a high point of a ridgeline that reaches approximately 2,320m. [*Previously unreported, this spire was likely first climbed in 2002 by Brian Delay and William Wacker, who suggested the name Canadian Import. It is located across from Castle Greyskull/ Kooshdakhaa E4 (AAJ 2004)*]. Our new route, Lichening Bolt Buttress (400m, IV 5.11-), ascends aprons and crack systems on the southwest aspect, with mostly moderate climbing and frequent more challenging cruxes.

After this climb, we hauled our gear over another pass to reach the headwaters

Kooshdakhaa Spire, showing the three routes completed by Bonnett and Fisher in 2014 and 2015. From left to right: North Couloir (600m, AI3 M3); Otter Water Boogie Man (2,000' V 5.11- A1); South Couloir (350m, AI3 M3 [*not to summit*]). Max Fisher

The Devils Paw massif from the west. Black Roses (1,000m, 6c A1 M4) climbs the prominent northwest ridge on the north summit (left skyline of left-most tower). The central couloir was climbed to the saddle in 2011 and then skied. The prominent right-hand couloir was climbed en route to the south summit (right-most tower) in 1976; it has also been skied. *Oli Lyon*

of the Nourse River, making to our knowledge its first complete descent. On river, we paddled sections of continuous class II to III+ whitewater over four days, portaging a series of beautiful waterfalls and two canyons that looked to offer excellent, harder whitewater.

After our trip, we learned that, since 2002, Alaskan climber William Wacker and partners including Brian Delay, Eric Forester, Kevin Forester, and Dave Sundas have made numerous trips into the Upper Chilkat and climbed approximately ten prominent summits and towers in the area, including the 7,550' main, flat-topped summit adjacent to (climber's left of) what we have called Kooshdakhaa Spire. (They called this main summit Mt. Agony.) Additionally, they have exited the area by packrafting the Chilkat River or Homan River. Their ascents had been previously unreported. 📷

— ERIK BONNETT

DEVILS PAW, NORTHWEST RIDGE OF NORTH SUMMIT, BLACK ROSES

DURING MAY 18 AND 19, Simon Gietl and I completed a new route on the north summit of Devils Paw (2,616m). Our ascent took 19 hours, including a short bivouac below the summit, and the downclimb took another five hours. We named our route Black Roses (1,000m, 6c A1 M4) after the rose-like black lichen covering much of the rock. The climb was a real "museum day," as I call the very special days that I put into the museum of my life memories.

[*Editor's note: Devils Paw (a.k.a. Boundary Peak 93) is a four-summited mountain in the Boundary Ranges, part of the Juneau Icefield, on the border of Alaska and Canada. The massif has walls up to 900m tall. The main summit, immediately south of the north summit climbed by Schäli and Gietl, was first climbed by its northeast side (Griscom-Michael-Putnam, AAJ 1950). The southernmost summit was climbed by its south couloir (Beckey-McCarty-Tackle-Zaspel, AAJ 1977). It's likely the main summit has not seen a second ascent, though a strong attempt was made up an icefall on its northeast aspect (AAJ 1984). Additionally, some of the prominent, snowy couloirs have been climbed and/or skied (AAJ 2012).*] 📷 📄

— ROGER SCHÄLI, *SWITZERLAND*

SNOW TOWER

BY WILLIAM WACKER

Snow Tower tops out at an elevation of 6,572' and has unusual prominence for its height: The peak ranks 61st among all peaks in the United States and 34th in the state of Alaska. Amazing, also, is that it was an unclimbed summit that was named on the USGS map. More significantly, for Mike Miller and myself, was that Snow Tower appeared to be another interesting, unexplored mountain in the vast wilderness of Southeast Alaska.

On the afternoon of June 7, Mike and I flew 40 miles southeast of Juneau with floatplane pilot Gary Thompson. We landed at Crescent Lake (174') and began a steep, forested ascent southward through cliffs and tangled forests toward the peak. As with many climbs in this region, the bushwhacking sections can make or break an attempt. After negotiating a few no-fall zones, we successfully exited the trees and pitched a high camp (ca 2,000'). Armies of mosquitoes attacked as we set up camp. From here, we were still too low on the mountain's shoulder to see anything but a rocky horizon swallowed in ice. It was unsettling not to see the summit.

We left camp at 4:30 a.m. and climbed to a point where we could see the north face for the first time. Warm temps had melted out the face, revealing large bergschrunds and exfoliating rock buttresses. We decided to gamble and traverse around the base of the tower toward the eastern aspect. To our relief we found a steep 1,500' snow slope that connected to the peak's east ridge. After four pitches of challenging, loose ridge climbing, through two deep notches, we topped out around 4 p.m. on June 8.

On the descent we spent another night at our high camp and descended the forest section the following day. The descent proved to be more involved than the ascent. As we neared Crescent Lake, we wandered off our approach route and got sucked into a more direct descent. Several sizable rock bluffs blocked the final quarter-mile exit to our resupply at the corner of the lake. To avoid climbing above and around the massive cliffs, we opted to leave our gear, swim the edge of the lake, and return with our pack rafts, which we had brought for a planned paddle out the Whiting River.

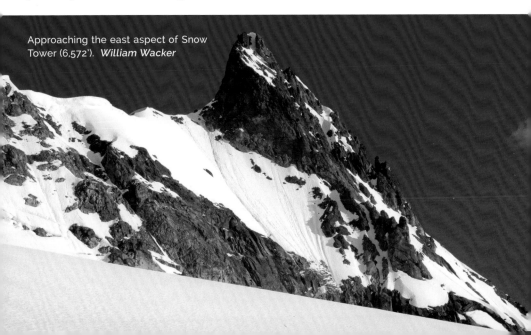

Approaching the east aspect of Snow Tower (6,572'). *William Wacker*

Mike Miller wonders what's next on the upper east ridge of Snow Tower, a previously unclimbed peak in Southeast Alaska. *William Wacker*

Following a cold and strenuous swim to base camp, Mike and I arrived barefooted and soaked at a camp devoid of our exit supplies. The intoxication of our successful climb of Snow Tower gave way to the realization that our possessions had been ravaged and dragged into a nearby swamp by an unidentified animal. Exhausted and demoralized, we waded through shallow water full of floating sticks and pine needles to find a flotsam of perforated supplies. After two nights out and 28 hours of climbing we took a pragmatic inventory of our items in the swamp, both aware that the animal might still be nearby. A chewed can of pepper spray was found floating in the debris. Soon our eyes began to burn.

One packraft was intact and we still had our SAT phone. Our bear canisters, filled with extra food, also survived a massive chewing. However, our plan to float to the ocean was out of the question, as Mike's packraft was ripped beyond field repair. I retrieved our climbing gear along the lake's edge and we phoned Gary for a pickup. As we waited an afternoon storm moved in. The lake became agitated and darkened into a deep black-green. The wind began to build and whitecaps sent waves of spray into the forest edge. Through a small opening in our tent, it was possible to see the intermittent flashes of lightning arcing above a dense forest and traversing the hanging fields of snow and blue ice, until, finally, a delayed boom echoed from the distant rock towers of the Stikine.

Sometimes it feels as if anything might happen. Lightning might strike you; that bear might come back; your pilot might not get you in time. When you finally relax during a brief moment of vulnerability, the magnitude of what you have done finally sets in. Avalanche, rockfall, and any number of disasters could have found you. Yet, still, you are here. Sometimes adventure shows us what a gift it is to be alive.

SUMMARY: *First ascent of Snow Tower (6,572') by its east face and east ridge, by Mike Miller and William Wacker, Coast Mountains, June 2015.* 📷

LUCIFER, NORTH FACE, AGUA SIN GAS

In the *AAJ 1947*, Fred Beckey wrote, "Although they do not rise so high as the great mountains farther to the N.W., these peaks of the Alaska-Canada Boundary are magnificent in their alpine grandeur and challenging in their technical difficulties. Here, indeed, is one of Alaska's neglected mountain regions, not without mystery."

In 2014, while approaching the West Witches' Tit (*AAJ 2015*), I spotted a very attractive north-facing wall to the south-southwest, on the other side of what local climbers call "The Cauldron" or "Witches' Cauldron." I later found out the point was called Lucifer (Point 7,872'), and it was first climbed by Peter Rowat and Rupert Roschnik, by its east side, in 1976. From the upper bergschrund, Lucifer's north face is ca 1,800–1,900'.

With a weather window shaping up in May, Doug Shepherd was available for a quick trip. We flew into the range by helicopter late on May 14. After the helicopter left, I discovered I'd left my stove at home. I think most trips would have ended right there, but with the warm temps and high pressure we found a few shallow glacial pools where we could collect water. Given the heat wave, we opted for a 2 a.m. departure from camp.

Our goal was a direct line up an ice runnel on the central, diamond-shaped face. But given the above-freezing temps and sloppy snow conditions, we opted for a safer, less direct line that first ascends the steep glacier/icefall below Lucifer, then up a gully climber's left of the steep face. We managed most of the climb before sunrise, encountering some vertical snow and sn'ice in places, but finding the majority of the terrain to be moderate. Atop the gully we joined the east ridge to the summit. From camp, the climb took us 12 hours.

From the summit we reversed our route, descending around 4,000' back to camp. We managed to snag a pickup the same day and were back in Petersburg late on May 15, making for a sub-24-hour Petersburg-to-Petersburg trip. Given my stove oversight, we named the route Agua Sin Gas (III WI4 and steep snow).

– JOHN FRIEH

The north face of Lucifer (Point 7,872'). Agua Sin Gas climbs up a snowy gully left of this prominent, steep face (out of picture). The 1976 first ascent of Lucifer, by Peter Rowat and Rupert Roschnik, climbed its snowy east ridge, left of the summit. *John Frieh*

CANADA

The route up the north face and east ridge of Mt. Malaspina.
Camilo Rada

MT. MALASPINA, NORTH FACE TO EAST RIDGE

On August 4, Natalia Martinez and I, as part of our Uncharted Project (which has focused mostly on the Cordillera Darwin and Cordillera Sarmiento in southern Chile), flew into Kluane National Park. We landed on the Seward Glacier, close to Mt. St. Elias. After traveling 12km we established a base camp (ca 1,862m) near the base of Mt. Malaspina (3,776m), our objective. To our understanding, this peak was owed the title of "highest unclimbed, officially named mountain of North America." [*There may be higher unclimbed summits that are unnamed.*] Regardless of title, it was without doubt one of the most prominent and attractive unclimbed summits on the continent. We believe it had been attempted only once, in 1976, by a Polish-Alaskan expedition, via its west ridge (*AAJ 1978*).

After three days exploring the heavily crevassed Malaspina Glacier, our only option was to follow a short section on the very edge of the glacier where avalanche debris had filled in the crevasses. Crossing that section in the early morning, we established a high camp below the north face of the mountain on August 9. Due to bad weather and high avalanche risk, we quickly abandoned that spot. Several sites nearer the wall seemed safe, but the seracs 1,000m above were capable of launching large ice and snow projectiles over the entire area.

Once the weather improved, we started a summit push from base camp on August 14, just after midnight. After three hours we reached our old high-camp cache and then continued east toward the col between Mt. Baird (3,550m, *AAJ 2001*) and Malaspina. The route to the col was extremely exposed to avalanches and rock and serac fall, diagonaling under a hanging glacier along 300m of snow and ice (45–60°), which we simul-climbed. Above this step we belayed two pitches of 55–65° ice to finally reach the col. After resting, we climbed a ramp for 350m to Malaspina's east shoulder. This consisted of a very sustained slope, involving nine belayed pitches on 50–65° snow and ice, with a final cornice that presented short vertical steps. We reached the shoulder (ca 3,377m) shortly after midnight and built an igloo-like bivouac, surrounded by the breathtaking spectacle of a northern lights storm.

On August 15, at 10 a.m., we started toward the summit, climbing easy snow slopes and some technical steps to overcome a few bergschrunds. After a false summit, we finally summited at 2 p.m., with the GPS reading 3,756m, relatively close to the recognized elevation. The view was dominated by the overwhelmingly large Malaspina Glacier, the largest piedmont glacier in the world, Mt. St. Elias to the west, Mt. Logan to the north, and Vancouver, Augusta, Cook, and Fairweather to the east. We descended our route, which entailed 15 rappels and downclimbing through clouds and spindrift. We reached base camp again at 8 a.m. on August 16 after 55 hours on the mountain. We graded our 1,900m route TD AI2 55–65°. 📷 🔍

– CAMILO RADA, *CHILE*

THE WEISSHORN, NORTH RIDGE, AND OTHER ASCENTS

EAMONN WALSH, CARL DIEHL, AND I spent approximately one month (mid-April to mid-May) in the northwestern pocket of the Lowell Glacier, within Kluane National Park. After flying in, we set up camp below the north side of the Weisshorn, with the south face of Mt. Kennedy to the north and Mt. McKim to the west. We hoped to climb new routes on the north-facing walls of the Weisshorn (11,620'; *see AAJ 1977 for information on the first ascent by its south side*) and Mt. McKim (11,995'; *McKim is an unofficial name for this peak, otherwise known as Kennedy South, first climbed in 2003*) but underestimated the danger of cornices and seracs. Thus, we turned our attention to less steep but safer lines.

We first completed the north ridge of the Weisshorn, a beautiful snow ridge with short bits of moderate mixed climbing (III). A few days later, we skied north and scrambled up a small peak east of Mt. Kennedy, possibly a first ascent. Finally, we climbed a straightforward line of snow and glacial ice up a tower-like peak on the ridgeline east of Mt. Kennedy.

– JAY MILLS, *CANADA*

NORTHWEST TERRITORIES / RAGGED RANGE

THUNDER MOUNTAIN (MT. NIRVANA) ATTEMPT AND OTHER ASCENTS

IN SUMMER 1965, Bill Buckingham and Lew Surdam made the first ascent of Mt. Nirvana (9,097'; *the mountain's name is being officially changed to Thunder Mountain by the Canadian government to reflect the local Deh Cho First Nation name.*) They first studied the southwest face but decided, "Any route here would be more of an undertaking than we were prepared for" (*AAJ 1966*). Instead, they made the first ascent via the north face and north ridge.

The southwest face has been largely forgotten since then. There were no published pictures from the 1965 trip, and the only description was that it had "great exfoliated slabs." I found one other reference, when Pete Ford and Bob Howell glimpsed the upper portion from a valley to the south (*Canadian Alpine Journal 1972*). Research revealed the southwest face could be up to 3,000' and a mile wide at the base. Could such a huge granite face on the tallest mountain in the territory really have gone unclimbed for so long?

On June 28, Dave Custer, Susan Ruff, and I helicoptered from Watson Lake to the edge of the unnamed lake at the base of the southwest face. We hatched a plan to gain the summit ridge just north of Peak 33—the rocky southeast summit of Thunder Mountain—by climbing a ramp and gully system and then traversing northwest to the summit. On June 29 rain developed and we retreated. On July 1 we returned and began our ascent. Once at the ridge crest, we

The southwest face of Thunder Mountain. (A) Summit of Thunder Mountain. (B) Peak 33. (1) 2015 route to summit of Peak 33. (2) Horizontal ledge system used on various attempts, showing the high point of the July 12 attempt. (3) July 4 attempt and high point. *Mike Fischesser*

peered north along the ridge to Thunder Mountain. There was still a lot of very technical terrain along the ridge to the summit. We turned our gaze to Peak 33. To our knowledge, it had no documented ascents, and there appeared to be a climbable crack system along the north ridge.

We descended several hundred feet, then climbed diagonally back up and right for three pitches to a flat area on the ridge. Two more pitches led to the airy summit. We were surprised to find a cairn and worn webbing rappel anchor leading off the northeast face. We later consulted Ragged Range experts Mike Fischesser and Jack Bennett, who had no knowledge of this earlier ascent. Our ascent would appear to be the second overall. Our new route up the southwest face and north ridge involved eight roped pitches to 5.8.

After an aborted attempt up the middle of the face on July 4, followed by some rain days, July 7 dawned clear and we headed up the same ramp we had used to climb Peak 33, hoping to cross a long, horizontal ledge system to reach a line leading toward the main summit of Thunder Mountain. By midday we reached a snowfield, and above this Dave led four pitches up wet chimneys with tricky chockstones until we were halted by rain.

On the evening of July 12 the skies cleared and we climbed back up to the ledge system. We brought bivy gear and slept for a few hours. The next morning, we continued past our previous high point for three pitches, with wet cracks requiring aid. Now on a right-diagonaling ramp just below the ridge crest, the rock turned unprotectable. My GPS read 8,530'. A system of wet, overhanging cracks directly above looked like they might continue, but this was as high as we could safely get in the conditions found. We retreated again and reached camp the next morning in pouring rain. Rain lasted the next few days.

A final weather window appeared as rain squalls pulled away the evening of July 16, but we retreated below our previous high point. On July 19 we climbed several rock spires. A small cairn atop one led us to believe it was one of the "grotesque" aiguilles climbed by Embick, et al (*AAJ 1976*). Our plan now was to rendezvous with another party on July 20 on the east face of Thunder Mountain and attempt the route pioneered by Bennett, et al (*AAJ 1997*). However, four days of solid rain prevented a helicopter flight. We decided on a new plan.

On July 23, Dave and Susan helicoptered to the Cirque of the Unclimbables, while I decided to hike out solo to Hole in the Wall Lake. From there I would take a float plane to Rabbit Kettle Lake and paddle out the Nahanni River with part of the other climbing team. I loaded my pack with 10 days of food and overnight and glacier gear, and set off following in the footsteps of Buckingham and Surdam. I had no particular plan beyond scrambling up interesting peaks I passed on the way. [*Visit the AAJ website to read the remainder of the author's story, with additional details on the many attempts on Thunder Montain and a map that describes in detail the many peaks climbed during this expedition.*] 🗎 📷 🔍

– **ERIC GILBERTSON**, *USA*

MT. WADDINGTON, NORTHWEST SUMMIT, SOUTHWEST BUTTRESS

ON AUGUST 17, I joined Ines Papert (Germany) and Mayan Smith-Gobat (New Zealand) for a four-day trip to Mt. Waddington (4,018m). We flew by helicopter to the Dais Glacier on the southwest side of the Waddington massif. Above camp, the rocky southwest buttress jacked out of the glacier like an 800m petrified shield, leading directly to the northwest summit (4,000m).

At 5:30 a.m. on the morning of the 18th, we crossed the bergschrund and quickly made progress up loose but moderate ground. Soon we joined the crest of the buttress, where the rock quality became superb and the sun revitalized our bone-chilled bodies. Taking stock of our rugged surroundings, it was hard to believe we were in such a savage wilderness just over 24 hours after leaving Squamish.

The line unfolded above, yielding stiff, technical rock challenges and spicy ridge and

Leading fractured rock on Mt. Waddington's southwest buttress. *Paul McSorley*

Colin Haley starts up 80m of AI4 in the crux portion of Heart of Darkness, Mt. Slesse. *Dylan Johnson*

mixed climbing. By 6 p.m. we had gained the summit slopes, worked but psyched. The final few hundred meters to Waddington's northwest summit played out like a power ballad, and the tippy-top was one of the wildest places any of us had ever been. In all we climbed 20 pitches (5.11+ M5 AI3). We bivied on the descent and reached camp again the morning of August 19.

Sean Easton, Craig McGee, and Eammon Walsh were the first to attempt the southwest buttress, climbing about 80 percent of the wall (*AAJ 2006*). In September 2011, Jason Kruk and Tony Richardson attempted this same route via a truly sporting approach. From Twist Lake they took a motorboat to Mosley Creek. From there they rafted to the outflow of the Scimitar Glacier and then bushwhacked up to the ice and over Fury Gap to the Dais Glacier. It took them a week just to get to the base of the wall. Once on the southwest buttress, rime ice high on the mountain forced them to retreat just shy of the summit ridge (we found their bail only two harder pitches from easier ground). In spite of the elusive summit, their effort stands as an all-time adventure. 🖸

— PAUL MCSORLEY, *CANADA*

BRITISH COLUMBIA / NORTH CASCADES

MT. SLESSE, HEART OF DARKNESS

DYLAN JOHNSON AND I drove to Mt. Slesse on March 7, hoping to climb the oft-attempted but unclimbed Heart of Darkness on Slesse's north side, a giant gash that goes straight up between the Northeast Buttress and North Rib. It had been attempted by a lot of the local hard core since the early 1980s. The route had been a serious hope of mine since 2005.

Hiking into the basin below Slesse's east face, it was obvious that conditions were exceptionally good, with little snow. On March 8 we left our tent at first light. Dylan crossed the bergschrund just after 8 a.m. and we started simul-climbing up the couloir.

The Heart of Darkness has three distinct sections: a lower couloir, a steep crux midway, and an upper couloir. We simul-climbed both couloir sections, which had difficulties to about AI3/4. In the middle crux section, the excellent conditions gave us a huge advantage. During Dylan's attempt with Roger Strong, a few years prior, Roger led a pitch of M6 R where I was able to climb an 80m pitch of straightforward AI4. This pitch brought us above any party's previous high point. From there, I led a short traverse with a mix of aid and free climbing. We were both blown away by how casually we had negotiated the crux—and it wasn't too scary.

From the top of the gully, I had always imagined difficult mixed climbing up the North Rib to reach the summit. However, at the upper col we were delighted to find the route almost free of snow and ice. Dylan led these last four pitches barehanded in the afternoon sun. What a combination: plentiful ice in the shady, north-facing couloir, followed by dry, sun-warmed rock! We reached the summit about nine hours after starting.

Our descent went smoothly, with just two short rappels near the summit and a bunch of downclimbing. Alpine climbing is often about timing, and in this instance ours was perfect. 📷

– COLIN HALEY, *USA*

CATHEDRAL PROVINCIAL PARK, BISHOP

IN JULY, Brandon Workman and I headed into Cathedral Provincial Park to climb the Deacon, a granite wall a few hundred yards from the USA-Canada border. We repeated a route on the Deacon and then set our sights on the 700' east-facing cliff a few hundred yards north. We dubbed this feature the Bishop. It's approximately the same height as the Deacon and has clean, steep rock. As far as we can tell it had not been climbed.

On the morning of July 19 we began climbing the Bishop via the right-hand of two obvious dihedrals, on the right side of the wall. After three pitches sharing leads up corners and seams (5.7–5.9), the cracks appeared to dead-end, but we had faith we would find a safe passage. Brandon worked his way up and left across an unprotected face and past a large roof. This led to rightward-trending ramps through otherwise steep and blank terrain. Two more strenuous crack pitches (5.10c and 5.10a) led directly to the summit. We descended a ramp to the northeast to the head of the basin. Our six-pitch route is called Faith (700', III 5.10c). 📷

– RAD ROBERTS, *USA*

SNOWPATCH SPIRE, EAST FACE, NEW ROUTES

OVER THE LAST DECADE, the 500m east face of Snowpatch Spire has been transformed into one of the finest alpine free climbing walls in North America. Formerly best known as an aid-climbing venue, it is now covered in free routes—mostly difficult ones, usually with at least a couple of 5.12 pitches. The climbing is almost entirely traditionally protected, with some bolts to connect crack systems via face climbing. Perhaps the most amazing thing about this wall is that almost every pitch is good! It has been one of my favorite zones for over 10 years now.

In the 2014 season, Michelle Kadatz and I investigated the lower-middle section of the east face, where a large flake had fallen off. We combined parts of several routes for the first three pitches, including Les Bruines Es Pentinen, Deus Ex Machina, and the original Sunshine Wall. It didn't take much effort to buff the terrain above into a nice free climb. After five

Alik Berg on a face climbing section of pitch four of Welcome to the Machine. *Jon Walsh*

pitches, we had established Minotaur Direct (5 pitches, 180m, 5.11+). This felt like a better start than the original Minotaur (14 pitches, 600m, 5.12a), a route I established several years ago with Colin Moorhead that started on Labyrinth before traversing in. Michelle and I returned to add belay stations to Minotaur Direct in 2015, and then continued up the amazing climbing on Minotaur.

Alik Berg and I teamed up in mid-July of 2015 to complete another route. We started on Minotaur Direct and then ventured left into Deus Ex Machina (at our sixth and seventh pitches). We were pleasantly surprised to get through the great roof system that spans the face at 5.11+ (previously rated A3). We then continued up new terrain until slowed by mossy cracks about 10 pitches up. We cleaned them and rappelled. Two weeks later, in early August, we were back. On the first day we climbed the first four pitches and fixed our two ropes. (Our friend Taran Ortlieb joined us on this day.) The next day we ascended the two lines and then made a continuous free ascent to the summit, adding four more pitches above our previous high point, sending every pitch first try. It was a very satisfying day on a fun route with a lot of varied climbing: Welcome to the Machine (13 pitches, 5.11+). Every pitch is between 5.10- and 5.11+, and I would recommend rappelling the route. 📷

— JON WALSH, *CANADA*

SOUTH HOWSER TOWER, NORTHEAST FACE, IT IS WHAT IT IS

In MID-OCTOBER, Toshiyuki Yamada and I climbed a new route on the northeast face of South Howser Tower. I was thrilled to try alpine climbing in the Bugaboos in October, as the winter climbing season in Japan runs December to March. I was fascinated first by the Big Hose (Krakauer, solo, *AAJ 1979*), and then by an obvious ice line on the left side of the wall. After climbing the Big Hose on October 14, we left our gear at the base and returned to the Kain Hut.

Early on October 16 we left the hut and retraced our steps to South Howser to climb the other ice line. We named the route It Is What It Is (320m, D+ M5 WI4 R). The upper portion of our climb shares terrain with Ethereal (*AAJ 2015*), and the climb took 14 hours round-trip from the Kain Hut. 📖 📷

— TAKESHI TANI, *JAPAN*

REINHOLD PUSSYCAT

BY CHRIS WEIDNER

The clock doesn't lie. But sometimes it seems to bend the truth. In the mountains, time seems fluid, its viscosity changing unpredictably. In a storm, tentbound, the sludge of time barely oozes forward. Yet when racing darkness on a climb, time rushes like snowmelt down a warm glacier—hours tick by like minutes. And so it was in the Bugaboos of British Columbia last August with Bruce Miller.

It was our fourth trip to the Bugs together since 2005, and we shared one clear goal: to free climb Reinhold Pussycat, a 1,700' route we had established in 2006 on the west face of the Minaret (*AAJ 2007*). During the first ascent we freed all but one 130' pitch right in the middle, where we resorted to banging pins and pulling on gear. Later that trip we climbed back up and tried to free that section, but time and weather got the best of us. We failed again in 2013 under cold, soggy conditions.

This year we flew in to East Creek Basin with three weeks of food and fuel, hoping time was on our side. Through repeat visits to these mountains we've learned approaches, descents, and weather patterns. Every trip becomes a little easier, the chance for success a little higher. Yet when the helicopter left us on a snowfield surrounded by duffel bags, I couldn't help but feel a visceral loneliness. Three weeks suddenly felt like a long time.

The crux of Reinhold Pussycat lurks 1,000' feet up the route. The sun illuminates this panel of granite for about five hours, starting at 2 p.m., which meant Bruce and I would climb for several hours up cold and sometimes wet or icy cracks before we could even begin to make progress. Over two weeks, as time flip-flopped between sludge and snowmelt, Bruce and I climbed to the crux five times to decipher a free variation and rehearse its moves. We eventually linked a dead-end crack into the seam we had

The west face of the Minaret showing Reinhold Pussycat, with the route of the first ascent (established in 2006) in yellow, an aid variation established while trying to free the climb in blue, and the full free line climbed in 2015, including a variation with two pitches of 5.12c, in red. *Chris Weidner*

Bruce Miller follows the upper part of the second crux pitch of Reinhold Pussycat. *Chris Weidner*

originally nailed by utilizing a horizontal section of very thin face climbing. This variation, the Murder of the Impussible, yields two pitches of 5.12c.

August 26 dawned calm, clear, and warmer than it had since our arrival, 16 days earlier. The forecast called for several days of cold and snow ahead, so our time was running out. It would be our last chance to free the Pussycat this year. I should have felt confident and relaxed on our sixth lap up the same chunk of rock. Instead, I felt more nervous. I think Bruce felt the same. We knew the moves well—I'd mentally rehearsed the two cruxes more than I'd actually practiced them—yet we hadn't led either pitch without falling.

For the first time this trip the sunny rock at the crux felt warm. Perspiration softened our fingertips, making the smallest holds feel slick. I somehow calmed my nerves before the traverse and executed the moves precisely. Bruce did the same, but only after greasing off the half-pad edges and restarting the pitch several times. After so much extra climbing his successful effort was nothing short of heroic. The second crux, a vertical seam with finicky footholds, went down first try for both of us. Meanwhile, the sun was setting and time hit warp speed.

We raced up the Minaret by headlamp, gained the east ridge of South Howser Tower, and then followed it to the summit. We bumbled around searching for the new, bolted rappels, and then settled for the old raps down the north face. Before we touched the glacier there was light again in the east. Back at our camp in the East Creek Basin, the clock told us our round-trip journey had taken 26 hours and 20 minutes. It also told us that the following day, when we flew out, was my 41st birthday. Maybe the clock does lie—I sure as hell don't know where all that time went.

SUMMARY: *First free ascent of Reinhold Pussycat (600m, V 5.12c, originally graded 5.10+ A2, Bugaboos, Minaret, west face, by Bruce Miller and Chris Weidner (USA), August 26, 2015.* 📷

BLOCK TOWER, SLIM PRINCESS; WALL TOWER, STATE OF WONDER

THE LEANING TOWERS are 50 miles south of the Bugaboos in the Purcell Wilderness Conservancy. They're practically an untouched part of the world, and the quality of the granite and wilderness setting were the main allures for Jasmin Caton and me.

On July 11, Jasmin and I, along with help from Stephen Stenecal, struck out with heavy packs for the two-day approach. After passing hot springs and talus, we found a winding trail through thick rhododendron. Many moraines later, we stood below Hall Peak, steep and spectacular, home to a handful of routes. We continued up and over the right shoulder of Hall to the basin below Wall Peak. The skies were dark with intermittent rain, which inspired a recon outing. Many of the towers here start with a smooth, crack-less slab that is capped by a sharp, square-cut roof about a hundred feet above the snow. The easiest passage up the unclimbed east face of Wall Tower seemed to start up a weakness between Block and Wall towers.

On our first day of good weather, we climbed this weakness in five pitches to the col between the towers. Here, we were intimidated by the terrible dark sky and steep wall, so we headed up to the easier summit of Block Tower before rappelling into a storm. It was a great adventure with all kinds of cracks—fingers, hands, offwidths—and perfect gray granite. We called the route Slim Princess (250m, 5.10).

After a few more rainy days, we rallied through the cold and damp to climb what we hoped would be our descent route from Wall Tower, the northwest ridge (300m, 5.7, Campbell-Jones-Palmer-Roxburgh, 1980), which follows the ridgeline above the steep east face. Our days were growing fewer and we pleaded with the weather gods. Our last day of eight was supposed to be rain-free. We read books, made art, and packed for a new route up the east face of Wall Tower, aiming for a striking black pillar leading to the summit.

We stepped off the glacier, heading up and left of the slabby nose of the wall, and found perfect golden hand jams. A pendulum, wild roofs, finger cracks, and world-class thin-hand cracks led us to a brutal, dirty crux pitch. Traversing back left under a truck-size boulder and into the chimneys of the black pillar was scary (and I recommend future parties quest straight up.) A handful of beautiful chimney pitches led us to the sunny summit. Golden light led the rappels; we were happy with our good fortune in this big granite paradise—State of Wonder (300m, 5.11- C1). 📷

— KATE RUTHERFORD, *USA*

MT. LOUIS, NORTHEAST BUTTRESS, BUCKING HORSE RIDER

FROM JULY 19–20, Jason Ammerlaan, Tony McClane, and Paul McSorley climbed a new route up the northeast buttress of Mt. Louis (2,682m), to the right of the route Homage to the Spider (Auger-Bunyan, 1987). They completed the approach and climbed the lower half of the route on the first day, reaching the terrace below the upper headwall, where they bivied. On day two they tackled a long and steep dihedral on the headwall to reach the summit. They called the route Bucking Horse Rider (600m, 5.11a A0).

— ERIK RIEGER, *WITH INFORMATION FROM* PAUL MCSORLEY

MT. LAWRENCE GRASSI, NORTH FACE, TAINTED LOVE

Juan Henriquez tackles a snow mushroom on pitch two of Tainted Love. *Raphael Slawinski*

NOVEMBER 2014. Ian Welsted and I were gunning for the Hole (*AAJ 2015*), a natural arch in the middle of the north face of Mt. Lawrence Grassi, a prominent yet obscure wall above Canmore. We missed the break leading up to the route and instead found ourselves below the Gash. The thin ice dribbling out of the giant chimney looked innocent enough. It was only when I was halfway up the 25m flow, picks wobbling in shallow placements, that I began to think I had strayed over the line separating scrambling from soloing. Pulling onto a steep snow ledge, I spied faded cord connecting two bolts: relics of previous attempts on the Gash. But we hadn't come for the Gash. Tying into the rope, we took off on a rising traverse in search of the Hole.

DECEMBER 2014. The Hole ended up being fun in an "alpine" kind of way, but the sport climber in me was drawn to the undone project. A couple of weeks later, Ian and I, joined by young Sam Eastman, slogged back up to the Gash. This time we continued straight up. After a few pitches—steep rock, slabby rock, unconsolidated snow, and the occasional token patch of ice—we entered the guts. With Ian and Sam bundled up at the belay, I started up the overhanging back wall, hooking frozen choss, hanging from tools, drilling bolts: an altogether too familiar, anything-goes dance to get up the pitch.

At this point in the game, Ian, always more of an alpinist than a sport climber, declared himself uninterested in my construction project. Finding partners for my newest obsession was proving challenging. All the same, I managed two more short, snowy December days on the Gash, prepping what was starting to resemble an alpine sport mixed route.

NOVEMBER 2015. "The route's rigged, it just needs to be sent." I thought it more likely that Juan Henriquez would be interested if he knew it wasn't to be another aiding, bolting, and standing-around mission. Colin Simon was also in the Rockies from Colorado. They were both game. For once it was a mild, windless day. Perhaps I'd earned a treat after all the blustery, snowy days working on the route. Now all that was left was to climb it.

A few hours later all three of us stood tethered to the station below the crux corner. I eyed the largely decorative icicles dripping from the dihedral. "I haven't really tried the moves before, so first I'll just go up a few bolts to check out the holds," I said, as Juan put me on belay. To my surprise, a few minutes later I was searching for a seam, an edge, anything to take a tool beyond the overlap, where the wall kicked back to vertical. Blindly finding a hold, I released my bottom tool. If I fell off here, they'd hear about it down in Canmore. But the hold was good. Slowly, carefully, I hooked and torqued my way up the last few meters. While I belayed my friends up, I strapped the headlamp to my helmet. We'd be finishing the route properly: in the dark—Tainted Love (320m, WI3 M9). 📷

– RAPHAEL SLAWINSKI, *CANADA*

STORM MOUNTAIN, KOGARASHI

IN MAY, Toshiyuki Yamada and I climbed a new route on the northeast face of Storm Mountain (3,191m). Storm Mountain is located on the Continental Divide in the Bow River Valley, across from Castle Mountain. An obvious ice line on the right side drew our eyes and hearts into longing and excitement for a new route. The climbing took six hours from the base to the summit. It wasn't too hard, and it appears to be the easiest and most natural line on the northeast face. We named it Kogarashi, which means "little storm" in Japanese (350m, D WI4 5.6). 📄 📷

– TAKESHI TANI, *JAPAN*

The northeast side of Storm Mountain showing: (1) East ridge (Boles-Greenwood, 1961). (2) Northeast face (Thomas-Wallator, 1988). (3) Canoeing to Cuba (Mills–Van Haeren–Welsted, 2015). (4) Kogarashi (Tani-Toshiyuki, 2015). (5) Northeast spur (Greenwood-Lofthouse, 1958). (5a) The col from which the climbers descended back to the glacier beneath the northeast face. (6) North spur variant (Kruszyna-Whipple, 1963). Note that many of these routes start lower than the route lines indicate, as they are obscured by a foreground ridge or out of frame. *Takeshi Tani*

STORM MOUNTAIN, CANOEING TO CUBA

"TRAVEL A THOUSAND miles by train and you are a brute; pedal five hundred on a bicycle and you remain basically a bourgeois; paddle a hundred in a canoe and you are already a child of nature," said Pierre Elliot Trudeau, a past prime minister of Canada. It was October, and the times were changing in Canada. A 10-year reign by Canada's Conservative Party and their fear-based policies had ended after a resounding victory by Justin Trudeau, son of the revered elder Trudeau. The mountains were dry. Things were headed in the right direction.

In mid-October, Jay Mills and I spent one day approaching and then a day and a night getting high above Moraine Lake (featured on the old $20 bill) on an unclimbed route. The road into the Valley of the Ten Peaks was closed, so we rode our bikes in 10km. There were only three alpine routes on the side of the valley that interested us, and the most recent one had

Ian Welsted leads the fifth pitch ice pillar of Canoeing to Cuba. *Maarten van Haeren*

been established 30 years earlier. That's why alpine climbing in Canada is amazing: You don't have to go anywhere obscure to find first ascents. In the end, we didn't make it up our objective, but for a backyard adventure it couldn't be beaten. There is nothing more Canadian than a trip into nature, no matter how brief. But contemporary climbers have made communing with the natural world a lesser priority. One of my friends recently challenged each of her "sport mixed" climbing friends to try establishing a new "non-sport" route this winter.

In 1988—just down-range from Jay's and my objective—Ken Wallator and Tom Thomas were getting chased around by the park wardens for pirate camping, so they figured they might as well spend time up in the mountains, and they completed the first ascent of Storm Mountain's northeast face over four days. The route they completed grew to mythical proportions, partly due to Ken's widely reputed hard-man abilities. [*Editor's note: In 2010, Wallator offered a free rope to anyone able to repeat the 1988 northeast face route. As of 2015, the route is unrepeated.*] By this point, I'd talked about going for a look-see for five years. This was during the same time period that my friends and I waited, wishing, for a change back to a more Canadian attitude in our national politics. We'd managed to get rid of the might-as-well-be-Texan politicians in Alberta. Maybe we could get up Ken's route, too? Jay and I decided to head out for another multi-day mission, this time to Storm Mountain, partly for the joy of camping out and reconnecting with nature. Maarten van Haeren would join us. He works in a wilderness center for addiction recovery, helping troubled young men find solace in nature.

As Jay chatted with our new team member, Maarten, about whether Alaska or Chamonix was better, I interceded, "Come on. Look at where we are. We've got it the best." It was October 28 and Jay, Maarten, and I managed to climb a new route up the center of the northeast face of Storm Mountain (3,191m) in 13 hours camp to camp. We didn't revisit the fierce-looking Thomas-Wallator route. Instead we shocked ourselves with how easy it was to get up this face we'd all looked at for so long. It was obvious we'd created an insurmountable problem in our minds, rather than just going for a look. We faced our doubts in the same way we voted the fear mongers out of power.

"Can I name it Canoeing to Cuba, after Pierre Trudeau? You know, he tried to canoe from Florida to Cuba to visit Castro. He worked in the cane fields there when he spent a year traveling the world when he was young," I recounted. "Sounds like a pretty Canadian thing to do," commented Jay—Canoeing to Cuba (350m, WI5 M6).

[*Editor's note: In 1999, Raphael Slawinski and Chris Geisler made it to the fifth, crux pitch of the nine-pitch Canoeing to Cuba; however, the ice pillar climbed by Mills, van Haeren, and Welsted in 2015 was not present on the earlier attempt.*] 📷

– IAN WELSTED, *CANADA*

MONT GROS BRAS, NORTH FACE, LE DERNIER RŌNIN

THE DAY WAS PERFECT—except for the date, Friday, March 13. Mathieu "Mat" Leblanc, François "Frank" Bédard, and I had decided to finish a project we'd started last year on the far right side of the north face of Mont Gros Bras. (The 200m wall, located on the eastern edge of Parc National des Grands-Jardins, previously had five winter routes in this right sector.) We hoped to climb a new route in memory of Yannick Girard. Yannick died not long after he and I made the first winter ascent of Sens Unique on the Acropole des Draveurs (*AAJ 2015*).

We had already tried five times to climb the second pitch of our project. There seemed like nothing more to do: It was almost like a mirror, with tiny crimps to place the tip of our picks, one or two micro cracks, and no protection possible. Even the hardman Nick Balan came to lend a hand but with no luck.

This time, our feelings were different, with a sense of conviction and of a last chance. When we arrived, we inspected the north face for other options to finish our route but found nothing. Even in mid-March, it was cold and the snow was firm. At the base of our route, we decided Mat would tackle the first pitch. Frank, the bravest, would have the difficult task of the second. I felt lucky to get the third pitch, which we hadn't tried yet. We didn't know who was going to climb the fourth pitch.

Gros Bras in winter inevitably means freezing hands and screaming barfies, plus the first pitch is difficult. It's all like a violent punch in the teeth. But we were off to a good start: Mat freed the pitch, a diagonal ramp into a beautiful crack. Now it was Frank's turn. It's a strange feeling to see your friend head up a climb knowing he has a good

Mat Leblanc engaging some hard dry tooling in the middle of the first pitch. *Louis Rousseau*

chance of falling with many sharp metal spikes attached. When he arrived at the crux, he climbed extremely delicately and slowly. When a hold broke, he took a large, jumbling fall. But after that he went off again in search of micro-crimps, probing with the blades of his ice tools. Eventually, he deciphered the sequence and engaged a long, icy section above.

I found the third pitch to be run-out but much less technical. Below the fourth pitch we packed into the belay like three frozen sardines. Mat volunteered to continue through an overhang and some loose blocks. When cracks petered out, he placed the smallest cam available to do a single aid move (C1). Above this, a slabby section crossed two short ice steps before the easy summit slopes. Before the descent, I thought about our friend Yannick, who had guided us all day from above. This was one of the Québec crags he especially liked to visit with good friends, in search of alpine adventures and the sound of his swinging ice tools. We named the route Le Dernier Rōnin (175m, M6 C1), which means the Last Ronin. 📷

– LOUIS ROUSSEAU, *QUÉBEC*

BLOW ME DOWN, THE BETRAYER OF HOPE

In September 2014, Sam Bendroth and I began establishing a free route on the 1,300' seaside cliff Blow Me Down. Our route is just right of Lucifer's Lighthouse (*AAJ 2007*) and shares its initial 20'. On this initial trip, we freed the first four pitches, including the crux, ground up. In summer 2015, we went from the top down to find a line through the upper section of the cliff. After a few days of work, we put it together and cleaned the fixed lines to climb ground up.

The route has 12 pitches, including one 5.12a and six 5.11 pitches—all 5.11c or harder, with the exception of one 5.11a pitch. It feels pretty stacked by the end of it. We called it the Betrayer of Hope (12 pitches, 5.12a), after a character from the Wheel of Time fantasy novel series, which Sam was reading. 📄 📷

–BAYARD RUSSELL, *USA*

GREAT CROSS PILLAR, DECONSTRUCTING JENGA

In early May, Cheyne Lempe and I traveled to the Sam Ford Fjord of Baffin Island and established a new route on Great Cross Pillar: Deconstructing Jenga (900m, 5.9+ A3+).

We spent our first day and a half preparing camp and hiking our gear to the base of the Great Cross Pillar, at the northeast corner of Sam Ford Fjord and the Walker Arm. We began climbing capsule-style on May 9.

The wind blew steadily down the fjord from the east and rarely changed directions or stopped for the entire trip. When it did, the sun almost felt warm. We climbed with the motto of the Polish big-wall experts Marek Raganowicz and Marcin Tomaszewski: Climb every day. Our second and third days on the route were in a proper Arctic blizzard, with temps below -20°F.

Our route began up Great Cross' right-side slab to reach the base of its right pillar (365m of climbing). We established our first camp here on a large talus ledge. From that point, we began climbing 30m left of camp, up the obvious cleft between the nose of the wall and its right pillar. Our friends Ben Ditto and Sean Villanueva had attempted this line to about one-third height in an all-free effort in summer 2014, but were turned back due to poor rock (*AAJ 2015*).

We encountered myriad rock types and qualities in the massive, steep, right-leaning corner and chimney system. While heel-toeing up difficult offwidth cracks in double boots and Arctic battle gear, Cheyne and I were thankful for our Yosemite roots. We found occasional towers of stacked rocks in the bottoms of the chimneys that required delicate deconstructing, like a game of Jenga. After 275m of climbing on the headwall, we reached the Nighttime Nibbler Bivy. And after another 155m of climbing above that camp, we exited the decomposing corner system to the right, via a sporty A3+ traverse. Now on a large, golden face right of the corner system, we climbed tiny cracks and shallow corners through immaculate rock, reminiscent of Reticent Wall on El Capitan.

On May 19, after a frigid 36-hour blizzard, we ascended 200m of fixed lines, climbed another 60m pitch, and then decided to push through the night hours to the summit of the route. The 24-hour daylight made the event surreal. Two short, snowy pitches and two difficult aid

Sam Bendroth on the Betrayer of Hope, a new route on Blow Me Down. *Bayard Russell*

pitches through crackless, bulletproof rock brought us to the summit. We descended our route over two days by two-bolt anchors we had installed on the way up. After two additional days on the ice, Levi Palituq picked us up on his snowmobile. 🖿

— DAVID ALLFREY, *USA*

CUMBERLAND PENINSULA ASCENTS

TWELVE YEARS AFTER traversing a major unnamed icefield east of Kingnait Fiord, Cumberland Peninsula (*AAJ 2004*), Louise Jarry and I returned to continue exploration of the region. In all, we traveled 120km and made four first ascents. [*See the AAJ website for the full report, along with photos and a map of peaks climbed.*] 🖿 🖿 🔍

— GREG HORNE, *CANADA*

GREENLAND

THE MILD BUNCH: COASTAL ROCK CLIMBS FROM A YACHT

MY CREW ABOARD the Dodo's Delight in Greenland last year was not the "Wild Bunch," those talented professional climbers from Belgium and America who joined me in 2010 and 2014, but the "Mild Bunch," a quartet of non-professional British climbers. Apart from one glorious exception they stuck to shorter routes within their comfort zone, but they proved there is plenty of new-routing potential in West Greenland for holiday climbers.

We sailed from Sisimiut around June 6 and first visited the Evighedsfjord (Eternity Fjord), an old stomping ground of H.W. Tilman and the location of 2,190m Mt. Atter, the highest mountain in West Greenland. This long fjord is bordered by many rock walls and side glaciers, with numerous alpine peaks awaiting first ascents. At the far end lies an offshoot, Sangmissoq Fjord, and about 3 km up-glacier to the southeast, Patrick Deacon and Trystan Lowe found a rock buttress they named Sangmissoq Buttress, where they climbed the Rocky Road to New York (100m, E1 5a).

In this fjord we faced a difficulty that became even more apparent when we moved south to the Hamborgerland/Maniitsoq area: snow down to sea level. As the manager of the Maniitsoq Hotel put it, "This year in Greenland winter has lasted longer than in the previous 47." We had only brought rock gear, expecting it to be summer.

To my knowledge, none of the rock walls in the Hamborgerland/Maniitsoq area had been climbed, and there is much scope for first ascents of prominent alpine peaks, rising 1,000m to 2,000m above sea level. The four lads found a partially dry cliff that we named Starter Walls, quite close to the Agpamiut anchorage, off Hamborgerland Sund. Here, Deacon and Lowe, Rob Beddow, and Mark McKellar climbed six new routes, up to 155m and E3.

We then moved to Maniitsoq Island and a smaller island off its southwest corner called Kin of Sal (a strangely English name on Danish maps; in Greenlandic it is the Big Heart; we called it the Shark's Fin, for obvious reasons).

Trystan Lowe during the first ascent of Midnight Sun on the Kin of Sal. Dodo's Delight is moored in the waters below. *Rob Beddow*

On the east face the four climbers outdid themselves, completing two bold climbs: Midnight Sun (280m, E4 6a, Beddow-Lowe) and Dusk Till Dawn (280m, E4 6a, Deacon-McKellar). Five days later they added two shorter routes high on the back (west) side of the second summit of Kin of Sal.

Farther south, on July 8, Rob and Patrick climbed the prominent ridge between the Itossoq and Umanap Suvdlua fjords, crossing over the summit of Nakaigajutoq (1,180m). They took 25 hours boat to boat, at an overall grade of TD. We later discovered a similar traverse had been completed in 2009 by two Norwegians (*see report below*).

Our final climbs were in the region of Kap Desolation (Nunarssuit), where we anchored in

Dusk Till Dawn (yellow) and Midnight Sun on Kin of Sal (a.k.a. Shark's Fin). *Mark McKellar*

the channel between Kap Thorsvalden and the line of islands at its base. On July 28, on the east side of a slabby face to the north of the Kap, the lads put up two routes. Then, after an attempt on the Thumb, a prominent spire on the other side of the fjord, we sailed to Scotland, with the usual stormy adventures associated with these high latitudes. Our expedition was supported by the British Mountaineering Council and the Gino Watkins Memorial Fund. [*The online version of this report provides area coordinates and more route details.*]

– BOB SHEPTON, *U.K.*

NUUK REGION, UNREPORTED ASCENTS FROM 2009

In 2008, AUDUN IGESUND from Norway went to the Nuuk area to meet local climber Aili Lage Labansen. The two put up Sortebærstien (ca 10 pitches, 5.8), on a wall at the southeast end of Storø, and climbed a handful of pitches at the start of the west pillar of Qupik. Back in Norway, Audun told enthusiastic tales of good rock in a fabulous Arctic landscape with relatively easy access. Bernt Bye, Laura de Steur, Tore Røysheim, and I took the bait.

In August 2009, Aili's parents took us by boat to our first target, Qupik (1,040m). This beautiful granite mountain is situated in the fjord northeast of Nuuk, on the way to Qooqqut. We landed with some difficulty on the shore southwest of the mountain. Next day we all started up the west pillar by three different lines. Finger cracks and thin dihedrals led in five pitches to a walk-off ledge. Tore and I continued up beautiful, steep hand and offwith cracks for several pitches. Then, easier but loose ground led us to the top (12 pitches, 5.10). I fell from a mossy offwidth during our ascent, but Laura and Bent managed to climb it clean the following day, while Tore and I climbed a new line from the walk-off ledge to the top (Flyfrisk, 4 pitches, 5.11 R). Later, Audun and Tore climbed the south wall in seven pitches on high-quality granite (5.10+).

Tore Røysheim climbing excellent granite on Qupik's west pillar. *Jo Gjedrem*

After a week of fun on Qupik, including hosting a trad-climbing course with a group from Aapakaaq, the climbing club in Nuuk, we moved camp to the bay of Itissoq on Storø. Here, Tore and I climbed the northeast ridge of Nakaigajugtoq (1,180m). We roped up for five or six pitches (5.8 max) and soloed easy but sometimes exposed, loose, and mossy terrain for at least a kilometer. From the top we descended low-angle slabs and talus fields westward to a point where four rappels down a northwest-facing wall brought us to walking ground. We also climbed the short northeast ridge of Naajat Inersuat (610m).

Our last camp was on the shore of the bay east of Sermitsiaq (1,210m), a relatively popular trekking mountain on Sermitsiaq Island (Sadelø). Tore and I climbed the south wall (seven pitches, 5.9) on clean, solid, white granite.

Aili had information that during the 1990s two Danes had climbed the impressive, steep, and loose-looking 1,040m peak to the north of Itissoq bay. We didn't find any traces of other climbers, but then again, except for some webbing, we didn't leave any traces ourselves. 📷

— JO GJEDREM, *NORWAY*

EAST GREENLAND / NORTH LIVERPOOL LAND

MANY FIRST ASCENTS ABOVE THE ICECAP

IN APRIL AND MAY, following two previous visits to this area (*AAJ 2009 and 2015*), I returned with regular partners Geoff Bonney and Sandy Gregson, plus new recruits Roger Gott, Richard Toon (all U.K.), and Ingrid Baber, a German living in Scotland. We flew from Iceland into Constable Pynt/Nerlerit Inaat, and from there were transported by Snow Dragons snowmobile service, operated by Tangent Expeditions, to the icecap zone of North Liverpool Land.

We set up base camp at 71°21.679'N, 22°07.389'W (525m), just 45m north of our 2014 site. The site was chosen because of its central position and maximum exposure to sunshine, very important at the tail end of an Arctic winter. The mountains and glaciers were well-cloaked with snow, yet there was ample sunshine to settle it and lower the avalanche risk.

On the Seven Dwarfs, which form the end of the ridge extending westward from 1,005m Mt. Mighty, we made the first ascents of Sneezy, Happy, Dopey, and Sleepy. The other three summits of the Seven Dwarfs remain unclimbed. To the west of the Seven Dwarfs, Geoff, Ingrid, Sandy, and I made the second ascent of Castle Peak (780m) by a new route, Postern Gate (PD), on the north flank, followed by a traverse and descent over the Eastern Ramparts Ridge.

On Mt. Mighty, first climbed by an Australian pair in 2012, Geoff, Ingrid, Sandy, and I climbed Snake in the Outback (PD+/AD-) up the northeast face for the peak's second ascent. East of Mt. Mighty, toward the inlet of Neild Bugt, Ingrid, Sandy, and I made the first ascent of Farfarer Peak (815m) via the northwest face and ridge (Dennis Davis Memorial Route, PD+). To the north, on the opposite side of the glacier from the Mt. Mighty chain, Roger and Richard made the second ascent of Longridge Peak (960m), following the original 2012 Australian Route (AD) up the west ridge. Two days later, Ingrid, Sandy, and I made the third ascent via a new route, Cryogenic (PD+), on the southeast rib and east face.

Further east, Ingrid, Sandy, and I made the first ascent of Hvithorn (825m) via Blanco (PD+) on the south face. This was particularly satisfying as Sandy and I had tried this peak by the west ridge in 2014 and were stalled at the 750m foresummit of Varmtind. The next summit east was climbed by Roger and Richard and named Lewty Peak (855m)—they ascended the snowy Memorial Ridge (PD+, 50°) on the south face to the rocky summit. South of the Mt. Mighty chain, Roger and Richard made the first ascent of Lancstuk (1,050m map height) via the northeast face and north ridge at PD+/AD-. The ascent started about 100m above sea level.

This area still has much to offer, but some base camp locations would increase the potential for polar bear encounters. More difficult rock climbing is available on the still-virgin Tower of Silence, ridges on the north side of Mt. Hulya, other exposures on the south side of the Seven Dwarfs, and possibly the large prow on the east side of Old Men's Peak. These would perhaps be better attempted in a warmer season, although access then would be more complex. [*The online version of this report has more details on many of the routes and coordinates of the peaks.*]

– JIM GREGSON, *U.K.*

[Photo] Looking across the northern branch of the Neild Bugt Glacier. (A) Hvithorn. (B) Lewty Peak. (1) West ridge of Varmtind (Gregson-Gregson, 2014). (2) Blanco (south face, 2015). (3) Memorial Ridge (south face, 2015). *Jim Gregson*

REFLECTIONS

BY MATT PICKLES

Other than expedition organizer Leo Houlding, the journey to Greenland was a first for us all. Joe Mohle from South Africa, Waldo Etherington, photographer Matt Pycroft, and I (U.K.) were relatively inexperienced and very apprehensive about the journey we were about to take. After a Twin Otter flight across the North Atlantic to Constable Pynt, we jumped into a helicopter on June 25 and flew ca 150km deep into Renland and onto the Edward Bailey Glacier. This really was the middle of nowhere.

Mirror Wall (ca 2,050m) is set back in one of the many tributary valleys coming down from the ice cap. In August 2012 the Swiss team of Basil Jacksch, Christian Ledergerber, Vera Reist, and Silvan Schüpbach made the first ascent via two beautiful routes up each edge of the 1,200m west face: Ledgeway to Heaven and Midnight Solarium (*AAJ 2013*). From our base camp 5km away the cliff looked surprisingly small: "How can this be bigger than El Cap?" But slowly we realized the scale was confusing us. The ice cap that hung like a huge serac above the neighboring cliffs was a serac 100m high!

Two weeks later, after several load carries up the highly crevassed glacier, we were alone on the wall, trying to find a way to the top. After a 200m, heavily loaded snow slope, we made good progress up the first 300m of rock climbing, swinging leads and climbing onsight. This led to our first wall camp, Bedouin Camp, named after the huge, Saudi Arabia–shaped flake it sat upon. It had a little roof above that we assumed would protect us. Many rocks whizzed by over the next few days, but nothing came close until one night we were awoken by unmistakable whistling, and then a rock the size of a tennis ball hit Leo right in the nuts. Lucky or unlucky? A meter to either side would have been a different story, but a head shot might have been the end.

Difficult and dangerous climbing led straight out from the portaledges. Joe aided and cleaned a stellar, 60m pitch up a loose corner before I returned to free it at 5.12b. After 200m we reached a sizeable ledge system over to the left via a tricky diagonal traverse followed by a diagonal rappel. This became our second wall camp—the Arctic Hotel—and provided a good base to launch our attack on the headwall.

Living up to its name, the central Mirror Wall is blank. With limited time and unstable weather, a wrong turn on the huge expanses of featureless granite could easily have led to failure. Taking advantage of the 24-hour daylight, and working in teams of two, we climbed around the clock to get through the harder pitches. We climbed until we were exhausted, rested until we recovered. Heading back right toward the center of the face, we climbed five pitches up to 5.12c leading to a 30m blank section. A crack line could be seen farther right, and we placed 10 bolts to get there. To our utter disappointment, the apparent crack system turned out to be a horrifically thin seam, and it took all of Leo's experience to overcome 45m of A3+ climbing, with 50 pieces of gear placed over six hours.

Thankfully this led to more featured rock, which gave several more great pitches up cracks and corners, typically around 5.11c to 5.12a. At this point a rock thrown from the wall

[Photo] Leo Houlding starts the first pitch (E5 6b) above the Arctic Hotel, 600m up Mirror Wall. *Matt Pycroft / Coldhouse Collective / Berghaus*

[Top] Leo Houlding above the Paper Flake, a 20m-tall, 10m-wide granite formation that was just 1cm at its thinnest. [Bottom] Mirror Wall seen from the glacier approach. (1) Midnight Solarium (2012). (2) Reflections (2015). (3) Ledgeway to Heaven (2012). *Matt Pycroft / Coldhouse Collective / Berghaus*

took 20 seconds to reach the glacier below. Finally, 200m of easier climbing led to the summit ridge. With a 1,200m drop on one side and a steep snow slope on the other, we precariously walked along a meter-wide rock ledge to the highest point. After 12 days on the wall, we took some time on the summit to look back over the long road we had followed to complete our goal. The route had stirred the soul of each of us.

SUMMARY: *New route on the west face of Mirror Wall in Renland, East Greenland: Reflections (1,200m, 25 pitches, E6 6b/5.12c A3+, 11 protection/aid bolts and 27 belay bolts), July 2015.* 🔲

GRUNDTVIGSKIRCHEN, EAST FACE ATTEMPTS, AND ASCENTS FROM SKILLEBUGT FJORD

IMAGINE SAILING TO YOSEMITE, amid an array of glaciers, with the ocean lapping the base of rocky slopes and walls. Enzo Oddo and I had arrived at Renland aboard Isobelle Autissier's yacht Ada II, and before our eyes lay more rock faces than we could ever climb, even if we stayed the rest of our lives.

Our first target was Grundtvigskirchen (1,977m), which looms above the fjord separating Renland from Milne Land to the south. In 2010 an Italian-Swiss team climbed the central pillar on the ca 1,300m east face (Eventyr, 7a+, *AAJ 2011*). After trying to climb a line up the steep, compact wall farther to the right, we headed back left along the face to attempt a dihedral on the right flank of the central pillar. We climbed six pitches in the corner, after which the logical line took us back to the Italian-Swiss route, which we decided to follow. Bad weather confined us to the portaledge for 36 hours during our fourth bivouac. We then went for the top but were forced to retreat just 150m below the summit in a hailstorm. We later made an attempt on the magnificent south ridge, climbed by Norwegians in 1999, but were again beaten back by rain and snow.

With the aid of the boat we transferred base camp to the head of Skillebugt Fjord. On one of the best days of our entire stay, we climbed a 400m ridge immediately above camp, Pointe de l'Observatoire (6a), which provided a fine viewpoint of the surrounding objectives.

A magnificent spire caught our eye, with a wall that featured huge dihedrals at its base. These led to a sandy chimney, an exposed roof, and a series of excellent cracks. A few pitches

Philippe Batoux after passing a roof about halfway up Pilier du Camp de Base (400m, 7a) , near the head of Skillebugt Fjord. *Enzo Oddo*

required aid from skyhooks and copperheads. We made three portaledge camps en route. As we started down from the summit, the short weather window closed and we made our descent in snowfall. We named the 600m route Midnight Rainbow (7a A3).

Our last route in the area was a fine pillar that we managed completely free, albeit with a little run-out climbing. Pilier du Camp de Base was 400m, mainly in cracks up to 7a, but with a face-climbing crux (7a) that was not protectable.

All three routes lie above the end of a narrow glacier running south into the Skillebugt from the Kloftbjerge Glacier plateau. Little gear was left in situ; we generally rappelled as directly as we could, most of the time away from the line of the route. 📄 📷

— PHILIPPE BATOUX, FRANCE

Midnight Rainbow (600m, 7a A3), north of Skille-bugt Fjord. The summit lies 150m behind. *Philippe Batoux*

JACOBSEN FJORD, PEAK 1,092M

AS A YOUTH I hitchhiked around a lot, but the best lift I ever got was the one going to Greenland last summer. Paddy Barry was planning a sailing and climbing trip from Iceland to East Greenland and back. There was one free space.

Ice prevented us from accessing the Mikis and Kangerdlugssuaq fjords, but as we were debating what to do a French schooner passed and told us by radio they had managed to find anchorage in nearby Jacobsen Fjord. We spent five days there, and our attention soon was drawn to a chain of peaks above the west side of the upper fjord. On August 2, Harry Connolly, Frank Nugent, Paddy O'Brien—all old Irish Mountaineering Club hands—and I set out in clear weather.

After a rising traverse up a glacier below steep rock walls, we found ourselves below a 250m, northeast-facing, snow-filled gully with an ice cap above and left. After debating the risk of serac fall, we went for it. It was sweet: dead straight and around 50° (Scottish II) at the most. On the crest of the main chain we continued southeast to the base of a snow dome. Onward we went, ascending the dome's narrowing spine. Soon we were at the top (1,092m, 68°10'8"N, 31°9'32"W). Although chuffed, we weren't hanging around—there's only so long a man can stand on a knife-edge ridge. In all, the round trip was nearly 13km, taking seven and a half hours. 📄 📷

— GERRY GALLIGAN, IRELAND

POLAR BEAR FANG

IN EARLY JULY my brother Andy and I boarded a plane to Tasiilaq on Greenland's east coast with the aim of reaching a remote fjord I had reconnoitered in 2014 with Andy Mann, and had failed to reach on three previous expeditions. I had flown to the east coast of Greenland seven times since 1998, but I had never witnessed as much sea ice as I now saw clogging the coastline. It was like a million-piece puzzle of white geometric shapes. After landing in Greenland, my brother and I planned to travel nearly 400km south by boat through this maze to reach Timmiarmiut Fjord. Already, the sea ice had damaged our first boat (which eventually sank), but that is another story.

A new friend, Bendt Josvassen, his wife, and two children agreed to try the voyage. We needed to take a second boat simply to carry enough fuel for the round trip. We expected the journey to take 45 hours. Before making a landing in our chosen fjord, Bendt sailed back and forth looking for polar bears; last time I was here, there were 11 bears in the area. We established base camp close to the shore and started carrying loads up the long valley toward an elusive tower I had dubbed Polar Bear Fang (62°50'49.30"N, 42°18'10.16"W), shotgun over my shoulder and flares and pepper spray in our pockets. We established a high camp at ca 900m, with food for at least 12 days. There was no doubt in my mind that no human had been here before.

After an easy crossing of the glacier and a bivouac at the foot of the tower, we set off. I planned to climb free, while Andy followed on jumars. My brother had only done two climbs before, both with me: a first ascent in China (2005), and another in Kyrgyzstan (2006). For the first time in Greenland, I took a satellite phone, which I felt would give him a fighting chance

The summit of Polar Bear Fang, a Year of the Ram mask, and a wealth of unknown and unclimbed East Greenland peaks. *Mike Libecki*

should something happen to me. We also took our Year of the Ram masks and a small bolt kit for emergencies.

We made one bivouac on the face and found the crux to be three pitches below the summit: a huge chimney filled with loose flakes and rotten stone-teeth. Andy finessed through the minefield without a problem, and our reward was an overhanging bombay chimney on the next pitch—one of the coolest 5.8s ever. The last technical pitch, a full 60m of clean 5.9 granite, took me to 20m of walkable, knife-edge ridge leading to the tip of the fang. My altimeter watch read 2,030m. We were on the highest summit for as far as we could see.

After a bivouac 3m from the top, we elected to forego the perils of the route we had climbed and instead descend the opposite side of the tower. After six rappels down really loose rock, we reached a ridge, followed it to a couloir, and made seven more rappels down this to the glacier. Not having brought axes or crampons, we crawled half a mile over a dangerous, crevasse-lurking glacier to our high camp, towing our bivy sacks as sleds behind us and laughing, just as we had our entire lives together. The Libecki-Libecki Route is ca 900m, 16 pitches, 5.11. Special thanks to the Mugs Stump Award and Shipton-Tilman Grant for helping to fund this expedition. 📷

– MIKE LIBECKI, *USA*

SOUTH GREENLAND / TASERMIUT FJORD

ULAMERTORSUAQ, PITERAQ, NEARLY FREE ASCENT

Silvan Schüpbach and Bernadette Zak free climbed all but 3m of the poorly protected aid route Piteraq. This climb on the ca 1,000m west face of Ulamertorsuaq (old spelling Ulamertorssuaq) was established in 2000 and previously unrepeated. From July 8–10, the two Swiss freed the route to within seven pitches of the top, finding many dangerous runouts. They retreated in wet weather, and then, from July 15–18, climbed the Geneva Diedre/War and Poetry variations to the tower's summit. On the 19th they rappelled the top seven pitches of Piteraq and freed all but a 3m pendulum across a compact wall. In all, they climbed 28 pitches on Piteraq (ca 1,200m) at 7c R/X A0, placing two bolts on variations. 📄 📷 🔍

– *INFORMATION FROM* SILVAN SCHÜPBACH, *SWITZERLAND*

SOUTH GREENLAND / CAPE FAREWELL REGION

MARLUISSAT PEAK, HAPPY MAEWAN; PAMIAGDLUK ISLAND, MICKEY PIED D'ACIER AND WARM SUMMER

Erwan Lelann and Emeline Son are on a four-year, round-the-world trip with their yacht, Maewan, and are being joined from time to time by different parties for sporting adventures. We joined them in the winter of 2014-'15 to ski in the vicinity of Aappilattoq (a.k.a. Appilatoq or Augpilagtoq), the last significant village east of Nanortalik before reaching Cape Farewell. The many surrounding rock faces motivated us to come back in summer. So, in mid-July, Charlotte Barré, Florence Pinet, Gérome Pouvreau, and I flew to Narsarsuaq, where we met the yacht and sailed to Aappilattoq.

Florence Pinet and the flared cracks of Warm Summer. *Maewan Adventure*

On our first day we climbed on a small crag near the entrance to the harbor, completing two routes, and then made a one-day ascent on Marluissat Peak, behind the village, climbing the east face via a 650m route we named Happy Maewan. The maximum difficulties were 7a. [*The steeper face on Marluissat, to the right of Happy Maewan, is home to the Polish routes Snake from Appilatoq (7a+), Three Hobbits from the Moon (6b), and Two Hobbits from the Moon (6b). See AAJ 2013 and 2014.*]

We then decided to visit Kangerdluarssuk Fjord, which penetrates deep into Pamiagdluk Island from the south. Here we climbed the 300m, south-facing Mickey Pied d'Acier (7a), dedicated to a friend, Mikael Fuselier, who had suffered a major accident in Turkey. The rock quality was high, and again we left no gear, walking from the top down to the shore.

We were attracted by a summit farther up the fjord that we dubbed Saga Africa (60°03.200'N, 44°21.468'W); it is the highest top accessible from this fjord. [*This 1,373m summit was named Twin Towers by a 2004 British expedition that was perhaps the first to climb from this fjord but did not climb this tower.*] It took three hours to reach the base of this steep wall, and we decided to climb straight up the middle via a perfect crack system. After 100m of 5 and 5+, we embarked on seven excellent pitches up to 7b+. We bolted the belays and used two sets of large cams up to number five. We needed three days (July 26, 28, and 29) to complete the 300m climb, which we named Warm Summer due to the cold temperatures we experienced.

After this we just had time to travel to Tasermiut Fjord and repeat the famous Moby Dick on Ulamertorssuaq. We found it very difficult to get an accurate topo of the route, and so we have created one of our own, which is included in the web version of this report. 🞖 🔍

– **MATHIEU MAYNADIER**, *FRANCE*

MEXICO

LA CRUZ DEL DIABLO, PUTA DE LA SIERRA

MIGUEL "MIKE" NORIEGA, of Sonora, and I had not previously met in person. With only a few messages online, we hatched a plan to head into the mountains of northeastern Sonora and establish a route in La Cruz del Diablo. This canyon has many large cliffs composed of what I believe is rhyolite. To our knowledge, climbers had not touched La Cruz, although the canyon had seen a few technical descents.

Upon arrival on December 19, we chose a line on what is likely the tallest cliff, a 200m south-facing wall at the head of La Cruz. We worked both ground-up and top-down to establish the route. On our third day of climbing, December 22, we started from the ground and freed all five pitches. We called our route Puta de la Sierra (600', 5.11).

The majority of the climb could not be protected with traditional gear, and we wanted to make a route that local Sonoran climbers would be able to climb, so we made the decision to bolt the entire route. Unfortunately, we only had 50 bolts so there are some runouts on the 5.9 and easier sections. Those solid at the 5.11 grade should feel comfortable, and a single rack of cams from 0.5 to 5 inches will supplement the bolts.

La Cruz del Diablo has a massive amount of rock with more potential for new routes. There are large chossy sections, but also many areas of immaculate steep rock. Driving across Sonora, we were impressed by the vast potential for climbing; currently, the only other development has taken place at a few nice sport crags close to the capital of Hermosillo. 🗎 📷

– KEVIN KENT, *USA*

PIEDRA BOLADA, WEST FACE, ARISTA MEXICANA

AFTER A 20-HOUR TRIP in a pickup truck with nine people and three dogs, we made it into Basaseachic very late and rested. The next day, Tiny Almada, José Vega, Oscar Cisneros (our base camp support), and I (all from Mexico) reached Valentin Grijalva's house in Cajurichi, where we prepared gear and food before taking Valentin's truck into Candameña Canyon.

Once down in the canyon, we hiked upstream and set up camp below the line we intended to climb on Piedra Bolada. [*Tiny Almada and Cecilia Buil made the first ascent of Piedra Bolada, located across from El Gigante, in April 2014. See AAJ 2015.*] However, we soon found that our intended line consisted of overhanging loose rock, so instead we chose the very aesthetic ridge on the left side of the wall. The next day, after carrying in more equipment, food, and water, José began our climb by heading up past loose rock, vegetation, and even a snake. After two days of climbing we had done three pitches, returning to the ground each night. From our high point we hoped to use portaledges the rest of the way up the wall.

The fourth pitch was maybe the hardest of the route. José began by placing a pair of pitons

Sunrise hits the team on day nine, pitch nine of Arista Mexicana, looking north toward unclimbed cliffs in Candameña Canyon. *Tiny Almada*

and then entered a face with no cracks but some pockets. He hooked his way up until the rock broke and he took an 8m fall, ripping his gear and falling onto the belay bolt. He was too beat up to keep climbing, so Tiny finished the pitch. I took the lead on the fifth pitch, and from here on we began climbing on either side of the prominent ridge to make the hauling easier.

A traverse on the sixth pitch led to a nice offwidth crack on the seventh. The hauling here was terrible. Above the offwidth, pitch eight had slabby, loose, and sketchy climbing with big runouts. This deposited us on a small needle along the ridge, and we had to rappel 12m. The next two leads ascended a loose corner and then a solid finger crack. The final pitch was difficult and confusing, up a dihedral and out a roof leading to the summit. Once on top, Oscar showed up to help us with our descent. We call our route Arista Mexicana (470m, 5.11 R A2), and we established the climb from March 29 to April 7. 📷 🔍

— DANIEL ARAIZA, MEXICO

PIEDRA BOLADA, SOUTHWEST FACE, RITÉ I´NAMÉ

FROM NOVEMBER 17–25, Israel Pérez (Mexico), Georg Pollinger (Germany), and I climbed a new route on the right side of Piedra Bolada, ascending its southwest face. Our route is a few hundred feet left of the Piedra Volada waterfall and well right of the route Rastamuri (*AAJ 2015*). I had dreamed of climbing this wall for three years, and it was easy to convince my partners.

After picking up Georg in Mexico City, we drove many hours to Chihuahua City, where we bought some supplies. We continued driving a second day, stopping at the home of Don Santiago Pérez in Huajumar. He organized five porters to carry all of our gear and supplies to a base camp below El Gigante. We departed early the next morning. On November 9 we walked to the base of the Piedra Volada waterfall, searching for a good approach. Three pitches of climbing

Rité I´namé (775m, VI 5.11+ A0) on Piedra Bolada.
The routes Rastamuri and Arista Mexicana are out
of view to the left. *Luis Carlos García Ayala*

were required to reach the base of the wall, near the pond formed below the falls, and this took us two days. Once at the wall proper, I led the first pitch of the route, while Israel and Georg hauled supplies for nine days on the wall. We bivied in sabine pines and bamboo that night, planning to launch up the wall the next day, November 17.

After three days fixing three more pitches and returning to the bivouac each night, we moved camp up the wall. The route to this point involved many changing corners. It took another three pitches of climbing before the rest of the wall unfolded. Now the days were passing and our water was slowly being depleted. By our eighth day on the wall the heat and thirst were debilitating. We did a three-pitch push that day before our last night on the wall.

On our ninth day, the final pitch finished up a big water gutter and slab. From the top we had to make one rappel into the Piedra Volada streambed. That night a big rainstorm caught us, and we spent the night all wet. The next morning we continued up the streambed. A slab to the left of a smaller waterfall connected us to the Rancho San Lorenzo—two hours' walking by easy trail. After three days of rain we returned to collect our gear from atop the waterfall (pitch 18).

The climbing was great on excellent virgin rhyolite. It was an adventure to climb it, with nine days hanging on the wall and 18 pitches in total. We climbed the route as free as possible; it relies mostly on natural gear plus some bolts where necessary. We called the route Rité I´namé (775m, VI 5.11+ A0), which roughly means "stone in the air" in the Raramurí language. 📷

– LUIS CARLOS GARCÍA AYALA, MEXICO

NUEVO LEÓN

PICO TATEWARI, SOUTH FACE, PAU

In March 2015, my wife, Marisol Monterrubio, and I opened a new route on the south face of Pico Tatewari in Parque La Huasteca. We returned in late December to try and free the route and both managed to free to the top of pitch 10, the 5.13c crux, in around four days, before rain arrived. We returned three days later and free climbed most of the route. After this, we only had two days to redpoint the two remaining hard pitches (5.13a and 5.12d) and climb the last pitch.

On the first day we free climbed the final pitch at 5.11c, finishing in the dark due to bolting time. We bivouacked on the summit. It was really cold, with thick fog and drizzle all night. We managed to make a fire with wet wood. Our intention was to free the final two hard pitches of our 14-pitch route the next day; however, when we woke it was still drizzling and too cold for the hands. We were tired, wet, and decided to just say fuck it. It was good enough.

Pau (520m) is spectacular, with smooth, technical, crimpy face climbing on perfect limestone. It's hard, clean, long, magic, and safe—a dream for many sport climbers. We equipped the route with 3/8" bolts. The route has mandatory 5.12a climbing, and it likely could be climbed in 10–12 hours by a strong team. [*Editor's note: This route climbs the center of Pico Tatewari and is located just left of Fiducia al Sentiero. It is the couple's second new route on Pico Tatewari. See AAJ 2010 for a photo showing other lines on this wall.*]

Marisol Monterrubio leading on Pau (520m), south face of Pico Tatewari. *Oriol Anglada*

— ORIOL ANGLADA, *SPAIN*

PICO INDEPENDENCIA, NORTH FACE, THE LIFE YOU CAN SAVE

ON APRIL 2, Carlos Flores and I made the first ascent of the Life You Can Save (350m, 13 pitches, 5.12d) on the north face of Pico Independencia in Parque La Huasteca. The route first required three weeks of preparation, alone on my part, which included 22 days of cleaning and eight days of bolting, both ground-up and top-down. Once the bolting was completed, I was glad to recruit the tenacious hands of Carlos Flores, a straight-talking, rope-savvy Mexican who is respected in the local community. Together, Carlos and I climbed ground-up to the summit in a single push. I was able to climb everything first go, except for the final 5.11 pitch near the top. We descended the south face via three rappels.

The route climbs a direct line up the central pillar of Pico Independencia, just right of the unrepeated route Directísima (300m, 5.9+ A3+). It has eight pitches of 5.11 or harder and is well-equipped with bolts in the harder sections. It would be possible to bivy under a roof on pitch seven, but I would recommend a hammock. [*Editor's note: Climbs on Pico Independencia have not been well-covered in past AAJs. Gareth Leah has prepared a PDF mini-guide to the routes which can be found with this report at the AAJ website.*]

— GARETH "GAZ" LEAH, *U.K.*

Carlos Flores climbing fine, white limestone on the Life You Can Save, Pico Independencia (see report on previous page). *Matthew Parent*

EL DIENTE, NORTH FACE, EL SON DEL VIENTO

FROM DECEMBER 2–21, Mexican climbers Tiny Almada, Octavio "Ocho" Aragon, and I established a new route up the north face of El Diente in Parque Nacional Cumbres de Monterrey, climbing and bolting ground-up over 18 days, fixing ropes as we went. Eventually we climbed the route from the bottom over two days, using a double portaledge and a natural ledge atop pitch seven. We were able to free every pitch except the third, which we climbed with some falls. We returned to free this pitch at 5.12d/5.13a two days after topping out. Our 15-pitch route, El Son del Viento (420m, 5.12d/5.13a), takes a more or less direct line to the summit through various limestone formations, including a number of tufa sections. We rappelled the route, using fixed draws along the way due to the route's overhanging nature. 📑 📷 🔍

— GARETH "GAZ" LEAH, *U.K.*

COLOMBIA

SIERRA NEVADA DEL COCUY AND SOUTHERN ANDES

2015–2016 SEASON SUMMARY

THE SIERRA NEVADA DEL COCUY was the area with the most new routes. The climbs below are described chronologically.

During the rainy season, on May 2, Roberto Ariano, Omar Lopez, and Luis Pardo made the first known ascent of Pico Espejo (5,173m), a distant summit in the central sector of Sierra Nevada del Cocuy. They climbed up the narrow south ridge (AD) and descended by the north ridge to the glacier below San Pablín Sur. Also during the rainy season, on July 11, Pardo and Angélica Gutiérrez made the first ascent of the south face of Cusirí (4,680m) at the southern limit of the Sierra Nevada del Cocuy. This new line was of low difficulty but very fun; they called it La Maja Acostada (300m, 5.7).

In the beginning of the normal dry season, Julio Bermudez and Santiago Zuluaga made the first complete traverse of the Ritacubas. Over five days, from

Julio Bermudez on the traverse of the Ritacuba peaks. *Santiago Zuluaga*

December 30–January 3, they climbed along this sharp 4km ridge, with altitudes over 5,000m. Along the traverse, they reached the summits of Ritacuba Norte (5,257m), Ritacuba Negro (5,300m), and Ritacuba Blanco (5,330m). For acclimatization, three days prior to the traverse, Bermudez soloed a new line up the north ridge (120m, D 75°) of Muela Peak (5,100m).

On January 9, Luis Quintero and Ricardo Rubio climbed a new route on Puntiagudo (5,019m), ascending the north face to the summit ridge: La Huella del Oso (250m, AD 60° 5.9). Later, Ricardo Rubio and Nicolas Beltran traveled to the center of Sierra Nevada del Cocuy and climbed a new route on the Portales (4,920m). This rock climb ascends the middle of the west wall; they called it El Bastón (150m, 5.10d).

Lastly, on January 19, Oscar Bonilla and Alejandro Restrepo opened a short but difficult sport route on the southeastern wall of Concavo (5,240m). The route is located just left of the route Conspiración Cósmica; they called it Conspiración Lunar (45m, 5.12d).

Beyond the Cocuy zone, the volcano Nevado del Huila, located in southwestern Colombia, went almost 12 years without access due to strong volcanic activity and incidents of violence in the region. On December 9 the team of Julio Cardona, Nelson Calcetero, Jorge Mancera, Anibal Pineda, and Carlos Valero ascended to the northern summit (5,280m) and two days later reached the highest, central summit (5,364m). 📷

– LUIS PARDO, COLOMBIA

VENEZUELA

ACOPÁN TEPUI, TIME IS THE MASTER

IN JANUARY 2015, Billy Brown, José Ramón Torre Zea, Alfredo Zubillaga, and I climbed a new route on the right side of Acopán Tepui. This part of the wall is approximately 2,000' tall. Our first trip up the wall—using a mix of free and aid—took nine days. After summiting we descended the wall and returned to the village of Yunek for a break from the jungle. Alfredo and José returned home at this point. After a few days of rest, Billy and I returned and attempted to free the route over an additional six days.

To begin our climb, we staged a convenient base camp below the wall, close to a spring and the start of our route. The first 150m circumvent massive 20' roofs by trending left for five pitches. The climbing in this initial section starts on potato chip–like patina but is mostly vertical 5.11 on solid, dark red, marbled quartzite. We reached our first wall bivy atop pitch five, where there is a nice ledge.

The next pitches dodge the neighboring route Purgatory (VI 5.12+, Albert-Calderón-Glowacz-Heuber, 2007), taking an independent line; however, we did utilize a few of Purgatory's bolted belay anchors. Pitch seven sews a straight line up a dripping, water-colored face comprised of yellow, orange, and purple rock. Small cams in horizontal cracks protect technical climbing up clean crimps (5.12b). Atop pitch eight, a cave in the wall provided a perfect roost for our second camp. By this point, we'd placed three bolts and bent one drill bit in the bulletproof rock.

Billy Brown on the water-colored face of pitch seven (5.12b) of Time Is the Master. *Eric Bissell*

Above our eighth pitch, we continued up ever-steepening rock. (The route Purgatory travels hard left at this point.) The quality of the rock pinnacled on our 10th pitch (5.12c/d) and then plummeted into choss—it appeared to be a mixture of salt and sand. Our first venture up pitch 11 was terrifying—the potentially leg-breaking aid pitch combined thin nailing and hooking on sheets of exfoliating rock, with high-consequence ledges. The entire route would have been a bust if we couldn't find a way through this band of choss. After two days of elaborate top-roping, we found the line we were looking for. The free climbing on pitches 11 and 12 orbits rightward and up adventurous but quality 5.11 corners. The top of pitch 12 trends back left toward the headwall, where we made our third wall bivy.

When we first landed in the fields outside Yunek we could see a smooth shield high on the wall from miles away. Pitches 13 through 16 tackle this sustained, gently overhanging headwall in short pitches totaling 80m. Here, the rock is hard and granite-like, with the texture of fine sugar and cheetah-skin patterns. We used up our last eight bolts on this section and spent multiple days figuring out the inspiring climbing.

A whiteout-like mist engulfed Billy and me as we sussed out the moves on the crux pitch. In jungle-stained shirts and with malnourished muscles, we laughed at the ridiculousness of redpoint attempts thousands of miles from home and 1,500' above the Gran Sabana. Unfortunately, an 8' span between horizontal cracks eventually shut us down (5.13b A0). We climbed one more bouldery pitch above this (5.12c), and, having barely survived the upper 400' of vertical jungle-pulling to the summit our first time up the wall, we happily descended from here to begin the long journey home to California. We called our route Time Is the Master (20 pitches, 5.13b A0). 📷 🔍

— ERIC BISSELL, *USA*

MORURCO, SOUTHWEST FACE, NITROGLYCERIN

ON MAY 1, Gonzalo Espinosa and I drove to the upper highlands below Cotopaxi's south face. From here we targeted our objective, Morurco (4,880m), a rarely climbed peak just south of Cotopaxi (5,897m). This peak was first climbed in 1971, utilizing a long approach and siege-style climbing. Its walls are steep, with a combination of loose rock, verglas, and mud.

Gonzalo and I started our approach at 3 a.m. on May 2 and reached the peak at first light. A 60m scramble brought us to a prominent gash on the vertical and unclimbed southwest face. For four hours we climbed meticulously, with very committing moves on both pure rock and mixed terrain. We were able to place only four pieces of protection and one untrustworthy anchor before reaching the summit snow slopes: Nitroglycerin (200m, 5.9 R/X M4). Summit glory came with a spectacular view of Cotopaxi from the tallest balcony in Ecuador. We descended the normal route on the neighboring southeast side. ☰ ◙

– FELIPE PROAÑO, *ECUADOR*

BRAZIL

PEDRA RISCADA, NORTHEAST FACE, VIAJE DE CRISTAL

PEDRA RISCADA is a granite dome in the state of Minas Gerais, located in southeast Brazil. In July, Argentine climbers Ignacio Elorza, Horacio Gratton, María José Moisés, and Cintia Percivati established a new route on this wall, just left of Place of Happiness (*AAJ 2010*); it shares some terrain with that route at the beginning and end, but 11 of the 19 pitches are new. They summited on July 23 after spending 12 days on the wall with portaledges, calling their route Viaje de Cristal (900m, 8a). The route is mostly bolted but requires a standard rack. ◙

– MARCELO SCANU, *ARGENTINA*

[Photo] María José Moisés climbing a thin slab on Viaje de Cristal (900m, 8a). *Noel Martinez de Aguirre*

Simon Gietl leading on Chappie (600m, 7b+),
La Esfinge. *Frank Kretschmann*

PERU

LA ESFINGE, SOUTHEAST FACE, CHAPPIE

ROGER SCHÄLI AND SIMON GIETL climbed a new route on La Esfinge (5,325m) in the Paron Valley in early July. Chappie (600m, 7b+) is situated on the upper right (shorter) side of the southeast face, between the routes Intuition (*AAJ 2001*) and Dion's Dihedral (*AAJ 2001*). The route climbs a prominent thin crack system, with bolts at the belays. It took the duo five days to complete; they suggest future ascents could be done in one to two days with a standard rack. 🔾

— *INFORMATION FROM* SIMON GIETL *AND* ROGER SCHÄLI, *SWITZERLAND*

CAYESH, WEST FACE, CHILEAN ROUTE

IN JULY, Chilean climbers Jimmy Mora and Francisco Rojas climbed a partial new route on the west face of Cayesh (5,720m). The duo began on July 18 from the Quebrada Quilcayhuanca. On July 20 the climbers spent the day at a high camp scoping the wall, which was in excellent condition. They saw one nearly complete line of ice rising to the left across the face, beginning on the Slo-Am Route (House-Prezelj, *AAJ 2006*) and eventually trending up and slightly right to finish on the upper portion of the British Route (Gore-Moore, *AAJ 1987*), on the upper left (northwest) part of the wall and summit ridge. Their route was made possible in part due to the absence of a large, hanging serac that had fallen off the wall.

Leading the initial part of the Slo-Am Route in the early morning, before heading into new terrain on Cayesh's west face. *Jimmy Mora / Francisco Rojas*

On July 21, at 4 a.m., Mora and Rojas left their camp. By 6 a.m. they had climbed the first "real" pitch, after ascending two initial pitches on snow. These first technical pitches ascend the lower part of a major couloir and dihedral system in the center of the west face; to this point the route is same as the Slo-Am Route. Above this, they headed left across a ramp into mostly new terrain, where three pitches of ice and mixed climbing brought them to a steep wall of bad ice. [*It's possible one pitch in this section shared terrain with the 1986 British Route, and this is also where the route crosses the path of the Amow-Fowler 1988 route (AAJ 1989).*] They climbed this ice directly, which was very exposed and difficult;

two pitches brought them to a rock wall. Here, they traversed hard left across ice and then back right across ice and mixed terrain, reaching a belay on the left margin of the face below large cornices. At this point, Mora and Rojas continued climbing up and somewhat right on mixed terrain to reach another ice wall in good condition. Around noon, they found a small ledge where they could sit, drink tea, and rest. Above this, they climbed two pitches up very steep snow, ascending through cornices to reach the summit ridge. They continued up the ridge for three pitches through dangerous cornices, using body belays, and reached the summit after 23 hours of climbing, at approximately 3 a.m. on July 22.

The climbers waited in a snow cave on the summit for dawn and then descended in the vicinity of the German and Czech routes (*AAJ 1989*) on the center-right side of the west face. The Chilean Route (MD+ WI5 M6 70°) had about 16 pitches; approximately half of these were on previously unclimbed terrain. 📷 🔍

— SERGIO RAMÍREZ CARRASCAL, *PERU*

Tomas Franchini heads up steep rock on La Divina Providencia. *Silvestro Franchini*

JANGYARAJU I, NORTH FACE

ON MAY 25, Basque climbers Kepa Berasategi and Odei Girado climbed the north face of Jangyaraju I (5,675m). They chose a weakness left of a prominent prow and climbed mostly good granite for 250m (6a+ A2). Atop the rock face they climbed 400m of lower-angle snow, ice, and mixed terrain (60° M5) to the summit. They descended the same day, rappelling back to the glacier. They named their probable new route Libre (650m, MD+). 📄 📷 🔍

— SEVI BOHORQUEZ, *PERU*

NEVADO CHURUP, SOUTHWEST FACE, LA DIVINA PROVIDENCIA

ON JUNE 2, my brother Silvestro Franchini and I climbed a route on the rocky right side of the southwest face of Nevado Churup (5,495m, a.k.a. Tsurup), directly in line with the peak's west shoulder and right of the typical snow/ice route on the south face. The approach took one hour from camp at Laguna Churup (ca 4,550m), with 75° slopes to reach the wall. It took us nine hours to climb to the top of the wall and west shoulder. There was good rock in the lower part and rotten rock up top. We abseiled down the southwest face's most commonly used descent route (Fear-Lahr-Malotoux-Ridgeway, *AAJ 1973*), which had rock anchors in place. We called our route La Divina Providencia (650m, M7 80°). 📷 🔍

— TOMAS FRANCHINI, *ITALY*

JIRISHANCA CHICO, NORTHEAST FACE, VIA DEI RAGNI

On August 9, Silvano Arrigoni and I climbed a new route on the icy northeast face of Jirishanca Chico, reaching a subsummit on its west shoulder. Our route Via Dei Ragni (400m, D+ 90°) climbs the right margin of this face and is mostly 65–70° with a short stretch of vertical climbing. We climbed just right of the Iwatani-Oestemer 1967 route, which ascends the central part of this face through seracs. [*Editor's note: The 1967 route is incorrectly noted as being on the northwest aspect in various publications; it clearly faces northeast.*] After reaching the subsummit on the west shoulder of the main Jirishanca Chico, our route connects with the main peak's west ridge (Albrecht-Bloss-Buncsack-Jordan-Wels-Wolf, *AAJ 1962*), which we climbed short of the summit due to poor conditions and witnessing an avalanche. Retracing our steps from the ridge, we descended our line of ascent. 📷

— LORENZO FESTORAZZI, *ITALY*

NEVADO SULLCÓN AND NEVADO PACA, VARIATIONS

In late May and early June, Eleazar Blass, Quique Apolinario Villafán (both Peru), and Frank Nederhand (USA) established variations to existing routes on Nevado Sullcón (5,650m) and Nevado Paca (5,600m) in the Cordillera Central. Photos and more info about these climbs and the Cordillera Central can be found in a PDF trip report at the AAJ website. 📄 📷 🔍

— ERIK RIEGER, *WITH INFORMATION FROM* FRANK NEDERHAND, *USA*

NEVADO PUMAHUANCA, SOUTH FACE

Nevado Pumahuanca (5,350m) is a quite accessible peak located between Halancoma and Chicón; however, it is a minor peak in the Cordillera Urubamba and does not have big pull as an objective. In November 2013, Jorge "Coqui" Gálvez and I tried Pumahuanca by the eastern ridge that extends from Nevado Capacsaya (5,044m). We found the ridge too broken by rock towers. We also saw that the peak could be more easily approached from the south or northeast side.

On April 23, 2015, Duncan McDaniel and I left Cusco to meet with Coqui at his home outside Urubamba. The three of us went to Yanahuara by car and then hiked up the valley to Pumahuanca and a bivy at about 5,050m. During the night it snowed lightly and became windy. Early the next morning we climbed good snow (45–60°), traversing up and right across Nevado Pumahuanca's south face. After arriving at a snow ridge, we followed it for the final 50m of altitude gain to the summit. We began our descent at 6:15 a.m. and were back in Cusco by late afternoon. Our route is 300m, PD+. 📄 📷

— NATHAN HEALD, *PERU*

NEVADO HUAYNA AUSANGATE, NEW ROUTE

Huayna Ausangate is the name used for two different peaks on the western side of the Cordillera Vilcanota. One of them is a subpeak of Nevado Ausangate that is located two miles west of the main summit, along its west ridge, and has a height of 5,700m. I believe this subpeak was first reached in 1953 during the main peak's first ascent (*AAJ 1954*). Carlos Buhler climbed a direct route up the west face in 1977. There have been a few other ascents, the most recent in June 2015 by local guide Daniel Chillihuani and two Swiss clients.

The other Huayna Ausangate is a pointy, prominent summit at the western end of the Colque Cruz massif, with a height of about 5,600m. Although not as high as its neighbors, it is steeper on all sides, and mixed climbing is required to reach the top. There are only a few references to this peak in past expedition accounts, and I believe it had been climbed three times previously. The first was by Fritz Mörz, Heinz Steinmetz, Jürgen Wellenkamp, and Heinrich Harrer in 1953, during the trip on which they made the first ascents of Ausangate, Cayangate, Colque Cruz, Jampa I and II, and Surimani. Huayna Ausangate was covered with more ice then, quite noticeable when you compare their photo with one I took at almost the same spot on the west ridge. The second ascent came in 1971 when the French Alpine Club was active in the area; Léon Carron and Annik Wates climbed it from a camp on the northwest side (*AAJ 1972*). In 1985 the Italian Alpine Club made a handful of ascents from the north side of the Colque Cruz chain. Their report notes that Italo Bazzani and Livio Lanari climbed "extremely steep ice via the north face" of Huayna Ausangate to establish a new route (*AAJ 1987*).

During my attempts to climb the south face of Colque Cruz in 2014, the sight of Huayna Ausangate raised interest every time. The south face looked quite dangerous low down due to a rock wall toped by a large serac that would have to passed to reach the upper glacier. I figured an easier approach would be from the north.

On September 27, Alexis Trudel (Canada) and I left Cusco and took the bus to Tinki, where we met Luis Crispin (Peru) and bought the last supplies for the trip. A taxi took us up toward Perhuayani Pass on the interoceanic highway, and we got out at the community of Yanacancha. Luis' father, Alejandro, and brother Macario were waiting for us with their horses near a restaurant on the roadside. After three hours we arrived at a base camp on the northwest side of Huayna Ausangate at ca 4,900m, in a flat moraine next to a clear lagoon the size of a football field. Here, we found the circular stone camps of one of the previous expeditions.

On the 28th, Alexis, Luis, and I took our climbing gear up a moraine ridge to the icefall coming down from the northwest side of the peak, which seemed to be the easiest access. We explored a way through the crevasses, so we could make quick work of it the next day, and left our equipment cached. We departed camp at 1 a.m. on September 29, and after weaving around and jumping a few crevasses we reached the north side of the west ridge, where we climbed 300m of easy mixed. We gained the west ridge at about the exact spot where the Austrians had taken their photo in 1953. It was light outside by now, but we were in the shadow of the mountain and there was still 300m of climbing on the summit pyramid to overcome.

Alexis decided to stay on the ridge and wait for us due to an altitude headache. With many cornices on the ridge, we made a short rappel onto its south side. Luis led first, heading up 60m of poor snow to reach a rock wall. From there we alternated 30m pitches of mixed climbing. The angle was about 70°, with good rock but bad ice and six inches of loose snow.

The Colque Cruz chain from the west, showing: (A) Huayna Ausangate. (B) Huayna Alpamayo. (C) Garache. (D) Colque Cruz I. (E) Colque Cruz V. (F) Colque Cruz VI. *Nathan Heald*

It took us five pitches to top out. The clouds had come up from the Amazon, but there was still very good visibility, and Laguna Singrenacocha looked surreal below. We stayed for half an hour. Around 10 a.m. I made a V-thread in the summit ice and we began rappelling down the southwest face, not wanting to go down the ascent route because of falling rock. Near a bergschrund, Luis and I struggled back up the ridge to meet Alexis. As we downclimbed to the icefall it started snowing hard, and we lost our way a few times. After jumping a few icy crevasses we made it out to the moraine and down to the tent by 4 p.m. Our route up the north face, west ridge, and south face is 600m, D AI3 M4. [image]

– NATHAN HEALD, *PERU*

NEVADO CAYANGATE IV, WEST FACE

THE CAYANGATE MASSIF lies 10km northwest of Ausangate in the Vilcanota Range, southeast of Cusco. This chain of five high peaks is aligned and numbered I–V, north to south, comprising a 4.5km-long ridge. The history of these peaks is confusing, due to a few peaks being known by other names. After analyzing the *Andes of Southern Peru* by Piero Ghiglione (1950), I believe the first of the peaks to be climbed was the northernmost, by its northeast buttress—Piero called the peak Cayangate III or Verena. Subsequent expeditions called this peak Cayangate I; it has an altitude of about 6,000m.

In 1953 a German-Austrian team led by Heinrich Harrer made first ascents of many of the big peaks on the western side of the Vilcanota. They first climbed Ausangate, then Colque Cruz, and then Cayangate IV (ca 6,100m), the highest of the Cayangate group. They climbed the northwest icefall to a bivouac at the col between Cayangate III and IV, and then finished on the northeast face to the summit (*Alpine Journal 1955*). The Japanese expedition of 1962 made first ascents of Cayangates II, III, and a subpeak of Cayangate I they called Pico de Victor. (I believe this subpeak was climbed and called Horrorhorn by subsequent expeditions.) It seems the Japanese climbed the northwest sides of these peaks (*AAJ 1962*). The southernmost, and last, peak to be climbed was Cayangate V, in 1966. The German Alpine Club named it

The west face of Cayangate IV, showing the line of ascent (900m, D+ WI3). *Nathan Heald*

Chimbaya, which is also the name of a couple of remote peaks in the Vilcanota (*AAJ 1967*). Even more confusing, the Peruvian IGN map has this peak labeled as Colque Cruz, while the actual Colque Cruz chain is to the north [*see previous report*].

Subsequent ascents of the Cayangate peaks have been few and far between. I will only note those going to the highest summit, Cayangate IV, which is also labeled Collpa Ananta on the Peruvian IGN map. In 1972 a French team made it to within 200 yards of the summit but had to turn back because of an arriving storm. Their report notes this was a new route; however, it appears they more or less followed the line of the 1953 first ascent (*AAJ 1972*). In 1985 four Polish climbers reached the summit by a new route, the technical rock buttress to the right of the northwest icefall. They bivouacked at the col between Cayangate III and IV, just like the Austrians and French before them. The most recent ascent, and the only one on the eastern side of the mountain, was completed in 2006 by three Americans: Chris Alstrin, Andrew Frost, and Mark Hesse. They climbed the technically difficult eastern ridge (about 1,000m of rocky terrain) and finished on the north face to make the third ascent to the summit (*AAJ 2007*).

I have long wondered about the imposing west face of Cayangate IV, and my compadre Luis Crispin and I decided to try it. We invited Caleb Johnson, who was working for the summer in Cusco. We left Cusco on April 18 and met Luis and his younger brother Adan in the village of Marampaki at about 1 p.m. The hike to base camp up the moraine south of Laguna Armacocha took us a few hours with horses. On the 19th we followed the moraine ridge on the west side of the west face icefall. It was easier than I anticipated, and we made good time to the end of the moraine, where it terminates below the shadow of the west ridge. We took in the face and made camp early and comfortably (ca 5,110m).

We left camp at about midnight, and early season gave us the advantage of snow-covered crevasses. We followed the most direct line up the west face, where there was plenty of funneled avalanche debris from the toppling seracs higher up. At the top of the funnel, midway up, the face steepened next to a serac barrier on our left. Here, I led a pitch of WI3 to bring us onto the clean snow slopes above. Dawn was just breaking, so we stopped to rest a moment and take in the views. Luis led the rest of the wall while Caleb and I simul-seconded up 60–70° snow and ice. Being well acclimated (he lives at 4,300m), Luis made quick work of the trail breaking and brought us up a final 70° snow runnel directly to the summit. It was 11:20 a.m., the clouds had rolled in from the jungle, but there was no wind and it remained pleasant. I took a GPS reading of 6,120m on the summit. Our route was 900m, D+ WI3.

We decided to descend a different route due to the warm day and fear of triggering an avalanche on the slopes we'd just climbed. We downclimbed easier slopes on the upper mountain, to the climber's right of our route—meanwhile it started snowing and reduced visibility. After finding a serac band we debated where to rappel. At this point a river of snow started flowing down on us from above. Nervous, I found a passage through a serac and we rappelled from a V-thread into a rockfall-prone chute where the seracs meet the west ridge. After one more V-thread rappel down the chute we were out of the difficulties. We reached camp by dusk and had just enough energy to get some food down before darkness arrived. Luis, who is always indefatigable, went down to base camp with some equipment and to meet his brother. We all hiked out to Marampaki the next day. 📷

– NATHAN HEALD, *PERU*

CORDILLERA VILCABAMBA

NEVADO PALQAY, WEST BUTTRESS

Nevado Palqay (5,422m) is a peak to the northeast of Salcantay. To my knowledge, it was unclimbed. On May 11, Edwin Espinoza (Peru), Waldemar Niclevicz (Brazil), and I climbed the west buttress to its main summit. Our route is 500m, D. 📄 📷

– NATHAN HEALD, *PERU*

The west side of Nevado Palqay, showing the line of ascent (500m, D). *Nathan Heald*

TUCARHUAY'S SOUTH FACE

BY NATHAN HEALD

In 2013, Edwin Espinoza and I climbed the lower east summit (5,700m) of Nevado Tucarhuay (5,943m GPS). The main, western summit remained a challenge to me. Lionel Terray called this peak Pico Soray, and the locals call it Humantay, but on the Peruvian IGN map it is labeled Tucarhuay. [*See AAJ 2014 for futher clarification and photos of previously climbed routes.*] The climbing history on this peak is short, with Terray and party making the first ascent in 1956 up the north side, and with its last known ascent by a Japanese expedition in 1968 via its south ridge (*AAJ 1957 and 1969*). The beautiful, triangular west face was first attempted by a Japanese team in 1980; it still awaits its first route (*AAJ 1981*). At the foot of the peak's south face is a glacial lagoon that tourists visit; a local rancher named Antonio Huari told me he once had to recover the bodies of two climbers who had perished attempting this face.

After acclimatizing on the normal routes up Pumahuanca (5,350m) and Cerro Soray (5,428m), Duncan McDaniel and I decided to try the south face of Tucarhuay. We spent the night of April 28 in Soray Pampa, having left a gear cache in the meadow west of the lagoon. On the 29th we hiked up to our cache and then gained 600m up to a camp on some ledges below the south ridge (ca 4,800m). At 11 p.m. on the same day we set out for the summit with a stove but no bivy gear. We easily gained the glacier below the icefall formed by the south ridge, but had to navigate immense seracs. Above the seracs, we traversed west underneath the south face, looking for runnels that would lead directly to the summit. We alternated leads up 30m pitches of 80–90° ice. At one point the angle lessened to 70° for a couple of pitches of mixed climbing.

It began snowing in the afternoon, and the rapid accumulation became dangerous. I could see what lay ahead: mixed climbing with loose snow covering it all, topped by hanging cornices that stretched up to the summit. We decided to look for a hole under one of the cornices to bivy and found a perfect, rocky roof to protect us. We laid out our ropes and gear on the icy floor and prepared tea while watching the last golden rays fade from the ancient Inca heartland. The long night was clear, with lights shining from towns in the valleys below. I would awake at times and look at them, almost forgetting about the shivering cold at 5,800m. As morning came on May 1 we began to stir into action. The sun would not touch us here.

At 6:45 a.m. we left the ledge, mixed climbing up runnels covered by fresh, loose snow. Two pitches later, we reached a large, hanging cornice. Dangerous simul-climbing followed over loose snow, brittle ice, and airy cornices—it felt like I was standing on clouds. The lip onto the final summit block was overhanging rime, in which I had to cut a gap to pull myself over. I could see the final summit 30m higher. As I got to the top, the cloud level was rising all around. The summit was about the size of a volleyball, so I straddled the ridge just below it. I was out of protection. Duncan fell as he pulled over the lip onto the summit block, but I held it. It took three hours to climb the final 150m. It was 9:45 a.m. and the GPS read 5,943m.

I made a V-thread below the summit and we made 11 rappels. On the last rappel we core-shot a rope, and on the final downclimb a bus-size block of ice fell from a serac. Duncan went ahead, and I finally made it to the tent about 7 p.m.

SUMMARY: *South Face Direct (1,000m, TD+ AI4) on Nevado Tucarhuay (5,943m), Cordillera Vilcabamba, by Nathan Heald (Peru) and Duncan McDaniel (USA), April 30–May 1, 2015.* 📷

[Top] Duncan McDaniel at a hanging ice belay on the south face of Nevado Tucarhuay. *Nathan Heald*
[Bottom] The South Face Direct on Nevado Tucarhuay. *Nathan Heald*

BOLIVIA

KASIRI-CALZADA MASSIF, VARIOUS ASCENTS

AFTER ACCLIMATIZING in the Condoriri region, Hugh Alexander, Nick Berry, John da Silva, Rafal Malczyk, Ken Mulvany, Lili Mulvany, Peter Yuen, and I (leader) made the five-hour drive from La Paz to a camp by a series of small lagunas on the 5,070m (GPS) col between Calzada and Kasiri. Mining activity in the area has led to marked improvements to the rough road crossing the Kasiri-Calzada pass, and with care it is now drivable using 4WD vehicles. The Kasiri-Calzada area is rarely visited, and there is little record of the climbing achieved from the col, although it is unlikely that any of the neighboring summits and tops have been left untrodden. Since access from both sides of the col is so much easier nowadays, we considered it prudent to hire a camp

Looking south from Peak 5,694m, across the Kasiri-Calzada pass. (A) Unnamed Peak 5,649m. (B) Main summit of the Calzada group (Calzada I, 5,843m), and behind it part of the Chearoco massif. (C) "Calzada West," 5,634m. (1) Approach and ascent to snow dome on the northeast ridge of "Calzada West," climbed by Ken and Lili Mulvany. (2) North-northwest ridge, climbed to ca 50m of the summit. (3) Northwest face, climbed by the Mulvanys. *Derek Buckle*

guard for the whole of our stay. We saw several mule trains crossing the pass and, surprisingly, met one vehicle close to the col a little after 4 a.m., just as we started out on one of the climbs. One can only guess which of the two was more taken aback by the encounter.

On June 11, Ken and Lili completed a more or less direct route on the west face of Calzada (5,634m, AD+). They returned the same way, rappelling the steeper sections. John, Rafal, and I attempted the obvious north-northwest ridge (AD UIAA III). This attempt failed ca 50m short of the rocky summit, when a steep, uncompromising rock step barred further progress.

After an exploratory day, John, Nick, Rafal, and I climbed directly up the southeast face of Peak 5,662m (map height; a southeastern outlier of the Kasiri group), until it was possible to cut right to the south-southeast ridge. Continuing along the ridge, we reached a foresummit (5,662m GPS, AD). From there a short traverse led to a second top, Peak 5,694m (GPS), which was separated from the main Kasiri massif by a steep and substantial drop. We returned the same way.

On the 15th, having set sights on an interesting snow dome on the northeast ridge of Calzada, Ken and Lili traversed the boulderfield below Calzada to reach the north-northwest ridge, crossed it, and dropped onto the northern glacier, which they crossed to a steep, slanting couloir (80° max) that gave access to Calzada's northeast ridge. From here they climbed up the northeast ridge as far as the snow dome (AD+/D). Meanwhile, Nick, John, and I attempted the long northeast ridge of Kasiri Chico (5,542m), which we accessed via a steep snow gully rising from the valley running southeast from the ridge. Unsurprisingly, this was an unconsolidated shale ridge, but without technical difficulty until around one-third of the way up, when a steep tower at ca 5,300m blocked safe progress. 📷

— DEREK BUCKLE, *U.K.*

Editor's note: Calzada is perhaps best described as a massif rather than a single peak, and, in common with a number of mountain groups in Bolivia, it has an enigmatic mountaineering history. The Calzada generally designated on maps is perhaps better called Calzada West (5,634m, as recorded by the 2015 British expedition). It is not the mountain referred to as Calzada I by Roland Hunter's British expedition, which made the first ascent in 1962. This higher peak, perhaps also known as Calzada Grande, has a map height of 5,843m and was surveyed in 1962 at 5,874m. Hunter's expedition also climbed four subsidiary summits of the Calzada group.

CONDORIRI MASSIF, COMPLETE TRAVERSE

In July, Juvenal and Sergio Condori made a 44-hour, alpine-style traverse of the Condoriri Massif. Starting with the summit of Aguja Negra, they continued over Ilusión, Ilusioncita, Pirámide Blanca, Pico Tarija, Huallomen (Wyoming), Ala Derecha, Cabeza del Cóndor, and Ala Izquierda. This amounts to a horizontal distance of more than 14km and total altitude gain of ca 2,000m.

At 3:30 a.m. on July 9, the two brothers left base camp on the shores of Lake Chiarkhota (4,600m), and three hours later, at sunrise, reached the summit of Aguja Negra. They immediately started their descent toward Ilusión, but the rock was so poor they were forced to place a bolt in order to anchor a 50m rappel. Poor rock continued all the way to Pico Tarija. Fifteen minutes before reaching the summit of Wyoming, the sun set and the two backtracked to find a bivouac site on rock. They used the ropes as mattresses, put their feet inside

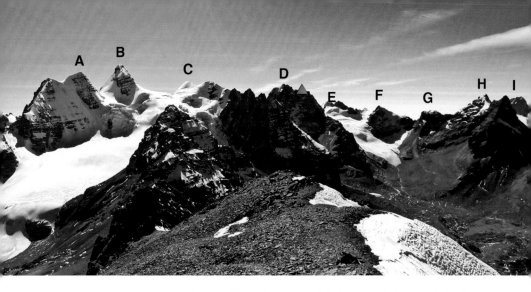

Looking northeast at the Condoriri Massif from Pico Austria. (A) Ala Izquierda (5,532m). (B) Cabeza del Cóndor (5,648m). (C) Ala Derecha (5,482m). (D) Huallomen (Wyoming, 5,463m, with red triangle marking bivouac site. (E) Pico Tarija (5,320m; the two pointed summits behind this are Pequeño Alpamayo (left) and Innominado). (F) Pirámide Blanca (5,230m). (G) Ilusioncita (5,150m). (H) Ilusión (5,330m). (I) Aguja Negra (5,290m). In July the Condori brothers traversed all these peaks, from right to left, in a 44-hour round trip from base camp. *Sergio Condori*

rucksacks, and covered themselves with a bivouac blanket. By 8 p.m. the temperature had fallen dramatically, and at 2 a.m. Sergio began to show signs of hypothermia, shivering, losing consciousness, and hallucinating. Juvenal was in better shape and kept his brother moving, and both were relieved to see the sunrise. They reached the top of Wyoming at 7:30 a.m. This summit gives the best view of the entire traverse.

They now began to descend unknown terrain, as they had been unable to find any information of a previous crossing of the ridge between Wyoming and Ala Derecha. The rock was loose and they made three rappels: the first of 20m from a length of rope wrapped around a pile of loose blocks; the second of 30m from a piton backed up with a small jammed knot; and a third of 15m, which led to the ridge leading up toward Ala Derecha. Tired, they reached this summit at 3:30 p.m., and two hours later the top of Cabeza del Cóndor. Now close to their goal, they descended a gully and then added more clothes for their ascent to Ala Izquierda. The pair climbed three technical mixed pitches by headlamp before reaching the summit at 8 p.m. They descended the southwest ridge, made a 30m rappel to the glacier, and after a shortcut across the pass in front of Pico Austria, reached base camp, exhausted but happy, at 11:15 p.m. They have named their difficult and often precarious traverse Alcanzando el Cielo sin Morir, and suggested a grade of ED2 6a AI5+ M4.

– SERGIO CONDORI, *TRANSLATED AND SUMMARIZED BY ALEXANDER VON UNGERN, BOLIVIA*

Editor's note: There is some confusion over the left (Izquierda) and right (Derecha) "wings" (Alas) of the Condor. Most reports, including those in past AAJs, name the peak to the left (west) of the condor's "head" (Cabeza), as seen from the south, as Ala Izquierda. We have adopted this convention here. However, Sergio Condori, in the original version of this report, takes the understandable view that the wings should be named from the perspective of the Condor itself, and thus calls the wing to the west Derecha.

CONDORIRI GROUP, ALA IZQUIERDA, SOUTH FACE, VARIATION

Pacifico Machaca and Alexander von Ungern climbed a partial new line on the south face of Ala Izquierda, starting on the 50–60° snow/ice slope of the Direct Route, then angling right toward the rocky section forming the right side of the face. They climbed this via a narrow gully line with four 60–70m pitches (M3+ and WI3).

— *INFORMATION FROM* ALEXANDER VON UNGERN, *BOLIVIA*

CABEZA DEL CÓNDOR, EAST FACE, DANZA DE CÓNDORES

On July 15, Juvenal and Sergio Condori left Condoriri base camp at 3 a.m., and after ascending the glacier toward Pequeño Alpamayo, crossed the watershed between Pico Tarija and Wyoming (a.k.a. Huallomen), descended the far side, and traversed beneath the northern flanks of Wyoming. Escaping from the bottom of the glacier on the northern flank of the watershed proved more difficult than expected, and involved careful downclimbing of loose rock.

The brothers reached the base of the east face of Cabeza del Cóndor (5,648m) at 9 a.m. and found the conditions worse than expected. They had hoped to simul-climb sections of the central line of weakness, but immediately found themselves belaying 60m pitches. Loose rock and stonefall proved a problem, and they encountered sections of ice up to 80°. In strong

Sergio Condori descending the normal route (southwest ridge) of Cabeza del Cóndor, with the north face of Ala Izquierda behind. *Juvenal Condori*

wind they reached the summit ridge at 3:30 p.m. Hurrying to keep warm, they arrived at the top an hour later. They descended to base camp by the normal route along the southwest ridge. The route was named Danza de Cóndores (700m, TD AI5).

[*Editor's note: There are rumors this remote face might have been climbed by Poles, but the line is unknown. There also are several reports of parties climbing new routes on the "east face," but it seems likely they refer to the much shorter southeast face*].

— SERGIO CONDORI,
TRANSLATED BY ALEXANDER VON UNGERN, BOLIVIA

The ca 700m east face of Cabeza del Cóndor with the line of Danza de Cóndores. The descent along the southwest ridge followed the lefthand skyline, above the much shorter southeast face, as far as the small notch, then continued down a short couloir to the hanging glacier. *Sergio Condori*

CONDORIRI GROUP, INNOMINADO (ALPAMAYO NEGRO), SOUTHWEST RIDGE DIRECT

AFTER THEIR PARTIAL new route on the south face of Illimani (*see page 219*), Marco Farina and Marco Majori discussed other climbing options with Aldo Riveros, a local mountain guide, and the three hatched a plan to attempt a little-visited mountain in the Condoriri group. The question was how to reach it. As the peak lies northeast of the popular Pequeño Alpamayo (5,410m), Riveros suggested the most convenient access would be over the top of this mountain.

Together with Riveros, the Italians left Condoriri base camp at 3 a.m. on June 20 and climbed the normal route up Pequeño Alpamayo in three hours. From here they descended the northeast ridge of the Pequeño (IV, with a couple of 50° snowfields) to reach the col, and then continued up the southwest ridge of the peak they called Alpamayo Negro, but which is better known as Innominado. The three climbed more or less directly up the ridge, which was not trivial and featured mixed climbing on often poor rock, especially in the upper section. On the summit they found an ancient tin can. They retraced their steps and returned to base camp in a round trip of 14 hours. The height quoted is 5,428m, though the peak is of similar altitude to (or lower than) Pequeño Alpamayo. The three have named the route Arista de Cice (250m from the col, 5c WI3 M4).

This peak was called Innomindo by the first ascensionists, a Slovenian expedition that made 10 first ascents in the Condoriri region during 1964. After first crossing Pequeño Alpamayo, the Slovenians reached the col beneath Innominado. Although their expedition report is not clear, it appears they traversed the face left of the southwest ridge to reach a couloir that leads easily toward the summit, probably finishing up the final section of the north-northwest ridge.

— LINDSAY GRIFFIN, *WITH INFORMATION FROM MARCO FARINA, ITALY*

PICO TRIANGULAR, SOUTH FACE, THANKS FOR COMING

ON SEPTEMBER 29, Gregg Beisly and I completed an unclimbed gully on the south face of Pico Triangular (5,600m), topping out more or less at the summit. Our route was left of the 2011 Baker-Beisly line called Baked. We climbed unroped up the first 160m of steep, narrow gully at WI3. As the gully narrowed, we broke out right and roped up for two mixed pitches (M4) before reaching the summit. To descend, we traversed along the south flank of Pico Italia and then connected

Marco Farina on steep mixed ground in the first section of Innominado's southwest ridge. *Marco Majori*

the gully on that peak's normal route with the lower part of the 1998 Monasterio Route on its south face. We rappelled only once (35m), leaving a piton and sling, and downclimbed the rest, following a straight line toward our parked car.

We named our new route Thanks for Coming (ca 500m, TD-), as this was the last route Gregg climbed in Bolivia after six years of residence, before moving back to New Zealand. It also reflected our pleasant surprise in discovering that this line, one of the last to be climbed on the south face, was among the best.

— ALEXANDER VON UNGERN, *BOLIVIA*

PICO MILLUNI, CLOUDY CONDORS

ON MAY 29, Pacifico Machaca (Bolivia) and I climbed what we think is a new line on the southwest face of the Pico Milluni ridgeline. After a two-hour approach, including a nasty boulderfield and 50° snow slope, we climbed two pitches of steep snow with short sections of vertical ice. The third pitch was mixed. As I was rather new to this discipline at the time, I took off my crampons, stowed my ice axes, and climbed 12m of vertical granite (5c/6a) in my mountaineering boots. This turned out to be the crux of the route. We then climbed one more steep pitch on snow before reaching the crest of a ridge that led to a top just east of and 10–15m lower than the central summit (ca 5,500m) of Milluni. We descended the south-southeast ridge to the gap before the southern top, and then made four 60m rappels down the large couloir on the southwest face. We named the route Cloudy Condors (D), after the pair of condors we spotted as we reached the summit, just before the clouds rolled in.

— ALEXANDER VON UNGERN, *BOLIVIA*

CHARQUINI, SOUTHWEST FACE, PARTIAL NEW ROUTE

JOSÉ CALLISAYA AND ROBERT RAUCH climbed a partial new line on the broad southwest face of Charquini (5,392m): Don't Let the Walls Cave in on You (400m, 8 pitches, WI3 M5). They followed Recuperated Abandonment (D- WI3 M5, Beisly-Bylinksi, 2014) until about half-height. From here, Beisly and Bylinski moved right while Callisaya and Rauch climbed directly to the summit ridge, with a section of M5 on the penultimate pitch.

— *INFORMATION FROM* ROBERT RAUCH, *BOLIVIA*

KHALA CRUZ GROUP, CONDORES Y PICAFLORES

ON MAY 17, Pacifico Machaca and I climbed a 200m, six-pitch route on the south face of the most prominent granite buttress of the Khala Cruz group (west of the 5,200m highest summit). We believe this is the same buttress mentioned in *AAJ 1982*, as we found a piton a few meters up the first pitch. Above, we found no other traces of previous passage. (*See editor's note below.*)

The route starts at ca 5,000m, after less than one hour of approach from the road leading to Zongo Pass. The first 15m is vertical to overhanging, and we overcame it using aid. Above, we climbed a 55m pitch (5a) to reach a vertical gully, which we climbed in two pitches (6a and 6a+). Above this, we moved up a large, snow-covered ledge and then slanted slightly left for 55m (5c). As the terrain eased off, we belayed one more pitch (5a) before simul-climbing to the top. We suggest the name Condores y Picaflores.

[*Editor's note: In November 1980, longtime La Paz resident Stanley Shepard soloed a route on this face that he named La Muesca (the Slot). By his own admission, it was an audacious solo climb. He appears to have climbed a similar line to the snow-covered ledge at roughly half-height. (Conditions would have been much snowier then.) Where the 2015 party moved left, Shepard continued up the giant chimney system, which was ice-choked and had sections of vertical, somewhat unstable granite.*]

— ALEXANDER VON UNGERN, *BOLIVIA*

HAMPATURI GROUP, JATI KHOLLU, SOUTH FACE, GULLY ROUTE

WITH SIGNIFICANT MIST obscuring their view of the face, Nick Berry, Derek Buckle, and John da Silva (U.K.) inadvertently climbed a variant (AD) to the 2014 route on the south face of Jati Khollu (5,421m), left of the original line.

— *INFORMATION FROM* DEREK BUCKLE, *U.K.*

Fu-Man-Chu on the tallest granite tower of the north ridge of Jati Khollu. The dashed line marks the 40m chimney/tunnel, "the most extraordinary pitch I have ever climbed." *Alexander von Ungern*

HAMPATURI GROUP, JATI KHOLLU MASSIF, FU-MAN-CHU.

On August 30, Juan Gabriel Estellano (Bolivia), Lilén Sosa (Argentina), and I established a new route on the tallest granite tower of the northern ridge of Jati Khollu (5,421m). After a 1.5-hour drive from La Paz and 3.5 hours walking up the valley on the left (west) of the long ridge falling southwest from Jati Khollu, we reached a pass at a little over 5,000m on the watershed between the Amazon basin and Andean highlands, then headed up right for 100m toward the northern ridge. Two 150–200m granite towers come into sight at the very end of this lengthy approach.

We climbed the most obvious line on the left tower. The third pitch was the most extraordinary I have ever climbed, as the crack widened into a chimney and then formed a tunnel, the outside edge comprising loose blocks. The chimney was relatively easy (40m, 5c), but protection was scarce. The fourth pitch (6a) was slab climbing with little protection, and the fifth led to the top of the tower at ca 5,280m. The name of the route, Fu-Man-Chu, is the derived from the "Rock, Paper, Scissors" game we use to determine who starts leading.

— ALEXANDER VON UNGERN, BOLIVIA

HAMPATURI GROUP, SERKHE KHOLLU, SOUTHWEST FACE, WATER WORLD

On October 6, José Callisaya (Bolivia), Robert Rauch (German, resident in La Paz), and I climbed a new route on the southwest face of Serkhe Khollu (5,546m). We began with the first two pitches of Tiers of Pachamama (350m, WI4, *AAJ 2012*), then followed a big ledge to the right and climbed three mixed pitches (M5-, M2, M3). The first had an almost vertical 20m section; the second and third gained less altitude, traversing toward big icefalls we had seen from afar. The last pitch (WI5) was 35m and divided into two vertical parts, the second of which finished with a 2m–3m overhanging section, with hollow and rotten ice. (The best season for ice is usually late July and August.) We topped out at ca 5,300m and from there went down the normal route to the northwest. [*This is Rauch's seventh new route on the face.*] We named our six-pitch climb Water World, alluding to the late-season ice and the effects of global warming—some local routes seem to have disappeared. 📄 📷

— ALEXANDER VON UNGERN, *BOLIVIA*

MURURATA, NEW ROUTE ON SATELLITE PEAK AND SOUTH FACE SOLO

IN SEPTEMBER, I went to Mururata (5,775m) with a group of Bolivian guides and friends, hoping to solo the south face. Gustavo Lisi and four friends were attracted by a couloir on the southeast face of an unnamed satellite peak opposite (west of) the main south face of Mururata and went off to climb it. This proved to be a nice new route of ca 450m with two steeper pitches in the middle section. I left base camp alone and climbed Goulotte Marie up the south face but turned around before the summit because I mistakenly assumed the rest of the group would be forced to wait for me. [*Although later claimed by several parties, Goulotte Marie was first climbed in June 1987 by Slovenians Filip Bertoncelj, Bojan Pockar, Bojan Pograjc, and Jernej Stritih. The face at this point is ca 600m high.*]

After another aborted attempt, I returned alone from La Paz and soloed Goulotte Marie to the summit, finding a short section of WI4 and another short but serious passage of M4 where the ice had not formed or had disappeared. During the last 200m the weather turned, and on top it was snowing heavily, so I opted to descend the glaciated normal route to the west—seemingly endless, with wet snow up to my knees—followed by a long walk into the main valley. Nine hours after leaving the summit, I was offered a blanket to sleep in a farmer's house.

This was most likely the first solo of the rarely climbed south face. The southeast ridge, to the right, was reported to have been soloed in the late 1980s by Bernard Francou. 📄 📷

— ROBERT RAUCH, *BOLIVIA*

PICO 5,540M AND ILLIMANI GRAND TRAVERSE

IN JUNE, as usual, I traveled to Bolivia to team up with New Zealand expat Gregg Beisly, who has been based in the country for the last five years. On June 2 we acclimatized by making the first recorded ascent of Pico 5,540m (Bolivian IGM 5946 III map) from the 4,700m low camp for Chearoco and Chachacomani. A better approach would be from Chearoco high camp at 5,200m. From there, head southwest to an obvious group of lakes, then climb west over a moraine field to the north ridge of Pico 5,540m. The last 200m along this ridge comprise a rocky crest leading to an elegant summit on a large, imposing gendarme (PD+ 4).

After climbing Chachacomani (6,048m) and then traveling south to climb the volcano Uturunku (6,048m), near the Chile/Argentina border, we decided to attempt the highly coveted Grand Traverse of the Illimani massif. This traverse crosses all five 6,000m summits of Illimani, and although attempted on a number of occasions, from south to north or vice versa, only three complete traverses have been recorded, each taking between four and six days. The shorter three-peaks traverse (north-central-main) is now done regularly, though

Robert Rauch on the third pitch (M5-) of Water World, where slippery, breakable slate did not make for easy climbing. *Alexander von Ungern*

Erik Monasterio approaches the summit of Pico del Norte during the north-south Grand Traverse of the Illimani massif's five peaks. At the end of the long corniced ridge behind lies the summit of Pico del Indio. *Gregg Beisly*

there are different accepted start and finish points. In 2015, Roberto Gomez, a guide from La Paz, and Andy Polosky, a German guide living in the USA, completed the three-peaks traverse in a single push of less than 19 hours.

On June 16, with Andy Baker (U.S.), Gregg and I set off at 6:30 a.m. from Mina Aguila (4,800m), just above Laguna Tijrac Khota on the northern flank of Illimani. We walked over moraine to reach an easy snow gully that gave access to the northwest ridge at 5,800m. We followed this ridge over a series of tops to Pico del Indio (6,109m), then climbed along a complex, undulating, heavily corniced ridge to a col, then upward over a series of tops to Pico del Norte (6,403m), which we reached at 6:45 p.m. We dropped down the southeast ridge and at 7:30 p.m. reached a col at 6,250m, where we made an open bivouac.

The following day we climbed the north ridge of Pico Central (6,362m), then dropped to the col between Picos Central and Sur, from which we descended east on a glacier with soft snow to climb Pico Layka Khollu (6,159m). We retraced our steps to the col and climbed Pico Sur (6,438m), then descended the normal route west to Nido de Condores, which we reached at 5:30 p.m. We continued down and off the mountain after an overall climbing time of about 22 hours.

The complex and stunning summit ridge of the Illimani massif runs for 13km, all over 6,000m, making it an Andean super-classic. The key to a successful crossing is adequate acclimatization, as developing altitude sickness once past Pico del Indio would present real difficulties—there is no easy way out from here without climbing over 6,000m. After two weeks at altitude I still found it extremely hard going. If you don't get through this section in a day, it will require sleeping at well over 6,000m. There is little chance of rescue and a real risk of frostbite, due to prolonged exposure to altitude and wind. Overnight temperatures dropped to -20°C. This was definitely one of the highlights of my more than 20 years of climbing. 📷

– ERIK MONASTERIO, *NEW ZEALAND*

Editor's note: The first recorded five-peak traverse was made in 1979 by Anton and Ria Putz, and the second in 1997 by Bernard Francou, Jean-Emmanuel Sicart, and Patrick Wagnon. Both teams climbed from south to north. In August 1998, Yossi Brain, Peter Grosset (both U.K.), and Alesandro Bianchi and Marcello Sanguineti (both Italian) made the first north-to-south crossing. They chose to climb Pico Layka Khollu after Pico Sur and then continue south down the long glacier, from the end of which they descended to scree slopes and eventually Cohoni.

ILLIMANI, SOUTH FACE, PARTIAL NEW ROUTE

Manu Chance and I left France with the explicit aim of climbing the south face of Illimani (6,439m). We acclimatized with new routes in the Quimsa Cruz (see below), and then, thanks to the Bolivian mountain guide Aldo Riveros, managed to reach the abandoned mine below the south face of Illimani by 4WD, saving half a day's walk. On June 3 we bivouacked at the foot of the face. Getting up at 1:30 a.m. to start the climb, we found our stove would not function. We decided to descend to the mine and see if we could scavenge any plastic bottles to fill with water. Four bottles inspired some confidence among a pile of others that were either broken or reeked of petrol.

We hiked back up to our bivouac below the face on June 5, planning to start early the

Thomas Arfi above 6,000m, heading for the southwest ridge during the first ascent of Por la Vida. *Emmanuel Chance*

The south face of Illimani showing the two partial new routes climbed in 2015. (1) Por la Vida (2015). (2) Hubert Ducroz (1988). (3) Laba-Thackray Route (1974, first ascent of south face). (4) Directa Italiana (2015). Other routes on this face are not shown. *Marco Farina*

next morning. By now we had modified our objective to a line we felt we could complete in two days. We swapped our stove, fuel, and freeze-dried meals for eight liters of cold water, some energy bars, and powdered chocolate drinks. Comfort would be for another time.

Above the bergschrund, the first few pitches were straightforward mixed climbing up to M4. We quickly discovered that the rock did not accept our Friends and were pleased that we'd brought along four pitons. Toward the end of the day I led a fine pitch of WI5+, on which I was forced to leave my pack behind. Above, 100m of 50° snow in the couloir led to a possible bivouac site. We spent two hours hacking with our axes before being able to pitch the tent. It was 5,800m and dinner that night was dried fruit and a cold drink of chocolate.

Next morning we continued left up the snow couloir to the foot of a rock barrier that had always been a question mark, as the base had remained invisible. However, we found a beautiful ice smear, which Manu quickly dispatched (WI5). We had now reached 6,000m, and the way ahead was not very difficult, with sections of ice no more than 70°. A final snow slope led to the southwest ridge, which proved long and exhausting. At 5 p.m. we reached the summit, drank our last water, admired the wonderful panorama, then headed down the normal route on the west side in strong wind. We reached base camp at 11 p.m., and our Bolivian friends met us with Coca Cola and crackers. Heaven!

We named the route Por la Vida (1,200m, WI5+). [*Editor's note: The two French alpinists climbed the first half of Hubert Ducroz, the line completed solo by Patrick Gabarrou in 1988. Where that route continues up right in a broad snow gully, the French followed a steeper left exit to the southwest ridge.*] 📷

– **THOMAS ARFI**, *FRANCE*

ILLIMANI, SOUTH FACE, DIRECTA ITALIANA

IN MID-JUNE, Marco Majori and I, from the Italian High Mountain Military Section, climbed Directa Italiana (ca 1,300m) on the south face of Illimani (6,439m). Prior to this we acclimatized by climbing Pico Milluni (5,600m) and Huayna Potosi (6,088m).

Early on June 13 we began the two-hour walk from a base camp at the abandoned Mina Mesa, at 4,800m, arriving at the bottom of the south face at about 6 a.m. Starting at the lowest point in the center of the face, we climbed directly through a large rock buttress at 5c WI3 M4 until reaching the great snow and ice slope above. Here the climbing became more physical than technical. At 6,200m we decided to bivouac below an ice wall at the left end of the upper serac barrier. It was neither comfortable nor pleasant. Next day we climbed onto the upper southwest ridge and followed it to the summit, which we reached at 11 a.m. The same day we descended the normal route to the west to reach the base of the mountain. [*Editor's note: This is a direct start to the 1974 Laba-Thackray Route, which gained the central snow and ice slope by slanting up much easier ground on the left flank of the large lower buttress.*]

— MARCO FARINA, *ITALY*

Marco Majori ascends the verglassed slabs of the initial rock buttress of Directa Italiana on Illimani. *Marco Farina*

CORDILLERA QUIMSA CRUZ

CRESTA LA VERTEBRA, NEW ROUTES

DURING ACCLIMATIZATION for the south face of Illimani, Manu Chance and I headed to the Cordillera Quimsa Cruz. Here, we first visited the cliffs at the Jardin de Porotos and then climbed on the Cuernos del Diablo. The lines here are superb, even if some of the cracks are vegetated. We then moved to the Cresta la Vertebra, where we put up several single-pitch lines and two longer routes: Maître Splitter (150m, 5 pitches, 6a, finishing on the crest of the ridge and snowline) and Pan Bagnat Connection (150m, 5 pitches, 6c; number 5 and 6 cams useful for the crux offwidth pitches). We placed bolts on some of the belays and rappel anchors. [*Editor's note: Cresta la Vertebra lies immediately southwest of the Cuernos, and the routes climbed by the French are at the head of a southwest-facing cirque on the south side of the ridge. The approach is steep and bouldery, taking about 1.25 hours from the upper lake at ca 4,300m.*]

— THOMAS ARFI, *FRANCE*

ARGENTINA-CHILE

VOLCÁN GRANADA, SOUTH FACE

VOLCÁN GRANADA (5,697M) is a volcano in the Puna region, a highland desert zone near the point where Chile, Bolivia, and Argentina meet. It was first ascended by Incas long ago for ceremonial purposes. On June 21, Argentine climbers Agustín Piccolo, Diego Simari, and Carlos Torino opened a new route on its steep south wall. After a five-hour trek through moraines, the group reached the south face and found many options for ca 400m routes, with mixed terrain and icefalls. After climbing for four hours, they ended their route on a lower summit (5,670m), calling the route Tata Raymi (400m, PD WI4). They descended the west ridge. 🔘

— **MARCELO SCANU**, *ARGENTINA*

MT. PAROFES AND OTHER VOLCANO ASCENTS

MT. PAROFES is a 5,845m volcano that rises between Pissis and Bonete in Argentina's La Rioja Province. It was said to be the highest unclimbed American summit, until Máximo Kausch (Argentina), Jovany Blume, and Pedro Hauck (both Brazil) ascended it on November 11. From camp, they climbed the cone by its northeast face in a 22km round trip.

This group also was active in the zone due north of Paso de San Francisco, where they ascended some remote and possibly unclimbed 5,000m volcanoes in October. On the 27th, they ascended the tallest peak in this zone by its west side: Sierra Nevada (6,137m). 🔘

— **MARCELO SCANU**, *ARGENTINA*

CERRO COLORADO AND CRESTA ESCONDIDA

ON NOVEMBER 14, Argentines Adrián Petrocelli and Ramiro Casas departed from Punta de Vacas, trekked along Quebrada Tupungato, and camped in Quebrada Potrero Escondido at ca 4,100m. The next day they continued to the foot of unclimbed Cerro Colorado (4,621m). On November 16 they attempted the east face of the peak, retreating at a high point of ca 4,500m due to avalanche hazard. The next day they witnessed a large avalanche sweep the face. With good weather on November 19, they started up the west face instead. Scree slopes led to snow runnels (30–40°, with some steps to 60°), a long leftward traverse, and a 4m rock step (V). Above this they gained a ridge that led to the summit.

The good weather persisted, and on November 20 they departed for an unclimbed and unnamed 4,970m summit west of Cerro Colorado. From the saddle between the two peaks (Portezuelo Cerro Colorado), they dropped to the base of the east face and then ascended an easy snow slope, which steepened near a rock band. Here, they climbed a 15m icefall with a vertical finish. Above this they gained the north side of the peak, climbing 40–50°. On the

[Left] A short section of steep ice on Tata Raymi, south face of Volcán Granada. *Diego Simari*
[Right] The route Dioses del Ocaso (1,100m, 6c) up the west side of Pico Los Zondinos. *Gabriel Fava*

summit ridge they observed three rocky high points with vertical walls, the leftmost being the highest. They used cams to protect the final rock wall (V) and reach the small summit perch. They called the peak Cresta Escondida. 📷 🔍

— MARCELO SCANU, *ARGENTINA*

CERRO TITO, EAST FACE

ON JANUARY 10, 2016, Argentine climbers Lissandro Arelovich and Glauco Muratti ascended an unclimbed 4,905m peak above Quebrada Potrero Escondido. They departed on January 7 from Punta de Vacas, making three camps west of the peak before beginning their climb up the east side. Their route started with 150m of 50° snow up a gully, with plenty of rockfall, and then they climbed poor quality rock to reach the summit (III). They named the peak Cerro Tito. 📷

— MARCELO SCANU, *ARGENTINA*

PICO LOS ZONDINOS, DIOSES DEL OCASO

FROM MARCH 20–22, Roberto Piriz and I climbed a new route on a rocky satellite peak of Cerro Tolosa (5,432m), known as Pico Los Zondinos (4,850m). [*See AAJ 2014 for more info about Cerro Tolosa.*] We started our journey from the town of Las Cuevas. Our route starts on a lower-angle ramp and then ascends the steep, upper west-facing buttress of the peak, with a five-star, dream bivouac. The climbing is connected by good cracks on okay rock and protects with cams. We roped up for approximately 15 pitches on the upper buttress (about 550m of climbing). We called the route Dioses del Ocaso ("Gods of the Sunset," 1,100m, 6c) because of the incredible views and sunset on the climb. 📷 🔍

– GABRIEL FAVA, *ARGENTINA*

FIVE NEW ROUTES

IN NOVEMBER AND DECEMBER, Oriol Baró (Spain) and partners climbed five new routes on five different peaks in the Central Andes. The peaks were Cerro Yeguas Heladas, Cerro Morado, Cerro San Francisco, Cerro Yeguas Muertas, and Gemelo Este, and the routes ranged in difficulty from D+ to ED.

On November 6, Baró and Andrés Zegers climbed a left-angling snow and mixed route up the west face of Cerro Yeguas Heladas (4,771m,), which they called Yeguas Salvajes (1,110m, MD M5). The route ascends snow, mixed ground, and unstable cornices and mushrooms. They descended by the south ridge and a couloir, and their round-trip time from base camp at 3,050m was 20 hours.

On November 13, Baró and Zegers climbed Gemelo Este (5,117m) by its west face. The route ascends snow, ice, and rock just left of this face's central rock rib, with a crux in the middle consisting of a 90m WI4+ icefall and two M4+ pitches on

[Above] **Cerro Yeguas Heladas, west face, showing the route Yeguas Salvajes.** [Next page] **Andrés Zegers walks across an exposed cornice on the summit ridge of Cerro Yeguas Heladas.** *Oriol Baró*

bad rock. They descended to the east. Their round-trip time from a camp at 3,550m was 13 hours. They call the route Turbera (1,100m, MD- WI4+ M4+).

On November 22, Baró, Aike Parvex, and Zegers climbed Cerro Morado's south summit (4,490m) by a significant variation to the Tangol-Vasquez 1961 south face route. After following the Tangol-Vasquez for 400m, the team traversed a snow ledge to the right, gaining a steep, unclimbed ice flow (sometimes called Cascada Central in topos). They climbed this section of steep ice and mixed ground for 350m, eventually reaching the upper snow slopes and the summit. They called their variation Fina y Sucia (750m, ED 6a WI5 M4+), and the route took 11 hours round-trip from a camp below the wall.

On November 30, Baró, Xavi Farré, Seba Rojas, and Zegers climbed Cerro Yeguas Muertas (4,912m) via a prominent couloir on the central-right side of the south face. The climb is predominately snow with some stretches of mixed climbing and waterfall ice. They descended to the east, then climbed over the southeast ridge and descended a west-facing slope

[Above] The south face of Cerro Yeguas Muertas, showing the route Wenatti. [Left] The south face of Cerro Morado's south summit, showing: (1) Tangol-Vasquez 1961 route. (2) The new variation, Fina y Sucia. The main summit of Cerro Morado is out of view to the right. *Oriol Baró*

to return to base camp, eight and a half hours after leaving. They called the route Wenatti (1,150m, MD-).

On December 3, Baró and Xavi Farré climbed Cerro San Francisco (4,307m) by a series of weaknesses on its southeast face. They started from a camp at Laguna El Morado (ca 2,400m) and, carrying a rope but never using it, ascended snow slopes below the face to reach a prominent, short, left-angling couloir. From the couloir's exit they made a couple of large traverses to gain weaknesses through the upper headwall and onto the summit ridge and the peak. They descended to the south and east, and their round-trip time from camp was 11 hours. They call the route Antiparkes (1,000m, D+). [*See the AAJ website for photo-topos and more information about these routes.*] 📷 🔍

— ERIK RIEGER, *WITH INFORMATION FROM* ORIOL BARÓ

CERRO MORADO, NORTHEAST RIDGE, FILO CONTIGO

AT THE END OF APRIL, Pablo Miranda and I left Santiago to attempt the unclimbed northeast ridge of Cerro Morado (4,647m) to its principal summit.

[*Editor's note: Cerro Morado is a twin-summited peak. Its main (north) summit was first reached in 1941 up a glacier on its southeast side (Foerster-Hein-Sattler). The subsidiary (south) summit (ca 4,480m), well known for its 900m south-facing big wall, was first climbed in 1934 (Melschner-Melschner), and its steep south face was climbed in 1961 (Tangol-Vasquez, 1961). See past AAJs, chilemountains.info/morado, or andeshandbook.org for more information.*]

On April 24 we started the approach, and around 3 p.m. we started climbing the ridge, just right of the 2007 Fainberg-Farias Route, via some easy fourth- and fifth-class terrain. We finished the day with a short section of 50° ice. That night we slept on a little ledge, waiting for the sun to hit us in the morning before continuing. On the second day we simul-climbed until reaching a short section of 5.9. After this, we continued simul-climbing, and a few hours later we were standing on the summit. We descended via the normal route to the southeast.

The descent took longer than expected due to late-season snow and glacier conditions. We made the decision to stop once it got late, spending one more night on the mountain. We reached our car around noon the next day. We call our route Filo Contigo (1,000m, 5.9 50°).

– PEDRO BINFA, *CHILE*

TORRES DEL BRUJO, CERRO ALTO DE LOS ARRIEROS

IN OCTOBER, Ricardo Hernandez and I traveled to the Torres del Brujo (a.k.a. Sierra del Brujo), in the VI region of Chile. We started up the University Glacier until the point where it intersects the Mañke Glacier—a two-day approach. It took one additional day to pass large seracs on the Mañke Glacier and make camp below our objective, the unclimbed southeast couloir of Cerro Alto de los Arrieros (4,980m).

On our fourth day we climbed the couloir for 750m, roping up for 10 pitches. Due to strong winds, we dug an improvised bivouac in an ice cave, where we spent the night at around 4,900m. The next day, at first light, we completed the final meters to the summit. The climb took us 36 hours round-trip from our camp (750m, D 80°). It was the fourth overall ascent of the mountain, with prior ascents in 1950, 1964, and 1971.

The climbing possibilities in this area are very interesting, with big rock walls, frozen cascades, and mixed terrain [*see AAJ 2005 and 2010 for examples of recent routes completed*].

– ELVIS ACEVEDO, *CHILE*

AGUJAS DEL SOSNEADO, TORRE BLANCA DE ECTELION, JUMANJI

ON MARCH 23, Argentine climbers Charly Contartese, Esteban Degregori, and Juancho Torres opened a new route in the granite towers known as Agujas del Sosneado, on Torre Blanca de Ectelion. This is the second route on the tower and is located left of Chaparral (*AAJ 2015*). The route begins with an easy 200m ramp, which was ascended unroped. Above, they took an obvious route up the center-right side of the tower, climbing five pitches to the summit. Part of the route has rotten rock. They called it Jumanji (475m, 6c). The group also climbed Torre Principal via the older route Nalgas de Loncho (450m, 7b+). [*See guiasosneado.blogspot.com for an online guide to this area.*]

– MARCELO SCANU, *ARGENTINA*

PIRITA CENTRAL

BY ALAN GOLDBETTER

PLANES, BUSES, TAXIS, truck beds, boats, horses, and feet—it was an exciting and lengthy journey just to get into the Piritas Valley, and it was all worth it for the stunning landscape, impeccable granite, and remoteness of the valley. It was January 26, 2016, and Tess Ferguson and I had just begun our 17-day exploratory climbing adventure into the Turbio Valley of northern Patagonia.

With the invaluable assistance of our local contact, Iván Larsen, we were able to arrange all the logistics needed to carry out our expedition. We began in the town of Lago Puelo and took a private boat to the far side of the lake. There we met our gauchos, and after a 24-hour delay due to high river levels, we continued deeper up the Turbio River on horseback.

Two days later, the gauchos dropped us off and we began shuttling gear up to the Refugio Osvaldo. Upon arriving, we were surprised to find a kind and welcoming Argentine couple living there. In addition to making renovations and expansions on Osvaldo, they were working

on a new refugio in the Mariposa Valley (*see AAJ 2014 for more info on this area*). They also informed us that a four-person climbing team was currently exploring the Rio Turbio. While this area is far from having an active scene, it is surely growing in popularity.

The next morning we started off for the Piritas Valley. Two long days of hiking, bushwhacking, and scrambling were required to reach the Piritas massif. [*Piritas is a tri-summited granite spike. Pirita Central was first climbed in February 2006 by Pedro Lutti and Bicho Fiorenza via its east corridor. See AAJ 2009 and 2011 for more info on past trips and routes.*] A comfortable bivy spot afforded us a brief rest before our ascent. To access Pirita Central, it was necessary to climb a 400m "approach." We found the first three pitches to be dirty and difficult. Four points of aid were required for us, though past parties have freed

Alan Goldbetter preparing gear beneath the Piritas. El Conono ascends the left skyline of the large left tower. See the online report for a route-line diagram showing the seven routes on the massif. *Tess Ferguson*

Tess Ferguson topping out on the summit block of Piritas Central with peaks and valleys to the west in the background. *Alan Goldbetter*

them at 5.11. The remaining terrain we found to range from third class to easy fifth class.

Upon reaching the base of Piritas Central on February 1, we began climbing our intended line up the center of the prow: pitch after pitch of clean, compact granite with plenty of gear placements and thoroughly enjoyable climbing. We shivered through a rather uncomfortable bivy just shy of the summit and topped out the following morning. We decided to name our route El Conono (800m, IV 5.9 C1) after one of our gauchos. We utilized five points of aid on the route, which could likely be freed at 5.11.

Our descent was more difficult than anticipated. After an all-day rappel session that involved limited anchors, rockfall, and many stuck ropes, we reached the glacier. More scrambling, talus, and a sketchy river crossing had us back at our bivy site well past midnight.

Following our climb we descended from the Piritas Valley and explored the Mariposa Valley. We climbed nine vegetated pitches on a feature called the Earlobe before deeming it not worthwhile. Many of the cracks in the Mariposa are vegetated and closed off. While there is certainly more rock to be had there, I believe it is better suited to harder lines, harder climbers, and a bolt kit.

We exited the valley on the Turbio River, using inflatable kiddie rafts and paddles fashioned out of sticks. The paddling was also more difficult than anticipated, though more likely due to our inexperience with whitewater and our inadequate boating setup than the river itself. After nine hours of rafting, the river spit us into Lago Puelo on February 11.

COCHAMÓ VALLEY, SUMMARY OF NEW CLIMBS IN 2014–2015

DANIEL SEELIGER has noted a number of long new climbs completed in Cochamó from 2014 to early 2015 that were not previously mentioned in the *AAJ*. They are listed below. Find more information about the climbs, including a library of hand-drawn topos, dating back to 1998, at *http://www.cochamo.com/topos*.

On Arco Iris Wall, Hillo Santana and Daniel Arcifa climbed La Luz Que Ilumina (5.8 A2+). On Cerro La Junta, Daniel Seeliger and Eric Blake climbed Gardens of the Galaxy (900m, 5.11 A0). On Cerro Noemi Walwalun, Logan Fusso, Oliver Abbitt, and Jordan Collins climbed Al Lado del Corazon (10 pitches, 5.11+), Andrew Andraski and Grant Simmons climbed 50 Años de Libertad (685m, 5.11), and Andrew Andraski and Logan Fusso climbed El Cambio Entre Sombras (15 pitches, 5.12-). On Pared del Perfil, Jim Taylor climbed Cocho Mojo (5.11+ A0). On the backside of Gorilla Wall, J.B. Haab and Nico Rivas climbed Tio Tiedro (8 pitches, 5.12). On El Espejo, Artemia Ramirez Acevedo, Luis Carlos Garcia Ayala, and Carlos Sandoval Olascoaga established Mapudungun (535m, 5.12b), a variation to Through the Looking Glass.

– **ERIK RIEGER**, *WITH INFORMATION FROM* **DANIEL SEELIGER**, *CHILE*

CERRO TRINIDAD, NORTHWEST FACE, EL CÓNDOR PASA

ON DECEMBER 28, Josef Kristoffy, Martin Krasnansky, and I (all Slovakia) flew to South America for a five-week trip to Cochamó Valley. After getting acquainted with the area, we decided to try a new route up the impressive 700m northwest face of Cerro Trinidad. We spent three days carrying 300kg of gear, food, and other necessary materials to our bivouac at the base and then

A foreshortened view up the route El Cóndor Pasa on the right buttress of Cerro Trinidad.
Jozef Kristoffy / Vlado Linek

jumped right on the project. It starts about 50m left of the route Nunca Mas Marisco.

Climbing through small, shallow granite cracks in the first few pitches, we soon realized that the climbing was not at all the kind we were used to. The route turned into a serious big wall with complex climbing, using the smallest micro-nuts, micro-cams, and hooks. Most of the cracks were dirty and full of weeds, the wall got unbearably hot around 1 p.m., and there were biting insects. We managed to climb the route with a mix of free and aid over a week, reaching the summit on January 14.

In the following days, from January 20–25, we climbed all the pitches free, in a team-free style, with Josef freeing the crux pitch. It was very technical climbing on vertical to slabby stone, with tiny holds: El Cóndor Pasa (710m, UIAA X). The 20-pitch route is fitted with 152 bolts (40 of these are at belay stations), and was named after the condors, with their 10-foot wingspans, soaring in the background while we ascended the final two pitches. Though at this time unrepeated, we believe it is the hardest free route climbed in Cochamó to date (approximately 5.13d).

Vlado Linek climbs the seventh pitch, an excellent crack. *Jozef Kristoffy*

— **VLADO LINEK**, *SLOVAKIA*

EL PERFIL, NORTHEAST FACE, COCHAMOJÓ

In February, Jim Taylor and I established a beautiful line he'd scoped out the year before, on a feature known as El Perfil in the Amphitheater. The route follows a crack system up to a short roof and then continues up a very prominent arête.

Our initial ground-up attempt came to a standstill after about four pitches (35m below a vegetated crack under the roof). The climbing on the pitch up to the roof turned out to be extremely thin and too vegetated for hooking. Thus, we decided to take a top-down approach, first climbing to the summit via a fifth-class gully to the southwest. Although the upper arête and three other pitches were bolted on rappel, we managed to establish several of the pitches on lead. We then cleaned the route from the top down over the course of the next two weeks.

Establishing this 11-pitch route in Cochamó was a wild learning experience. We fondly referred to this process as "finding your Cochamojó." Our climb, Cochamojó (400m, 5.12a A0), is all free aside from a short pendulum to connect pitches six and seven, and it includes incredibly fun and varied crack and face climbing.

— **NICK ROTHENBUSH**, *USA*

CERRO TORRECILLAS, VARIOUS ROUTES

On March 20, Cristian Mono Gallardo, Jorge Chispa Sepulveda, Favian Zandoval, and I reached the area called La Junta in Cochamó. Our goal was to reach an area called Cerro Torrecillas, a little-known glaciated zone that I reconnoitered with aerial photos and satellite images, and which is known to have been visited once before.

We began our approach through the Trinidad Valley, crossing below El Monstruo. We gained much elevation from the forests to reach the upper alpine amphitheater, and after about 10 hours, when we had the Torrecillas in sight, we decided to bivouac.

In the morning we reached the glacier below the Torrecillas. On the west side of the group, a short but very aesthetic needle—what we've called Aguja Don Pipor—hypnotized us immediately. We found the rock to be very good and very clean, unlike the valley, which has more vegetation. We rappelled back to the glacier and climbed two additional towers on our trip: Aguja Nahuel and the main North Tower. 🄾

– JOSÉ DATTOLI SELKNAM, *CHILE*

CERRO TORDILLO

During September and November, Rodrigo Chabalgoity, Pablo Cuadra, Jacob Perkinson, Christian Steidle, and I, along with 17 NOLS students, completed an expedition in Jeinimeni National Reserve in the Aysén Region. On October 17, our group made the first ascent of Cerro Tordillo (2,310m, 46°48'33"S, 72°14'36"W) by its east face, from a high camp in the Ventisquero Valley. The route was 1,000m, 40°. 🄾

– PEDRO BINFA, *CHILE*

CERRO CASTILLO NATIONAL RESERVE, NEW ROUTES

In September 2015, Pedro Binfa and Marcelo Mascareño climbed a new route in winter up the south face of Cerro Sahne Nuss. The climb contained steep snow, ice, drytooling, and some aid, taking a prominent right-angling gash to the

The southwest aspect of Cerro Sahne Nuss, showing the route Las Vueltas de la Vida on the left and La Invernada on the right. *Pedro Binfa*

summit ridge, which they followed to the top. They called the climb La Invernada (300m, 5.8 A1 WI2 M4). Binfa returned with Marissa Bieger in January 2016, and the two climbers ascended a new route up a snow/mixed gully on the broad southwest ridge (left of the previous route). High on the ridge, a long traverse right and then back left allowed them to gain the north aspect and then the summit. They called the climb Las Vueltas de la Vida (350m, 5.8).

– ERIK RIEGER, *WITH INFORMATION FROM* PEDRO BINFA, *CHILE*

AVELLANO TOWERS, NEW ROUTES

In January 2015, Dave Anderson, Matt Hartman, Jared Spaulding, and Szu-ting Yi traveled to the Avellano Towers. They first made an attempt on the east face of South Avellano Tower, climbing approximately 400m of the 800m wall, with difficulties up to 5.10- and 5.7 R. After this they made the first recorded ascent of the north ridge of the Tooth (100m, 5.7). Lastly, they climbed the Tooth by its southwest ridge: Filo Suroeste (305m, 5.10). Jared Spaulding has compiled a PDF with notes and photos of all known climbs, attempts, and exploration in the Avellano Towers—see the AAJ website for this PDF.

– ERIK RIEGER, *WITH INFORMATION FROM* MATT HARTMAN *AND* JARED SPAULDING, *USA*

CENTRAL PATAGONIA

CERRO HERMOSO, SOUTH FACE; CERRO SAN LORENZO, NEW ROUTE TO PILAR SUR–SOUTH SUMMIT COL

In November, my partner Domen Petrovčič and I, along with Rok Kurnčič, Boštjan Mikuž, and Dejan Koren (all Slovenian), decided to go to Cerro San Lorenzo. Our main objective was, until our arrival, a new route on the east face. The planned time for our expedition was one month, of which three weeks were expected to be in base camp.

After flying into Rio Gallegos, we purchased our food and remaining supplies and then continued by bus to Gobernador Gregores, the closest town to Perito Moreno National Park, where Cerro San Lorenzo lies. From here on we needed a 4WD to travel into the park, and we were lucky to secure it beforehand, thanks to Rolando Garibotti, who generously helped us with logistics and forecasts on our trip. It took us three round-trip carries to get our equipment to base camp at an old shepherd's shed.

The south face of Cerro Hermoso and the Slovenian line. *Domen Kastelic*

On our second day at base camp, Domen and I hiked up to scope the east face. The wall seemed fairly dry: Snow and ice climbing conditions looked bad, and the temperature was completely spring-like. While waiting for better conditions, we hoped to try the south face of Cerro Hermoso. [*Prior climbs exist on this side of the peak, but their location is not certain.*]

[Above] The south end of San Lorenzo (3,706m), showing: (A) Aguja Antipasto. (1) Romance Explosion. (B) Pilar Sur. (2) 2013 Argentine attempt. (3) 2016 Ecuadorian attempt. (4) 2015 Slovenian route to the col. (C) Cumbre Buscaini. *Pablo Pontoriero* [Below] The east face and main summit of San Lorenzo. (1) No Fiesta, the 2015 Slovenian line, with a high point at the junction with the Sudafricana Route on the east ridge at about 3,450m. (2) Sudafricana Route (1986) to summit. *Rolando Garibotti*

On November 11, from a bivy close to Cerro Hermoso, Domen and I started climbing early, ascending easier terrain during the night and reaching the main snowfield at dawn. After we crossed the snowfield, we reached the steeper south-southwest face, where we climbed straight to the summit up the fall line. The conditions were generally good, but warm, and the ascent took six hours (ca 500m, 80° M4). From the summit, we first descended toward the east summit and from there down the southern snowfield until we reached the foot of the wall.

After this the weather worsened, the temperature dropped, and our base camp got covered in snow. After days of waiting, reading, playing tarot card games, and loitering around the base, some good news reached us: A nice weather window, though not 100 percent fair, would arrive during the final days of our trip. Still, for days, the mountain stayed engulfed in clouds.

Domen and I decided to try Pilar Sur via the northeast couloir between it and San Lorenzo's south summit (Cumbre Buscaini). We packed for three days and headed up. After an eight-hour approach, we reached the edge of the glacier, right under the wall, and pitched a tent in the shelter of a large boulder. In the afternoon we had time to examine the chosen line up close.

We started climbing at 2 a.m. on November 21 with our bivouac gear. With fresh snow, we progressed more slowly than expected. After 13 hours we reached the col between Pilar Sur and the south summit, where we found steep and crumbly walls leading to either summit. For our taste, the climbing would be too dangerous. Still, we were content with our route to this point (ca 900m, 90°).

We descended with many rappels down the south side of the mountain, dropping into the glacial tongue of the Buscaini-Metzeltin Route (1986). Meanwhile, on the same day, the rest of our party climbed a line on San Lorenzo to reach the Sudafricana Route (east ridge) [*see following report*]. 📷

– DOMEN KASTELIC, *SLOVENIA*

CERRO SAN LORENZO, EAST FACE TO EAST RIDGE, NO FIESTA

IN NOVEMBER, five Slovenian alpinists traveled to Cerro San Lorenzo (3,706m) as two semi-independent teams: Domen Kastelic and Domen Petrovčič, and Dejan Koren, Rok Kurinčič, and Boštjan Mikuž.

On November 10, Koren, Kurinčič, and Mikuž made an attempt on the east face of San Lorenzo, turning back in deteriorating weather. During this short weather window, Petrovčič and Kastelic climbed a new route on Cerro Hermoso (*see previous report*).

On November 20, while the other two Slovenians were climbing on the far left side of San Lorenzo's east face, Koren, Kurinčič, and Mikuž began an attempt on the far right side. They started from base camp at midday and reached the base of the southeast-facing section of the wall by 5 p.m. They started climbing at 7 p.m., moving unroped up 70° snow slopes. By midnight they had covered 800m and reached the icefall that connects the lower and middle parts of this face. Here, they roped up and climbed mixed terrain to the first serac. At this point they traversed left on a diagonal for five pitches, across very hard ice, to find a passage between the second and third seracs.

By dawn on November 21 they had reached the base of the third serac. Despite a windless weather forecast, a southeasterly wind had picked up around midnight and became quite strong after sunrise. The wind prevented them from stopping to melt water, so upon intersecting the Sudafricana Route on the east ridge (ca 3,450m), they decided to call it good without continuing on to the summit. To this point, they had climbed 1,600m. It was 3 p.m. and they had climbed for 20 hours.

To descend, they rappelled the northeast face, which was more protected from the wind, making around 40 rappels (1,000m). They reached base camp at dawn on November 22, after being on the go for 40 hours. They call their line to the ridge No Fiesta (1,600m, ED+). 📷

— DEJAN KOREN *AND* DOMEN KASTELIC, *SLOVENIA*

CERRO SAN LORENZO, CUMBRE BUSCAINI, NEW ROUTE

MANY CLIMBERS throughout the years have turned their eyes to one of the biggest walls in Patagonia, the east face of Cerro San Lorenzo (3,706m). Our team from Ecuador—Nicolas Navarrete, Felipe Guarderas, and I—was no exception. We hoped to climb the peak's south pillar (Pilar Sur).

We knew little about this place, so we took all sorts of equipment to allow us to attempt our objective in the style that seemed most appropriate. Starting in early January 2016, we first spent a week carrying loads to the base of Pilar Sur, where we waited for good weather.

In late January, we set off from our advanced base camp at 3 a.m. A long approach over the glacier got us to the base of the wall at sunrise. We chose a line on the right side of the wall, left of the couloir climbed by the Slovenian team [*see previous report*], between the south pillar and San Lorenzo's south summit. We climbed for 250m but decided to retreat due to constant rockfall. During the descent, a serac collapsed and Felipe was struck by debris, breaking his arm.

With not many options on the east face, Nico and I decided to go on a big adventure around the mountain while Felipe returned to our camp. We hiked for 10 hours until we reached the southwest arête of Cumbre Buscaini (ca 3,300m, the south summit of San Lorenzo). We waited at the base for a couple of hours, hoping for better snow conditions; unfortunately, conditions never improved.

Cerro San Lorenzo's southwest face, showing: (A) Cumbre Buscaini. (1) Haba-tar. (2) Buscaini-Metzeltin Route. *Groupe Militaire de Haute Montage*

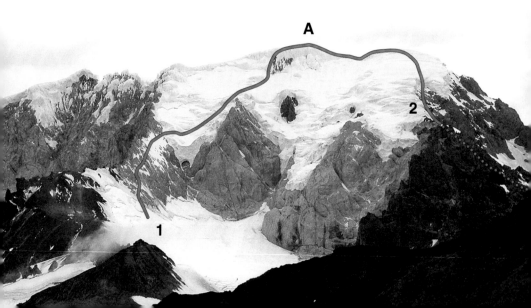

At 3 a.m. we started our climb, heading up through deep snow until we reached the bergschrund. Some steep snow took us to a mixed ridge, where we traversed right. Magically, we found a way through the big serac that guards the ramp to the summit. From there we climbed perfect ice up to 75° to the south summit. We enjoyed the view for a few minutes in strong winds and then started our long descent, downclimbing the majority of our route and rappelling one section. We reached camp again after 40 hours out.

We named our route Haba-tar (800m, 75°). It was definitely a big adventure in a wild place, and we learned a lot, taking our good experiences home with us. [*This route is located west (looker's left) of the Buscaini-Metzeltin Route (1986) up the south face and west arête.*] 📷

– ROBERTO MORALES, *ECUADOR*

SOUTHERN PATAGONIA / CHALTÉN MASSIF

2015–2016 SEASON SUMMARY

ALTHOUGH THERE WERE hardly any accidents in the area this past season, one of the incidents unfortunately resulted in the death of Argentine climber Iñaki Cousirrat. He was hit by rockfall while attempting a route on the east face of Cerro Fitz Roy.

The extreme heat of the last few summers, including the heat of the five good weather weeks we had this season, have had an impact on permafrost depth, making the mountains more unstable. The freezing level should be an important consideration when choosing an objective, and it might be time to go further: During particularly warm summers, certain objectives might have to be considered "off limits," regardless of the freezing level on a particular day. A similar evolution in thinking has taken place in the Alps over the last couple of decades.

The following summary of activity is organized geographically from south to north along the Torre group, then from north to south along the Fitz Roy crest.

In the Agujas del Río Túnel, Julian Casanova and Tomas Müller (Argentina) did the first ascent of agujas "2" and "5," now called Lise and Leo, climbing two new routes: La Vida Boba (450m, 5.8 60˚) and El Dealer de la Bicicleta (500m, 5.8 60˚). In the same area, Quentin Lindfield Roberts (Canada) climbed a new route on T48: M23 (300m, 5.6). Just to the east, Colin Haley soloed a new route along the west ridge of Cerro Solo: El Dragón (300m, 5.8 R).

On El Mocho, Martin Marovski and Viktor Varoshkin (Bulgaria) climbed a new line on the north face, right of Grey Yellow Arrow: The Approach Team Line (13 pitches, 5.11 A2). Also on El Mocho, Marc-André Leclerc (Canada) completed the first solo ascent of Voie des Benitiers (400m, 5.11 C1); he also soloed Rubio y Azul (350m, 5.11) on the nearby Aguja de la Medialuna.

Cerro Torre's southeast ridge got its second free ascent, by Andrew Rothner, Mikey Schaefer, and Josh Wharton. All three of them freed all the pitches (800m, 5.12d WI5). They believe the crux is around 5.12d (down from the original rating of 5.13b). Three other parties repeated the southeast ridge with aid, climbing the crux via the "Haston Crack."

On Torre Egger, Tomy Aguilo (Argentina), Korra Pesce (Italy), and Roli Striemitzer (Austria) completed the second ascent of Psycho Vertical (900m, 6c A3 90°, Karo-Jeglic-Knez, 1986) on the south face. They climbed alpine style over two days, descending on day three. They were followed by Iñaki Coussirat and Carlitos Molina (Argentina), who initially climbed

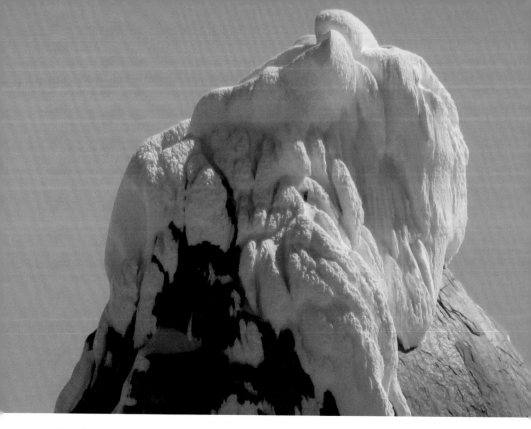

Colin Haley soloing the ice mushrooms on Torre Egger to complete the peak's first solo ascent. He did the first solo ascent of Punta Herron, en route to Torre Egger, earlier in the same day. *Korra Pesce*

independently but later jugged ropes fixed by the first team for at least a third of the route.

Colin Haley brought the house down with the first solo ascents of Punta Herron and Torre Egger. From Col Standhardt he traversed across the east face of Aguja Standhardt (400m, 5.9 65°), then rappelled to the route Tobogán and followed this to the Col del los Sueños (100m, 75°), between Standhardt and Punta Herron. He then tackled Spigolo dei Bimbi (350m, 5.10d 90°) to reach the summit of Punta Herron. After rappelling south to the col below Torre Egger, he climbed the Huber-Schnarf (200m, 5.11- 80°) to the top. He reached the summit of Torre Egger in 13 hours 30 minutes from Col Standhardt. He free-soloed everything except for a short tension traverse near the start, four pitches along Spigolo dei Bimbi, and another four pitches along the Huber-Schnarf, where he rope-soloed. He descended the south face of Torre Egger, then down the American Route. The round trip from the Noruegos camp took 27 hours. In 2010, Haley completed the first solo ascent of Aguja Standhardt, so he now has under his belt the first solo ascents of three out of the four summits in the Cerro Torre group.

On Aguja Standhardt, one day after the winter equinox, Marc-André Leclerc free-soloed the stout Tomahawk-Exocet link-up (900m, WI6 M7), reaching the summit 12 hours after leaving Niponino camp. Later, Luca Bianco, Giacomo Deiana, and Francesco Salvaterra (Italy) climbed the first two-thirds of the unfinished Chaverri-Plaza attempt and then joined Exocet, along which they continued to the summit. The result: a very sustained 900m route—stellar rock climbing in the lower half, stout ice climbing in the upper part.

Further north, Matt Burdekin and Tom Ripley (U.K.) climbed 13 new pitches into Cogan on the east face of Aguja Bifida's south summit: The Siren (400m, 5.9). Pete Fasoldt and Eli Simon climbed ten new pitches into Su Patagonia on the west face of Punta Filip: Shelter from the Cow (5.11 A0). On the neighboring Aguja Pachamama, Gediminas Simutis and Saule Simute climbed a new route on the west face: Ziggy Stardust (300m, 5.10a).

There was a lot of action in the peaks above the Marconi Sur Glacier. Two new routes were climbed on the left side of Cerro Piergiorgio's west face. Katsutaka Yokoyama and Takaaki Nagato (Japan) climbed Pilar Canino (500m, 5.12), and soon afterward Pete Fasoldt and Jonathan Schaffer (USA) climbed Skull Fuck (500m, 5.11c), immediately to the right. Just to the north, on the west face of Aguja El Tridente, Yokoyama and Nagato climbed Knob-mania (10 pitches, 5.12d). The crux pitch was freed with preplaced gear; all other pitches were redpointed.

Across the valley, Jonathan Schaffer and Joel Kauffman (USA) climbed a new route on Aguja Volonqui's east face: Chorblito (14 pitches, WI4 M7). On Los Colmillos, Nicola Castagna, Jacopo Pellizari, and Francesco Salvaterra (Italy) climbed Colmillo Central from the east and south by the route Matetang (55° M4) and did the first ascent of Colmillo Sur with Marcello Cominetti: Anonima Sequestri (300m, 90° M6). In the same area, Stefan Gatt, Andreas Reinhardt, and Markus Stockert (Austria) climbed a new route on Cerro Pollone that they called Escama del Dragon (200m, 5.11-). They climbed another new route on a small tower south of Aguja Tito Carrasco that they called Alegría (180m, 5.11-), and did the first ascent of a slender tower just north of Aguja Volonqui: Voluntad y Cuidado (250m, 5.11-).

Cordón Marconi saw two new routes. Henry Bizot (France) and Gabriel Fava (Argentina) climbed the south face of Aguja Dumbo: André y Sophie (600m, 65° M3; see Henry's report at the AAJ website). On Cerro Marconi Sur, Markus Pucher (Austria) soloed a new route on the west face: Into the Wild (800m, 80° M5).

Cerro Fitz Roy received a lot of attention, including a new speed record. Colin Haley and Andy Wyatt smashed the "car-to-car" mark for running and climbing Fitz Roy, summiting via

The west face of Cerro Piergiorigio, showing: (1) Via del Hermano. (2) Greenpeace. (3) All You Need is Love. (4) Pilar Canino. (5) Skull Fuck. *Colin Haley*

the Supercanaleta in a 21:08 round trip.

On the north face, Pete Fasoldt and Jonathan Schaffer climbed a major new route. They started at the lowest point of the wall, following a 1985 attempt, then joined the Afanassieff Route briefly before continuing to the Gran Hotel. On the headwall above, they climbed a 12-pitch crack, mostly offwidth (difficulties to 5.12), later rejoining the Afanassieff to the summit. In all, they climbed 1,600m on their new route Pretty Bird (7a+ A0), of which 25 pitches were new. They bivied at the Gran Hotel twice, on the way up and during their rappel descent of Tehuelche.

On the south face of Fitz Roy, Michal Sabovčík and Ján Smoleň (Slovakia) climbed 400m of new terrain left of the Canadian Route: Asado (M8 7a+ C2). On the east face, David Bacci and Matteo Della Bordella (Italy) did the second ascent of Pilar Este (Ferrari-Meles, 1976), climbing alpine style over three days and managing to free many of the pitches. El Corazón (Ochsner-Pitelka, 1992) saw its first one-day ascent, by Jorge Ackermann (Argentina) and Tony McLean (Canada) in 20:30.

At the south end of the Cerro Fitz Roy chain, on Aguja de l'S, Nico Gutiérrez and Carlos Vasquez (Colombia) climbed a new route on the west face: Los del Maipo (5.11), with 21 pitches total and 18 new pitches.

The north face of Fitz Roy, showing the new route Pretty Bird. See *www.pataclimb.com* for the many other routes on this aspect. *Doerte Pietron*

As a closing remark, Colin Haley had the most successful single season in the history of Chaltén Massif climbing. In addition to the climbs mentioned above, he soloed the California Route on Cerro Fitz Roy and climbed a new route on Cerro Huemul with Alex Honnold. His two speed traverses in the Torre and Fitz Roy groups are described in a feature story earlier in this *AAJ*. The quality and number of ascents he pulled off in barely two months is staggering.

– ROLANDO GARIBOTTI

CERRO ADELA NORTE, EAST FACE, BALAS Y CHOCOLATE

EL CHALTÉN is a vast playground where the possibilities for new routes are still infinite. So when Dani Ascaso and Santi Padrós showed up at the hostel where Jerôme Sullivan and I were staying and told us they had the exact same plan as us for a new route the next day, we were surprised, to say the least. Given the randomness, we decided right away to combine forces and share the adventure.

Our plan was to climb the right side of Cerro Adela Norte, which leads to the Col de la Esperanza, and then climb the Ragni Route on Cerro Torre. This required hiking around Cerro Torre for two long days in order to get to the base of the route.

On October 23, the alarm went off at midnight. Getting past the bergschrund went smoothly, but the steep, narrow gully that came next was steeper than expected. The ice wasn't always that solid, and some sections were hard to protect. The upper part of Cerro Adela Norte's east face is directly exposed to the first rays of sun in the morning, and almost immediately after sunrise we were bombarded with falling ice. Fortunately, we had timed things fairly well. A nice step led us to base of the two crux pitches of the route. The first crux involved a delicate mixed traverse that led to a thin, unprotectable section of ice approximately 20m long. The next pitch was a mix of aid, mixed, and unconsolidated snow climbing with a bit of tunneling; it was also virtually unprotectable. These two pitches slowed us considerably—we spent about eight hours on them. As night encroached, we continued climbing up 250m of easy gullies.

After gaining Col de la Esperanza, we dug a snow cave to protect us from the strong wind. We had been awake for 28 hours and had climbed nonstop for 24 hours. We didn't set an alarm, but

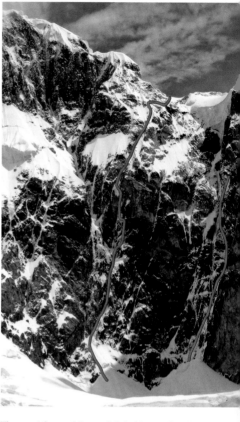

The east face of Cerro Adela Norte, showing Balas y Chocolate (left) and Los Tiempos Perdidos (right). *Rolando Garibotti*

the sun woke us from our slumber five hours later. We were still motivated to continue up Cerro Torre, but the accumulation of little problems compelled us to retreat. After descending to Circo de los Altares, two long days of hiking awaited us. The route name Balas y Chocolate ("Bullets and Chocolate," 900m, WI5+ M6 A2) hints at the difficulties we faced while climbing, but also all the happiness and simple pleasures these climbs bring us.

[*Editor's note: This climb is located to the left of Los Tiempos Perdidos (900m, 90° M5+, Marsigny-Parkin, 1994). A large serac sits between the two routes. In 2007, Colin Haley and Kelly Cordes made the first and only integral ascent of this lower wall to the Col de la Esperanza and then up the Ragni Route (approximately 1,500m of climbing, see AAJ 2008).*]

– LISE BILLON, *FRANCE, TRANSLATED FROM FRENCH BY TODD MILLER*

CERRO FITZ ROY, SOUTH FACE, COLORADO ROUTE

OGLING OVER PHOTOS at home in Colorado, on the plane ride down to Patagonia, and even from a vantage point at Niponino camp, Max Barlerin was doing his best to convince Mike Lukens and me there was a new line to try on Fitz Roy. Just one day back from climbing Aguja

Looking up pitch two of the Colorado Route, south face of Fitz Roy. *Quinn Brett*

de l'S we jokingly started a cost-benefit analysis to aid our decision-making for the next adventure. A few glasses of wine later, Max's vision for a line on the south side of Fitz Roy found itself at the top of our list.

Warm spells this past season in southern Patagonia made crack climbing on south faces more feasible, as they were likely to be free of ice. Our approach across the Piedras Blancas Superior Glacier, on the other hand, was made more complicated by the warm weather. We delicately walked two thong-like snow bridges over gaping crevasses, finally weaving our way to a bivy below the east face of Fitz Roy. The intimidating 4,000' gray monolith towered over our heads.

The following morning we simul-soloed the 60° snow slope left of La Brecha. At our bivy, we rested, refueled our bodies, and worked on our alpine sunburn, all while watching the light change on the south face in hopes of revealing a line. It looked plausible, but portions were hidden. Alarm set for 2:30 a.m., we brewed and finished packing our kit.

Leaving camp required ascending a small buttress to gain a snowfield that hugs Fitz Roy's base. We paused for a bit, allowing the sky to lighten. We now had a visual on our possible entry point (between the Washington Route and Asado) as we shoed up in the snow at 6 a.m. The route began up a beautiful finger crack and a short offwidth, the first of many, many splitter cracks to come.

Roughly 12 hours later, we had finished the ten steep pitches of the headwall. Three more pitches of simul-climbing up blocky terrain had us on the summit of Fitz Roy. We brewed a quick dinner and retreated to our three-man bivy sack, spooning under the summit block. Morning blanketed us in blue sky. We rappelled the Franco-Argentine and finally hit the isothermic snow of La Silla in early afternoon. After a brew and packing up our gear at the base, we made the rappels down La Brecha and began a slushy walk out the Piedras Blancas. We bivied one last time on the shore of the electric-blue Laguna de los Tres, below the glacier.

We couldn't believe that a line so beautiful and clean had been untouched: a golden granite headwall with nary a loose rock and splitter cracks for over 1,000 feet. The climbing varied from ring locks to fists (tons of fists), with an occasional wider section, for 13 pitches. I am still trying to convince Max to go climb it again—the Colorado Route (500m, 5.11c). 📷

— QUINN BRETT, *USA*

ALETA DEL TIBURÓN, NEW ROUTES

ON JANUARY 9, 2016, I arrived in the British Camp in the French Valley of Torres del Paine with my wife, Heather Baer. We were intent on repeating the normal route on Aleta del Tiburón (Shark's Fin), but information on the climb is scarce and the low-angled south and west faces of this formation can be climbed virtually anywhere. In camp, we met two Italians, Antony and Andrea (last names not known), who had just completed a new route on the east face of Aleta del Tiburón. Their route, El Sonido del Viento (600m, 5.10 A2), was left with the necessary pitons in situ so that a standard rack and rivet hangers are all that is needed.

On January 14, Heather and I started at the high point of the talus on Aleta del Tiburón, about 200' left of the fin that defines the south ridge, beneath a dark, blocky feature that we deemed the Black Onion. From the top of the first pitch, I reasoned that Charlie Fowler, who had soloed the route about 20 years prior, had probably gone up the lower-angle ground to the left of the Black Onion. Heather and I went up and right, gradually edging closer to the arête on the right, which we joined on pitch 10 after climbing about 1,000' of new ground.

We underestimated the length of the climb—a total of 13 pitches—and coupled with a late start (5 p.m.), we found ourselves midnight-ed on pitch 11. We were forced to make an open bivy in a quaint hole. Eventually the sun came up and warmed our shivering bodies. Around 9 a.m. we continued climbing the final two pitches to the south summit. Totally spent by our night out in the open, we did not go to the true summit, which is 5m higher and involves another 40m of horizontal climbing along the summit fin. We descended the rappel route from the south summit, which is totally separate from our climbing route, replacing many ratty anchors along the way. We called our route When Does the Sun Come (V 5.9). Except for the crux 5.9 pitch, every pitch is 5.7 or 5.8, mostly following thin cracks, but with 40' runouts on edgy face climbing midway up the climb.

A few days later, Heather and I were joined by climber/photographer Claudio Carocca from Puerto Natales. On January 18 we hiked into the Agostini Valley, a higher tributary of the French Valley. Five minutes from base camp, Heather suffered a bad ankle sprain in the soft snow. After stabilizing her ankle, Claudio and I left to explore a crag at the very top of the valley, climbing a three-pitch route (5.10b) to a virgin summit we dubbed the Helmet. The climbing was stellar on thin cracks, arêtes, and underclings, not unlike climbing at Joshua Tree. Over the next two days we descended toward town. Heather toughed it out and self-rescued by crawling, limping, and eventually walking back to the trailhead.

– STEVE SCHNEIDER, *USA*

CENTRAL TOWER, RIDERS ON THE STORM, FREE VARIATIONS

IN EARLY 2016, Ines Papert (Germany), Thomas Senf (Switzerland), and Mayan Smith-Gobat (New Zealand) repeated Riders on the Storm (1,300m, 7c A3, Albert-Arnold-Bätz-Dittrich-Güllich, 1991) on the east face of the Central Tower of Paine. Papert and Smith-Gobat were the first women to climb the route. They also climbed two pitches (up to 7c+) that had not yet been freed and discovered a five-pitch potential free variation in the middle of the climb, freeing two of these pitches.

– DOUGALD MACDONALD

ANTARCTICA

HALL PEAK, SOUTH FACE AND SOUTHEAST RIDGE

THE 2015-'16 SEASON was stormier than normal, which led to challenging conditions for getting to and climbing on Mt. Vinson (4,892m). However, the summit success rate remained relatively high, as usual. The only new climb of the season was the first ascent of Hall Peak (2,190m) on the eastern side of the Heritage Range. On January 6, 2016, François Chateau, Eric Crown, Chris Haver, and Alison Levine went to the summit with ANI guides Nick Lewis, Todd Tumulo, and Scott Woolums. They approached from the south, slanting up right across the south face and onto the southeast ridge. This was followed to the summit, negotiating some moderate mixed terrain in the middle section. Hall Peak lies to the north of Mt. Spörli (2,263m), which had its first ascent in December 2011 by an ANI team. 📷

— DAMIEN GILDEA, *AUSTRALIA*

FILCHNER MOUNTAINS, VARIOUS ASCENTS

IN NOVEMBER, Michael Guggolz (Germany), Kjetil Kristensen and Kjell Olav Gjerde (Norway), and I visited the Filchner Mountains and skied from Jøkulkyrkja (3,148m), the highest point in Queen Maud Land, along Trollslottet toward Rakekniven in the east. On the 19th we climbed a nameless 2,775m peak that we called "Thor's Altar," the next day Jøkulkyrkja, on the 22nd Peak 2,670m and Peak 2,240m, and on the 25th the high point of a rocky ridge of 2,231m (there were three rocky summits that we named "Tre Trollungane"). Apart from Jøkulkyrkja, all were first ascents. [*See the website for coordinates of these peaks.*] 📷

— CHRISTOPH HÖBENREICH, *AUSTRIA*

VARIOUS SKI ASCENTS

IN NOVEMBER AND DECEMBER, Marc Rioualec and I led a group of seven ski mountaineers to the Peninsula through exceptionally icy waters, aboard the good ship Podorange. The ice prevented all vessels from moving south of Cuverville Island (which is pretty far north), and in suboptimal weather we had only one clear day out of 12 days on skis.

We enjoyed some fine skiing from anchorages in the bay at the head of the Sikorsky Glacier, south of Cierva Cove. Our first day was on the 495m peak to the east of Charles Point, which we named "Gentoo Peak." [*See the online version of this report for all summit coordinates.*] This summit offers numerous great ski lines, and by Antarctic standards the crevasse hazard

Ascending "Tarka Lookout." On the left is Mt. Tennant, which has been climbed by the left ridge. In the background: the east tip of Anvers Island (Clifford Peak), and to its right Schollaert Channel. *Jim Blyth*

is easily manageable. Our second summit was a fine little peak of 797m to the south of the bay. We climbed an easy snow ramp in wind and poor visibility, hence the imaginative name "Windy Top." We also enjoyed the 450m hill to the north of the bay, which we called "The Faff."

After attempting to explore the mountains to the south of Tournachon Peak and climbing a summit we call "Tarka Lookout" (730m), east of Mt. Tennant on Rongé Island, we made our way to Brabant Island. Here, we ascended an unnamed 1,343m peak between Mounts Ehrlich and Cook that we called "Nevis Australis" or "Mt. Jenner," as it lay at the head of the Jenner Glacier. Subsequent research leads me to believe this was not one of the many summits climbed during the 1984-'85 British Joint Services expedition to Brabant, but I cannot be sure. 📄 📷

— JIM BLYTH, *FRANCE*

SIKORSKY GLACIER, PEAK 1,475M

FROM DECEMBER 2011 TO FEBRUARY 2012, I led an Eagle Ski Club party to the Peninsula, where we made ascents from the Sikorsky Glacier (*AAJ 2012*), southeast of Cierva Cove. In the 2015-'16 season I returned to the Sikorsky with a group of Australians to attempt the last significant unclimbed peak in this region, which lies on the south side of the glacier. From a camp on the upper Sikorsky we traversed "Central Peak" (unofficial name, ca 1,300m) to reach the northwest side of our mountain, which we climbed on skis without any significant difficulty (1,475m, 64°15.372S, 60°45.147W). 📷

— PHIL WICKENS, *U.K.*

LIVINGSTON ISLAND, FALSA AGUJA AND SOFIA PEAK

AAJ 2015 BRIEFLY reported the first ascent of False Aguja (1,680m), the second-highest summit on Livingston Island. A complete report from the Bulgarian climbers is now available at the AAJ website. 📄 📷

— LINDSAY GRIFFIN

NORWAY

BREITINDEN, NORTH FACE, THE ICE PRINCESS

FROM FEBRUARY 20 TO MARCH 7, Paul Bride, Jesse Huey, Michael Pennings, Jon Walsh, and I visited the island of Senja, north of the Arctic Circle. During the first few days, Jon and Jesse climbed Finnkona (400m, WI6+), which they agreed was one of the wildest ice routes anywhere. They also attempted the still unrepeated Ines Papert testpiece Finnmannen (WI6+ M9+, 2013), finding hard, insecure, and spicy climbing. Mike and I enjoyed a Polar Circus–like route called Hesten, a 450m WI5 classic.

Conditions then became very coastal, and the danky rains mirrored the health of our team as we battled a flu-like sickness that took us down one after the other. During a down-day ski tour to Senja's highest peak, Breitinden (1,010m), we scoped the "Scottish Wall," finding the 400m to 600m north face ripe with potential. Jesse and I returned in better conditions and launched up an unclimbed system of goulottes and mixed ground to the left of the original route, Fantasia (Nesheim, Olsen, and partner, 2007).

Right away we knew it was game on. I found only a couple of pieces to protect the 60m AI4 first pitch. That theme continued for the remainder of the route, but when the difficulties increased and the terrain got steep, we always found just enough gear to make the next move. As a full moon began to rise, we topped out on the summit ridge, howling as you do when

The "Scottish Wall" on the north face of Breitinden. (1) Grasshopper Gully (400m, AI5 M5, Perrin-Visscher, 2014). (2) The Ice Princess (450m, AI4+ M6+ R, Huey-McSorley, 2015). (3) Fantasia (450m, TD WI4+, Nesheim, Olsen, and friend, 2007). (4) Crazy Maze (600m, 8+/IX WI4+, Papert-Senf, 2014). *Paul McSorley*

a fist pump just isn't enough. A rappel off the back led to long snow slopes and a circumnavigation of the mountain to get back to the car. We arrived home 17 hours after leaving. Our 450m route, the Ice Princess, was AI4+ M6+ R, but like most mountain experiences the grade only tells part of the story.

– PAUL MCSORLEY, *CANADA*

GRYTETIPPEN & BREITINDEN, POSSIBLE NEW ROUTES

IN FEBRUARY 2014, Vincent Perrin, Bas Visscher, and I climbed a possible new line on the southwest side of Grytetippen (890m), near Fjordgård. According to the local mountain guide Bent Vidar Eilertsen, this 600m face had only one line on it, an easy snow couloir. Our route follows an obvious couloir in the center of the face. We called it No Time for Tea (WI4 M4) because of the British team climbing close to us, Tim Blakemore and Twid Turner, who did a new line that was quite hard (WI5 M7+). They called their route Pass the Dutchie.

Jesse Huey searches for pro on the run-out Ice Princess, north face of Breitinden. *Paul McSorley*

Visscher and Perrin also climbed a possible new line on the north face of the Breitinden: Grasshopper Gully (400m, AI5 M4).

– BAS VAN DER SMEEDE, *THE NETHERLANDS*

THREE NEW ROUTES

IN LATE FEBRUARY, Daniel Burson, Chris Guyer, Shawn Gregory, and I visited Senja for a week of mixed climbing. I had been there before, in 2013, with Steve Berwanger and Tanner Callender, and established five new climbs on the island, including two mixed routes above Ersfjord with 365m of climbing each and two shorter routes in Ballesvika, above the tunnel to Gryllefjord. But since Senja was relatively unknown to climbers at the time, we tried to keep things hush. On this trip the crew established three lines, ranging from four to six pitches.

Tidal Roulette (200m) rises straight out of the ocean on the south-facing cliffs above Ersfjord and involved a 2.5-mile rock-hopping approach along the shore. As we climbed the tide came in, forcing us to post-hole in snow for hours to get back to the car.

Deliberation Corner (270m) was on Luttinden's high east-facing cliffs above Ersfjord. This route, the most difficult climbed on the trip, involved very thin dry-tooling up seams to a small ledge. Above, the second pitch was a thin ice smear up a corner. Halfway up you had to step out of the corner system on a thin smear where everything beneath your feet was space—perhaps the climb's most memorable moment.

We spotted Smoke Show (150m), the last route on the trip, on Hatten, the next mountain east of Luttinden. After approaching on skis, we climbed a thin smear that rises directly up the peak. I recall an incredible long pitch of thin alpine-like climbing, leading into a chimney system with moderate alpine ice and mixed terrain above.

I declined to rate these mixed rock and ice adventures because the conditions change so often here, and I wouldn't want to deter anyone from doing the routes because of a grade.

— AARON MULKEY, *USA*

VÅGAKALLEN, NORTHEAST FACE, NIGHT CROSSES THE CROWN

OVER TWO MONTHS of a Lofoten winter, a couple of friends and I managed to add a few new routes to the Magic Islands' collection. The first is the biggest and proudest, with a feel more Alaskan than its low altitude might suggest.

On the morning of February 16, fellow American Kurt Hicks and I clicked into our skis and skinned away from the lodge at Kalle, where we were both employed as ski guides for the season, thus able to spend two months in pricey Norway. As the sun lit the Hopenfjord, we racked up below the northeast face of Vågakallen. The mountain has three distinct features on its northern aspect, the most conspicuous being the central Storpillaren, which bisects the face. Taking the most appealing line on the northeast face, we climbed a series of runnels, benches, corners, and freshly iced slabs to the ridge at the top, well left of the Scottish Route (Benson-Robertson, 2001). The climbing was consistently thin and bold, but overridingly good, and we arrived at the ridge around 6 p.m.

The ca 750m northeast face of Vågakallen, showing (1) Night Crosses the Crown (2015) and (2) the Scottish Route (Benson-Robertson, 2001). The prominent buttress in center is the Storpillaren, home to several difficult rock routes. The north face is to the right. Various other routes are not shown. *Chris Wright*

after roughly 18 quality pitches.

We believed we had overcome the bulk of the climbing, but the next eight hours to the summit exposed a gross underestimation on our part. The many pitches up the ridge included memorable levitations up foam on rock, a skittering fall down a slab into a pile of snow, and an overhanging rappel from a bollard chopped out of a rimed cornice. Finally we reached the summit at roughly 1 a.m.

We descended the summer route to the south and west toward Djupfjorden. Owing to an inconveniently missed text message with details of the egress, we scrambled over sea ice and frozen kelp before a sheer wall forced us to contemplate the merits of either swimming or sleeping. We instead retreated and stumbled along the fjord's opposite side, bringing us to a waiting car and back to the lodge around 8 a.m., some 26 hours after leaving. We named the 750m route Night Crosses the Crown and graded it V WI4+ M6 R, though I remain curious exactly what number to apply to inch-thick vertical ice with a Spectre in turf some distance below.

In the ensuing seven weeks I made multiple attempts on a variety of objectives, finding success only on a single pitch (WI5 M5) on a promising buttress near Eide, which we believe to be the first on the wall.

After so many failures, I got lucky again on April 6, the day before I had to leave, when my friend Danny Uhlmann and I set out for a line I had seen while ski touring near Falkfjorden. Our climb ascended one of a few iced gully systems on the west face of a 720m sub-peak on the ridge running south from Middagstinden (520m) to Nissvasstinden (750m). We climbed the route in eight pitches, with a thin, strenuous crux on an iced slab down low and another on steep rock and turf up high, with moderate terrain in between. We named the route Morning Bread (360m, III WI5 M5), and I left for the Alps the next day.

Two months and two big routes: When conditions in Lofoten are on, the climbing is otherwordly, a dream. The number of days when they are not explains why there is yet much to be done. Still, I'm going back. 📷

— CHRIS WRIGHT, *USA*

HELVETESTINDEN, NEW ROUTES; SEGLTINDEN, SOUTHWEST PILLAR

IN JUNE, Guillermo Cuadrado, Gerber Cucurell, Salvador "Muna" Llorens, and I visited the Lofoten Islands, seeking adventure and unspoiled rock. After two flights and a day by car, we arrived at Moskenes. A little boat ride and a short walk completed our journey to the base of Helvetestinden (602m). We installed our camp on the beach, about 100m from the base of the west face, near a whalebone that served as our dinner table, complete with seats.

We had a very clear style in mind: two 45m ropes, 12 cams, and a rack of nuts—no pitons and no bolts. We had never tried to climb a wall of this size in this style, and we enjoyed the feeling of nervous anticipation. After a night

The southwest pillar of Segltinden has two intertwining routes (2014 and 2015). *Gerber Cucurell*

Helvetestinden with the approximate lines of (1) Left Approximation, (2) Terra i Mar, (3) Helvetesvegen (Russian Route), (4) Catalan attempt, (5) Noensfoten, (6) Ticket To Greenland, and (7) the French Pillar, Norwegian Sheep Ranch, the Next Best Thing, and Tradicionarius. *Jordi Esteve Collection*

without stars, Gerber and I were first to attack the wall. Our attempt finished in just 80m below a compact wall without a clear crack system. We returned to the tent to have a coffee and rethink our strategy. Half an hour later, we returned to try a line on the left side of the cliff. We climbed quickly until a blank wall blocked the path. However, a little ledge led over to a dihedral system that opened the path to the top. At 11 p.m. we completed Terra i Mar (630m, Norwegian 7- A0).

Meanwhile, Muna and Guille climbed a line they called Tradicionarius on the southwest pillar. [*The right side of Helvetestinden's face is generally known as the French Pillar, with several intersecting lines.*] The following day we rested while they made an impressive ascent up the middle of the wall, solving a great puzzle. Their new route Noensfoten (570m, ED+ 6c) crosses Ticket to Greenland (Maracek-Svihálek, 2009) high on the face and was climbed in 15 hours.

After a several days we left the beach and went to investigate the Kirkefjord area. Guille and Gerber climbed a new route on the southwest pillar of Segltinden (Achilles Tendon, 340m, 7-), but on the way down Guille suffered a serious accident, sliding 100m down the northwest slopes. He miraculously survived but had multiple contusions and fractures, including a serious fracture of the cervical vertebrae. The rescue service responded quickly, moving Guille in less than two hours to the hospital in Bodø. 📷

[*Editor's note: The first ascent of the southwest pillar of Segltinden was completed in June 2014 by Norwegians Lars Martin Solberg and Johanne Broch Hauge: Hoist the Colours (8 pitches, 7+ A0). Detailed information on this route is posted at the AAJ website along with this report. The Catalonian route intersects Hoist the Colours several times but stays mostly to the right.*]

– JORDI ESTEVE, *CATALONIA, SPAIN*

THE ALPS

The following climbs appeared on the "Big List" of notable 2015 ascents in the Alps prepared for the annual Piolets d'Or jury by Lindsay Griffin, with help from Claude Gardien.

WESTERN ALPS

AILEFROIDE ORIENTALE (3,847M), NORTH FACE. On October 26, Alexandre Michel, Stefano Morino, and Pierre Sauget (France) put up Winter is Coming (700m, 550m new, 5 M5+ 80°).

PIC SANS NOM (3,913M), NORTH FACE. Benjemin Brochard, Fred Degoulet, and Jonathan Joly (France) climbed Le Prestige des Écrins (1,000m, M6+ 6a) over three days in October. 🗎 📷

AIGUILLE DU FOU (3,501M). Fabien Dugit and Cédric Lachat completed the first free ascent of Balade au Clair de Lune (Bellin-Boivin-Moioli, 1983). After working the route, the two Frenchmen climbed it free in a day, with pitches of 7b+, 8b, and 7c+ and some serious runouts.

SIX NORTH FACES. Tom Ballard (U.K.) became the first person to solo the six "classic" north faces of the Alps in a single calendar winter.

EIGER (3,970M), NORTH FACE. Simon Gietl, Robert Jasper, and Roger Schäli (Italian-German-Swiss) completed the Odyssee (1,400m, 33 pitches, 8a+). The route has been redpointed but awaits a continuous free ascent. 🗎 📷

MATTERHORN (4,478M), SOUTH FACE. Patrick Gabarrou (France) and various partners over 13 years, finishing with Pierre Gourdin, completed a new line: Padre Pio, Une Échelle Vers le Ciel (1,300m, 7a). 🗎 📷

EASTERN ALPS

MONTE QUALIDO (2,707M), EAST FACE. Paolo Marazzi, Luca Schiera, and Matteo de Zaiacomo (Italy) climbed King of the Bongo (ca 800m, 18 pitches, 7c+, no bolts).

TORRE VENEZIA (2,337M), SOUTH FACE. Emanuele Pellizzari and Nicolas Tondini (Italy) made the first winter ascent of Rondo Veneziano (470m, IX-).

CIVETTA (3,220M), NORTHWEST FACE. Martin Dejori, Marta Mozzati, Titus Prinoth, Giorgio Travaglia, and Alex Walpoth (Italy) climbed Via Degli Studenti (1,000m, VIII- A0).

SCHNEEFERNERKOPF (2,875M). In February, Joachim Feger and Michael Wohileben (Germany) climbed Optimist (1,300m, M6) on the west face of the Wetterstein massif in Austria.

GREAT BRITAIN

Scott Borden traversing Swanage limestone. *David Coley*

BOULDER RUCKLE, WONDERLAND

THE IDEA WAS SIMPLE. The cliffs in southern England are short—very short—so we would climb sideways.

Swanage already had a long traverse: the Girdle Traverse (1,070m, given E1 but rumored to be XS), climbed by Richard Crewe and Kenny Winkworth in 1969. It follows the mid-height horizontal fault line on Boulder Ruckle. As far as we can ascertain this has only been repeated once, in 1978. It might seem strange that a route of this length, only two hours from London, has had only two ascents. However, as we quickly found out when we tried to make the third ascent, the fault line provides some of the worst rock on the cliff, and the climbing is highly repetitive. Moreover, several parts of the route had fallen into the sea.

Having climbed in the Ruckle a reasonable amount, I was convinced there must be an alternative traverse on the solid limestone above or below the fault line. The Boulder Ruckle is around 40m high. Measured in a straight line, the cliff is 1km long. We guessed we were looking at 50 or so pitches for the full traverse. Pete Callaghan and I chose to start on the left end; we rapped in and started climbing toward the east.

Knowing we weren't going to able to do anything like 50 new pitches in a day, we decided to break it up into natural sections. This would create a series of routes, so climbers could spread the experience over several winter days of fun above the sea, like Munro bagging (Scottish peakbagging) for rock climbers. I was joined by a cast of characters on the route, some of whom were on a sea cliff for the first time. The youngest was 12, the oldest nearly 70.

On August 21, my son Theo and I climbed the final crack of Second Sight to finish the last section of the traverse. The full route covers 1,278m and 67 pitches. However, if you complete the route using the 12 suggested sections, starting from the base each time, much as the first ascensionists did, you will climb 1,625m in 84 pitches. We called the full traverse Wonderland (E1).

Wonderland is a very British big wall: above the sea, never more than two miles from a tea shop, and within walking distance of one of the world's best pubs. Don't forget your swimming trunks. 📄 📷 🔍

– **DAVID COLEY**, *U.K.*

SCOTTISH GRADE X ONSIGHTS

BY SIMON RICHARDSON

Scottish winter climbing continues to go from strength to strength and remains a fascinating blend of the traditional and modern. Bolts are not allowed and protection needs to be placed on the lead. Several years ago this was thought to be a limitation, but leashless tools and dry-tool training have increased skill and fitness levels, and recent seasons have seen an explosion in activity and standards. Not long ago, a new grade VIII was headline news, but nowadays several grade IXs are put up each season, and grade XII has been climbed. [*Scottish winter climbs receive an overall difficulty grade using a Roman numeral, and a second grade, using an Arabic numeral, for the technical difficulty of the hardest moves.*] The vision is to climb ever more challenging lines in perfect style.

In 2013 the chilling prospect of an onsight grade X became very close to reality with a winter ascent of Nevermore on the Tough-Brown Face of Lochnagar. This rarely repeated summer E2 (hard 5.10) was first climbed by Dougie Dinwoodie and Bob Smith in August 1981 and takes a direct line up the face between Post Mortem and Mort. Guy Robertson had made four attempts on the route, spread over three seasons, when he teamed up with Nick Bullock in April 2013. Bullock led the challenging second pitch (thought to be IX,10 in its own right),

Greg Boswell onsighting pitch three of the Messiah, an eight-pitch climb on Beinn Bhan in the Northern Highlands. *Guy Robertson*

leaving Robertson the crucial fifth pitch. After some hesitation, Robertson pulled over the roof but then fell.

With the onsight lost, Robertson handed over the ropes to Bullock, who soon passed the high point and pushed into the unknown. The climbing difficulties above the second overlap increased, and there was no more gear until the angle eased. "I took a long time, as the technicalities were brain ache–inducing, stomach-churning," Bullock wrote later. "Terror was the tang of battery terminals licked." Bullock kept his cool, and a winter ascent of Nevermore was finally a reality.

A dozen or so grade IX first ascents had previously been climbed onsight—Nevermore was graded X,10. Of course, given the prior attempts, Nevermore was not a perfect first ascent, but it had been climbed in better style than the handful of grade XI and XII winter routes in Scotland, which typically benefitted from pre-inspection, multiple attempts, or prior knowledge from summer ascents.

The 2014 winter was poor for mixed climbing, and the 2015 season was stormy and started late. However, a wet autumn meant that as the mountains cooled down in January, the mid-level gullies and smears began to weep copious amounts of ice. Activity levels were high, but the clear highlight was three new grade X's by Robertson and Greg Boswell.

They started their remarkable run on January 19, when they made the first ascent of the Greatest Show on Earth (X,10) on the north face of Cul Mor in Coigach. This awe-inspiring route takes the blank wall on the right side of Coire Gorm, which is defended by a large overhang. The line had been considered a problem for the next generation. Robertson led the first pitch, a steep icefall leading to a small terrace below the overhang. Boswell then made one of his finest ever leads, pulling through the roof and climbing the poorly protected wall above. A new grade X had been climbed onsight at last!

Four days later, Robertson and Boswell turned their attention to the 100m-high Broad Terrace Wall on Creag an Dubh Loch in the Southern Cairngorms. The angle tips considerably the wrong side of vertical between the lines of Sword of Damocles and Culloden, and in summer this section is breached by two mythical climbs: Flodden (E6) and Range War (E4). The first pitch of Range War is very vegetated, and the route has only been climbed a handful of times (in summer) since its first ascent in July 1983.

Boswell had visited the remote Dubh Loch seven times to attempt the route, and finally, on January 22, the stars aligned. Boswell and Robertson climbed an alternative first pitch left of the original line, and Boswell then led the daunting 35m crux pitch (graded 6a in summer), pulling on huge reserves of physical and mental strength, and leaving Robertson the top pitch of thick bulging ice. The pair gave Range War (winter variation) X,10.

Ten days later, Robertson and Boswell teamed up with Uisdean Hawthorn and succeeded on the long-sought first winter ascent of the Messiah on the forbidding vertical walls of Beinn Bhan in the Northern Highlands. This route was first done by George Shields and Bob Jarvie in the summer of 1972, but their ascent was not recorded, and the route had passed into climbing folklore. At the beginning of February, the trio climbed the eight-pitch winter route onsight, grading it X,10, and thus completed a remarkable hat trick of hard new routes—a significant step forward in the development of Scottish winter climbing.

[Previous page] **Pete Benson climbing the challenging second pitch of Nevermore (X,10) on Lochnagar during the fourth attempt in March 2013. Extreme cold and dwindling daylight forced retreat two pitches above. The first ascent finally fell to Nick Bullock and Guy Robertson several weeks later.** *Guy Robertson*

MODERN WATER ICE IN TURKEY

BY TUNÇ FINDIK

The history of ice climbing is not at all old in Turkey. Except for long alpine ice gullies in the high mountains, few ice climbs had ever been done, and nowhere in the country was there a real water-ice area. However, in eastern Turkey, near the town of Uzundere in Erzurum province, the altitude is high, the winter season is generally cold and long, and the terrain is mountainous—perfect conditions for waterfall ice buildup.

The ice climbing history of Uzundere began in January 2012, when my friend Çetin Bayram, the head of ATAK (an Erzurum-based sports and search and rescue club), invited me to climb an icefall he had found in the winter of 2011. The 30m Serafin (WI3+/4) may have been the first frozen waterfall route climbed in Uzundere.

In January 2014, Doğan Palut and I returned to Uzundere to climb new routes, following more exploration by Çetin. I was very happy to make the first ascent of Lucifer, a massive 45m icefall (WI4+/5) in Uzunkavak village. In February of that year, an "icefall meeting" incorporating most of the committed climbers in Turkey was sponsored by the Hotel Xanadu of Erzurum. During the meeting, Efecan Aytemiz, Emrah Ozbay, and I climbed the first multi-pitch true water-ice route in Turkey: Sarıgelin (85m, WI5+). By the end of that winter, Uzundere had at least seven outstanding new water-ice routes, with good potential for rock climbing as well.

As a consequence, the municipality of Erzurum sponsored the first International Erzurum-Uzundere Ice Climbing Festival in January 2015, hosting 25 foreign climbers as well as 175 Turkish climbers. Before and during the festival, a number of new ice routes were opened, including the longest water-ice

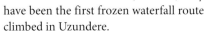
Anatolia Pillar (100m, WI6), climbed in January 2015 by Anna Torretta, Cecilia Buil, and Tunç Fındık. *Zhang Wei*

route in Turkey: Nakavt (300m, WI6, Findik-Şarkoğlu), on Mt. Güllü, near the Kirazlı village pasture, at an altitude of nearly 3,000m. Visiting climbers established a number of very impressive ice routes, including Anatolia Pillar (100m, WI6), above Cevizli village, climbed by Anna Torretta (Italy), Cecilia Buil (Spain) and me; Çetinceviz (100m, WI5+), the extreme left icefall near Cevizli village, by Charlotte Barre, Mathieu Maynadier, and Thomas Vialettet (France); and two more routes on Mt. Güllü: Tovaritsch (260m, WI5+ and grade III, V mixed climbing), by Roman Abildaev, Sergey Seliverstov (both Russia), and Anıl Şarkoğlu (Turkey), and Sugar Couloir (450m, WI5 and grade IV mixed), by Torretta and Buil.

At the end of the winter, Uzundere region boasted 14 frozen waterfall routes, with a potential for many more. This is not a lot compared to regions such as Cogne in the European Alps, but, remember, this is a very new climbing area.

Uzundere is 84km and one hour's drive from Erzurum, the biggest city in eastern Turkey. The best ice climbing generally is found from mid-January through the end of February, with temperatures averaging -10°C at night and 0°C to 2°C during daytime. Even in the driest and warmest winter seasons, the icefalls at 2,000m or above offer thick, stable ice and season-long

Lucifer (WI4+/5) in Uzunkavak village, the first of seven new routes climbed in the Uzundere area in early 2014. *Çetin Bayram*

climbing, while in warm winters some icefalls at around 1,000m will never form. Some of the remote alpine settings can be difficult to approach after heavy snowfall or risky due to avalanche danger.

The online version of this story has additional logistical information and descriptions of all ice routes in the area as of February 2015. Information on newer routes can be obtained through the contacts listed in the online article.

MIDDLE EAST

Sivridağ in Antalya, showing the line of the first route up the north face (580m, 10 pitches). *Tunç Fındık*

KAÇKAR DAĞI, WEST FACE; NEW ALPINE ROCK ROUTES IN ALA DAĞLAR AND ANTALYA

THE PROLIFIC ALPINIST Tunç Fındık has climbed many long new routes in the mountains of Turkey in recent years. In 2015 he completed about a dozen, with various partners, ranging from 100m to 600m. These were mostly in the Ala Dağlar mountains or on the huge limestone pyramid of Sivridağ in Antalya. Fındık's brief descriptions and photo topos of these new climbs can be found at the *AAJ* website.

In the summer of 2013, Fındık, Emrah Ozbay, and Serkan Ertem climbed the west face of Kaçkar Dağı (3,932m), the highest peak of the Kaçkar Range in northeastern Turkey, via a complex mixed route up a gully system, with wet, loose rock and some steep ice and snow pitches: 700m, TD+ VI WI4+ M6. 🗒 📷 🔍

— DOUGALD MACDONALD,
WITH INFORMATION FROM TUNÇ FINDIK

Editor's note: Most Turkish climbers oppose the use of bolts on alpine routes or high mountain walls. Several bolted mountain routes recently have been chopped by local climbers, and in 2015 the police halted an attempt to create a new route on the north face of Demirkazık (3,756m) in the Ala Dağlar mountains. Sport routes and bolted anchors are acceptable on certain lower-elevation cliffs in mountain areas, and visiting climbers are urged to contact local activists to determine which cliffs are open to bolting, especially in the Ala Dağlar and Antalya regions.

JEBEL MISHT, SOUTHEAST FACE, PHYSICAL GRAFFITI

IN NOVEMBER 2013, Andrea Migliano and I hiked along the huge southeast face of Jebel Misht and checked out a line on the right side, apparently unclimbed, though attempted by a French team some years ago. (We didn't know this yet.) We planned a fast ascent, with two ropes, cams, a couple of pegs, and two bottles of water. We started climbing the following day at dawn in a big corner. After a couple of pitches we started simul-climbing. The limestone was quite solid, and the line was clear. In the afternoon we arrived at the steepest part of the wall—in front of us was an overhanging corner. The rock was rotten and covered by sand. After 20m virtually unprotected, I managed to place a peg with one hand and then reached a good ledge. After some steep but safer pitches, we arrived at the big ledge three-quarters of the way up the wall. It was too late to finish, so we lit a fire and bivied there; unfortunately, during the night it started raining. The next day Andrea led a corner with very nice features, then we simul-climbed fast to the flat summit: Physical Graffiti (1,000m, 6c). [*This route may share some ground with Riddle in the Sands (Barlow-Bishop- Chaudhry, 2001), but the key sections are completely independent and well to the right.*]

The southeast face of Jebel Misht showing the routes (1) Boys Don't Cry (1,000m, 7c+, 2016) and (2) Physical Graffiti (1,000m, 6c, 2013). Half a dozen other routes lie between these two. *Ondřej Beneš*

After a couple of days exploring canyons, we opened a route on the northeast face of a tower northwest of Al Hamra that we later learned was called Jebel Ghul. We started in the middle of the wall and then trended to the right, where we found the steep crux pitches (650m, 6b+). The rock was good. We descended the opposite side, leaving one rappel anchor. [*The Italians began their climb on the 2002 British Route (Davison-Hornby-Sammut, 650m, VII), of which they were unaware, before moving right on the upper pillar. In 2006, a French trio also climbed a route in the same area as the British Route.*]

– LUCA SCHIERA, *ITALY*

JEBEL MISHT, SOUTHEAST FACE, BOYS DON'T CRY

At the start of January 2016, my friends Jiri Lautner, Filip Martinek, David Michovsky, and I, all Czech, climbed a new route on Jebel Misht. We choose a line 50m to the right of the route Make Love Not War (2003) on the southeast face, the steepest part of huge southern wall. We finished our route after seven days, including three nights on the wall. There are big ledges, so you do not need portaledge. We drilled 35 protection bolts and 22 belay bolts. Because of some loose rock, we had to follow Make Love Not War for two pitches, but most of our line is completely new: Boys Don't Cry (1,000m, 21 pitches, 7c+ redpoint).

– ONDŘEJ BENEŠ, *CZECH REPUBLIC*

New routes on the Said Wall, a relatively shady sector of Jebel Kawr. (1) Passer Fritz. (2) Vacca Loca. (3) Interruptio. (4) Sab Kuch Milega. *Simon Messner Collection*

JEBEL KAWR, SAID WALL; JEBEL MISHT, SÜDTIROLERFÜHRE

JAN KOBALD, Markus Kollmann, Philipp Prünster, and I (all South Tyroleans, age 23–25) couldn't wait for our Christmas holidays. Markus and I had already made one climbing trip to Oman in 2012–'13. Ever since, we knew we would return for more time with the friendly people, the moon-like landscape, and the simple life in the desert.

Just after finishing our last course at university, we flew to Muscat on December 17, 2014, and headed into Oman's desert. Near Jebel Misht and Jebel Kawr, we set up camp at the foot of the same acacia that two years earlier had provided us with shade, hammocks, and a fridge for our food. The centuries-old tree was our only refuge from the sun.

During the last weeks of 2014, we climbed almost every day and put up 10 new routes. [*At the AAJ website you can find a link to a report (in German) with photos and topos of the new routes. The Italians' earlier routes are found in* Climbing in Oman *by Jakob Oberhauser (2014)*]. After a trip south to the sea, where we nearly lost our Jeep when it got stuck on the mudflats and flooded by the incoming tide, we spent two days climbing in Wadi Tiwi and then returned to our original camp and our beloved acacia. We were well adapted to the rock and highly motivated to try some bigger lines. We had already climbed two easier routes on a shady sector of Jebel Kawr that we came to call the Said Wall, after a hospitable old man named Said who lived nearby and came out again and again to watch us with binoculars. In the center of the Said Wall was an incomplete line with the promising name Interruptio, begun in 2004 by Hanspeter Eisendle and friends. Markus and I had tried this route in 2012, but were scared off by a huge, slick overhang in the upper third of the wall.

On New Year's Day in 2015, this impressive roof once again did not appear climbable, so Markus bypassed it to the left. After some loose rock, he reached a small stance where he was able to place a piton. The next 8m were unprotectable and crimpy, requiring all of Markus' expertise. Fortunately, he reached a 4cm-thick hourglass thread that offered the only possibility for anchoring a hanging belay. The very bad piton backing up the thread did not give us a good feeling while belaying the next pitch. Again a long runout led straight upward, than we traversed back right into a prominent dihedral leading to the exit of the wall. For sure, Interruptio (500m, VII+) was one of the most inspiring routes I have ever climbed!

While descending, Markus spotted another line on the right part of the wall. He and Philipp climbed this challenging new route the next day. At one point, Markus broke off an undercling and took a long fall onto the only piece above the belay anchor. He was lucky to get away with no more than a scare and some scrapes. The duo named this difficult-to-protect route Sab Kuch Milega ("Everything is Possible," 450m, VIII-).

At the end of our trip, we succeeded on a new line on Jebel Misht—the only route we climbed together as a team of four. We had noticed a pillar on the left side of the south face that seemed to have no routes, probably because of the long approach and full sun. (*This pillar is between the Second Tower and Third Tower, right of the route Madam Butterfly, Chaudhry-Hornby, 2000.*) We got onto the wall early in the morning and planned for a bivouac. We were all surprised when we stood on top of the mountain after only six hours of climbing—a fabulous miscalculation on our part. We named the route Südtirolerführe (800m, VI+). All 16 routes we opened on this trip were climbed from the bottom up and all free. We used a total of ten pitons, which we left fixed. 📄 📷

— SIMON MESSNER, *ITALY*   Climbing on Sab Kuch Milega. *Philipp Prünster*

IRAN

SHAH DEJ GROUP, NEW ROUTES

NORTH OF TEHRAN, a spectacular road leads to the Caspian Sea, passing numerous high mountains, including Alam Kooh (4,851m, a.k.a. Alamkouh or Alamkoh), with one of the biggest granite walls in the country. Many rock towers in the area are still unclimbed. Close to the Amir Kabir reservoir, about 1.5 hours' drive from Tehran, is a huge, rocky summit called Shah Dej ("Kingdom Castle," also spelled Shahdzh). In October, after three attempts, I climbed a 300m wall on this peak with Zohreh Ofoghi: Golden Eagle (8 pitches, 6c).

The second wall we climbed, Loodar, is in the same area, near Khozenkola village. Because of security concerns, permission to access this area must be arranged with the dam security forces. In November, Ofoghi and I met with a local climber, Majid Azimi, and after an hour-long approach we reached the base of the wall around sunrise. I thought the route would be 400m long, but I made a big mistake—it was more than 800m. Most of the pitches were easy, but others were up to 6c/5.11. On the ninth pitch a falling stone broke Majid's finger, and he was obliged to climb the rest of the wall with his broken hand. The descent was long (next time I would rappel the route), and we made it back at 11 p.m., after a hard day of around 17 hours. We named the route Marathon because it needed stamina and patience! 📄 📷

— HAMID REZA SHAFAGHI, *IRAN*

AFRICA

Steffen Krug following pitch eight (6c) of Into the Blue on Jebel Taoujdad. *Jens Richter*

JEBEL TAOUJDAD, SOUTHEAST PILLAR, INTO THE BLUE

ON OCTOBER 14, Steffen Krug and I returned to the beautiful limestone area of Taghia Gorge. The year before, we were very unlucky and got stuck in extremely bad weather for three weeks, with heavy rain, snow, and even ice—very unusual in this area. Because of the bad free climbing conditions we used aid to put up a new route on the southeast pillar of Jebel Taoujdad. We were sure it was going to become a great free line under better circumstances.

Starting on October 15, we enjoyed 10 days of great weather and repointed the route. The climb goes up some of the best limestone on one of the most impressive summits in Taghia, between the West Pillar and Au Nom de la Réforme. It is almost entirely bolted, but there is some distance between the bolts. The final two pitches require traditional protection. We called it Into the Blue (513m, 7c). There is obligatory 7a climbing, and the pitches are as follows: 7a, 7a+, 7b+, 6b+, 4a, 7c, 6b+, 6c, 6b+, 6c, 3, 5c, 5b.

[Editor's note: Jebel Taoujdad contains at least three other long routes, in addition to shorter climbs: Au Nom de la Réforme (340m, 6c), Fata Morgana (500m, 15 pitches, 7c), and Les Rivières Pourpres (545m, 7b+). Search the AAJ website for more info on these three routes.] 📷 🔍

– JENS RICHTER, *GERMANY*

JEBEL TIMGHAZINE, BERÉBER STYLE

IN MAY, Javier "Pitxi" Gonzalez (Spain) and I went to Taghia to put up a new line on Jebel Timghazine. We installed 88 bolts, over 13 pitches and 500m of climbing, in six climbing days. We didn't have time to free the whole route, but we estimate the grade to be 7a A1+, with obligatory 6b free climbing. We called it Beréber Style. 📄 📷 🔍

– RYAN ADOBE, *USA*

RECENT CLIMBING DEVELOPMENT

[*Editor's note: An influx of new-route submissions from the Anti-Atlas Mountains has prompted the AAJ to provide more background on this area, which we've only covered sporadically in the past. It is not possible to report all new routes from this zone, but we hope the following information will be useful to readers.*]

The climbing potential of the Anti-Atlas Mountains was first explored in 1991 by British climbers Les Brown and Trevor Jones, when the first Gulf War diverted them from a planned climbing trip in Jordan to the ancient market town of Tafraout, on the northern fringe of the Sahara. Throughout the 1990s, there followed extensive development by a team of well-known veteran mountaineers, including Sir Chris Bonington, Joe Brown, Derek Walker, and Claude Davies, who wrote the area's first guidebook in 2004. Today, although the secret was slow to get out, Tafraout is fast becoming something of a rock climbing mecca, particularly for British and northern European climbers, for whom it offers high-quality traditional climbing with reliably good weather throughout the winter months.

James Lam climbing Wall Street (5.10b) on the crags at Tizi Gzaouine. Along with many lengthy, adventurous climbs, Tafraout is home to dozens of high-quality, easily accessible roadside crags. *Steve Broadbent*

Given the background of Tafraout's early developers, it is no surprise that climbing here has maintained a very traditional adventure ethic—in contrast to the predominantly bolt-protected climbing that exists around much of the Mediterranean coast. The rock is high-quality quartzite, offering superb, positive handholds and good natural protection. This has produced satisfying low- to mid-grade routes in a remote mountain environment. Indeed, although numerous hard lines have been climbed, it is the lower-grade climbs for which Tafraout is becoming popular, and a number of long, adventurous climbs have already become established as classics of the region.

The Great Ridge (2,600', HVS/5.9) was the first of the big routes to see an ascent, back in 1998 at the hands of Les Brown and Pete Turnbull, before attention shifted to the northern side of the massif. There, on the huge cliffs above Asseldrar, Guy Robertson and Trevor Woods climbed Adventures Beyond the Ultraworld (1,200', E5/5.12a) in 2003—this remains one of the hardest routes in the range.

Between 2007 and 2011 there was an explosion of new route activity. This period saw the

The Thumb at Asseldrar. The 12-pitch route Adventures Beyond the Ultraworld climbs a pillar up the left side of the face at 5.12a. *Steve Broadbent*

first ascent of the now very popular Pink Lady (750', VS/5.7) on Afantinzar's Grand Wall, by Pete Johnson and Lun Roberts. In Samazar, home to some of the biggest cliffs in the Anti-Atlas, Jim Fotheringham and Mike Mortimer climbed the Great Ridge of Samazar (1,700', VS/5.8). Alongside this route is one of the most sought-after routes in Tafraout: Labyrinth Ridge (2,600', VS/5.8) on Samazar's Great Rock, climbed by Steve and Katja Broadbent in 2008.

Other notable ascents include Aylim's Central Buttress (1,500', E1/5.10a), by Steve Broadbent and Caroline Culwickm, and, on the Waterfall Wall, the very adventurous Daffodils, Kittens, and Pink Bunny Rabbits (1,000', E5/5.11b) by Topher Dagg, Davide Cassol, and Luca Vallata.

Today there are in excess of 2,000 documented climbs within one hour's drive of Tafraout, with new routes still being reported at the rate of about 150 per season. Most of these are on easily accessible crags and are between one and three pitches, spanning the grades from 5.6 to 5.12. More route information, maps, and guidebooks are available from the Oxford Alpine Club at www.climb-tafraout.com. 📷

— STEVE BROADBENT, *U.K.*

ETHIOPIA / GONDAR MOUNTAINS

MOLALIT TOWER, ABYSSINIA ÁLAINN

ON JANUARY 7, 2016, Barry Watts and I climbed a new route on Molalit Tower in the Gondar Mountains, in the Amhara region of northern Ethiopia. [*French climbers Alain Bruzy and Magali Salle made the first ascent Molalit Tower in 2012 (AAJ 2014)*]. We called our route Abyssinia Álainn (200m, HS), which means Beautiful Ethiopia. 📑 📷

— GERRY GALLIGAN, *IRELAND*

LUPUPA ROCK AND PEDRAS NEGRAS, NEW ROUTES

FROM AUGUST 31 TO SEPTEMBER 12, Stacy Bare, Maury Birdwell, Ted Hesser, and I went to Angola to sample the climbing and do some nonprofit solar-energy installations through the Honnold Foundation. The climbing exceeded expectations, particularly in Pedras Negras, which someday could be a world-class sport climbing area. The main difficulty is just getting a visa to enter the country, since this requires invitation. Once there, it was relatively easy to get around and climb. We had an outfitter, Eco-Tur, which arranged logistics.

We first visited the area around Lupupa. On big granite domes with super-compact rock, wide cracks and chimneys were pretty much all we could climb. Everything was very vegetated. (The country is equatorial.) On September 1 we climbed our first route, Bare Wrestling (450m, 5.10). This takes one of the proudest lines up Lupupa Rock: the big right-facing corner and chimney system on the main wall. It was the most sustained and strenuous chimney climbing I've ever experienced.

After this route we established two shorter climbs. Bare Trap (5.13-) is an overhanging, leaning offwidth crack, requiring number 4 and 5 Camalots—heinous!—and Maury's Roof (5.12+) is a splitter roof crack, perhaps the Separate Reality of Angola. These two routes, probably the hardest in Angola, are around the right side of Lupupa Rock, on the ridge with the prominent orange boulder. We hoped for good sport climbing here but had to settle for strenuous cracks.

After this we traveled to Pedras Negras. This was the real gem, an area of amazingly solid and featured conglomerate stone that someday could rival Margalef in Spain and is certainly better than Maple Canyon in Utah. It just needs a ton of bolts. Here, we established the Bare Hug Arête (2 pitches, 5.13c) up the southeast corner of the Sentinel, after climbing the standard north face route. The second pitch isn't fully bolted, and we didn't manage the redpoint.

In short, Angola offers some adventurous rock climbing and some major potential. It felt totally safe for traveling and was not nearly as expensive or intense as things previously written about it would indicate.

— ALEX HONNOLD, *USA*

ANGAVOA WALL, MAHAGAGA

IN MID-SEPTEMBER—after I climbed in Tsaranoro Valley in July and August—a local Tsaranoro climber from Madagascar named Rakotomalala Herynony Samuel (a.k.a. Hery) raved to me about an unclimbed wall a few hours away, in the little village of Ambohimahamasy. "Just as big and as impressive as Karambony," he told me.

I was skeptical. But just like a man getting married for the second time, hope prevailed, and I had to go and check it out. Sure enough, Angavoa Wall (Malagasy for "bat") is not quite as impressive as Karambony (few walls are), but it's a nice-looking wall nevertheless.

Hery (who had very little big-wall experience, especially at this difficulty) and I made the first ascent of the wall on September 13. It turned out to be quite the challenge. It's an excellent climb and, even though it has bolts, it is not to be taken lightly. We encountered loose rock, poisonous plants, bat guano, a lot of lichen and moss, jungle scrambling, and a little bit of bird shit. So it was right up my alley! We called our five-pitch route Imahagaga (250m, 7c+). The pitches are as follows: 7a, 6a+, 7c+, 6b+, 6c. 📷 🔍

— SEAN VILLANUEVA, *BELGIUM*

Climbing the arête on the fifth pitch. of the Change Experience. *Hamid Reza Shafaghi*

KARAMBONY TOWER, NORTHEAST ARÊTE, THE CHANGE EXPERIENCE

IN APRIL, Hassan Gerami, Farshad Mijoji, and I opened a new route up the stunning right (northeast) arête of Karambony Tower. We mainly aided at first, using hooks and bolts to make progress up the wall, then did our best to climb the route free. In total we spent six days opening the route, and then another three days climbing it from the ground up. Our route crosses Rain Boto (Albert-Arnold, 1995, 450m, 7b+) twice—once at the big midway ledge and again close to the summit—but does not share any notable amount of climbing. We called our climb the Change Experience (440m, 8b A2, 7c obligatory). [*See the full report from the team, containing first-hand beta on traveling to and climbing in Tsaranoro, at the AAJ website.*] 📄 📷 🔍

— HAMID REZA SHAFAGHI, *IRAN*

TSARANORO BE, EAST FACE, CUENTO DE HABAS

AFTER FIVE DAYS OF TRAVEL from Ecuador, Felipe Guarderas, Nicolas Navaraette, and I reached the Tsaranoro Valley. The village below the walls was much like in Ecuador, where people live quiet agricultural lives.

Our aim was to open a new route on these beautiful walls. First, we decided to become familiar with the area's climbing, which is characterized by granite patina and face climbing on small, fragile holds, mainly with bolts for protection. We chose two routes on the sprawling Tsaranoro Massif: Out of Africa (600m, 7a, Motto-Pellizzari-Piola-Robert, *AAJ 1999*), on Tsaranoro Kely, and Life in a Fairy Tale (500m, 5.11+, Luebben-Luebben, *AAJ 2000*), on Tsaranoro Atsimo. These climbs were enough to motivate us to find our own line.

We chose a path up the sheer wall of Tsaranoro Be, between Old Master and Short Cut.

After a problem charging batteries for our drill (the voltage here is 220V and we had a 110V charger), essential for a new route here, we began our journey up the wall. Our line begins on a slab washed smooth by years of African rains and then continues on vertical ground for most of the way—usually up patina. We occasionally crossed a huge black vein in the rock, and the final 100m of our route climbs it directly. We called the route Cuento de Habas (750m, 7b+/c).

In total the route required six days. We often hooked and aided ground-up to add bolts to the route, but we also utilized bolts from the nearby routes to assess the best line. In all, we placed about 250 bolts. We free climbed all the pitches but not in a single push. No cams or nuts are needed. [*Editor's note: Some past AAJ reports contain inaccurate descriptions or illustrations of routes on the four walls of the Tsaranoro Massif. In particular, AAJ 2001 shows a very inaccurate route-line overlay for the Tsaranoro Massif. Please see Roberto Morales' PDF in the online version of this report for the most up to date and accurate route lines on the Tsaranoro Massif.*]

— ROBERTO MORALES, *ECUADOR*

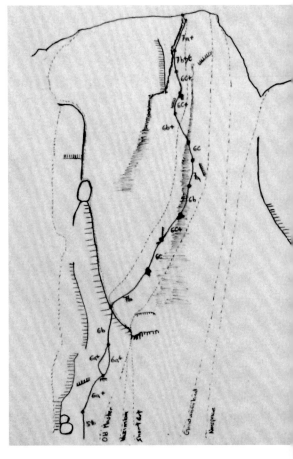

A topo of the new route Cuento de Habas on Tsaranoro Be. *Roberto Morales*

TSARANORO ATSIMO, FIRE IN THE BELLY

AFTER HAVING CLIMBED some of the classics in the Tsaranoro Valley with Argyro Papathanasiou (Greece) in July, I was joined by Siebe Vanhee (Belgium) in August. He had spotted a major unclimbed line on Tsaranoro Atsimo. The route is located right of Mora Mora (Blanco-Vales, 1999, redpointed by Adam Ondra in 2010 at 8c) and another, unknown route.

Armed with a drill, skyhooks, and thirst for exploration, we tackled the face ground-up. With much uncertainty, it took us six days to reach the summit. The route involved 700m of face climbing on black and green granite, with a very blank headwall at the top. We were convinced the route was out of our reach to free climb and thought we would have to leave it for future generations. However, we decided to give it a proper hard battle anyway, just for the fight. We returned and, to our own surprise, managed to free climb the line after a three-day effort. We called it Fire in the Belly (700m, 8a++). It's a great line, and even the easier pitches are demanding. The 11 pitches are: 5c, 6c, 7b+, 6b+, 6c, 7c, 8a+, 6b, 7a, 8a++, 7b.

— SEAN VILLANUEVA, *BELGIUM*

NEVER THE SAME

BY **CARLO GIULIBERTI**

It is the summer of 1998. A team of alpinists composed of Rolando Larcher, Marco Sterni and Erik Švab arrives at the still untouched Tsaranoro Atsimo. Its east wall is the first thing a climber will notice. The three climbers finish the expedition with a new route: Never the Same 670m, 8a+ A0, *AAJ 1999*). Beyond the numbers, it was a great route for the beauty of the line, the amazing rock quality, and the style—a challenging climb that requires concentration, finger strength, and perfect technique. The only drawback was Marco's hang on the hardest pitch.

Now it is summer 2015, 17 years later, and numerous routes have been opened in the Tsaranoro Massif. Our friend Marco still vividly recalls the un-freed pitch, and, to celebrate his 50th birthday, he proposes to Andrea Polo, Gabriele Gorobey, and me to return to Madagascar and complete the free climb. The four of us fly to Antananarivo on September 17.

Although we camp in the bungalows of Tsarasoa Camp, instead of in a tent under a mango tree, as Marco did on his first expedition, this does not prevent us from appreciating the local setting. Life here is timed by cycles of rice cultivation, along with the making and firing of clay bricks. A working day starts at sunrise and ends at sunset. A very different world, simple and poor, but where every person greets you, more or less surprised yet always with a smile.

Never the Same starts an hour's walk from camp. The east-facing wall allows only a few hours of climbing before the sun gets too hot. We have no portaledge, and the Tsaranoro granite does not offer places to bivy, so we decide to move ahead on the route day by day, climbing only during the shady hours and equipping the wall with fixed lines.

The route is stunning: a succession of increasingly difficult slabs up to 7c, where every move startles us due to the small holds. The climbing is enhanced by the incredible colors and the beautiful afternoon wind, and also by the Jurassic Park–style "music" that comes from the sacred forest below. Nevertheless, the real masterpiece for rock lovers is the crux eighth pitch, a smooth overhang with a single possible line of ascent along perfect and variously shaped and colored crimps, leading to a tough crux on tiny crystals.

After a day's rest to redeem energy and skin, Gabriele, Andrea, and I each manage to free the crux on our second try. We think it is solid 8a, but the main fulfillment is in having freed a route that was opened 17 years earlier along with the first ascensionist himself. The next day we climb to the summit. After the crux pitch the difficulty decreases (7a+ max), but the style is very technical and the spacey bolts demand concentration right to the top. After a well-deserved rest day, Andrea and I manage the ascent in one push, with Andrea freeing all 13 pitches in a day without mistakes (670m, 13 pitches, 8a+ [7b obligatory]).

Satisfied with these results, we next repeat the beautiful, and by now classic, Out of Africa on Tsaranoro Kely, and then Marco returns to Italy. The rest of us then climb the new route Fire in the Belly (700m, 8a++, *see report above*). Again we stay in the shade, use fixed lines, and climb team-free. The seventh pitch (8a+) is freed by Gabriele on his second attempt; the tenth (graded "8a++" by the first ascensionists) is freed by Andrea in three attempts. It takes us five days to climb the route, with one bivy below the crux pitch on the fourth day. We now understand the usefulness of portaledges! 📄 📷

Photo| Carlo Giuliberti climbing pitch six (7c) of Never the Same. *Andrea Polo*

RUSSIA

MAMISON, NORTH FACE, TRIANGLE DIRECT

IN FEBRUARY, Dmitry Romanenko and Vladimir Roshko (Ukraine) climbed the first route up the center of the Triangle on the north face of Mamison (4,319m), a peak in North Ossetia on the Russia-Georgia border. Using snowshoes, the two reached the Nikolaev Hut on February 4, and the next day established a camp at the head of the North Tseyskiy Glacier, where in clear weather the temperature dropped that night to -15°C. Their first attempt was halted by poor weather after they had climbed only 100m.

On February 12 they returned to high camp and the next day climbed 10 pitches. It took 1.5 hours to construct an adequate tent platform. The following morning, one more pitch led to the top of the Triangle, and then they followed the east ridge to the summit, arriving at 3 p.m. They regained the tent that night and the following day rappelled their route. The 820m new route (1,060m of climbing) was rated 6A. No bolts were taken. 📷 🔍

— LINDSAY GRIFFIN, *WITH INFORMATION FROM* ELENA DMITRENKO, *RISK.RU, RUSSIA*

CAUCASUS ACCESS NOTE

CLIMBERS SHOULD BE AWARE that, for the last five years or so, access to the frontier regions of the Caucasus has been complicated by tightened security along Russia's border with Georgia. Officially, a party needs to get a permit from the local security detachment. This may take one month. Without a permit, it will not be possible to pass roadblocks, even for ski touring or simple walks in the "high altitude zone." With a permit, a party can go to the mountains for any type of activity, but no closer than 100m to the border, which follows the summits of the main Caucasus ridge. (Patrols at these elevations are unlikely.) Mt. Elbrus sits to the north of the main chain and is entirely in Russia, so no permit is required.

— ANNA PIUNOVA, *MOUNTAIN.RU, RUSSIA*

SAYAN MOUNTAINS, ZVEZDNIY, NORTHEAST FACE, KOSINUSOYDA

I HAD LONG DREAMED of climbing a new route up the big northeast face of Zvezdniy (2,265m) in the Ergaki massif of the Western Sayan. After listening to our coach, Valery Balezin, Nicholas Matyushin and I decided to try a logical line on the left side of the face.

We left Krasnoyarsk, where we are both students at the university, in the evening of December 2. We started our approach on the 4th, spending that night in our portaledge, hung from a tree in the forest. Moving our ca 100kg of equipment through blowing snow, we reached a good site for advanced base on the 7th, close to the northeast face.

At 4 a.m. on December 9 the wind seemed to be almost hurricane force, and we feared to venture outside the portaledge, but by 10 a.m. we realized that if we didn't start soon we

Difficult iced slabs on day three of the 29-pitch new route on Zvezdniy, climbed in December. *Alexander Zhigalov*

[Top] The northeast face of Zvezdniy seen in drier, more summerlike conditions than during the 2015 winter ascent, when it was plastered in snow and ice. (1) Kosinusoyda (2015, 5B). (2) Temerev (2013, 6A). (3) Hvostenko (2001, 6A). (4) Balezin (1997, 5B). (5) Balezin (2001, 5B). *Alexander Zhigalov*

[Bottom] Sites of new routes in southern Siberia: (A) Zvezdniy, Western Sayan Mountains. (B) Sever, Eastern Sayan Mountains. (C) Moryan, Barguzin Range. © *Mapbox*, © *OpenStreetMap*

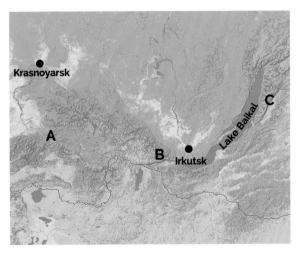

would run out of time. We set off in improved conditions, climbed five pitches to the first snow terrace, then moved along it to the right for about four rope lengths to a place where we could erect the portaledge. Next day we managed to fix our two ropes on the difficult terrain above, and on the 11th we climbed to pitch 22 before stopping for the night. The 12th dawned sunny and windless, and we added six more pitches, climbing through overhangs, slabs, cubic meters of snow, and wide cracks choked with ice, almost reaching the summit ridge. On the 13th we crawled up the last bit of the southeast ridge through gale-force wind to reach the summit.

With beta provided by Ivan Temerev, we found the top anchor of his 2013 route (6A) and began a series of rappels down his line, reaching the bottom of the wall at 5:30 p.m., after which, in a blizzard, we attempted to locate our base camp, where we had left gas and food. Eventually we had to suspend our portaledge from a boulder, mix coffee with snow, eat this, and wait until morning, when we discovered we were only 100m from our cache.

Our route, which we named Kosinusoyda, was 570m, but the climbing distance was much longer, involving 29 pitches to the ridge. The route was 5B, with free climbing to around F5a/b and aid to A3+. Bolts were placed on all belays and occasionally for aid. 📷

– LINDSAY GRIFFIN, *WITH INFORMATION FROM* ALEXANDER ZHIGALOV *AND* ELENA DMITRENKO, *RUSSIA*

SAYAN MOUNTAINS, SEVER, NORTH FACE

ON AUGUST 20, Eugeny and Sergey Glazunov climbed a new route up the center of the north face of Sever (2,826m) in the Barun Handagay Valley of the Eastern Sayan Mountains. The peak lies ca 150km west-southwest of the large city of Irkutsk, close to the southern end of Lake Baikal. The new route ascends a very steep, 400m granite pillar and then continues along the west ridge to the summit, for a total of 600m of climbing (5B, mostly free). The brothers descended the east ridge (3A).

– LINDSAY GRIFFIN, WITH INFORMATION FROM ELENA DMITRENKO, RISK.RU, RUSSIA

BARGUZIN RANGE, MORYAN

IN APRIL, Dashi Ayusheev, Alexander Baguza, Anton Fedotov, and Purbo Norboev made the first ascent of Moryan (2,070m) on the east side of the Barguzin Range. Their route, up the eastern pillar of the south-southwest face, then along the southeast ridge to the summit, had a vertical gain of a little over 500m (but 742m of climbing) and was graded 5B.

– LINDSAY GRIFFIN, WITH INFORMATION FROM ELENA DMITRENKO, RISK.RU, RUSSIA

CHUKOTKA REGION / BILIBINO – CHUVAN MOUNTAINS

THE GENERAL & THE COMMANDER, EIGHT NEW ROUTES

AFTER THE DISCOVERY by two Australians in 2014 of an exiting area of big granite walls north of the Arctic Circle (*AAJ 2015*), Hansjörg Auer (Austria), Jacopo Larcher (South Tyrol, Italy), Eneko and Iker Pou (Spain), and Siebe Vanhee (Belgium), accompanied by photographers Elias Holzknecht from Austria and me (Spain), spent a month in the area, opening eight new routes, most of high quality.

We split into two teams. In eight hours on July 6, Eneko and Iker put up Aupa! (300m, 6c) on the General. They followed this on the 11th with the first ascent of Into the Wild (425m, 7a) on the Commander, and then returned to the General on the 14th to add Mosquito Rock Tour (450m, 7a+) in 11 hours. Finally, on the 24th, they made an 8.5-hour ascent of the Two Parrots (320m, 7a) on the Commander. All routes were climbed in continuous pushes.

Auer, Larcher, and Vanhee started their collection of new routes on July 6 with Wake Up in Siberia (240m, 6b) on the General, and then on the 11th, 12th, and 14th put up Red Corner (450m, 7c+) on the Commander, to the right of a line attempted in 2014 by Australians Chris Fitzgerald and Chris Warner. This route was team-freed on the final day. They placed four hand-drilled 8mm bolts, including three on belays, and left two beaks and two knifeblades. On the 18th and 20th, the same three put up Sketchy Django (400m, 6a+) on a previously unclimbed wall leading to the summit of a formation they named the Monk. Finally, over the 21st, 22nd, and 24th, the three worked and then completed From Zero to Hero (490m, 7a) on the General.

The team spent 23 days at base camp and felt this was one of the best trips they had been on, despite having a constant fight with a harsh, unexpected enemy in the form of Siberian mosquitoes. [*See route photos on next page.*]

– JORDI CANYI, SPAIN

THE GENERAL, EAST FACE, ILIUM

SOMEWHERE ABOVE US the walls were making their presence felt, unfriendly and brooding in the impenetrable mist. Tantalizing photos of granite formations—the Commander and the General—had drawn us more than halfway around the world to far eastern Russia. Sooner or later we hoped to get at least a glimpse of them!

Our Russian contact, Evgeny Turilov, had arranged with friends to drive us into the mountains from nearby Bilibino. After comically overloading two quad bikes with gear, it became apparent that I had drawn the short straw. Graham Dawson watched gleefully from the rear of a quad as I nervously clambered on the back of a battered Yamaha motorbike, held together with a thorough mummification of tape. The white-knuckle ride through the mist along rough, disused mining tracks was punctuated in true Russian style with frequent beer stops and the occasional round of vodka and pickles. The following heavily loaded slog through boggy tundra was either made easier or much harder by the constant boozing, depending on which member of the party was asked. After hours of marching we finally reached our base camp, a fact that could only rightly be celebrated with more vodka and an array of dubious tinned meats and probable mollusks.

After a few days the lingering clag lifted and we finally clapped eyes on our objectives. We set our sights on the east-facing side of the General. On August 19, in barely warm enough temperatures, we skirted icicles at the base and scrambled up an easy gully to what appeared to be a compelling and continuous crack system. Some offwidth grunting led to precarious tiptoeing up mostly verglas-free slabs, with just sufficient protection dug out of shallow, flaring seams. Some

[Top left] **North face of the Commander. (1) Into the Wild (2015, 7a). (2) Red Corner (2015, 7c+). (3) Australian attempt (2014). (4) Two Parrots (2015, 7a).** *Jordi Canyi* [Bottom left] **The east face of the General. (1) Wake Up in Siberia (6b). (2) Ilium (E4 5c). (3) Aupa! (6c). (4) From Zero to Hero (7a). All these routes were established in 2015.** *Jordi Canyi* [Next page] **Siebe Vanhee makes thin bridging moves during the first ascent of Red Corner (450m, 7c+) on the Commander.** *Elias Holzknecht*

fine finger cracks, spiced with a few worryingly loose flakes, run-out "necky gardening," and the occasional enjoyable and diverting move of 5c, led us to the summit. We named the route Ilium (285m, E4 5c).

Unfortunately, any sense of momentum was quashed when we awoke to steadily falling snow and equally descending temperatures. We repeated the first three pitches (up to 7a) of the Australian line Basil Brush on the General (*AAJ 2015*) and fixed 150m of static for a quick push the next day, but the unseasonable weather had other ideas. After many days of tent-based boredom, we moved our base camp to a neighboring valley to the east, called Finger Crack Cirque, in search of climbable rock and fresh banter with a group of Aussies. A rare glimpse of the sun encouraged another vertical foray. After 90m of entertaining climbing we reached an impasse in the shape of a finger crack that looked like it would offer an incredible E4 pitch if not choked with ice and frozen moss. A fresh fall of snow then saw us resort to mixing pure ethanol with boiled Haribo gummy bears, resulting in a catastrophic hangover hardly conducive to the next day's task: carrying 35kg loads for 12km out of the massif.

Simon Smith on pitch one of Basil Brush (Fitzgerald-Warner, 2014), north face of the General. *Graham Dawson*

— SIMON SMITH, *U.K.*

FINGER CRACK CIRQUE & WEASEL TOWER

FROM JULY 23 TO AUGUST 30, Australians Chris Fitzgerald, Natasha Sebire, and I completed several routes on the previously unclimbed rock wall of Finger Crack Cirque, and also made the first ascent of a rock tower. Our expedition almost didn't happen when, two weeks before we were due to arrive in Russia, we were informed that a special permit (*propusk*) was required to enter the Chukokta autonomous region. In 2014, Fitzgerald and Chris Warner were the first to climb in the area (*AAJ 2015*), but they did not have, nor even know about, this *propusk*, as very few people visit this area in far northeastern Russia. Luckily, our contact in Bilibino, Evgeny Turilov, managed to smooth things out, and we were allowed to enter the region with no permit. However, we were required to pay small fines. [*The online version of this report has additional notes about the permit procedure.*]

Finger Crack Cirque is in a valley 8km east of the Commander and the General, where Fitzgerald and Warner had climbed the previous year. The main wall of the cirque faces north-northwest, is nearly 500m at its highest point, and has quality granite for more than 1 km of its total length, with many crack lines. These lines usually have sections of dry, perfect rock, as well as damp parts with moss or grass, requiring a bit of cleaning.

Our first route on the wall followed a fairly continuous crack system to the right of a blunt buttress. After 290m of climbing we reached a diagonal ledge of loose rock that we scrambled for 300m to complete the Propusk (Australian 18/F6a). Descent from the top of the cirque is easy—we just hiked down the long ridge to our camp.

After some days of marginal weather, during which we established a short, splitter hand crack (Lemming Meringue Pie, 110m, 16/5a), we all climbed a route starting just to the right. We followed a series of cracks for seven full pitches, after which a few pitches of fourth- and fifth-class scrambling led to the top. Vodka and Lemming (505m, 18/6a) finishes at the highest point of the wall, and at 10 p.m. the Arctic sun remained only on this upper section, bathing us in an orange glow.

We next set our sights on a steeper and very impressive part of the wall, where it looks as though a giant orbital sander had scoured its way up, leaving arcs in the rock. Although we found a continuous crack line, short sections of moss-choked cracks led us to place four protection bolts (on two pitches) and others for belay anchors. We climbed Orbital Sander (440m, 8 pitches, 22/6c) over three days, using fixed ropes.

Snow arrived on August 17, early for this area. However, we still were keen to visit a nearby valley and climb a rock formation that we'd named Weasel Tower. On the 20th we climbed the front face of the tower, with Natasha racing up the first pitch and me leading the rest, with wooden toes and numb fingers. This forced me to pull on gear for two moves: Siberian Summer (160m, 20/6b+ A1, bolts placed for two rappels).

The Bilibino walls have huge potential for new routes, and there are valleys in which no climbing has so far been done. The summer is very short in Siberia, and climbing here is a balance between going too early and enduring the mosquitoes or going a bit later and risking colder weather. When we left at the end of August, our last day was enjoyed in sunshine, hiking 12km down a wide valley, where there were still berries for the picking and the ground was almost glowing with splashes of warm autumn color. ▤ ▣

— GEMMA WOLDENDORP, *AUSTRALIA*

Gemma Woldendorp leading the slabby second pitch of Vodka and Lemming, with the walls of Finger Crack Cirque stretching behind. *Natasha Sebire*

KYRGYZSTAN

ARCHAKANYSH GORGE, RYZHII AND SAUK DZHAYLYAU WEST I

DURING JULY, Eugene and Sergey Glazunov and Alexey Tyulyupo explored peaks in the long-forgotten Surmetash Valley. The expedition was only two weeks, but this was enough time for the team to make two first ascents of primarily rock routes, one on a previously unnamed 4,300m peak and the second on Sauk Dzhaylyau West I (4,866m).

Exploration of this region culminated in the 1970s and early '80s, when the area was used for the USSR Mountaineering Championships. Since the start of the 1990s, no mountaineer had visited the Sauk Dzhaylyau cirque.

The trio drove south from Uch-Korgon, through Shigay, and then penetrated the Archakanysh Gorge to a base camp at ca 2,300m. They then climbed a new route on a peak they named Ryzhii at the head of a cirque to the north of the main valley. The ascent of the southeast ridge was completed in 6.5 hours on July 14 with an overall difficulty of 4A (600m, V). According to a note found in the summit cairn, the last ascent was made in 1978, when the peak was given 4,160m; the GPS measured 4,300m. As the peak was unnamed they called it Ryzhii ("Ginger") after the reddish color of the rock and also a late friend of that name.

Their second new route was on Sauk Dzhaylyau West I (39°46'0.47"N, 71°56'4.48"E), one of the higher glaciated peaks to the south of the main valley. The three climbed the 900m north ridge at an approximate grade of TD (6A, mainly free climbing at 5b/5c, with maximum 6a, some A2, and sections of WI4). They started at 6 a.m. on July 18, summited at 3:30 p.m. on the 19th, and were back in base camp at 1 p.m. on the 20th. Four bolts were left as rappel anchors. This was only the second recorded ascent of the peak—the first was 38 years earlier, during a complete traverse of the Sauk Dzhaylyau massif.

Looking southwest into the Sauk Dzhaylyau cirque. (A) Sauk Dzhaylyau Main (5,120m). (B) Central. (C) West II. (D) West I, climbed in 2015 by the north ridge (right skyline). *Sergey Glazunov*

Steep ice runnel on the north ridge of Sauk Dzhaylyau West I. *Sergey Glazunov*

Editor's note: Although many routes climbed under the official system in the former Soviet Union are documented, at present this information is difficult for non-Russian speakers to access. Climbers wishing to visit lesser-known areas such as the Sauk Dzhaylyau massif are encouraged to contact Russian climbers or outdoor journalists for information. Otherwise, go to the area, have an adventure, and be prepared for the fact that you may be making second or third ascents. 📷

— **ELENA DMITRENKO**, *RISK.RU, RUSSIA*

PAMIR

BOR DOBO GLACIER, PEAK 5,143M, NORTHWEST FACE

HAVING A SPARE WEEK at the end of August between expeditions, James Monypenny, Heather Swift, and I made a quick exploratory hit in the mountains close to the Kyrgyz-Tajik border at Kyzyl-Art Pass. We caught a taxi from Osh to just south of the Kyrgyz checkpoint, and then hiked up the valley to the southeast and onto the Bor Dobo Glacier. Vladimir Kommissarov (ITMC owner and mountain guide) said there had been very few expeditions to this area east of Pik Lenin, and that most peaks remained unclimbed.

From a base camp at ca 4,300m, we climbed the prominent, icy northwest face of Pik 5,143m (Russian map; 39°28'15"N, 73°19'19"E Google Earth). The angle was relatively sustained at 55–60°, with slightly steeper sections at the bottom and top of the face. We topped out on the west ridge 50m shy of the final chossy rock pillar. Heather belayed James onto the summit, but with no possibility of a belay or rappel anchor, she didn't follow and James downclimbed, declaring this to be "one of the most terrifying things I've ever done." We descended the face in 18 full-length rappels from Abalakov anchors as a blizzard built from the west. The face we had guessed would be about 300m was more like 1,100m.

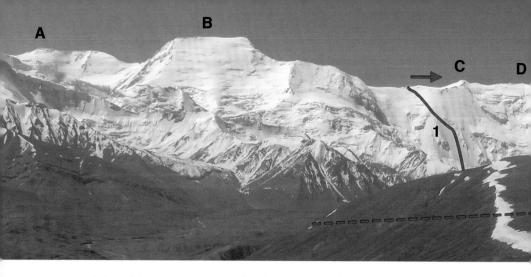

The blizzard kept us tent-bound for the next three days, after which Heather and I climbed the much shorter north face of Pik 4,875m (ca 50° with bomber névé), situated on the main ridge to the west. Sadly, the weather closed again so we were unable to reach the summit. We walked down to Bor Dobo that afternoon, and border guards plied us with vodka and tomato chasers before we started our cramped hitch back to Sari-Tash. 📷 🔍

— EMILY WARD, *FRANCE*

PAMIR / ZAALAYSKIY RANGE

TRAVERSE OF KURUMDY AND UNCLIMBED SATELLITE PEAKS

MELANIE GRÜNWALD (21), James Lam (21), Katharina Pfnaisl (23), and I (46) wanted to be the first to cross the central section of the Zaalayskiy Range, taking in the main summit of Kurumdy I (6,613m), a mountain climbed only once before. [*Kurumdy I was climbed October 12, 2001, by Vitaliy Akimov, Alexander Gubayev, Mikhail Mikhailov, and Oleg Turayev by the north spur and east ridge. Despite previous reports that the mountain was first climbed in 1932 from the south by Nikolay Krylenko's expedition, it now seems most likely they reached the summit of 6,154m Kurumdy Southwest II.*]

We located base camp at 3,770m beyond the western moraine of the East Kyzylsu (Kyzilsy) Glacier, and on July 14 put advanced base at 4,100m to the southwest. Over the next week we acclimatized and put our next high camp at 4,800m, positioned for an ascent of Gorlova Orla (5,440m). Melanie had been fighting an illness since Osh, so she remained in camp on the 20th while James, Kathi, and I climbed Golova Orla by the north flank and east spur, a new route. This was mainly 50° but ended with a huge, vertical, rotten summit cornice. This was only the second ascent, the first taking place in 2000, when a British-Russian team climbed the northwest ridge.

On July 26 we headed for the main ridge between Zarya Vostoka (6,349m) and Kurumdy East II (6,259m). Two days later we were at a 4,500m high camp, where the forecast for the coming nine days and Melanie's continuing illness caused her and James to abandon the ascent. Kathi and I opted to continue. After another night at 4,500m, we set out with provisions for eight days, with rucksacks weighing about 30kg each. At times we needed to wade through

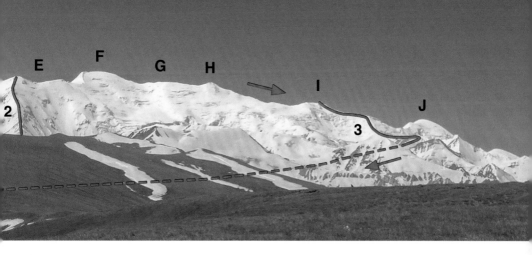

[Photo] **The central Zaalayskiy Range from the north. (1) Start of 2015 traverse. (2) Spur climbed during 2001 first ascent of Kurumdy I. (3) Descent from 2015 traverse. (A) Pik 5,995m. (B) Zarya Vostoka (6,349m). (C) Kurumdy East II ("Pik Kathi"). (D) Kurumdy East I. (E) Kurumdy Sharqi III, II and I. (F) Kurumdy I (6,613m). (G) Peak 6,585m. (H) Kurumdy West I. (I) Kurumdy West II. (J) Turkvo.** *Markus Gschwendt*

hip-deep snow, sometimes making no more than 10 vertical meters an hour. We made a camp on the north flank before reaching the crest on August 1 at ca 6,000m. The view was poor as we progressed westward to a camp at 6,120m. Next day we reached the previously unclimbed Kurumdy East II, naming it Pik Kathi. It was the first 6,000m peak she had climbed.

In knee-deep snow we continued along the ridge toward Kurumdy East I (6,384m), making another two camps en route, the latter because of complete lack of visibility. We had now spent our proposed eight days on the traverse. However, next morning the visibility was a little better and this spurred us on. We reached East I quickly, descended the far side, and joined the route of the first ascensionists of Kurumdy I.

In increasing wind we crossed the three Kurumdy Sharqi peaks to a camp below the ridge leading to the main summit. Next morning, August 5, it was very cold and windy, but by 3 p.m. we reached the highest point of the range, and as a reward the sky began to clear and we soon had a perfect view in all directions. What a gift!

We continued to the west, crossing another small top of 6,585m, which might be considered a previously unclimbed summit, and a few hours later were preparing camp below the striking double summit of Kurumdy West I. In barely two meters of visibility we reached its northern top (6,554m), but due to the bad weather we decided to forego the higher south top (6,558m, possibly unclimbed). Instead we headed down the west flank of the ridge and over Kurumdy West II (Chorku, 6,283m, first climbed in 2000). We stopped at 6,150m, at the junction of the main ridge and a spur that descends north over Peaks 5,532m and Golova Orla. That night was extremely windy, and by next morning the tent had been ripped in several places.

Next day we descended the spur, and yet again it took far longer than anticipated. We ended up having to camp close to the top of Golova Orla, and it took us until after dark the following day, reversing our previous route on the east spur, to reach advanced base, where we were very happy we'd left a little food, clothing, and gas. Ultimately, our traverse took 15 days: ten to the main summit and five on the descent. It was exciting, exhausting, and beautiful. 📷 🔍

– **MARKUS GSCHWENDT**, *AUSTRIA*

Gabe Oliver approaching the summit of Peak 4,361m during the traverse of Podkova Ridge. The view south shows peaks at the head of the Karakol Glacier. The high summit to the left is Peak 4,750m, while the prominent Castle Ridge, with its three or four rocky tops, is in the far center. *Paul Josse*

TIEN SHAN / FERGANA RANGE

KARAKOL VALLEY, HIGH TRAVERSES OVER UNCLIMBED PEAKS

AFTER BEING DENIED access to the Kokbel Valley, our original objective, by a team of armed hunters, Pete Duguid, Pete Nugent, Gabe Oliver, John Venier, and I made two long traverses above the Karakol Valley, where British teams previously had done numerous first ascents (*AAJ 2011 and 2012*). On August 30, I soloed the Vershina Ridge (PD), crossing four summits on the ridge between Piks 4,203m and 4,701m (Russian military map). Two peaks had no previously recorded ascents. On September 4, Gabe and I traversed the Podkova Ridge (F+), crossing five summits between Piks 3,870m and 4,330m in winter-like conditions. Four of these had no recorded ascents.

Pete Nugent and John Venier made an attempt on impressive Pik 4,485m at the head of the valley, climbing the north ridge to within 50m of the summit.

– PAUL JOSSE, *U.K.*

TIEN SHAN / TORUGART-TOO

MUR SAMIR, NORTHWEST FACE

AFTER AN ATTEMPT on Pik Karakol in July foiled by warm weather (freezing level above 5,000m), Sebastian Conrad, Stephan Rath, and I drove east via Naryn to the Torugart-Too, on the border with China. In the Mustyr Valley we headed up the John Charles Glacier (as a 2010 expedition named it) to establish base camp below Mur Samir (5,035m GPS, 5,008m Russian military map). We first attempted to repeat the northeast ridge, climbed in 2010 by John Proctor and Robert Taylor for the first ascent of the mountain (*AAJ 2011*). We followed a couloir to the right of theirs (400m, PD) to reach the crest at 4,800m. However, the very rotten rock on the ridge was unfrozen, making it almost impossible to climb or find anchors. We turned around without reaching the top.

Next day, July 27, we headed for the unclimbed northwest face. Above the bergschrund we climbed steepening ice in good condition, leading toward two narrow couloirs, each 50–60°. We took the left, which gave short passages of mixed climbing. After 700m we reached the north ridge and followed this on snow to the summit. The overall grade was AD. We continued down the northeast ridge and used Proctor's descent along the eastern part of the north face. This proved more difficult than described, due to dangerous rockfall and large crevasses that on several occasions we had to rappel. 🖻

— SEBASTIAN WOLF, *GERMANY*

TIEN-SHAN / CENTRAL REGION

ALA ARCHA RANGE, FREE KOREA PEAK, NEW ROUTE

In late January 2016, Russian climbers Max Krivosheev, Igor Loginov, and Alexander Zhigalov spent four days climbing a hard new route up the left side of the north face of Free Korea (4,778m). The route ascends the steep 690m wall between the 1991 Balezin Route (5B) and the 1982 Svab Route (5B), on what is referred to as the Lion Triangle (*AAJ 2011*). The climbers traversed the long east ridge over the summit and descended the ice couloir soloed by George Lowe (USA) in 1976. Their route was graded ED, mostly free with ca 150m of A3/A4. 🖻

— LINDSAY GRIFFIN, *WITH INFORMATION SUPPLIED BY* DMITRIY SHALYGIN, *KYRGYZSTAN,*
AND ELENA DMITRENKO, *RUSSIA*

TIEN SHAN / TERSKEY ALA-TOO

KONGURLONG VALLEY CLIMBS

IN SEPTEMBER, Dominik Bednar, Miroslav Dusek, Tibor Majer, Pavel Mezera, Pavel Simandl, Tomas Vemola, Borek Zelenka, and I, all from the Czech Republic, visited an easily accessible but rarely visited valley in the western part of the Terskey Ala-Too. From the main road alongside Lake Issyk Kul, we drove 25km south to Kalkagar village and then walked four hours to establish base camp at the confluence of the Kongurlong and West Kongurlong rivers at 2,950m. This point can be reached by a 4WD truck and/or mules.

Our first climb was Karakoo (4,289m), reached by a long approach up the East Kalkagar Valley, followed by a 45°, heavily crevassed, north-facing glacier to gain the east ridge. Bednar, Majer, Simandl, and I followed an easy snow crest to the top.

Merzera and Vemola climbed Lama (4,096m) and Verblud (4,040m), two rocky pinnacles above the Kongurlong Glacier, via a steep gully on the east flank to the col and then short rocky ridges to each top (UIAA III and IV).

Bednar, Majer, and I then made a long and winding approach up the Kongurlong Glacier, heading west at the top to reach the northeast ridge of Ak Bashi (4,610m), which we followed to the summit.

Dusek, Mezera, and Vermola climbed the highest peak in this part of the range: Kongurlong (4,747m). From the head of the Kongurlong Glacier, they crossed a difficult and heavily crevassed col, and then climbed the southwest face of the mountain (55° ice). They found signs of a previous visit, but we have not been able to find a description in Russian journals. [*Editor's note: A Swiss expedition visited this glacier in July 2014 and appears to have climbed Kongurlong, which they called Kundebe Peak, and also Ak Bashi, which they named White Melon and measured at 4,630m.*]

We also attempted Peak 4,399m on the upper western rim of the West Kongurlung Glacier but ran out of time at 4,250m on the north-northeast ridge. All ascents apart from Karakoo required one bivouac above base camp. 📷 🔍

– **MICHAL KLESLO**, *CZECH REPUBLIC*

KYZYL ASKER GLACIER, VARIOUS ASCENTS

MATJAZ COTAR, Anze Jerse, Uros Stanonik, and I landed in Bishkek to find one of our rucksacks had not boarded the plane. After three days of waiting, we were left with no other option than to buy the missing gear and move on. Two days of driving and five days' load carrying saw us established in base camp at the foot of the Kyzyl Asker Glacier.

After an initial reconnaissance, Anze, Uros, and I bivouacked below Gronky (5,080m) and the next day, August 29, climbed a new ice line on the west face of Carnovsky (4,860m). It was not exactly the warm-up we wanted: Because of bad conditions, the line required nine hours of difficult and often dangerous climbing: Mr. Mojo Risin' (500m, V/5+ M5 R/X). We determined to shift our activity to ridges, as the snow and ice was so bad.

After an acclimatization climb along the ridge forming the eastern rim of the glacier, all four of us packed four days of food and headed for the west ridge of Kyzyl Asker (5,842m). A heavily crevassed area, and then deep, fresh snow higher up, forced us to camp at ca 5,000m. Next day, September 7, we continued through more fresh snow toward the saddle at the foot of the west ridge. Here, we realized conditions were too bad to reach the main summit, so we left our sacks below the saddle and climbed the ridge southeast for ca 100m vertically (M4) to reach Kyzyl Asker West Shoulder (Pik 5,632m). [*This summit was first climbed around 1985 by Soviets via the ridge over Rock Horse and Raven Peak to the north-northwest (AAJ 2011).*]

We had just enough time for one more climb, and we split into two teams, planning day climbs, more or less. Uros and I left at 11 p.m. on the 11th and spent the whole night approaching the northwest face of Panfilovski Division (5,290m). At daybreak we were horrified to see the seracs on the east face of Kyzyl Asker directly above us, so we started climbing away from them—fast. Above a lower rock barrier we found steep ice, which brought us to a snowfield. We moved right below a broken pillar, and then—a surprise!—an entire wall of concrete-hard névé. The sound of the tools squeaking could be heard half a pitch away.

[Facing page] Uros Stanonik, belayed by Miha Hauptman, leads thin ice on Mr. Mojo Risin'. *Anze Jerse*

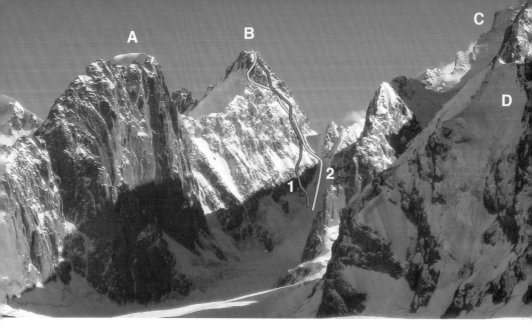

Looking south up the east fork of the Kyzyl Asker Glacier. (A) Vernyi. The very steep northwest face has three routes (*AAJ 2010–2012*). (B) Panfilovski Division. (1) White Walker (2015). (2) Popenko Route (1980). (C) Northeast ridge of Kyzyl Asker. (D) Part of the north flank of Ljosha (4,713m). *Miha Hauptman*

We reached the top half an hour before dark. We got lost twice during the descent and finally returned to base camp after nearly two full days without sleep. We named our 900m route White Walker (V/5 M6). [*Editor's note: The northwest face of Panfilovski Division was climbed in the summer of 1980 by Popenko and team to make the first ascent of the mountain. The new Slovenian route would appear to lie close by, but largely separate from, this line, which was likely climbed as a rock route.*] Meanwhile, Anze and Matjez had climbed a new route on the southwest face of Gronky. Their line, which followed obvious couloirs interspersed with icefalls and a few detours onto rock, was completed in a round trip of 14 hours from base camp: Take a Walk on the Wild Side (700m, V/4+ M6 6a). 📄 📷

– MIHA HAUPTMAN, *SLOVENIA*

PANFILOVSKI DIVISION SOUTHEAST, FLIGHT OF THE ZEPHYR

MY MOTHER WOULD PROBABLY SAY that going on a blind date to a foreign country like Kyrgyzstan is a bad idea. Ben Erdmann and I corresponded for months prior to the expedition, but we only met in person on the plane from Seattle to Dubai. However, the signs all pointed toward the potential for a productive partnership with a shared desire for adventure.

We reached base camp at the toe of the Komorova Glacier (3,800m) in the second week of August. I had been here once before, in May 2012, when Ryan Johnson and I attempted the southeast couloir of Kyzyl Asker (*AAJ 2013*). This time Ben and I hoped for less snow and better weather. After nine days of heavy load hauling, we finally arrived at our advanced base camp (4,400m) below the unique and cathedral-like 1,300m southeast face of Kyzyl Asker (5,842m).

We constantly monitored weather reports sent by friends back home, but each time we received a good forecast and packed for an attempt, a sudden storm would shut us down. At one point we decided to use a marginal window (read: snowstorm) to attempt a line on

Panfilovski Division's southeast summit, a peak on the southeast ridge of Panfilovski Division that is ca 100m lower than the main top. This stunning, 600m golden granite spire rose directly from the glacier near our advanced base camp.

Our blind-date partnership unfolded over initial pitches of moderate Styrofoam ice, as we carefully raced warming temperatures and falling ice to establish ourselves at the base of the thin mixed system defining the route's upper half. We then embarked on iconic mixed terrain that required all the tricks in the book, until finally a layback with my body horizontal got me through the last of the technical ground. Our line, Flight of the Zephyr, went in 12 pitches at AI4 R M7, without the use of bolts. Ben and I concurred that this line could be a classic in another range. We arrived back in camp at 6:30 p.m., 14 hours after walking out that morning.

Early on August 29 we decided to make an attempt on the Kyzyl Asker couloir, in what appeared to be an acceptable if not ideal period of moderate diurnal precipitation cycles. Eclipsing my previous high point of 5,300m in only seven hours, we found technical difficulties up to WI5 M6, as well as dangerous melting, hazardous precipitation, and punishing spindrift. We spent around 50

Flight of the Zephyr follows the obvious couloir and then ice runnels up to Panfilovski Division Southeast, the right-hand top. *Ben Erdmann*

hours on the face, with the final 36 hours mostly pinned down by the frightening conditions. We believe our high point of about 5,500m is the second highest attained so far on the route; Ines Papert reached 5,600m on one of her several attempts.

Our trip ended with much of our remaining food lost in a crevasse and multiple delays in our pickup due to vehicle and driver health breakdowns. For six days we watched our bodies deteriorate, remembering the deeper meaning of hunger. Finally, our transport arrived with four U.K. climbers inside. They'd heard about our plight and brought us an enormous cake.

– **SAMUEL JOHNSON**, *USA*

SEDOY STRAZH AND OTHER FIRST ASCENTS

OUR EXPEDITION CONSISTED of nine people, divided into three teams, including several very inexperienced climbers. The original goal was Byeliy, but after we discovered it had been climbed in 2011 by Slovenians, we focused on virgin Peak 5,481m (sometimes referred to as Byeliy East). Although it had been the aim of several parties, there had not been a serious attempt.

From August 8 to 13, we climbed above the Sarychat Glacier, where various teams made

first ascents of three mountains (Piks 4,585m, 5,020m, and 4,990m), from Russian 1B to 3A. We also completed a new route on Pik Novey (4,978m), the east face and north ridge, 2A.

On August 14, four climbers headed home and the rest of us moved to the Fersmana Glacier. On the 16th, while Dmitry Grigoriev, Sergey Nilov, and I started an ascent of the northeast face of Pik 5,481m (the steepest aspect, but also the safest), Vladimir Nikitin and Ruslan Sharifullin reached the col north of Korsun (5,320m). On the 17th they climbed Chudo ("Miracle," 5,100m, 2A), and on the 18th they summited Prozrachnaya ("Transparent," 5,070m, 2A). On the 19th they descended the Malitskogo Glacier and returned to base camp.

Meanwhile, Dmitry, Sergey, and I climbed Pik 5,481m over five days, reaching the top at 2 p.m. on the 20th. We had to wait there for two hours as a storm moved in and eliminated visibility, but once it was possible to see the way down, we set off to the northwest and descended to a bivouac in the bergschrund that night. The following day we were back on the Fersmana, having traversed the mountain. We have named the peak Sedoy Strazh ("Gray-haired Guardian"), and our ascent route Devjaty Val ("Ninth Wave"), from the famous 1850 painting of the same name: 1,230m, with 1,885m of climbing, Russian 6B (ED 6c WI5 M6 A2, minimal aid).

Ninth Wave on Sedoy Strazh (a.k.a. Byeliy East, 5,481m) with the higher summit of Byeliy (5,697m) behind. The first-ascent party descended to the north and northwest, between Sedoy Strazh and Byeliy. *Dmitry Golovchenko*

After a day's rest at base camp we returned to the Fersmana, and on the 25th Ruslan, Sergey, and I made the second ascent of the Polish Route (2009) on Granitsa (5,370m), while Dmitry and Vladimir made the first ascent of Pogranichnik ("Border Guard," 5,270m, 4A). 📷

– DMITRY GOLOVCHENKO, *RUSSIA*

PIK PALGOV, WEST FACE AND NORTH RIDGE

IN JULY AND AUGUST, Vaughan Snowdon and I climbed from the Palgov Valley, where we were fortunate to make the first ascent of Pik 5,602m, one of the highest unclimbed summits of the range. We were probably the third party to climb from the Palgov, after Moscow teams in 1998 and 2003. [*The former made the first ascents of seven summits, including neighboring Krylya Sovetov (5,480m).*]

[Above] The untouched southwest (Chinese) face of Pik Kosmos (5,940m), seen from the summit of Pik Palgov. The shoulder in the left foreground is Point 5,495m. *Paul Knott* [Below] Looking west-southwest from the summit of Pik Palgov to unclimbed 5,000m peaks on the Xinjiang (Chinese) side of the range, south of Pik Byeliy. *Paul Knott*

In two days from Bishkek, our agents ITMC took us by Gaz-66 truck to the nearest established vehicle access, by the Kotur River at 3,900m. From here we spent several days ferrying loads via the Aytali and Sarychat valleys to a base camp by the confluence of the Palgov and Grigoriev rivers, a distance of 20km and rather hard work.

On July 31, for acclimatization, we made the first ascent of Pik 5,190m on the east side of the valley. Scree and dry glacier led us to snow runnels on the west side of the north ridge. From the summit we descended over Pik 4,973m to the north.

After several days of intermittent rain, on August 8 we ascended the Palgov Glacier to its upper névé, at 4,600m, to tackle our main objective, Pik 5,602m. The most aesthetic route, the west ridge, looked exposed with sustained technicalities. Instead, on the west face, we found a twisting snow and ice couloir right of disintegrating rock buttresses and left of the most

[Above] Pik Palgov (5,602m) from the upper icefall of the Palgov Glacier. The first-ascent route reached the north ridge (left skyline) via a hidden couloir between the buttresses in the left foreground and the large seracs behind them. *Paul Knott* [Below] Vaughan Snowdon on the Palgov Glacier. Behind him to the south lie Pik Palgov (left) and Krylya Sovetov (5,480m, in the sun). The latter has had two known ascents (*AAJ 1999 and 2003*). *Paul Knott*

threatening seracs. Unfortunately, an overnight electrical storm and persistent heavy snowfall forced us to descend to base camp, wary of avalanche risk in the upper cwm.

Cooler and seemingly settled weather persuaded us to use our last available days on a second attempt. On August 14 we climbed up the couloir and onto easier, west-facing slopes, which led to a rounded foresummit and the exposed but straightforward upper north ridge. The summit was a spectacularly sharp point overlooking the impressive southern buttresses of Pik Kosmos and some striking unclimbed peaks on the Xinjiang (China) side of the border. [*See the AAJ website for excellent photos of the surrounding mountains.*] Thanks are due to the Mount Everest Foundation, which provided funding for this expedition. 📷

— PAUL KNOTT, *NEW ZEALAND*

PIK 5,190M, EAST FACE

IN SEPTEMBER, Mike Abrahamsson, Harry McGhie, Heather Swift, and I set out from Naryn to climb the north face of Pik Kosmos (5,940m) at the head of the western branch of the Grigoriev Glacier. Our first reconnaissance of Kosmos was not encouraging: Every day at least 10 significant seracs would carve from all areas of the north face. We decided to look at alternatives!

Harry, Mike, and I opted to try a mixed route on the east face of Pik 5,190m. I was not fast enough soloing the initial 700m couloir, and the sun reached the ice before I did. Harry and Mike continued and found four pitches of good climbing up a series of icefalls and mixed steps (AI 3/3+ M3), before snow-covered ice slopes led northward to the summit. In descent they downclimbed the snow/ice slopes and descended the steeper cliff band in two 60m rappels from blocks. At the time we believed the mountain was unclimbed, but in July it had been climbed from the Palgov Glacier, to the west, by Paul Knott and Vaughan Snowdon (*see report above*).

We spent our last few days on the Kotur Glacier, where I soloed a variation up the east side and north ridge of Pik Oleg (4,657m). We'd like to thank the British Mountaineering Council, Mount Everest Foundation, and Goretex Shipton-Tilman Grant. 📄 📷 🔍

— EMILY WARD, *FRANCE*

BORDER CROSSING RUMORS

TEAMS ARRIVING in the Western Kokshaal-Too from August onward were treated to a widespread rumor that, one month earlier, two Russians who had approached the mountains from the north had been caught on the Chinese side of the border, spent a month in jail, and then required the assistance of the Russian government to get home. As a result, a Slovenian party planning to attempt Kyzyl Asker's coveted southeast face decided against crossing the border at Window Col (the usual approach) and instead climbed on the Kyrgyz side of the range.

The two Russians, from Novosibirsk, approached the Kokshaal-Too via the hunting lodge at Bulat-M. Exactly what they planned to climb is unknown, but for whatever reason (lost, out of food) they opted to descend into China. Despite the rumors, they were helped by the Chinese and taken back to the border at the Torugart Pass, well to the west, where a main road crosses into Kyrgyzstan. It appears there were no problems with Chinese authorities.

— LINDSAY GRIFFIN

Nearing the summit of Pik 5,023m, with the North Inylchek Glacier below and, from left to right, Pik Piramida (5,332m), Pik Ignateva (5,488m), and Pik Panoramnyi (5,300m). *Will Kernick*

TENGRI TAG

PIK 5,023M, NORTHWEST RIDGE

CAMERON HOLLOWAY, Will Kernick, Tim Miller, and I arrived on the North Inylchek Glacier in July. After Will and Tim climbed Khan Tengri and Cameron and I succeeded on Karly Tau (5,450m) on our second attempt, we joined forces to attempt an unclimbed peak.

The original plan had been to trek 25km down the North Inylchek to attempt unclimbed Razor Peak (5,576m), one of the targets of a 2009 Singaporean expedition led by David Lim (*AAJ 2011*). Unfortunately, the glacier proved too broken to negotiate for such a long distance, so after making camp 10km down the glacier at 3,750m, we resorted to our reserve plan, an attempt on Pik 5,023m. This summit lies to the south of the North Inylchek, between the Ryzhova and Mikailova glaciers.

After a miserable four-hour glacier traverse to the base of the peak, we all headed up a loose scree slope into worsening weather, reaching the snow line at about 4,100m. Above, we simul-climbed 45–65° icy slopes for the next three hours, then traversed right to the northwest ridge, where we placed camp at 4,350m.

The following day we headed up the remaining 700m to the summit in perfect weather, negotiating networks of crevasses and climbing sections of 55–60° ice, a chossy rock ridge, and a small serac to gain a small shoulder 100m shy of the summit. Here we were faced with a 50m serac that could not be skirted, so we were forced to climb a 25m pitch of Scottish 5, followed by 25m of unprotectable 60° terrain to reach gentle slopes beneath the top.

We suggest the mountain might be named Nutcracker Peak, given that Tim had whistled the theme to "The Nutcracker" on the mountain—and the peak proved to be a bit of a ball breaker! *A complete expedition report is available at the AAJ website.* 🗐 📷 🔍

– SETH FORD, *U.K.*

TAJIKISTAN

LOUKNITSKY AND BAGRITSKY ASCENTS

In August, Vilnis Barons, Eduard Skukis, and I climbed in the Shakhdara Range of the southwest Pamir, south of Seydzh village. Finding the local Pamiri people very friendly, we were able to hire donkeys for two days to transport our equipment up the Seydzh River valley to Lake Zardiv (ca 3,700m), where we acclimatized for three or four days. After this we went to Zardiv Pass (4,706m), from which we saw a wonderful mountain, Dzharkh (a.k.a. Jarkh or Bayconur, 6,038m), a peak climbed two or three times, from 1973–'76, by Soviet mountaineers. There are three routes to the summit but potential for more. On August 8 we climbed Louknitsky (5,802m) via the Chibud Glacier, icefall, and east ridge (Russian 3A). This peak had been climbed four times from 1975–'81, with TD routes on the north face.

After this we moved into the valley that rises southeast from Lake Zardiv, where the peaks of Asham (5,858m), Granatovy (5,446m), and Borovikova (5,848m) are located. We climbed to the Latvian Rifleman's Pass (5,580m), first reached in 1987, and from there climbed Bagritsky (5,725m) via the southwest ridge at 3B. This peak was climbed once before, in 1977, by Nataly Tikhonkova's Russian team, via the northeast face. We followed a similar line to their descent route. We then crossed the pass and continued down the Ganzek Valley to Yamchun (3,500m), just north of the Oxus River. 📷 🔍

— OLEG SILIN, *LATVIA*

Dzharkh (local name; the mountain is also called Bayconur) from Zardiv Pass to the north-northeast. There are only three known routes: the north ridge, running toward the camera (D+, Nekrasov and team, 1976) and two routes up the hidden south face (D+, Lipchinsky, 1976; TD, Solonnikov, 1983). *Oleg Silin*

AK BAITAL ASCENTS

In 1940 the Soviet military officer V.S. Yatsenko visited the Ak Baital (Ak Baikal) Valley, gazed up at the five peaks forming the ridgeline at the back of the basin, and declared, "The passage of this route would have done credit to any master mountaineer." In the intervening years, only one expedition had attempted any of these summits—Oleg Silin's Latvian expedition (*AAJ 2015*), which climbed a peak at each end of the ridge—so our team of five set out to prove ourselves as master mountaineers. As it turned out, 75-year-old Russian climbing beta is not always of the highest quality, and while we climbed four new routes, a traverse of the ridge eluded us. Its chossy, fractured mess was more suited to master levitators than to climbers.

We established a base camp at 4,700m and then an advanced base on the glacier at just over 5,000m. On August 11, James Monypenny soloed the unnamed peak at the east end of the ridge. He climbed the north face by a route he named DofE Bronze (500m, PD+ 50°), a new line on this ca 5,570m summit, which was first climbed via the northeast ridge in 2014. (*This is the Latvians' Pik 5,560m, which they climbed at 2B.*) On the 14th, Emily Ward also reached this summit solo, this time via the west face and south-southwest ridge,

[Top] Western rim of the Ak Baital Glacier, showing attempt on Pik ca 5,700m. The peak to the right was climbed in 2014; the peak to the left is unclimbed. *Emily Ward* [Left] The team's 4WD stranded in the Ak Baital River. *George Cave*

close to the route descended by both Monypenny and the Lativans (500m, F).

James soloed Pik 5,792m (Russian map height), lying in the center of the watershed ridge, on the 14th. He climbed the serac-threatened northwest face on hard, brittle ice, then the northeast ridge, and finally the east face to reach the summit, naming the route DofE Silver (800m, D 75°). We propose the name Mt. Emily. Two days later, Clay Conlon and I repeated James' route on the ca 5,570m peak to make the fourth ascent of the mountain. On August 18, Emily and James attempted the second peak (ca 5,700m) along the ridge from the western end. They climbed an east-facing snow couloir to a col and then moved north along the ridge until stopped by a steep, loose rock wall. Their route as far as the col was named Pie Josh Horrowshow (500m, AD 55°). 📄 📷

— GEORGE CAVE, *U.K.*

Emily Ward during the attempt on the second peak (ca 5,700m) along the ridge from the western end. *James Monypenny*

BORDERSKI EXPEDITION

Alison Criscitiello, Kate Harris, and Rebecca Haspel's Borderski expedition, which took place during February and March, set out to document tightened border security and fence construction along Tajikistan's frontiers with Afghanistan, China, and Kyrgyzstan, and the resulting impacts on the natural migration of wildlife, specifically Marco Polo sheep, ibex, and snow leopard. The three women skied for two weeks in and near the Zorkul Valley, just north of the Wakhan Corridor in Afghanistan. They also attempted to ski along the Tajik/China border, but were stymied by Chinese soldiers, and then spent a final week skiing in the Alai Valley, just over the border in Kyrgyzstan. In all, they skied 22 days and 265km of borderlands.

They also climbed several summits, one of which, Peak 5,372m, ca 20km north of Alichur, may have been a first ascent. The expedition was supported by the AAC's Lara-Karena Bitenieks Kellogg Memorial Conservation Grant and Scott Fischer Memorial Conservation Grant. A full account may be found at the AAJ website. 📄 🔍

— LINDSAY GRIFFIN, *WITH INFORMATION FROM* ALISON CRISCITIELLO, *USA*

PAKISTAN

NANGA PARBAT, FIRST WINTER ASCENT

At 3:17 p.m. on February 26, 2016, Simone Moro (Italy), Muhammad Ali Sadpara (Pakistan), and Alex Txikon (Spain) stepped onto the summit of Nanga Parbat (8,125m) to make the long-awaited first winter ascent. Sadpara and Txikon, along with Adam Bielecki and Jacek Czech (Poland) and Daniele Nardi (Italy), had worked on the standard Kinshofer Route on the Diamir Face since January, fixing rope and establishing camps. Moro and fellow Italian Tamara Lunger were trying the Messner-Messner-Eisendle-Tomaseth Route. At the end of January they joined forces with the Kinshofer team, which by then had fixed rope to 6,700m.

Bielecki, Czech, and Nardi left the expedition, for various reasons, and the remaining four started their summit push on February 22. On the 25th they reached Camp 4 (7,200m). Next morning, climbing unroped, they reached the steeper face below the summit, where all but Sadpara continued up the usual couloir. The Pakistani mountaineer, who had climbed the Kinshofer in 2008 and 2009, opted for rock to the right. About 100m below the summit Lunger decided to descend to Camp 4 while the others continued to the summit.

From the 1988-'89 winter season to the 2015-'16 season, a total of 37 expeditions attempted to make Nanga Parbat's first winter ascent. Of the 8,000ers only K2 remains unclimbed during winter. 🖸

– LINDSAY GRIFFIN

NANGA PARBAT RANGE, TOSHE RI, ATTEMPT AND TRAGEDY

In August an expedition from Pakistan attempted to climb Toshe Ri (6,424m, a.k.a. Toshain I, Sarwali, or Dabbar) from the south. There is no confirmed ascent of this peak. (*See the online version of this report for a history of attempts.*) In 2015 the five-member Pakistani expedition approached via the Sarwali Glacier to the south and established Camp 2 at 5,000m. On August 31, Imran Junaidi, Khurram Rajpoot, and Usman Tariq were spotted at 5,500m, after which they made no communication with the team. A later aerial search provided no clues as to their disappearance. Junaidi and Tariq climbed Little Trango in 2014 (*AAJ 2015*). 🖸 ≣

– LINDSAY GRIFFIN

LUPGHAR GROUP, VARIOUS ASCENTS

Murilo Lessa and I visited the Lupghar Mountains in the northwest corner of the Karakoram in July. We approached via the Batura Glacier and, after difficulties with inexperienced porters, made base camp at 4,150m, midway up the Yukshgoz Glacier. After a couple of days of acclimatizing, we set our sights on one of the peaks at the head of an unnamed valley extending north-northeast from our base camp. [*This valley was explored in 1925 by Philips Visser and Jenny Visser-Hooft, a Dutch couple.*] We made a high camp in the first of two side valleys forking north-northeast from the unnamed valley. Next morning we attempted Peak 5,665m, but after a critical route-finding error we stopped at a broad shoulder (ca 5,600m) well to the south of the rocky summit pyramid. Two days later we returned to the same high camp and made what we believe to be the first ascent of neighboring Peak 5,702m

View of Lupghar peaks from an earlier trip (2006). Behind and to the east are (A) Khush Dur Sar and (B) Qalha Sar, both climbed in 2015 from the opposite sides. (C) Peak 5,665m was climbed from this side by the snow slopes leading up and to the left of the final rocky summit pyramid. *Lee Harrison*

via its southeast face (AD-, 35–45° snow). We named this Khush Dur Sar (36°42'54.5"N, 74°31'21.9"E). Subsequently, we traversed to the west-northwest ridge of Peak 5,665m and followed it to a point just 30m below the summit, where we were stopped by soft snow.

In unsettled weather we then made the first ascent of Peak 5,589m from a high camp at 5,050m in the second of two side valleys branching north-northeast from the unnamed valley. We ascended the southeast face (AD, 50° snow) and named the mountain Qalha Sar (Bastion Peak). The following day we made a third attempt at Peak 5,665m from our first high camp. From the head of the glacier, easy snow slopes led us to the west-northwest ridge, but the final pitches of snow (55–70°) were again in poor condition, despite it being only 7 a.m. To our surprise, the final section of rock was adorned with abseil cord. Though no more than British V-Diff, the rock was disturbingly loose and brittle, so we ventured one at a time to the highest point. We graded the full route D. Our porters knew of no other expeditions to the Yokshgoz for around nine years. Given that the peak can be approached from the Lupghar Nala, to the north, in half the time, it is possible the previous ascent was from the north. 📷 📄

— LEE HARRISON, *NORWAY*

HARJOLDUR SAR, SOUTH FACE AND WEST RIDGE

IN 1925, PHILIPS VISSER and Jenny Visser-Hooft, a Dutch couple, explored the Virjerab Glacier and described it as "the very worst glacier of the whole Kara-Korum.... The whole valley was filled with stones and boulders often of a tremendous size." Possibly due to this account, there has been very little mountaineering activity in the area ever since. Of the 30 or so 6,000m peaks above the Virjerab Glacier, I could only find a record of one having been climbed: In 1991

Seen from Harjoldur Sar, these peaks above the First West Virjerab Glacier and Spregh Yaz Glacier are thought to be unclimbed. (A) 6,172m. (B) 6,099m. (C) 6,316m. (D) 6,140m (attempted in 2015 from the north). (E) Khurdopin Sar. *Pete Thompson*

a New Zealand expedition summited Peak 6,460m above the Second West Virjerab Glacier, approaching on skis from Snow Lake.

Our expedition consisted of Phil De-Beger, Aiden Laffey, and me. Our aim was to climb Khurdopin Sar (6,310m) and other unclimbed 6,000m peaks above the Spregh Yaz Glacier and in the Chot Pert Nala, both of which branch from the lower Virjerab Glacier. On June 3, after a three-day trek from Shimshal Village, our porters and guide left us at a 4,095m base camp at the junction of the Virjerab and Spregh Yaz glaciers. This was near the base camp used in 2012 by a Polish expedition, which made the first ascent of a 5,900m peak above the Spregh Yaz Glacier that they named Khushrui Sar (*AAJ 2014*).

After establishing an advance base camp in the Spregh Yaz valley, we attempted Peak 6,140m by the north face, but gave up due to avalanche conditions. We also abandoned our planned attempt on Khurdopin Sar due to the number of seracs and avalanche risk.

Next, we decided to attempt peaks in the Chot Pert Nala, on the other side of the Virjerab Glacier. At one point this valley narrows to a gorge, and there are two short rock climbing sections to pass. After establishing another advanced base at 5,100m, we attempted the first ascent of Peak 6,020m by the west face and west ridge. Climbing without a rope, I was above the others in a very deep section of snow when I heard a muffled boom and started tumbling in an avalanche. Fortunately I managed to brake, leaving the others on a plinth of snow on a ridgeline below. Fault lines a meter deep on either side of the ridge indicated that I'd triggered two avalanches simultaneously. We retreated.

The next day we reconned the approach through an icefall to Peak 6,104m, the highest in the Chot Pert Nala. Setting off at 1:30 a.m. on June 19, we climbed a wide couloir up the south face and then continued along the west ridge to make the first ascent of this summit (PD), returning to our bivouac at 8 a.m. Later, locals suggested the name Harjoldur Sar, which in Wakhi means "the mountain of the valley of the black and white yak."

After returning to base camp, we trekked a short distance up-valley and photographed unclimbed peaks of the upper Virjerab. Some of these appear to be fairly easy objectives. [*A full report with maps can be downloaded at the AAJ website.*] 📷 🔍

– PETE THOMPSON, *U.K.*

OGRE AND OGRE II ATTEMPTS

Marcos Costa (Brazil), Jesse Mease, Billy Pierson (both USA), and I (U.K.) went to the Choktoi Glacier in June and July to attempt the unclimbed north face of the Ogre. This Eiger Nordwand of the Karakoram is accessed by a short walk over the Sim La (5,300m) from the upper Choktoi. It features serac-laden snow and ice slopes to 6,600m, topped by a rock ramp to an upper snowfield at 7,100m and a steep headwall to the summit (7,284m).

We shared permits with Scott Adamson and Kyle Dempster (both USA), who were planning to climb the north face of Ogre II and the north ridge of Latok I (*see report below*). Our liaison officer, one of the most inept any of us had encountered, informed us that the new and especially time-wasting military regulations being introduced this year in the wake of the Nanga Parbat massacre were intended to make things safer for all climbers, primarily by making it difficult for them to come at all. Once again the livelihood of the locals plays no role in the thinking of Pakistani officialdom.

After all four of us made an acclimatization trip up Baintha Ahrta (ca 6,300m, soloed by me in 2013), the forecast called for excellent weather and we rushed off to the north face of the Ogre and launched up it. However, at sunrise on the first ice pitches beyond our 2013 high point (ca 5,900m), we found ourselves in the firing line of very significant stonefall, with Jesse in particular being hit several times in our extended run for cover. Marcos and I spent the morning digging a four-man snow cave, and we sheltered in this until midnight before retreating. Rivers of slush flowed past us at sundown, providing our first hint that nothing was normal about the summer of 2015 in the Karakoram.

Marcos Costa during an attempt on the northwest ridge of Ogre II. *Jesse Mease*

The unclimbed north face of the Ogre. The line attempted in 2015 and camps are marked. Above the high point, the proposed route was the obvious ramp cutting right through the rock barrier to the snow patch below the summit tower. *Bruce Normand*

Sure enough, stiflingly hot days, with the freezing level far above 6,000m, dragged into weeks. Marcos and Jesse repeated the latter's 2013 all-free rock route on Biacherahi Central Tower. Billy and I attempted a new line up the snow couloirs leading to the north side of Porter Peak (ca 5,700m), directly east of base camp, but were closed down 10m below the summit by an impassable cornice. A team including the Huber brothers, trying a new route on Latok III, was lucky to escape uninjured when their tents were nearly blown off their platforms by the blast wave of a collapsing serac. With no break in the weather in sight, we gritted our teeth, chose our targets, and prepared for nighttime operations.

Billy and I returned to the Ogre. On the first night we regained our cave and spent a comfortable day. On the second night we breached an ice barrier in the main rockfall gully and exited left to shelter under a serac at 6,400m. On the third night we climbed to the top of the snow at 6,600m and here were shut down unequivocally. The rock band to 7,100m is by no means the excellent granite for which the Ogre is famous, but a slabby, friable, red- and black-streaked stone, which takes no protection and would not even remain in place for long enough to host a tool or a crampon. With no ice or snow cover, which could perhaps be expected only in September, progress was impossible. We rappelled the next night and were back in base camp the following day.

Marcos and Jesse decided to try Ogre II (6,960m) by the northwest ridge, climbed by Koreans in 1983 for the first ascent of the peak. On their first day they could only reach the basin below the col connecting the two Ogres before things became too warm. On their second night they climbed to the col, and then they were free of objective hazards and could continue up excellent ice and mixed granite. On their third day they reached a high camp around 6,600m on a precarious perch with stunning views of the Ogre. Their fourth day found them on steep, technical rock with insufficient equipment either to climb or to protect, and they were forced to retreat from a high point of ca 6,700m, regaining base camp safely the day after us. I would like to thank the MEF, BMC, and Alpine Club for their generous support of our effort. 📷

– BRUCE NORMAND, *U.K.*

NEAR MISS ON OGRE II

BY KYLE DEMPSTER

Scott Adamson and I arrived at Choktoi base camp on July 4 with permits for Ogre II and Latok I. This was my sixth expedition to Pakistan, and it was by far the warmest Karakoram season I have experienced. As Scott and I acclimated during the first two weeks of July, we climbed and traveled on the glacier solely through the hours of midnight to 10 a.m. Extreme temperatures forced us to stop during the day as we watched the mountains disintegrate.

On July 18 we woke at 1 a.m. and left advanced base to begin our attempt on the unclimbed 1,400m north face of Ogre II. We carried a stove, two-person sleeping bag, a tarp, six ice screws, a single set of cams, nuts, six pins, and two 60m, 7.3mm ropess. We were able to move quickly on the lower part of the mountain, climbing past short mixed bulges with good gear, and connecting snow and ice systems. Increasing cloud cover (as forecast) and cooler temperatures higher on the face contributed to minimal rockfall.

At 9 p.m., under light snow, we arrived at a 60° band of snow and ice ridges, where we hoped to bivouac. The bulletproof ice allowed for excavation of a ledge 50cm deep, and Scott and I pulled the two-person sleeping bag over our heads and sat shoulder to shoulder for the evening. At dawn light spindrift filled our sleeping bag. Unable to sleep, Scott rappelled a full pitch and found a better place to dig into the ice. We made a ledge large enough for us to lie nearly flat, wrapped ourselves in the tarp, and dozed off.

At 1 p.m. we decided to climb toward the summit ridge, which likely held a decent bivouac site. I led a delicate 150m leftward traverse and climbed up and into a massive dihedral that pointed us toward the ridge. Two more elegantly steep and technical pitches, the crux of the face, put us just below a short overhanging section. It was dark when Scott arrived at the anchor and I passed him

The north face of Ogre II. (1) The Adamson-Dempster attempt. (2) The descent route, with (R) marking the site of the anchor failure. (3) Approximate high point of the 2015 Costa-Mease attempt on the northwest ridge (Korean Route, 1993). *Kyle Dempster*

Scott Adamson and the remains of the ropes, back at base camp. *Kyle Dempster*

the rack. I remember looking at his watch and seeing 6,613m, indicating how close we were to the 6,980m summit. He climbed past the overhang, into the low-angle corner, and out of sight. The rope began moving faster and I felt relieved, thinking he had found easier ground. Several minutes later I heard him yell. Assuming this meant "Rock!," I swung close to the wall on the hanging belay. Suddenly: sparks, a headlamp, and Scott came flying past. "Holy shit! Are you okay?" I yelled. He had come to a stop more than 15m below me. I could see his headlamp slowly scanning his surroundings, and I gave him a minute. "Well, I think my leg is broken," was his response.

Before starting down, we had to cut nearly 12m from one of our ropes because of damage from the fall. It was hard for Scott to rappel at an angle, so I tried to build anchors directly down the fall line. After only three rappels, the sheath peeled down the rope we'd already cut, exposing another long section of core. We continued down, watching our rack diminish. After we rappelled over a 6m horizontal roof, the second rope became completely stuck and I had to cut about 33m from it. On subsequent rappels I remember thinking both ropes now seemed to be about 30m.

What had been swirling snowflakes was now a torrent of spindrift down the snow-covered granite slab. With only three cams remaining, I urgently searched for V-threads. At first light, around 4:30 a.m., Scott and I could see the glacier below; we had perhaps three or four short rappels to go. For the next anchor, I settled on a small patch of marginal ice that was covered in fresh snow. I built the anchor and clipped in. Scott rappelled down and also clipped to the anchor. There was no backup. We pulled the ropes and I began rappelling. Four meters below, as I went over a small bulge, the V-thread popped and we both fell 90m to the glacier. Scott had no additional injuries; I had only a bloody nose.

For months after our accident I beat myself up over the mistake that nearly killed both of us. As I ponder the events leading up to the anchor failure, I view them as both important to analyze and also as potential excuses for the inexcusable. Anchors can't fail. Every single one, no matter how tired you are or how bad conditions become, needs to be placed in a state of complete awareness. Scott and I both have recovered well. We would like to thank the Mugs Stump Award and AAC's Lyman Spitzer Award for supporting climbers' dreams, and sometimes their hardships, in the mountains. 📷

SUMMARY: *Attempt on the north face of Baintha Brakk II (Ogre II, 6,980m) to ca 6,600m, by Scott Adamson and Kyle Dempster (USA).*

Link Sar's main summit (7,041m) is the rock pyramid to the right. The high point on the left is Link Sar West (6,938m). (1) Fever Pitch on the northwest face. (2) The committing descent of the southwest face to an unnamed glacier basin. *The North Face / Jon Griffith*

LINK SAR WEST, NORTHWEST FACE

SITUATED BETWEEN K6 AND K7, the unclimbed Link Sar (7,041m) derives it name from being the "linking" peak between these two giants. Compared to neighboring peaks, it has seen very little attention, mainly because it is hard to approach or even see in its entirety.

This was Jon Griffith's fourth attempt on the mountain and my second. In 2014, Jon and Kevin Mahoney, climbing the northwest face through a storm, topped out on an unclimbable section of ridgeline. Armed with this knowledge, Jon and I planned to start up the same line but continue farther up and left (northward) to reach the top of the face at a much better spot.

As we left base camp on July 12, knee-deep trail-breaking in wet sleet on the glacier produced a very Scottish feel. We got soaked and nearly bailed then and there—starting up an unclimbed 7,000m peak with totally wet gear didn't feel too appealing. However, the next day we continued up the glacier, crossed the bergschrund at ca 5,600m, and started up the face, reaching our first bivouac at ca 6,100m. The weather cleared, but given the amount of fresh snow on the face, we decided to stay at this relatively safe bivouac site for the entire day and let the face shed the new snow. It was one of the wiser choices we've made.

On July 15, after a hard 17-hour day, we exited the northwest face and made a bivouac on the summit ridge at ca 6,800m. The climbing had not been too technical: several mixed pitches, with the hardest being a short pitch of M4. However, the face is consistently steep with lots of black ice. On top of that was the altitude, heat, and large packs. The effort destroyed us.

That evening Jon came down with a fever, and we decided to stay put the next day to see how much he would recover. On the 17th we continued up the ridge, and by midday we had reached the point we're calling Link Sar West (6,938m).

We had wanted to continue to the main summit of Link Sar, which is nearly a kilometer away along a complicated and corniced ridge. But we'd run out of food and weather. Jon's fever returned that afternoon, so we bivouacked right next to the summit and waited for cooler, safer conditions before heading down. Starting at 3 a.m. on the 18th, we descended a large couloir on the southwest face, then continued down an unnamed glacier and through a time-consuming icefall to reach the main Charakusa Glacier. We eventually reached base camp at 5 p.m., seven days after leaving. We named the ascent route Fever Pitch.

We've deliberated over whether we reached a separate summit, and therefore whether our route was a "success." Jon felt the line had been completed: We had climbed the northwest face and continued to the point that dominates the west side of the mountain. On other large massifs (including K6) there are often separate summits, and on maps the western summit is designated Point 6,938m. Having been there, I too feel the west peak justifies being classified as a separate summit. Either way, we had an amazing adventure getting to it and back. 📷

— ANDY HOUSEMAN, *U.K.*

KHANE VALLEY, EXPLORATION AND SHORSA TOWER I

OUR EXPEDITION from the Scuola Guido della Torre took place in August and comprised Matteo Filippini, Tommaso Lamantia, Luca Monfrini, Emanuele Nugara, and me as leader. Our goal was not only to climb virgin summits but also to thoroughly explore and document the Khane Valley. From a base camp on the First Terrace, at about 4,000m, we explored the main valley as far as the Khane Glacier icefall, at about 4,900m, as well as several side valleys.

During exploration of the valley leading toward what we called Hope Col (4,780m), we made the first ascent of Peak 45, as designated on Jerzy Wala's 2012 sketch map. We climbed the ca 300m east ridge (VI+/VII) and adopted the local name for this peak: Shorsa Tower I (ca 4,900m). The rock was generally good though blocky; it was more compact for the final pitches.

We attempted the south face of Peak 42, but the cracks turned out to be grass-filled and dirty, and we abandoned the attempt after only one pitch. Investigation of the lower sections of neighboring towers led us to the same conclusion, and we made no more attempts in this area.

We attempted to reach Saws Col (5,270m) between Meligo and the Twins (or, more precisely, between peaks 64 and 66), and from there hoped to climb Peak 66. However, we were stopped on the glacier at 5,000m by frequent stonefall from the west face of the Twins. We attempted Peak 23 but again failed due to poor ice and stonefall—one large rockfall missed our

Max Fisher on the third day on the southeast face of Tangra Tower. *James Monypenny*

tent by only 80m. Finally, we attempted a satellite peak near base camp and close to Peak 42. We climbed 300m up to III+, but the poor rock stopped us just 30m from the summit, which we named Nail I (4,500m).

Throughout our stay the weather was favorable, but constant high temperatures made climbing dangerous. Also, despite appearances, the rock quality was poor. *A full report appears on the website, along with numerous photos.* 📷 🔍

– *INFORMATION PROVIDED BY* WALTER POLIDORI, *TRANSLATED BY* VITTORIO BEDOGNI

KHANE VALLEY, TWIN II AND TANGRA TOWER ATTEMPTS

LAST YEAR, when my good buddy, climbing partner, and fellow adventurer Cory Hall passed away in a tragic climbing accident, I knew a memorial expedition was in order. The granite spires of Pakistan were a long-held dream for Cory and me, and I wanted to forge an uncompromising line, in good style, up a remote, untouched spire. Tangra Tower (ca 5,620m) fit the bill perfectly. After months of research, fund-raising, and preparation, I met Max "The Bear" Fisher, also one of Cory's climbing partners, in Delhi in early September.

Max and I bought Royal Enfield motorbikes and learned to ride in the deep end. After three days of dodging traffic and cows through the foothills of the Himalaya, we reached the Pakistan-India border. Try as we might, we were unable to bribe the bikes into Pakistan, so we continued by public transport up the infamous Karakoram Highway.

Entering the Khane Valley, our psych was running high—however, fate had other plans. After an initial day of reconnaissance, we spent the next nine days pinned at base camp while a foot of snow fell and I suffered badly with giardia. On day 10, only partly recovered, we moved our heavy big-wall kit to the base of Tangra, only to find fresh powder covering the lower slabs. We opted to acclimatize on Twin II. Endless trail-breaking through knee-deep snow finally gave way to some great ice climbing on the northwest face. We reached a point about 150m below the summit before Max ran out of gas. Our rappel through the night went reasonably well, and we stumbled back to advanced camp after 20 hours on the go.

After only one full day at base camp we returned to Tangra, collected water, and got established on the wall. Four days of climbing led us to a headwall, where wild splitter cracks, which required a mixture of free and aid climbing, with pendulums, brought us to a chimney where we spent the night. After an hour of trying to get the stove going using cheap Asian lighters, we succumbed to a depressing meal of dry noodles. Day five did not go well. After taking two hours to achieve 20m of horrendous offwidth climbing, loose rock, and tricky aid, I had to admit defeat. As we stumbled for the last time back to base camp, the weather remained mockingly good. 📷 📄

– JAMES MONYPENNY, *U.K.*

LACHIT VALLEY: GOAT PEAK, DREAM WALKER PEAK, "OGRE"

The line of Rolling (D)Ice on Dream Walker Peak (5,809m). *Tomasz Klimczak*

BETWEEN AUGUST 18 and October 2, four members of the Polish National Alpine Team—Maciej Bedrejczuk, Maciej Janczar, Marcin Wernik, and I—visited a previously unexplored region of the southern Tagas Mountains. Our goals were peaks in the Lachit Valley, north of the village of the same name in the lower Kondus Valley, above Dansam. We were the first expedition to receive a permit to enter this valley, which rises toward the south side of K6. It was the third year I had tried to obtain this permit.

After an initial reconnaissance we established base camp at ca 4,000m in one of the first western side valleys of the Lachit. During the next month we explored this and one other arm of the Lachit. Both side valleys were surrounded by beautiful ca 6,000m peaks.

On August 27, we made an easy acclimatization ascent of a rocky summit from a ca 4,700m snowy col. We named it Goat Peak (4,991m, UIAA IV).

For our second climb we chose the soaring peak we could see up and left from base camp. On September 4, from an advanced base camp at 5,000m, sheltered by a serac, we crossed the glacier and simul-climbed the initial 300m of the north face. We were caught out in the dark and spent the night on a small ledge at

The Polish Couloir on the "Ogre," with the main summit to the right. Dream Walker Peak is out of view to the left. None of the summits visible has been climbed. *Tomasz Klimczak*

5,600m without bivouac equipment. Unfortunately, it snowed. Next day, with no improvement in the weather, we decided to continue. The first pitch that day was the crux of the route, a 1.5cm-thick, unprotected ice smear (AI5). We reached the summit ridge and continued to the top at 3 p.m. Our descent followed the route, with 14 rappels from ice threads and pitons, plus some downclimbing. We eventually reached advance base in the middle of the night in continuous snowfall. We propose the name Dream Walker Peak (5,809m, 35°15'18"N, 76°33'01"E); our route is called Rolling (D)Ice (ED1/2 AI5 M5 80°, ca 1,450m of climbing).

Our third goal was a mountain seen on the right from base camp, a large tower with airy ridges and a pointed summit, difficult on all sides—the dream of every alpinist. Because of its character, we gave it a working name of the Ogre (35°16'12"N, 76°31'43"E).

There was a promising ice couloir on the northeast face, which was easily accessible from base camp. We first made an advance base at 4,500m, below the ca 1,500m face, and then climbed the couloir in three days, with two sitting bivouacs on snow ledges. On the third day, September 20, we reached a saddle on the ridge at 6,004m. We hoped to keep going, but it was now 3:30 p.m. and the weather had turned bad. We estimated we would need a full day to get to the summit and back. Given the forecast, this meant we would have to rappel our couloir in heavy snowfall, under the threat of avalanches. We started to rappel immediately and late at night reached our first bivouac. The following day we continued rappelling, reaching the glacier in the afternoon, after 27 rappels from the saddle. That night it began to snow heavily, continuing over the next couple of days. When we went back up to collect the tents we found them buried in snow, the poles broken. We called our route to the col the Polish Couloir (ED2 AI5 M7- 90°), but the Ogre remains unclimbed.

We believe the Lachit Valley will give future expeditions many unforgettable mountain adventures. [*Additional photos of this area can be found with the online report.*] 📷 📄

— TOMASZ KLIMCZAK, *POLAND*

INDIA

RONGDO VALLEY, PYRAMID PEAK, SOUTHEAST RIDGE, ATTEMPT

On June 21, after 18 months of planning, Andrew Basford, Katie Farrell, Matthew Fuller, Steve Hutton, Katie McKay, Dan Slome, and I left London for the East Karakoram, our aim to summit an unclimbed 6,000er via the mostly unexplored upper Southeast Shukpa Kunchang and Rongdo glaciers. Permits to this part of the Karakoram are very difficult to obtain. We received ours four weeks prior to departure, leaving just enough time to get everything sorted.

With our liaison officer, we left Rongdo village (3,200m) and trekked six days to base camp (4,800m), arriving on July 4. Our main objective was an unclimbed summit referred to by the 2013 Indian Air Force Expedition as Pyramid Peak (6,215m). This mountain distinctively guards the upper Rongdo Valley and is symmetrical and very aesthetic.

On July 5 we established an advanced base at 5,200m, and the following day moved this to 5,430m, just below the Southeast Shukpa Kunchang Glacier. On the 8th, Andrew, Katie McKay, Matthew, and I left advanced base and climbed a snow slope onto the Rongdo Glacier and then up to the col between Pyramid Peak (Peak 6,215m) and Ngapo Kangri (Rongdo I).

At 4 a.m. we started up the southeast ridge of Pyramid Peak, immediately seeing that it was corniced and steeper than expected. We made good progress up short snow ramps (PD, 50–60°) and had incredible views of 6,000m and 7,000m peaks. But at 6,050m we turned around due to approaching poor weather and concerns the sun would weaken the cornices. On returning to base camp, we noticed a marked change in the clear, settled weather we had been

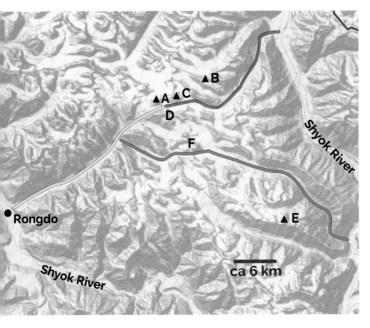

In 2015, three expeditions explored various valleys inside the great bend of the Shyok River, east of Rongdo. Yellow line: British climbers attempted (A) Pyramid Peak via the Rongdo Valley. Red line: An Indian expedition climbed (B) Peak 6,195m and (C) Peak 6,305m via the Ryong Kharu Valley. After these climbs, this team crossed (D) Sagtogpa Col and exited the mountains via the Rongdo Valley. Blue line: An Indian Air Force team explored the Kunzang Valley, climbing (E) Tak Jaal and other peaks. The military climbers crossed (F) Kunzang Col and exited via the Rongdo Valley.
© Mapbox, © OpenStreetMap

The British team's intermediate advanced base at 5,200m in the upper Rongdo Valley. Unclimbed peaks west of Gazgazri (6,160m, *AAJ 2013*) are seen behind. *Ed Poulter*

experiencing, with rain, snow, and poor visibility. Eventually we packed up and descended. Huge thanks must go to the BMC and MEF for their financial support. *A comprehensive report can be found on the AAJ website.* 📄 📷 🔍

— ED POULTER, *U.K.*

RYONG KHARU VALLEY, PEAKS 6,195M AND 6,305M

FOR THE LAST FOUR DECADES the Shyok Valley has been closed to trekkers and mountaineers, due to its proximity to the Line of Control with China. Also, the Shyok River is in spate from July to September, and movement up the valley impractical. However, recently the Border Roads Organisation has made improvements to enable the road to be used even in the summer months. Until the summer of 2015, the entire area south of Mandalthang remained unexplored. The Ryong Kharu Lungpa (valley), eventually leading to the Sagtogpa Glacier, had never been entered by a mountaineering expedition.

Our team comprised Rajesh Gadgil, Vineeta Muni, Sagar Shinde, Nikunj Vora, Kushala Vora, and me. We employed four climbing Sherpas, two high-altitude support staff from the Garhwal, and five Kumaoni people as cooking staff and low-altitude support. We all camped next to the road on July 23 and then spent three days walking to base camp at 4,665m. A further four hours led to the site of advanced base (5,070m), at the junction of the various branches of Sagtogpa Glacier that form the catchment area for Ryong Kharu valley.

Just above advanced base lay the first (eastern) subsidiary of the Sagtogpa Glacier, and we decided to attempt Peak 6,195m at its head (34°33'N, 78°04'E). On August 6, after a few days of acclimatizing, we established Camp 1 at 5,765m, and a group of us set off for the summit at 6 a.m. on the 8th. We approached up the easy glacier to the east-southeast of the mountain and climbed onto the southeast ridge via a pitch of 60° snow. The crest to the top

The view northwest from Sagtogpa Kangri. (A) Argan Kangri (6,789m) and (B) Amale (6,312m) in the Arganglas Group. (C) Saser Kangri Group (Saser I, 7,672m). *Divyesh Muni*

was gently angled, with a couple of 10m steep sections, and we reached the summit at 11 a.m. Views were excellent and showed that the next valley west (the Sagtogpa Central Glacier) had little of interest, but the western glacier had many enticing peaks. This is the main branch of the Sagtogpa Glacier, and we decided to attempt Peak 6,305m at its head (34°32'N, 78°02'E).

After traversing a lush green ridge, we established Paradise Camp at 5,270m by a stream fringed by beds of flowers. The distance to our peak was long, so we put in an intermediate camp before making summit camp at 5,860m on the 17th. On the 19th, ten of us approached up the glacier to the south of the mountain and started up the west ridge. We found that this culminated in steep rock towers, so we skirted the summit pyramid to the east until we found a 70m, 50° snow and ice gully leading to the top of the southeast ridge. We arrived on the summit at 11:30 a.m. We named our peak Sagtogpa Kangri, since it is the most prominent summit of the Sagtogpa Glacier.

We now spotted a possible route over to the upper Rongdo Valley, and the prospect excited us more than climbing another peak. With three days' rations and minimal gear we crossed Sagtogoa Col (5,915m) and were fortunately greeted by a gentle glacier going down toward the lush Rongdo Valley. It took another two days to reach Rongdo village, a devastating cloudburst having destroyed the path in several places, requiring the use of our climbing skills to negotiate the route. 📷 🔍

– DIVYESH MUNI, *INDIA*

KUNZANG VALLEY, EXPLORATION AND FIRST ASCENTS

Standing on the summit of Odgsal I during the 2013 Indian Air Force Rongdo expedition (*AAJ 2014*), our attention was captured by a huge glaciated valley to the east: the Kunzang. Locals told us this had never been traversed. In 2015 we planned to explore this valley, climb new peaks, and open a route across the col at its head to the Rongdo Valley.

The Kunzang River flows from the northwest and empties into the Shyok at the 63km milestone along the road that runs from Shyok to Daulat Beg Oldie. We arrived in very early summer, as later the Shyok swells and floods frequently. At this time the Kunzang River was also frozen for large sections and made movement up the valley easy. We were a 12-member military expedition, accompanied on the climbs by six Sherpas.

Seventeen kilometers inside the valley is a prominent stream flowing into the Kunzang on its true right (south) side. A steep valley was visible, and at its head was an irregular peak with a prominent rock face. We named this peak Tak Jaal ("Rocky Face" in Ladakhi). We went up the Tak Jaal Lungpa (valley) to a glacier nearly 1km wide and 10km long that ran in an east-west direction. We named the glacier Dhing Srehen ("Floating Clouds"). From an advanced base on the lateral moraine, on May 11, we climbed Tak Jaal (6,123m, 34°23'19.1"N, 78° 11'44.9"E) via the north ridge, using fixed rope on an exposed rock face below to the summit. The following day we climbed the neighboring Khemtses ("The Neighbor," 6,083m), less than 2km west of Tak Jaal, via its northeast flank.

In bad weather we returned to the main valley and moved our base camp farther up. We went up the Goskap Lungpa ("Valley of Opportunities"), which bisects the massif between the main Kunzang Valley and the Dhing Srehen Glacier, but poor weather thwarted our plans to attempt three peaks at the eastern end.

Near the head of the main valley is the large lake of Kunzang Tso. We crossed the frozen lake and ascended a gully at its northeastern end. After a two-hour climb we arrived at a large glacial field, which we named Stan Urkaan Glacier ("Flying Carpet"). To the west were half a dozen peaks of more than 6,000m, begging to be climbed. However, we were only able to climb one, due to the adverse weather. This peak, Jaksang ("Opportune Time," 6,152m), was just across the glacier from our camp.

One hour's walk under a hazy moon on May 23 brought us to its base, and from there we followed the northeast ridge to the summit (40–60°), fixing rope on two sections.

After this ascent we crossed the main glacier to the northwest and camped below Kunzang Col at 5,446m. Next day we crossed the col (ca 5,800m). It took nearly three hours, as almost 80cm of snow had fallen. We rappelled to the glacier on the far side, descended below Island Peak, and trudged down to the Rongdo Glacier. Another half day's walk across treacherous moraine brought us to the hot springs in upper Rongdo Valley. 🗐 📷

– GP. CAPT. V.K. SASHINDRAN, *INDIA*

[Top right] Tak Jaal (6,123m) seen from the approach to the northeast. The route of ascent lay behind the right skyline ridge. [Bottom] The Stan Urkann Glacier and a collection of unclimbed 6,000m peaks. *V.K. Sashindran (both photos)*

PEAK 5,600M

IN THE SUMMER OF 2014, Kathy Connelly and I wanted to explore a wild place without seeing other people—or even traces of them. If we could, we wanted to make the first ascent of an obscure 5,000m to 6,000m peak. In the end, we met all these goals.

After traveling the rough new road to Skarchen (3,600m), we trekked a day to Hundar Drog (4,100m). From here we reached the seldom-visited Sniu Valley—we saw no other people, nor prayer flags, though we did find prehistoric drawings. The next day we reached base camp at 4,900m in the southwestern branch of the Sniamo Valley. Gurmat, our guide, Lotus, his assistant, and I headed south up what we named Valley 3, reached a glacial lake, and cramponed up the left side of the glacier above to a saddle. From here we turned southwest and climbed the ridge to a 5,600m summit (ca 34°22'20"N, 77°22'13"E, Google Earth).

– ED HARSTEAD, *USA*

CHOMOTANG, NORTHWEST FACE

I FIRST NOTICED Chomotang on Google Earth during one of my regular cyber-tours of the world's mountain ranges. It seemed to stand out from its surrounds, and the imagery was of sufficient quality to indicate it had a few nice lines. It also caught my eye as it was clearly near a road—something I've come to appreciate after many Himalayan trips that were more approaching than climbing.

Chris White and I approached from Leh, via the village of Hanupata (3,790m), reaching base camp at 4,885m on June 26. The next day we set off at 5:30 a.m. for the peak immediately above us, the southernmost of a stretched massif that runs south from Nigutse La (ca 5,100m). We went straight up the south face and reached the summit at 8:30 a.m., where the GPS read 5,678m. We named this Nigutse South, and from it got a good view of the glacier on the north side of Chomotang. This convinced us to abandon our original plan of attempting it from the southeast and instead try from the northwest.

On the next day we reached the glacier and camped at 5,425m, then at 6:15 a.m. on the 29th set off for the right-hand of two broad gullies on the northwest face of Chomotang. We climbed unroped, mostly at around 40°, but a little steeper in the upper section and occasionally icy. We reached the top at 9:20 a.m.; the GPS read 6,065m and 34°05'08.7"N, 76°41'18.8"E. We returned to our tent at 11:30 a.m. and base camp at 3:15 p.m.

Maps designate this peak Chomotang II and clearly show it higher than Chomotang I to the northeast, which we can confirm. It would be far simpler and more accurate to reverse the names and designate our peak Chomotang and the lower peak to the northeast Chomotang II.

After an ascent of the normal route on Stok Kangri with Lars Svens, he and I traveled to Zanskar to reconnoiter a 6,000m peak, possibly named Babang, in the Chelong Valley, before returning to Hanupata and crossing the Sirsir La to attempt a 6,000m peak west of Photoksar Village via the north flank. Though we didn't know it at the time, this was Machu Kangri (*AAJ 2015*). However, we never got on the mountain because it rained for six days straight.

– DAMIEN GILDEA, *AUSTRALIA*

Chomotang (left) and Nigutse South seen from Sirsir La to the northeast. *Damien Gildea*

KANG YATZE III, NORTHEAST RIDGE

In August, William Newsom, Simon Ridout, and I made the probable first ascent of Kang Yatze III in central Ladakh. The expedition was hampered by heavy rain and flash floods in the Markha Valley, where many bridges were washed away. Base camp was made at 4,980m, about 1km below the normal base for Kang Yatze I and II. After acclimatizing with an ascent of Kang Yatze II, we trekked up the glacier beyond Kang Yatze I to make camp at 5,700m in the upper cirque between Dzo Jongo, the unnamed 6,300m peak at the valley head, and Kang Yatze III. On the 10th we climbed steep, loose scree slopes and shattered ribs to gain the ridge crest between Kang Yatze III and I at 6,110m. This terrain would be rather more pleasant with a covering of spring snow. A beautiful, curving snow arête—the northeast ridge of the mountain—then led to the summit tower. The final rocks were steep, loose shale, and the top tower was climbed on the right side (6,310m GPS, AD UIAA III). 🖾

— MARTIN MORAN, *ALPINE CLUB, U.K.*

PANGONG RANGE, KAKSTET KANGRI, FIRST WINTER ASCENT

Kakstet Kangri (6,561m) is an attractive mountain on the south bank of the Pangong Tso and is named after Kakstet village, from which it can easily be seen. It was climbed on September 3, 2001, by 11 young members of the Eighth Mountain Division of the Indian Army. From a camp at 5,400m, they climbed the southeast face and southeast ridge. In February 2015 this route was followed again by an 11-member expedition organized by the Indian Mountaineering Foundation to make the first winter ascent. The Pangong Range lies north of the true crest of the Ladakh Range and is an eastern extension of the Karakoram. *See AAJ 2011 for a sketch map of the peaks.*

— LINDSAY GRIFFIN, *WITH INFORMATION FROM* THE HIMALAYAN CLUB

Lisa Van Sciver checking out a rock peak toward the head of the Dalung Glacier. *Rachel Spitzer*

TAARE PARBAT, EAST RIDGE TO NORTHEAST TOP

ANNA PFAFF, LISA VAN SCIVER, AND I traveled to Zanskar in late August. We took the bus for two days from Leh into the Suru Valley. This broad valley first runs east to Ringdom Gompa, passing the Shafat Fortress, a massive granite wall dominating the roadside, and then south toward the Pensi La. Our goal was to investigate the Dalung Valley, the first valley to the west when traveling south from Ringdom.

Over the next few days, with the help of horses and after crossing the braided but relatively slow-moving Suru River, we established a base camp north of the Dalung River, about two miles up the valley, at approximately 4,250m. We found many inspiring unclimbed peaks, coupled with rugged approaches and a lot of loose rock, and settled on trying to climb a large massif that divided the Dalung from the Chilung Valley to the south.

In early September we established a high camp (4,800m) at the base of our intended objective, after crossing the Dalung River and ascending steep, grassy slopes and moraines for approximately 600m. On the 5th we left our high camp at about 4 a.m. and began to approach the east ridge of what we called Taare Parbat ("Star Peak" in Hindi), as it looked like a point on a star. The initial headwall leading to the ridge was primarily excellent water ice and mixed terrain. Once we reached the prominent ridge, the rock quality greatly deteriorated, and we took great care while climbing a 200m section of loose and detached slabs. Above, we unroped and made our way through third- and fourth-class terrain. The final pitch consisted of mixed terrain and some alpine ice to the summit ridge.

We ascended about 600m to the northeast top at 5,600m. (The main summit, across a chossy saddle, is about 5,630m.) We left one rappel anchor on the summit pyramid and then found a third- and fourth-class walk-off descending toward the Chilung Valley, until we could circle back to our high camp. We named our route Unattached (600m, 5.6 WI3 AI4 M4, no bolts) in reference to the large amount of loose rock and generally feeling unattached to anyone and anything in this remote corner of the globe.

This expedition could not have been possible without the support of the American Alpine Club via the Copp-Dash and McNeill-Nott grants. We found it especially inspiring to be climbing in the same region where Jonny Copp and Micah Dash had climbed in 2007. The locals still remember both men and told us stories of their charismatic personalities. 📇 📷

– RACHEL SPITZER, *USA*

GOMPE TOKPO GLACIER, PEAKS T19 AND T20, ATTEMPT

A STUDENT TEAM from Nippon University Alpine Club reached the col between T19 (6,162m) and T20 (6,157m), on the north side of the Gompe Tokpu. However, they were unable to ascend either ridge above the col (ca 5,600m). There is no evidence of either peak having been attempted previously.

– *INFORMATION FROM* KIMIKAZU SAKAMOTO, *JAPAN*

GOMPE TOKPO GLACIER, T18 (PEAK 6,184M), WEST RIDGE

IN JULY 2014, the Kolkata section of the Himalayan Club organized a trip to climb a virgin peak above the Gompe Tokpo Glacier. With the help of four Sherpas, the team climbed steep ice to the broad col between Peak 6,431m (T16) and Peak 6,162m (T19). Standing on the col between the two mountains is the rocky pyramid of Peak 6,184m (T18). Various team members fixed rope to the foot of the west ridge of T18 and then up over loose rock and snow to the summit, which they measured at 6,212m. 📇 📷

– LINDSAY GRIFFIN, *WITH INFORMATION FROM THE EDITORS OF* THE HIMALAYAN JOURNAL

KORLOMSHE TOKPO, KUSYABLA AND TEMPLE

IN AUGUST I led a small team of Alpine Club members to the Korlomshe Tokpo, which had received only one known previous visit. In 2012, Kamikazu Sakamoto's non-climbing expedition entered this valley but ventured no higher than 5,100m to photograph peaks (*AAJ 2013*).

From Leh we made a two-day, bone-shattering drive to Padam, via Kargil, and then continued by road for a short distance to just beyond Bardan Gompa. From there, a two-day trek took us to a 4,153m base camp close to the confluence of the Tamasa Nala and Korlomshe Tokpo. This site proved much lower than we had hoped, forcing us to make an advanced base below the Korlomshe Glacier at 5,130m.

Knut Tønsberg on the final slopes of Temple, with Kusyabla behind. *Derek Buckle*

From here, Drew Cook, Gus Morton, Knut Tønsberg, and I extensively explored the lower regions of the glacier to identify potential climbing objectives. On September 1, Cook, Morton, and I made the first ascent of Peak 5,916m (northwest of T10 and due east of T9 on the Sakamoto sketch map, *AAJ 2013*) via its glacial southeast ridge (AD). On the 4th, Tønsberg and our liaison officer, Malkeet Singh, followed the same route to the top. We called the peak Kusyabla (33°20.159'N, 76°47.747'E), the Ladakhi word for Monk.

Following a reconnaissance of the upper Korlomshe Tokpo, a high camp was established on a glacial plateau at 5,500m. From this camp, Morton, Tønsberg, and I attempted the impressive Matterhorn-like peak close to the head of the valley. On September 8 we ascended a prominent southwest-facing ice ramp to reach the steep (50°), glaciated east face, which we climbed to just below the rocky south ridge at ca 5,900m (D). At this point, insufficient time—rather than technical difficulty—dictated a retreat.

On the 10th, and from the same high camp, Tønsberg and I climbed unroped up the glaciated east-northeast face and southeast ridge of Peak 5,947m (AD). This peak, which is situated northwest of Kusyabla and north-northeast of T9 (6,107m), was given the name Temple on account of a pulpit-like rock formation on the summit ridge.

We gratefully acknowledge generous financial support from the Alpine Club Climbing Fund, the Mount Everest Foundation, and the Austrian Alpine Club.

– DEREK BUCKLE, *U.K.*

TETLEH NALA, EXPLORATION AND FIRST ASCENTS

FROM LATE JULY TO SEPTEMBER, Anastasija Davidova and I spent 35 days in the Tetleh Nala, one of the three main offshoots of the Raru Valley. Prior to our visit there had only been one reported climbing party here, the 2011 Imperial College (U.K.) Expedition (*AAJ 2012*). There are numerous mountains between 5,700m and 6,250m, some having steep faces up to 1,000m high. India still bans the use of satellite phones (though we did carry walkie-talkies to report our position each night to our liaison officer), and it was refreshing to be in remote mountains more or less on our own.

On July 29 we reached base camp at 4,623m in the Tetleh Nala, and on August 5, from a bivouac at 5,549m, made what we believe to be the first ascent of Khumchu Ri (R7 on Kimikazu Sakamoto's map, 6,064m, 33°14'32"N, 76°50'52"E) in a 13-hour round trip. We climbed snow

[Below] Mountains on the east side of the Tetleh Nala. (A) Kun Long Ri (climbed in 2015 by left skyline ridge). (B) Peak 5,890m. (C) Peak 5,790m (attempted in 2011). (D) Peak 5,750m. (E) Twin summits of 5,940m and 5,950m. (F) Peak 5,980m. *Matija Jost*

Entering the Tetleh Valley just above Onkar, showing peaks on the west side. Left: Ri Pok Te. The new route From East to West lies near the left skyline ridge. Right: Unclimbed R3 (6,036m). *Matija Jost*

from the north onto the southeast ridge, and then continued for 400m on high-quality rock (UIAA IV) before finishing up 600m of snow (50° maximum) on the east ridge. The climbing distance was ca 1,000m, but the height gain only 550m. We descended the south face and then traversed to the southeast ridge, which we used to regain our bivouac. The overall grade was D+.

We now felt suitably acclimatized to attempt an attractive peak on the east side of the valley. On August 13 we climbed 200m of good granite on the west face and bivouacked at 5,533m. After a night of rain we continued with 200m up to V+ to reach the north ridge at ca 5,700m. For the next 300m the crest was narrow with gendarmes. We made an initial foray, but it was tricky, so we returned to a point where we could bivouac, and on the 15th climbed along the east side of the ridge on less than perfect rock to the beginning of a snowy section (V 60°), where we bivouacked again at 5,689m. Next day we continued along the crest (65°), then across the west face (IV and 70° ice) to reach the summit, which we dubbed Kun Long Ri (6,058m, 33°14'19"N, 76°54'26"E). We called our ascent route Happy Journey (750m, TD+). We reversed the ridge as far as our last bivouac, from which we descended east to a glacier (dubbed Slovenian Glacier) and followed this down to the Raru Valley. We got back to base camp on the 17th.

In 2011, Joe Prinold and Virgil Scott from the British expedition attempted a fine pillar on the east face of R4, retreating in bad weather from 6,000m. We thought their line looked safe, so on August 25 we followed it to a good bivouac site at 5,920m. We first climbed unroped

and then did ten 50m pitches (IV+ maximum) on fine slabs of good granite. Next day we continued in the warm sun with rock shoes, climbing six excellent pitches (up to VI-) to reach the southwest ridge at 6,149m. We first climbed the west flank and then the ridge crest to the summit (V+). Locals in Raru village refer to this as Ri Pok Te (6,210m, 33°15'59"N, 76°52'41"E), and we named our line From East to West (1,000m, TD+/ED1), feeling the climbing was worthy of five stars. We reversed the route, mostly by rappel.

There is great potential in this valley. The upper section is rarely visited, even by locals, so feels unspoiled. We saw almost no evidence of the British and appreciate their respect of the natural surroundings—they left no rubbish, just a very nice report and part of their souls. Every expedition causes pollution, but we can minimize this by operating in small teams with minimum comfort. We hope future parties in this valley will be satisfied with our efforts. [*A full expedition report with much useful information and panoramic views of this valley is available on the website.*] 📄 📷 🔍

– MATIJA JOST, *SLOVENIA*

Editor's note: A large Swiss team led by Stéphane Schaffter and Yannick Flugi visited one of the other two Raru side valleys and had completed a successful ski expedition when, during the walk out, Schaffter was swept away during a river crossing and drowned. No details of their ascents have been forthcoming.

SURLE PUH VALLEY, SGURR A MHADAIDH FUAR (L5), EAST FACE

IN AUGUST, Struan Chisholm, Sam Newmark, Calum McLellan, and I arrived in Leh and headed to a maze of unclimbed peaks brought to light by the 2009 Kyoto Zanskar expedition (*AAJ 2012*). In Raru (3,400m), on the Tsarap River, we learned that onward travel to our proposed valley was blocked: All bridges and the continuation road to Char, connecting the Tsarap villages, had been annihilated by floods two months earlier and may take several years to repair.

We were forced to walk southeast for 15km on a rocky track high above the river, where an Indian Army dynamite team was working its loud magic to clear landslide debris. We had to rope up and belay some sections of this loose, exposed path perched above the river, although the locals were quite happy to charge across without such precautions. We reached the village of Surle after two days and then proceeded south up the Surle Puh Valley to base camp. This section was only 8km but rose continuously to 5,200m, so took us nearly three days.

Toward the end of August we wound south through moraine and passed beneath the hanging glacier of L5 (5,897m). [*L stands for Lenak. See sketch map in AAJ 2012.*] Left of the glacier zone we ascended scree and ice patches (45°) on the east face for 500m to reach the summit plateau. We named the peak Sgurr a Mhadaidh Fuar ("Hill of the Cold Hound" in Scottish Gaelic; 33°09'27"N, 77°04'20"E Google Earth) as a tribute to a dog that had followed us up the mountain. He came along on a whim and climbed hard and with great agility up to the summit without so much as a pair of socks. His English was limited, his personal hygiene questionable, and his continuous shouting during the night was disruptive. But he made it to the top like a true pioneer. We didn't see him again after the ascent.

The most prominent peak to the south was L4 at the head of the glacier. We attempted it following the same route as on L5, moving left (south) near the top of the scree to gain the long west ridge of L4. However, threatening clouds and lack of time ended our bid. If attempting it again we would make an advanced base farther up the valley (above the glacier) to shorten the approach over moraine. We are grateful for the support of the Alpine Club, Mount Everest Foundation, and BMC. 📄 📷

– CALUM NICOLL, U.K.

KISHTWAR HIMALAYA

BHALA, NORTHEAST FACE AND RIDGE; TUPENDEO, SOUTHWEST PILLAR; MAHA DEV PHOBRANG, EAST SPUR VIA TE

IN SEPTEMBER, Swiss alpinists Dres Abegglen, Thomas Senf, and Stephan Siegrist returned to the Kishtwar Himalaya to attempt Bhala (Spear), a Matterhorn-like peak they had seen during their 2014 expedition (*AAJ 2015*). Bhala lies on the western rim of the Kaban Valley, which flows southwest into the Chenab Valley, a little east of Atholi. (*See map on page 20.*) Base camp was established close to the foot of Bhala, and on September 12, in excellent weather, the three reached the col on the northeast ridge, where they bivouacked. Next day they climbed an obvious ramp up the 700m northeast face and ridge to the summit, which they gained at 3 p.m. Despite the aesthetic beauty of the mountain, the rock quality was extremely poor. Maps give the altitude of this summit as 6,000m, but the team recorded 5,900m, naming their route Copa-Kaban.

Back at base camp, the weather became more unsettled, with regular afternoon storms. The team's attention was now held by Tupendeo (a.k.a. Druid, as coined by a 1981 British expedition), a spectacular pointed peak that had nearly been climbed in 1992. In the early afternoon of September 18, the three reached a bivouac below the southwest pillar. They fixed a

Tupendeo from the Kaban Valley to the southwest. Yellow line: 1992 attempt. Red line: southwest pillar (Deokhal, 2015). *visualimpact.ch / Thomas Senf*

couple of pitches that day, and the following morning set out for the summit. Contrary to their experiences on Bhala, they found some of the best rock climbing they had ever encountered at altitude, completing their 800m route by 1:30 p.m., and returning to base camp at 9:30 that night. They climbed 21 pitches with difficulties up to 6a/b, recorded an altitude of 5,700m, and named the route Deokhal.

Poor weather pinned them down for a week at base camp, after which they set off for their third objective: Maha Dev Phobrang. This had previously been attempted in 1984, when it was known as Mardi Phabrang. [*The online version of this report recounts the British attempts on these peaks in 1984 and 1992, including a very serious accident on Tupendo.*] Conspicuous on the east spur of this mountain is a 200m tower the Swiss called Te ("Crystal" in Hindi). After a bivouac on the east spur on October 1, they reached the east face of the crystal-shaped tower and climbed it in four excellent pitches up to 5c/6a. As it was only 2 p.m, they rappelled the far side of Te and climbed snow slopes (up to 60°) to reach the main summit of Maha Dev Phobrang at 3.30 p.m. They measured an altitude of 5,900m. They were back in base camp by 9 p.m. and have named their route Chaprasi. Siegrist remarked, "The biggest superlatives don't even begin to explain the conditions we had on this mountain—it was quite simply unique." 📄 📷

— LINDSAY GRIFFIN, *WITH INFORMATION FROM* STEPHAN SIEGRIST, *SWITZERLAND*

CHOMOCHIOR VALLEY: WHITE SAPPHIRE, SOUTH RIDGE; MANASUNA, WEST-SOUTHWEST FACE; LAHARA, SOUTH FACE

WE ARRIVED IN DEHLI on July 6 and after a road trip of nearly five days reached the small town of Gulabgarh, the last section traveling along one of the most dangerous roads in the world, the "Kishtwar Killer." We then trekked for four days via Machail and the Darlang Nullah to the entrance of the Chomochior Valley, where we established base camp on a rock-strewn, grassy field at 3,900m. Our Swiss team comprised Mazal Chevallier (leader), Vincent Haller, Jonas Jurt, Christelle Marceau, Johan Martin, Axel Meyrat, and us.

On July 27, from a camp at 5,200m, we summited White Sapphire, a summit climbed once before, from the opposite side. We first climbed an east-facing couloir for 300m to reach the crest of the south ridge. Then 50° snow and ice slopes and two steeper mixed pitches brought us to the final ridge and summit. [*The south ridge was partially descended by Denis Burdet and Stephan Siegrist (Switzerland) after their first ascent from the west. The 2011 team measured an altitude of 6,040m for the main summit, while the 2015 team quotes ca 5,820m for the same summit, but also commented on the difficulty of obtaining accurate altitude measurements in this region.*] The route was graded TD.

We then split into two teams, the first planning to try an unclimbed peak of ca 6,100m (the next major peak on the ridge north of Kishtwar Kailash). This team established a camp on the moraine at 4,300m and then climbed a west-facing side glacier, beginning with a steep section exposed to objective danger. This was followed by less steep, ice-covered rock to a camp at 4,920m below an icefall with impressive seracs. Next day this ice slope (70°) was climbed in six pitches to reach the glacier plateau above, where a third camp was made. A 60° slope led to a broad 5,500m shoulder below the west-southwest face of the peak, leaving plenty of time to rest and study the face above.

[Previous page] **Stephan Siegrist climbs the fantastic granite of Te, a huge, crystal-shaped tower on the east spur of Maha Dev Phobrang.** *visualimpact.ch / Thomas Senf*

[Above] **Manasuna from the west-southwest with the line of the first ascent. Kishtwar Kailash is just off picture to the right.** [Below] **Looking south from Lahara. (A) Unclimbed. (B) Manasuna. (C) Kishtwar Kailash. (D) Rohini Sikhar. (E) Cerro Kishtwar. (F) Chomochior.** *Swiss Expedition Kishtwar 2015 (both)*

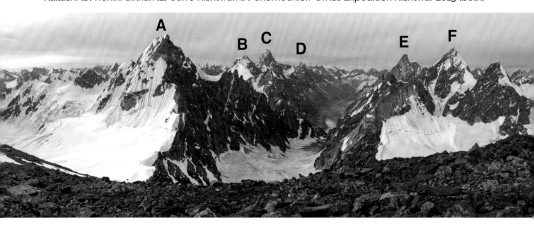

The following day, August 6, the team climbed the snowy face and then a snow/ice gully (60–70°), in surprisingly clear weather, to a final rocky section leading to the summit. The route was rappelled to top camp, and the next day base camp was regained, again after numerous rappels. The peak was named Manasuna ("Monsoon" in Hindi; 33°20'35.28"N, 76°38'6.30"E) in memory of the mostly wet weather experienced during the ascent. The grade was TD and the elevation measured at 5,965m, although we have no confidence in the accuracy.

Meanwhile, the other team made an exhausting walk over unstable moraine farther up the Chomochior Glacier, camping where a smaller glacier came in from the right. A short day then took them over more moraine slopes and through a serac band to a glacial plateau at 5,200m, below Peak ca 5,700m. On the 6th they climbed this summit, christened Lahara ("Wave;" 33°24'7.02"N, 76°38'11.56"E). They climbed the right side of the south face at PD (including 100m of 50–60° ice and a final snow ridge).

Before leaving the valley we made an attempt on Rohini Sikhar (5,990m, climbed once, by a Scottish team in 1989, via the southwest face, *AAJ 1990*), but a big stonefall on our planned route put an end to this idea. We used the remaining few days bolting several nice sport routes on a good granite crag close to base camp, an occupation that, in comparison with previous activities, we found quite relaxing. For more detailed information, please contact the expedition leader: maz_chevallier@hotmail.com. 📷

— REGIS MEYRAT *AND* MARTIN LUTHER, *SWITZERLAND*

HIMACHAL PRADESH

MIYAR VALLEY, UNNAMED PEAK, POORNIMA

ON SEPTEMBER 29, Crystal Davis-Robbins and I climbed a new route on a possibly unclimbed sub-summit east of Castle Peak. After filling our bellies with chai and momos in Shukto, the last village up the Miyar Nullah, we loaded horses with 10 days of food and fuel and began the 34km hike, arriving at the standard Miyar base camp eight hours later. We spent the next five days waiting out spells of bad weather before clear skies led us to pack for four days and set off up the Takdung Glacier, with the intention of trying the east face of Neverseen Tower. However, once we saw how much snow was on the peaks, we opted to stay lower on the glacier.

We had spotted a rocky summit (ca 5,100m) east of Castle Peak, with a chimney/offwidth system that split the middle of the south face. Thinking the climb would only be five pitches, we started around 11 a.m. Sustained stemming and chimney climbing brought us to a false summit after about eight pitches. The ridge above eased off and we switched into boots for a couple of hundred meters of simul-climbing over snow and blocks. We finally reached the summit around 8 p.m. Luckily for us, the moon rose full and bright, helping to show our path as we climbed back down some of the easier terrain on the ridge and then made many rappels down the east shoulder into a large gully. We made it back to camp around 2 a.m. under a brilliant night sky. We named our 600m route Poornima (5.10) and found no sign of other ascents of this summit. 📄 📷

— WHITNEY CLARK, *USA*

UPPER DARCHA VALLEY, GOAT PEAK, SOUTH RIDGE

ON SEPTEMBER 4 an Indian expedition made the second ascent of Goat Peak via the complete south ridge. The 10-member expedition, under Dipankar Ghosh, had planned to attempt both Peak 6,115m and Peak 6,125m on the Indian Survey map, unaware that the latter was Goat Peak, first climbed in 2013 by a British team (*AAJ 2014*). The British had climbed the lower south ridge, then made a rising traverse left to the southwest ridge, which they followed to the top, measuring the elevation at 6,080m (GPS). The Indians used fixed ropes throughout their ascent of the full south ridge.

— LINDSAY GRIFFIN, *WITH INFORMATION FROM* THE HIMALAYAN CLUB *AND* ANDY NISBET

PEAK 6,010M, SGURR KUDDU; PEAK 5,970M, ATTEMPT

ROBERT ADAMS, Tom Adams, Steve Kennedy, and leader Andy Nisbet (all U.K.) and Bill McConachie and I (both U.S.) visited an east-west side valley of one branch of the

The new route on the southwest face and south ridge of Peak 6,010m, seen from high camp on Peak 5,970m. *Paul Swienton*

Darcha-Mayar Valley, immediately north of Ramjak (6,318m). Our objectives were to climb unnamed peaks 6,010m (32°53'17"N, 77°08'46"E) and 5,970m, and to explore the valley for additional opportunities. This area was explored in 2013 by an expedition that included Robert, Andy, and Steve. They climbed Goat Peak (6,080m) and identified the peaks above as good objectives (*AAJ 2014*).

On May 31, Bill, Andy, and high-altitude porter Mangal Singh approached Peak 6,010m along a rocky ridge, followed by a traverse across an easy glacier, to reach the foot of the southwest face. They climbed snow and then a couloir on the face to reach the south ridge at 5,730m, where they camped for the night.

The weather deteriorated, leading to a windy and snowy night. However, the following morning the weather improved and Bill climbed the ridge to the top. There were several short rocky steps, and the fresh snow was safe. Bill found bamboo wands on the summit; we had thought the peak was previously unclimbed, but it now appears to have been climbed unofficially (as far as we can tell) from the Shingo La side. Our probable new route was given a grade of PD+/AD-.

During this same time, Rob, Tom, Steve, and I attempted the east ridge of a 5,970m satellite peak northwest of Ramjak, camping that night on a rock outcrop at around 5,550m. On June 1 we continued to 5,720m, where we encountered dangerous avalanche conditions about 250m below the summit and retreated.

During the afternoon of June 6, Steve and I, with the assistance of Lakpa Sherpa, set out to attempt an unclimbed peak of about 5,300m on the east side of the valley we used to approach base camp. This valley lies north of Kuddu. After climbing to about 4,700m, we camped in the lower reaches of an enclosed cirque to the northwest of the peak. Lakpa returned to base camp.

We set off at 2:30 the following morning in excellent weather, climbing on good névé via the cirque to reach a prominent col close to the base of the summit snow cone at an altitude of around 5,170m. Thereafter, more technical mixed climbing led to the summit, with the final 130m consisting of 60–75° snow slopes and a final exposed rocky corner and snow arête. The summit comprised two rock pinnacles, the westerly being slightly higher. We named this summit Sgurr Kuddu. We graded the route AD.

We would like to thank the Mount Everest Foundation and Mountaineering Council of Scotland for financial aid. 📷

– PAUL SWIENTON, *USA*

CB6A, SOUTH FACE AND EAST FLANK, NIBBIJIBBI

ON SEPTEMBER 16, Crystal Davis-Robbins and I made the first ascent of the south face and east flank of CB6A (5,450m). I had found a picture of this beautiful peak, yet had no idea where it was or how to get there. After arriving in Manali, we spent two days talking with locals in Vashisht and eventually learned the mystery peak was located near the small village of Chhatru on the Chandra River.

A few days later, our bags were packed, mules were loaded, and we were ready to go. We started up the Chhatru Nullah toward our proposed base camp, where we intended to spend the next 10 days. [*The Chhatru Nullah forms part of a classic trek across the 4,270m Hampta Pass, rising south from the Chandra River toward 6,220m Indrasan.*] However, two hours into the hike, our horseman informed us he could go no farther, due to hazardous terrain. We decided to bivouac on uneven ground, unsure what to do. The next morning Crystal and I decided to go forth alone, taking only what we would need for five nights. We repacked and began the trek up steep, loose talus, finally setting up camp at 4,300m in a beautiful meadow.

Three striking peaks shot into the sky, but the middle pyramid drew our attention, and we eventually opted for a line that began up the south face. We moved camp to 4,900m, just above the glacier. That night snow fell and we prayed to the weather gods for clear skies the following morning, as we only had one more night of food. At 4 a.m. we set off across the glacier toward a steep and loose gully. The gully was frozen, so we climbed with crampons and tools until we reached solid rock. We swapped leads up 5.8–5.10 terrain until we reached the ridge above. From there we moved onto the east flank and simul-climbed a few hundred feet before it steepened. We finished with three more pitches of nice 5.9 crack climbing.

To our surprise, we found a cairn on the summit and later discovered that a Finnish party had climbed the east side a couple of years earlier. We located their rappel line as snow began to fall. We named our route NibbiJibbi (400m, 5.10-).

Editor's note: In 2010 the Finnish team of Pasi Kyto, Samuli and Jussi Pekkanen, Mikko Tukiainen, and Janna Ylipelto climbed the east face of this formation to the summit ridge (400m of climbing, 5.10-), but did not continue along the last sharp section to the top. They returned in 2013 and finished their route directly to the highest point. The Finns refer to this group of rock peaks, which lie on the east side of the Chhatru

CB6A (5,450m) from the southwest. NibbiJibbi (2015) generally follows the right skyline. The Finnish route climbs the face on the opposite side. *Whitney Clark*

Quinn Brett climbing pitch one of the American attempt on the big wall below Raldang. Whitney Clark

Nullah, as the Charas Towers. As for the peak name, CB stands for the Chandra Bhaga Range, and 6A is how the name of the Finns' hometown is pronounced in their local dialect.

– WHITNEY CLARK, *USA*

PYAGSKI, NORTHWEST FACE

ON JULY 4, 2014, almost two months before a Singapore University team made the first ascent of Mt. SUTD (6,056m, *AAJ 2015*), a small group from the Japanese Alpine Club made the first ascent of nearby Pyagski (6,090m). This peak lies on the eastern rim of the largest of the four main glaciers that rise south from the Karcha River, its head forming the watershed with the lower Bara Shigri Glacier. Approaching from Batal, Kazuo Hoshi, Miyo Suzuki, and Masayo Tsuchiya, with four high-altitude porters, established Camp 2 on the glacier at 5,100m. Two days later, they climbed a steep, northwest-facing slope of deep snow to the rock-strewn summit. This peak appears to lie about 2.5km north of SUTD.

– *INFORMATION FROM* TOM NAKAMURA *AND* THE JAPANESE ALPINE NEWS

HIMACHAL PRADESH / KINNAUR

BASPA VALLEY, BIG-WALL FREE ATTEMPTS

IN MID-OCTOBER, Whitney Clark, Crystal Davis-Robbins, and Quinn Brett (USA) attempted two big-wall free climbs: one on the southern flanks of Raldang (5,499m), left of Naufragi (Vidal, 2010), and the other on Shoshala (ca 4,700m), to the right of the Swiss route Trishul Direct (*AAJ 2012*). Details of these attempts can be found at the AAJ website.

– *INFORMATION PROVIDED BY* QUINN BRETT, *USA*

WESTERN GARHWAL / GANGOTRI

BHAGIRATHI IV, WEST FACE, ATTEMPT

IN SEPTEMBER, Matteo De Zaiacomo, Luca Schiera, and I attempted to make the first ascent of the west face of Bhagirathi IV (6,193m), a rock wall attempted a number of times during the 1990s by Slovenians, Americans, and Spanish, overcoming difficulties up to UIAA VII and A2.

[One year Silvo Karo attempted it no fewer than 11 times without success.] After 200m of vertical or near vertical granite, the face overhangs for the next 500m.

We first opted for a central line, heading toward a big corner in the middle of the face, but we soon realized we didn't have the gear necessary to aid the hard sections, and they looked too difficult and scary for us to free climb. We bailed.

We started again 50m down and to the right of our previous attempt, where it is less steep. Luca led all the first day to the snowpatch below the upper half of the wall, where we installed our portaledge. I led the second day, with the temperature well below 0°C. At least the climbing suited my style: a corner with a crack that succumbed mainly to jamming and stemming. Eventually, ice, fatigue, and the steepness of the final corner forced me to abandon the dream of an onsight free ascent and begin aid climbing. The difficulties to this point had been around 6c, with short sections of 7b+ and C2. We set the portaledge at around 5,900m. Next day we discovered the schist band that tops the face was much steeper than it had looked and very loose. Luca tried a number of lines, but there was no good protection and holds broke in his hands. The decision was obvious, though hard to accept.

Even though we failed, we felt we had done well. It seemed similar to a soccer game where you score a goal and control the entire game until the last few minutes, when the opposing team scores twice and wins. What makes alpinism interesting is that even if you do well there is still the possibility of failure. *[Editor's note: The team later climbed the peak by the "normal route" up the east face.]*

– MATTEO DELLA BORDELLA, *ITALY*

THALAY SAGAR, NORTHWEST RIDGE, PARTIAL NEW ROUTE

IN AUGUST AND SEPTEMBER, a team comprising Felix Criado, Adrian Legarra, Txus Lizarraga, Ekaitz Maiz, and Alex Txikon (all Spain), together with Daniele Nardi (Italy), climbed a new line up a pillar on the northwest ridge of Thalay Sagar (6,904m), ending their ascent with a 50m rappel to join the normal route (west ridge), ca 500m below the summit. They descended from here. The northwest ridge was climbed to the summit in 2004 by a Swiss quartet (*AAJ 2005*). The Spanish-Italian team followed the Swiss route for 700m and then broke right onto the pillar. They climbed this in 11 pitches (A3 WI4+ M5/6) to their exit onto the west ridge.

– LINDSAY GRIFFIN, *WITH INFORMATION FROM* DANIELE NARDI, *ITALY*

CENTRAL GARHWAL

NILKANTH, SOUTHEAST AND WEST RIDGES, ATTEMPTS

JASON THOMPSON AND ANNE-GILBERT CHASE received a Mugs Stump Award and a Lyman Spitzer Cutting Edge Award from the AAC to attempt the unclimbed south face of Hathi Parbat (6,727m). When their permit was denied, they and Caro North instead tried the southeast ridge of Nilkanth (6,596m). This long and tortuous ridge was attempted six times between 1937 and 1992. The 2015 party climbed 300m of the ridge on very loose rock and faceted snow before retreating. A subsequent attempt on the west ridge ended at 6,400m on the summit ridge, where they were hit by a strong storm. A full report is at the AAJ website.

– *INFORMATION FROM* ANNE-GILBERT CHASE, *USA*

NANDA DEVI EAST, NORTHEAST RIDGE, ATTEMPT

MARK THOMAS AND I (U.K.) attempted the unclimbed northeast ridge of Nanda Devi East (7,434m) in the autumn. Nanda Devi East has only one existing route to the summit: the southeast ridge, climbed by a Polish team in 1939, by far the hardest prewar climb in the Himalaya. The northeast ridge has a height gain of 2,000m, starting at a 5,331m col between the Pachu and Lawan valleys, and features complex snow and ice terrain throughout. The first 1,400m follow the lateral east-facing spur on this divide, meeting the true northeast ridge at 6,700m. Although it's an obvious challenge, the only team known to have considered an ascent was Julie-Ann Clyma and Roger Payne (U.K.), who approached from the Pachu Valley in 1994 but were unable to find any safe access to the ridge. By contrast, the Lawan Valley approach is quick and simple.

Our initial team included Tom Coney, Kenton Cool (both U.K.), and Dave Morton (USA), and we established base camp on September 16 at Bhital Gwar in the Lawan Valley at 4,275m. On the 18th an advanced camp was established at 5,300m, close to the starting col. An attack of sinusitis and a family bereavement then reduced the team to two: Mark, 40, and me, 60 years old. Between the 19th and 22nd, Mark and I made an acclimatization climb on the route. The main feature of the lower section is a beautiful snow and ice arête with an angle in excess of 55°. From a camp at 5,850m in a bergschrund, this ridge was climbed in six 60m pitches. The arête was capped by a band of ice cliffs, but a way was found on the right-hand side (WI4) to a high point of 6,100m.

After a rest at base camp we set off for our summit attempt on September 24. Unstable weather produced regular snowfalls in the afternoon and evening. The fresh snow helpfully stuck to the ice on the steep sections, but made easier-angled slopes arduous. A camp on a small perch was made at 6,200m, above the ice cliff. Then the ridge broke into a complex zone of ice walls and labyrinthine crevasse fields. Bad weather on the 27th enforced an early camp at 6,400m. After we escaped from the labyrinth, easier slopes of deep powder led to a campsite at 6,640m under an ice cliff. Here we decided to go for the summit with bivy gear and two days' supplies. There was a direct route to the final slopes, but this climbed under the summit seracs for some way and was loaded with fresh snow. There was no choice but to break out right to gain the crest of the northeast ridge lower down at 6,750m.

Our hopes were high, but 100m higher the ridge narrowed into a sensational knife-edge of unconsolidated snow. Faced with a 500m horizontal section with 65° powder-snow flutes to the north and overhanging mushrooms on the south, the decision to retreat was obvious and immediate. Our high point was at 6,865m. Through the night we descended 1,300m to the bottom of the ridge, with 14 abseils from ice threads and much downclimbing. With more stable snow conditions and careful assessment of the state of the summit seracs, the alternative line up a broad couloir to bypass the fluted section of ridge could be feasible. 📷

– **MARTIN MORAN**, *U.K.*

Editor's note: Following their attempt on Nanda Devi East, Moran and Thomas crossed the 5,595m col between the Shalang and Poting valleys. This was probably the first traverse of this col since 1905, when Tom Longstaff and his Swiss guides Alexis and Henri Brocherel made the passage. In 2015 the climbers graded the traverse AD. A detailed report is at the AAJ website.

[Above] Mark Thomas exiting from the labyrinth of crevasses on day five of the attempt on Nanda Devi East's northeast ridge. Nanda Kot (6,861m) and the pointed Changuch (6,322m) are behind. [Below] Looking northwest from Changuch to Nanda Devi (left) and Nanda Devi East. (1) The 1939 Polish route up the southeast ridge. (2) The 2015 east spur and northeast ridge attempt. *Martin Moran (both photos)*

NEPAL

LIMI HIMAL, ASHVIN, WEST RIDGE

LANDING JUST AFTER DAWN at Simikot airstrip with all our baggage was already a great success. Our goal was to explore the Limi Group, a large "blank on the map" with more than 15 peaks over 6,000m (*see AAJ 2015*) and make the first ascent of Ashvin (6,055m). However, early on the approach we were surprised to meet a team of young Japanese mountaineers from Doshisha University, returning from making the first ascent of this mountain, from the valley of the Chuwa Khola. I was happy for their success because it marks another stage in my project to promote climbing in West Nepal, but also disappointed because it was I who proposed that this peak be opened and I had hoped to climb it as far back as the spring of 2013. We would follow the same route as the Japanese on the mountain, though our approach to the base would be different.

Ashvin has two summits, north and south, the former a less inspiring peak. The Ashvins are the two Vedic gods in Hindu mythology, and unfortunately a spelling mistake has crept into the official list of open peaks, on which the ministry refers to the mountain Aichyn, a name without meaning.

On September 24, from a high camp, nine of us reached the summit of Ashvin North (30°17'35"N, 81°52'22"E, 6,025m, F). The following day we first climbed the northeast ridge of a subsidiary peak, Kaya Ko Himal, then descended from that summit southeast to reach what we called Cosmos Col, and finally finished up the west ridge of Ashvin (30°16'15"N, 81°51'28"E, PD).

As part of the Limi Himal Project, my website soon will have a page where all can share their experiences in this area. It may go some way toward convincing the Nepalese government to open the entire range under a special permit system, encouraging mountaineers to think "outside the box," have adventures in this remote area, and in so doing help improve its economic situation. Currently only Ashvin and Ardung (6,034m) are on the permitted list in this region.

[Editor's note: The Japanese team reached the summit in two groups on September 3 and 8. The summiters, on their first climbing venture outside their country, were Shintaro Salto, Yuki Senda, Yuto Kamaki, Kaya Ko, and Yumo Uno.] 🗎 ⌑

– PAULO GROBEL, *FRANCE*

[Next page, top] The Limi Glacier with unnamed, unclimbed summits to just over 6,000m. [Middle] The village of Til and Peak 6,369m (Til Kang), part of a small range on the south side of the Nalakankar. [Bottom] Ashvin (6,055m). In 2015 the French team first climbed the northeast ridge of the subsidiary peak Kaya Ko Himal, then descended southeast to Cosmos Col, then followed the west ridge to the top of Ashvin. Retracing their steps to Cosmos Col, they descended directly, as shown. The peak had been climbed just a few weeks earlier, by a similar route, by a Japanese expedition. *Paulo Grobel (all photos)*

MUKOT HIMAL, FIRST OFFICIAL ASCENT

ADDED TO THE PERMITTED LIST in 2014, Mukot Himal (6,087m) is located in a remote and wild corner of Nepal, nestled into the flank of the rarely seen but phenomenal Dhaulagiri II. KE Adventure Travel organized three groups to attempt the peak in the autumn. In mid-October, Kami Sherpa, Mingma Dorje Sherpa, and Gelgin Sherpa equipped most of a 600m route to the top with fixed rope, and then two international teams climbed the peak, the first on October 17. The climbers ascended glaciated snow slopes on the northwest side to a col on the north ridge (45–50°), then followed the ridge (30–35°) to the top, for an overall grade of PD+. The third team was prevented from an attempt by 48 hours of continuous snowfall. Although these were the first "official" ascents, this peak, as noted in AAJ 2015, was most likely first climbed in 1967. 📖 📷

— *INFORMATION FROM* **RODOLPHE POPIER**, *FRANCE, AND* **TOM RICHARDSON**, *U.K.*

DHAULAGIRI I, SOUTHWEST PILLAR, ATTEMPT

THE SOUTHWEST RIDGE of Dhaulagiri (8,167m) descends 3km from the summit to a point where it divides into the south-southwest ridge and southwest pillar. The steep southwest pillar was climbed by a French team in 1980, reaching 7,500m, but they could not continue up the southwest ridge to the summit. It was left to Zoltan Demjan (Czech), Yuri Moiseev, and Kasbek Valiev (Kazakhstan) to complete the route in 1988, in a magnificent alpine-style ascent (16 days round trip from base camp), with climbing up to UIAA VI+ A2 on the 450m crux section above 7,000m.

In October, Yannick Graziani and Patrick Wagnon (France) climbed a variation start to the southwest pillar via a couloir on the south flank, reaching the crest at 5,900m (mainly 50° with sections of 70–80°). They continued with bivouacs at 6,600m and 6,900m before attempting to outflank the upper pillar on the west side. They were hit by a storm at 7,100m, and after a difficult bivouac at 7,050m they managed to make an equally difficult retreat. Wagnon was full of praise for the exceptional performance of the 1988 trio. 📖 📷

— **RODOLPHE POPIER**, *FRANCE*

NILGIRI SOUTH, SOUTH FACE, AND TRAGEDY

FROM OCTOBER 22–26, Hansjörg Auer, Alex Blumel, and Gerry Fiegl made the first ascent of the south face of Nilgiri South (6,839m), only the second overall ascent of this mountain. Nilgiri South was climbed in 1978 by a Japanese team that approached from the north and climbed the east ridge. Attention then turned to the south side. In 1981 the south face was attempted to 5,740m by Japanese climbers. (Later the same year Japanese also climbed the southwest ridge to 6,100m.) Japanese climbers were back in 1985 but only reached 5,900m on the south face. In 1996 the advanced base of a Slovenian expedition, sited at the bottom

[Photo] **Gerry Fiegl on the steep mixed ground of the south face of Nilgiri South.** *Hansjörg Auer*

Nilgiri South, showing the line of ascent (right, over Nilgiri Spire), descent via the southwest ridge, and bivouacs. *Elias Holzknecht*

of the south face, was swept away before the team had a chance to begin an attempt, but they returned in 1999. Finding the central part of the face too objectively dangerous, they climbed the left side to reach the southwest ridge at 6,100m, then continued up to 6,600m, where they were forced to retreat in strong wind and snowfall.

The three Austrians first spent time establishing a higher base camp than previous parties, so they could better see the south face. Auer had just returned from Mt. Kenya and was quite well acclimatized, but the other two were not. The three spent two nights at advanced base (5,300m) below the south face. After a rest at base camp, they started their ascent on October 22. On the 23rd they crossed the bergschrund at 5,400m and started up the ramp used by the Japanese on their 1981 attempt (60–90°). At 6,000m they continued up right on the more difficult terrain (M5 70°) of the west face of a subsidiary summit to the southeast of Nilgiri South, which they christened Nilgiri Spire (6,780m). After surmounting a big serac barrier at about 6,500m they found a good bivouac site.

Leaving at 6 a.m. on the 24th, the three climbed up to the south ridge of Nilgiri Spire at 6,600m and continued to its summit at 11 a.m. They descended to the col between this and Nilgiri South via an exposed and corniced ridge, at one point making a 30m free rappel. At 3 p.m. they came across a nice, flat bivouac site at 6,740m.

Starting out at 8 a.m. the following morning, Fiegl was very slow. The team continued the 1km traverse to reach the top of Nilgiri South at 11 a.m., having surmounted a steep cornice on the last pitch. They immediately began a descent of the unclimbed southwest ridge, which proved far more technical and difficult than expected. Fiegl was now extremely exhausted, and on reaching 6,500m at 3 p.m. the other two realized they had to stop and bivouac in order to give him a chance to recover. He was now suffering badly from altitude sickness and appeared to be no longer aware of the situation.

The forecast predicted strong winds the following day, and after a cold night the three set off down a sharp snow ridge, climbing unroped for speed. At 2 p.m., at the end of this section (ca 6,100m), there was a small step. While downclimbing it, Fiegl slipped and fell 800m down the south face in a complex couloir system. Shocked, the other two made three rappels on the south flank and then continued downclimbing, rappelling the last section. All the way down they found traces of the fall, but did not locate the body. They gained the glacier at 6 p.m. Auer commented: "When a good friend falls and dies in front of you, everything else loses importance. Our expedition could not have ended worse."

— LINDSAY GRIFFIN, *WITH INFORMATION FROM* HANSJÖRG AUER, *AUSTRIA*

MANASLU HIMAL

CHAAR BAATSA HIMAL

APRIL 25 WILL REMAIN FOREVER in our memories. We were at Manaslu base camp when the earth began to tremble, causing a national disaster. Rather than add to the confusion by attempting an untimely repatriation, we decided to remain in the mountains with our Nepalese team. The crevasses on Manaslu were destabilized by the earthquake, and most of our climbers turned around between camps 1 and 2; only two continued to the summit, in alpine style.

We then trekked to Larkya Pass. Just to the north of the pass, southeast of Panbari, is a group of mountains including unclimbed Chaar Baatsa Himal (6,621m). Frank Bonhomme, Christian Hurgon, Dhane Magar, Dhepeen Bothe, Jangbu Sherpa, Rajan Lama, and I headed up this peak from the pass with two tents and the minimum of equipment. Thanks to good acclimatization, weather, and snow conditions, we made rapid progress, and by midday had reached 5,800m and a suitable campsite. The following morning, May 9, we left at 4 a.m., making quick progress up fine snow slopes until the sun softened the snow. The summit ridge had no nasty cornices, and we were on top at 11 a.m. Our ascent route, via a hanging glacier to the south, up onto the east ridge, and so to the summit, was III/PD+. 📷

— PAULO GROBEL, *FRANCE*

THULAGI, WEST FACE AND NORTHWEST RIDGE, HAPPY BIRTHDAY

I'VE BEEN THINKING about how to write this report so that you will not be bored. Apart from a small incident with an avalanche, everything went to plan, and we achieved our goal without epics. But I will try to stop you from falling asleep.

There had been six previous attempts to climb Thulagi (7,059m). Several of these had tried from the north, and some of our team had been on one of those unsuccessful expeditions, so we were not interested in that approach. Belorussians Nikolay Bandalet and Sergei Belous had tried the south face, approaching from the southeast via the long and convoluted Thulagi Glacier, but tragically disappeared (*AAJ 2012*). Ivan Dozhdev, Rusian Kirichenko, Valery Shamalo, and I decided to try from the southwest, where there is a glacier flowing down from Thulagi below Phungi (6,538m) to the northwest.

On September 10 we reached base camp at 3,665m in a government rest house at

Thulagi (7,059m), showing the Russian route Happy Birthday (2015) up the west face and northwest ridge. *Alexander Gukov*

Dharmasa. Porters explained how to get onto the glacier above, but we found it hard to believe them—the slopes looked steep, with rock climbing that could hardly be termed "an approach." However, we found a canyon that proved to be relatively straightforward, and above it a grassy path led almost to the glacier, where we found a comfortable place for an intermediate camp at 4,700m. Despite bad weather, on the 13th we cairned a route to the glacier at ca 5,100m, and the next morning went to inspect the mountain. We were surprised to find an old rope running through a crevasse and a package of gas cartridges. Who had they belonged to and where had they been going?

There were several options, on the left and right side of the face, but we decided to go left, where the glacier seemed quite passable. A day or two later, we established an assault camp at 5,750m, setting it carefully below a deep crevasse that would catch all possible avalanche debris. We then descended to base for a rest.

Imagine our surprise when we returned to find our high camp demolished. An avalanche had come from the wall above, and the tent had been exactly in the middle of its flow—10m right or left and it would have been untouched. The tent was destroyed. Most of the gear inside was fine, but our ice tools, which had held it down, were gone. After a diligent search the next day we found three tools, which would be enough for four people if we took the easiest line.

We set off on the 24th in beautiful weather, with three days' food, two sleeping bags, and a small frameless tent. We climbed 14 pitches in 11 hours that day, including three on very loose rock and the rest on ice (55–70°). This brought us to the northwest ridge at 6,700m, where we dug a small snow cave for the night. Next day, taking only ice gear and a couple of ropes, we raced up the ridge. There was a section of vertical ice on the upper serac, after which we dropped ropes and gear and plodded to the summit. It was Ivan's 29th birthday, so we let him be first to step onto the top. We reversed the route, spending a second night in the snow cave, and were back at base on the 27th. We named our route Happy Birthday (1,200m, 1,850m of climbing, Russian 6A, TD+ AI4+ 5c M4).

– ALEXANDER GUKOV, *RUSSIA, SUPPLIED BY* ANNA PIUNOVA, *RUSSIA*

LANGTANG STUPA

WEST OF THE NAYA KANGA GROUP and the mountain recently renamed Baden-Powell Scout Peak lies the Chimisedang Lekh, a cluster of steeper, more difficult, and unnamed peaks rising to nearly 5,900m. Anna Boldinger and my main goal was the highest top at the northwestern end of this group: Peak 5,822m (DAV map; unmarked but ca 5,750m on the HGM-Finn map). We approached from Langtang village in April, and a reconnaissance immediately showed that snow conditions on our proposed route were too dangerous, so instead we turned to the southeast pillar of an unmarked peak to the northeast of Peak 5,420m on HGM-Finn. It is the most easterly of the steep rock peaks.

On April 7 we started up vertical rock on the lower section of the southeast face, which led to mixed terrain. The warmth of the morning sun made it perfect for rock climbing, but by the time we reached the top of the pillar at ca 5,350m, it was late afternoon and snowing. Due to lack of time and bad weather we descended after completing the pillar, down the east ridge and east face. We called the pillar Langtang Stupa. Our 300m route had difficulties of UIAA V+ M4 AI2 50–65°. Much of the rock was friable. 📄 📷

— EDUARD BIRNBACHER, *GERMANY*

CHHOPA BAMARE, EXPLORATION

ONE OF THE NEW PEAKS brought onto the permitted list in 2014 by the Nepalese government is Chhopa Bamare (a.k.a. Chobba Bamare or Chomo Pamari, 6,109m). It lies northwest of Lamabagar on the border with Tibet and most likely refers to the highest peak in a small, neglected range immediately east of the Friendship Highway, between Kodari and Nyalam.

A team of young alpinists from the FFME (France), guided by Dimitry Munoz and Antoine Pecher, were most likely the first mountaineers to explore the access valley running southeast from the peak. Their approach in October was difficult due to the road to Lamabagar being totally destroyed by the spring earthquake. After establishing base camp at 4,100m, the team found the mountains to be very dry, with frequent rockfall. The climbers tried to find an approach to Jobo Bamare (ca 5,700m), on the east side of the valley, and other objectives to the west, but failed. Nonetheless, the expedition considers the area to have climbing potential, and the predominantly loose rock suggests a snowy season would be preferable.

— ROLDOLPHE POPIER, *FRANCE*

BEDING GO, SOUTH FACE AND SOUTHEAST RIDGE

I HAVE BEEN LUCKY to become friends and climbing partners with a great group of Sherpas from the Rolwaling Valley. These include Mingma Tsiri Sherpa of Ascent Himalayas (first Nepalese to summit K2), with whom I climbed Everest in 2012. One mountain he had always wanted to climb was Beding Go (6,125m) in his home valley. When it was officially opened

The steep, loose southeast ridge of Beding Go, led by Tsering Pemba and Nima Galzen. *Dino Camargo*

for climbing in 2014, we made an unsuccessful attempt, then planned to try again in October 2015 with a larger team of clients and Sherpas. After the devastating earthquakes in the spring, we felt a climbing trip would be a great way to assist the people of Rolwaling and bring more business to the area.

After acclimatizing and completing a solar project to bring electricity to people in the village of Beding, we established base camp at 4,900m below the south face of Beding Go. Our Sherpas checked the route and spent two days putting in anchors and fixing rope up the south face. After three days in base camp, we left for a summit attempt at 2:30 a.m. on October 21.

We made good time across the glacier and got to the start of the 600m south face at sunrise. Aiming for the southeast ridge, we climbed a very steep gully of snow and ice to reach the rocky section of face. This proved very loose, and it was difficult to place protection. On a traverse near the start there was a big rockfall, but thankfully nobody got injured. The exit onto the ridge involved climbing a steep snow slab that looked as if it would detach at any moment.

Once on the crest we could see six towers we had to cross before reaching the summit. Tsering Pemba and Nima Galzen went ahead to fix more rope. The first three towers turned out to be more difficult than expected, especially with so much rockfall. At this point several of the party went down. Mingma Tsiri Sherpa, his brother Pasang Tenzing Sherpa, Nima Galzen Sherpa, Tsering Pemba Sherpa, Dean Carriere (Canada), Dino Camargo (Brazil), and I decided to keep going.

Tsering Pemba and Nima Galzen continued to put in fixed line, and when we reached the final pillar it was obvious it would be the hardest. I had now been on the go for 12 hours and had to use all the remaining energy I had in the tank. One section was overhanging and I inadvertently swung onto the Tibetan side, thankfully held by the fixed rope. A scramble led to the narrow summit. The view was incredible, but we didn't linger. It was a relief to get off the ridge just after dark and start carefully descending the south face. We finally reached base camp at 1:30 a.m. 📷

– CIAN O'BROLCHAIN, *IRELAND*

CHOBUTSE, WEST FACE, DORJEE SHERPA ROUTE

IT TOOK ME THREE YEARS to decide whether to go for a solo attempt on Chobutse (6,686m). I grew up in the Rolwaling Valley, seeing the mountain from my home. Each time I go back it seems so close and attractive, especially the west face, which remained unclimbed. In the 2014-'15 winter, I thought about trying the peak without an official permit, as it is our own domestic mountain. However, the weather turned bad and I had to cancel at the last moment.

In 2015 I got a permit on October 12 and started my approach three days later. With a team from Austria, Slovenia, and Italy, I climbed Parchamo (6,187m) on the 25th and arrived at base camp below Chobutse on the 27th with three friends, who were there to take photos. A valley elder suggested I make the attempt on the second day of the full moon, so I left camp at 4 a.m. on October 28.

It took one and a half hours to reach the snowline. At first I followed a rocky spur, then descended 60m to reach the bottom of the face. I initially climbed more toward the left, then slanted right to pass left of the hanging serac. The ice was covered by thin layers of snow, which proved good for tools but poor for crampons. As there was no natural resting place, I found the climb very tiring. I stopped at two points, cutting ledges out of the ice. The last part of the climb, to reach the summit ridge, was the steepest and most difficult, but 13 hours after leaving camp I arrived on the crest, which is long and flat, and was covered in deep snow. I followed it south to the highest point, planning to go down the southeast ridge.

On the summit, clouds moved in and I was quickly in a whiteout. I continued along the ridge and began my descent, but I soon realized I was confused. I could see hardly anything, so I decided to dig a snow hole and wait. I had no bivouac equipment, and the whole of that night I had to rub my body to keep warm. Next morning the weather had not improved, so I decided to ask for a helicopter rescue. However, this was not possible because the weather was bad throughout Nepal.

Chobutse (6,686m) from the west. (1) Dorjee Sherpa Route (2015). (2) Southwest ridge (1985). *Mingma Gyalje Sherpa*

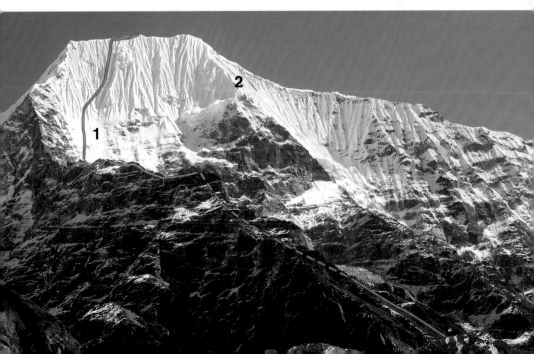

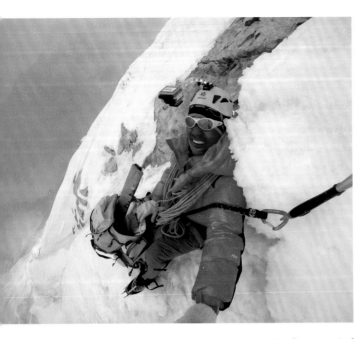

Mingma Gyalje "resting" at around midheight during the first ascent of the west face of Chobutse. *Mingma Gyalje Sherpa*

When it started to clear at 11 a.m., I immediately started to descend. I rappelled 120m before I was again in whiteout. Trying to move down, I fell over an ice cliff and decided it was time to stop again. While traversing 10m to a place where I could dig another snow hole, I was almost taken away by a slab avalanche. I was now forced to spend the rest of the day and the following night at this spot. It was cold and windy, and I had a hard time. At 7 a.m. the weather began to clear on the mountain, though it remained cloudy in the valley. I radioed my brother and friends to tell them a helicopter should be able to reach me, and within one hour it had arrived. On the second attempt I was rescued and flown down to my family home in the valley, where I was greeted with tears.

Chobutse is the hardest mountain I have climbed. I named my new route Dorjee Sherpa, in memory of my late father. As with my friends who climbed the three peaks above the Drolambau Glacier (*see report below*), I wanted to show that Nepal is safe for climbing again. It was not enough solely to write about this in the media—I had to do it with action.

– MINGMA GYALJE SHERPA, *NEPAL*

Editor's note: Chobutse has received only four ascents. See the online version of this report for a complete history of climbs and known attempts. Mingma Gyalje's ascent of the west face is the only known serious attempt on this difficult line and the first technical new route to be soloed in the country by a Nepali.

DROLAMBAU GLACIER, THREE ALL-SHERPA ASCENTS

IN THE FIRST WEEK of October three Sherpas, who all originate from the Rolwaling Valley, climbed three peaks flanking the Drolambau Glacier, one of which was likely a first ascent. Dawa Gyalje Sherpa, Nima Tenji Sherpa, and Tashi Sherpa are all experienced mountaineers, with multiple ascents of Everest and other high peaks. Nima Tenji is an IFMGA guide, and Dawa Gyalje a practicing member of the Nepal National Mountain Guides Association (NNMGA), formed in 2004.

The three Sherpas took the big step of organizing an expedition of solely Nepalese climbers with the aim of showing the world that, while Sherpas are well-known for their hard work on foreign expeditions, there is a growing band of young Nepalese climbers who are interested in mountaineering for themselves, and not just for business. The venture was also timed to prove to the outside world that trekking and climbing are practical and safe after the destructive earthquake earlier in the year.

The Sherpas aimed to climb three peaks that were added to the permitted list for climbers in 2014: Langdak (6,220m), Raungiysar (6,224m), and Thakar Go East (6,152m). From the perspective of the Nepali government, all three were unclimbed, though two of them undoubtedly have seen at least one previous ascent.

The three arrived in the village of Na on September 29, took one rest day, and by October 3 had reached the Drolambau Glacier. On the 4th they established a high camp toward the northern end of the glacier, between the peaks of Langdak and Raungsiyar, which lie on the eastern rim. That same day they headed up the west flank of Raungsiyar. Deep snow gave hard going, but once they reached a ridge, snow conditions improved. The summit crest proved quite long, but at 3:15 p.m., less than three hours after leaving the glacier, they were on top. The descent was uneventful, and they were back in camp at 6 p.m.

The following morning the three headed up the southwest flank of Langdak, reached the west summit (6,177m), and, after descending 100m, continued east-southeast along the ridge to the main top, which they reached at 11:45 a.m. With six 8,000m peaks in clear view, from Xixabangma to Kangchenjunga, Nima Tenji felt this was the best viewpoint he'd climbed, an aspect that would make this peak quite attractive to commercial expeditions.

The team returned to camp and then moved it down the glacier to below Thakar Go East. On October 6, all three climbed this mountain via the northeast ridge. This gave a trickier ascent than the previous two peaks, at first on rock and then a continuous snow arête. They reached the summit at 11:30 a.m., and by the end of the following day had returned to Na, having made three ascents in three consecutive days.

Both Langdak and Raungsiyar were climbed by British teams in the 1950s, likely by similar routes to those followed by the Sherpas in 2015. No ascents have been documented for Thakar Go East, or Takargo East, the low summit at the end of the long east ridge of Takargo (6,771m). [*The online version of this story has more details about the three Sherpas' climbing careers, as well as the history of these peaks.*]

—LINDSAY GRIFFIN, *WITH INFORMATION FROM* DAWA GYALJE SHERPA *AND* MINGMA GYALJE SHERPA, *NEPAL*

PEAK 6,166M, SOUTH RIDGE (ATTEMPTS)

IN SEPTEMBER, American climbers Erik Larsen and Ryan Waters twice attempted the elegant south ridge of Peak 6,166m, which lies along the ridge south of Takargo, but were halted by a difficult corniced knife-edge. They then summited the peak on September 16 via the relatively straightforward northeast flank (snow up to 55°). This appears to be the same peak, and indeed the same route, climbed in 1972 by Klaus Harder and Peter Vogler, repeated the following day by Michaela Wegert and Wolfgang Weinzieri, from the German expedition that made the first ascent of Chobutse.

— LINDSAY GRIFFIN

The west face of Chugimago in very dry conditions. (1) Hennessey-Kastelic (2014). (2) Mucic-Strazar. (3) Mucic-Strazar descent and Bajde-Kramer second attempt, with (H) showing their high point. (4) Bajde-Kramer first attempt. *Luka Strazar*

CHUGIMAGO NORTH, NORTH FACE; CHUGIMAGO, WEST FACE

Enthused by the stories and photos of countryman Domen Kastelic after his first ascent of Chugimago (*AAJ 2015*), with American Sam Hennessey, a team of four young Slovenians—Ambroz Bajde, Blaz Kramer, Matej Mucic, and Luka Strazar—visited the Rolwaling in October. The climbers made their base camp in the village of Na (4,020m) and acclimatized with an ascent of Chugimago North (5,945m, first known ascent in 2014 by Argentine and Spanish climbers, via the west face, *AAJ 2015*). The Slovenians climbed the north face (500m, 50–60° with a few sections of 80°) via a rightward-slanting snow and ice ramp, exiting onto a shoulder from which they followed the north ridge easily to the summit. They returned by the same route, making the round trip from their 5,100m advanced base in around nine hours.

On October 15, Mucic and Strazar started from an advanced base at 5 a.m. and climbed a direct line in the center of the west face of Chugimago, arriving on the summit at 8 a.m. the following morning. They took a line to the right of the Hennessey-Kastelic Route, reaching the summit ridge a very short distance north of the highest point. The pair then climbed down the southwest ridge a short distance before descending the west face. The 800–900m route (WI4 with one pitch of M5) was thought to be about the same overall difficulty as the Hennessey-Kastelic.

Meanwhile, Bajde and Kramer had left advanced base at the same time and started up a line to the right of the Mucic-Strazar line. They climbed 60–80° ice and by midday had reached 5,800m. However, there had been much deep snow and plenty of spindrift, so at that point the pair retreated. On the 23rd they attempted the line descended by Mucic and Strazar. They started at 3 a.m. and reached a high point of 6,000m by 1 p.m. This time they had found more ice (up to 80°) and no spindrift but very cold temperatures. They descended from this point, but nonetheless recommended this line over the first one they attempted. 📷

– RODOLPHE POPIER, *FRANCE*

DZASAMPATSE, NORTHEAST FACE, A LA VERTICALE DE LA PEINE

ON SEPTEMBER 30, Mathieu Détrie, Julien Dusserre, Pierre Labbre, and I arrived at our 5,130m base camp below the south side of the Nangpai Gosum peaks. [*All three Nangpai Gosum peaks, as designated by the Nepalese government, are still officially unclimbed; III has hardly enough prominence to be deemed a separate peak.*] During the approach we found the moraines to be unstable and chaotic, probably the result of the spring earthquake. The monsoon had been weak, but at first sight the faces looked to be in reasonable condition. However, seven days of warm weather completely changed conditions, and waterfalls were seen to appear up to 6,500m every afternoon on the south face of unclimbed Nangpai Gosum I (7,321m), our proposed line.

We switched to Plan B: Nangpai Gosum I via the Japanese route up the south spur to the 7,240m south summit. On October 16, having sat though bad weather in base camp for 10 days, Pierre and I went up to the bergschrund below the face and bivouacked. Next morning the weather was worse than expected, so we descended.

Not wishing to leave the area empty-handed, we decided to try a new route on the northeast face of Dzasampatse (6,295m). On October 17, Mathieu and Julien left base camp at 6 a.m., and at 3:35 p.m. were standing 20m below the summit, where they stopped because of extremely unstable snow on the narrow ridge. They descended the original Slovenian Route on the south-southwest ridge (650m, Azman-Golob, 2004), finding it very much easier than the grade of TD+ quoted by the first ascensionists. At 8 p.m. they reached the col at its foot.

The 700m line was named A la Verticale de la Peine and graded TD+ WI5. Next day, Pierre and I repeated the climb to the same high point, starting from base camp at 3 a.m., reaching the top at 9 a.m., and descending to the col by 11:30 a.m. It was a good line that saved our trip a little. 📷

— MATHIEU MAYNADIER,
FRANCE

In the couloir of A la Verticale de la Peine on the northeast face of Dzasampatse. *Mathieu Maynadier Collection*

INTO THE LIGHT

BY SKIY DETRAY

My most recent expedition to Nepal was filled with great joy and success, but also with immense sorrow and tragedy. When we dance with the extremes of nature we feel incredibly alive, close to the divine. It's these moments I hold dearest in my heart. Sadly, after one such dance my partner and good friend Justin Griffin fell to his death, on November 14, while descending from our climb.

We arrived in Kathmandu on October 19 with the generous support of a Lyman Spitzer grant from the AAC. In conjunction with our climbing ambitions, we had volunteered for two weeks with the Alex Lowe Charitable Foundation to further the construction of the Khumbu Climbing Center's new building in Phortse. The village sits at 3,800m, giving us a great chance to acclimate. We made substantial progress on the building, and were also lucky to make some new friends in the Sherpa community and get a glimpse into their magical lives.

On November 5 we left the village to set up base camp in a small lodge at Thugla (4,620m), below the massive north faces of Cholatse and Tawoche (6,495m, a.k.a. Taboche or Taweche). [*While Tawoche is the usual spelling, the author notes that during his two weeks in Phortse the locals only referred to the mountain as Taboche and rejected any other name. We have retained the traditional spelling for consistency.*] The forecast looked promising, and we established an advanced base at 4,800m. On the 8th we made a reconnaissance climb to 5,100m and found solid ice, good névé, and quality rock. We also made a final decision about which route we would attempt—there were many potential new and inspiring lines.

On the 9th we regained our high point, chopped a tent platform, and rested. The following day we climbed four technical pitches of AI4 M6 and were treated to spectacular views of the south faces of Nuptse and Everest. On the morning of the 11th we were slow to start and morale was low. The summit seemed miles away, and with difficult and unknown terrain ahead we were battling tremendous internal fears. But the first two pitches were spectacular and steep AI4 M6, and we were delighted to be in such technical terrain. The rock continued to be solid and the névé perfect. We next opted to follow a sparsely protected AI3 R gully for 250m. Thankfully, we found a bivouac site at 5,725m on a sheer ridge at the top of the gully and got to sleep by 2:30 a.m.

On our fourth day we were gifted with three hours of sunlight, the only time we saw it on the route. We lounged until 11 a.m. and then climbed four intricate traversing pitches, feeling very committed and exposed. Amazingly, the pitches kept connecting. Our final bivouac, like the others, required hours to construct.

At this juncture we opted to leave most of the kit behind and push for the summit. While this left our asses hanging in the breeze, we felt we would move much faster, and we reasoned we could collect the gear during our rappel descent of the route.

On the 13th we were moving by 5 a.m., and after three awesomely exposed and technical traversing pitches we reached the crux at 6,100m. From the ground we had spotted an ice seam through the final headwall, but would it go? We both led exhilarating 70m pitches of thin ice, rock, and névé at AI5 M5 R, coining the name "Five Star Hot Chinese Mustard" for the feature we climbed. Fear melted away and we moved with confidence and grace—the higher we climbed, the more we were able to let go.

Darkness began to settle and the temperature dropped. We were both exhausted, but Justin found a hidden level of motivation and took the sharp end for hour after hour. We reached the summit plateau at 6 a.m. on November 14, having completed Into the Light (1,500m, AI5 M6 R). What we thought would be a quick jaunt to the true summit now looked involved and time-consuming. Standing in the warm sunshine, looking at a possible descent by the easy southeast ridge, we made the decision: Let's get the hell out of here!

[Previous page] Justin Griffin leading hard mixed ground on day two of Into the Light on the northeast buttress of Tawoche. *Skiy DeTray* [Right] Tawoche from the north. (1) East face direct (Lowe-Roskelley, 1989). (2) Northeast buttress, British Route (Fowler-Littlejohn, 1995). (3) Northeast buttress, Into the Light, not to summit (DeTray-Griffin, 2015). (4) North face direct, not to summit (Ichimura-Narumi, 2009). *Angel Salamanca*

Justin Griffin on steep névé during the third day of the 2015 ascent of the northeast buttress of Tawoche. *Skiy DeTray*

We set off down the ridge and after two hours dropped into the east couloir. We downclimbed the easy terrain unroped. Several hours later, and no more than 100m from the base of the mountain and safety, I saw Justin turn around to downclimb a low-angle section of ice. He slipped, and with our ice tools dulled to nubs from thousands of feet of dry-tooling, he was unable to gain purchase. He fell over a final 60m vertical icefall. I rushed to his aid and administered CPR until I was choking on my tears. I descended the rest of the mountain alone in complete disbelief. Upon arriving in Pheriche, I contacted Global Rescue. Amazingly, six Sherpas hiked through the night from Phortse to assist in any way they could, proving that Justin had touched many in that village. A helicopter was called and a skillful recovery was performed.

Not a day passes when I don't think about Justin or of the accident, and I know that I will be forever haunted by this climb. But I know if Justin were here, he would look me squarely in the eyes and say, "Get over it, bro! This is what we do. We take chances. We train like athletes to stack the odds in our favor. We go to the mountains to push our personal limits, to get closer to nature, to get closer to our friends." I can only hope his memory will inspire future generations of alpinists to dream big and try hard. [*See the In Memoriam section of this edition for more about Justin Griffin.*]

Summary: New route Into the Light (1,500m, AI5 M6 R, not to summit) on the northeast buttress of Tawoche in the Khumbu, by Justin Griffin and Skiy DeTray (USA), November 8–14, 2015.

NUPTSE, SOUTH FACE, ATTEMPT

Two teams shared a permit during the autumn for attempts on the south face of Nuptse. Colin Haley (USA) and Ueli Steck (Switzerland) hoped to make an alpine-style ascent of the 2003 Babanov-Koshelenko Route on the southeast pillar of Nuptse East I (7,804m), while the French climbers Benoit Guigonnet and Hélias Millerioux hoped to complete a new route to the main summit (7,864m), between the 2008 Benoist-Glarion-Rappaz line and the Cobweb Wall.

After acclimatization and observing conditions, the four realized their chances for either project were slim, so they combined forces to attempt an alpine-style repeat of the original British Route on the face (1961). Starting from Chukung (a.k.a. Chhukung, 4,700m), and with Steck breaking trail throughout, they reached a bivouac at 6,900m after 9.5 hours—a vertical gain of 2,170m! The difficulty was about D, similar to the Jaeger or Macho couloirs on Mont Blanc du Tacul. With an uncertain forecast, and after a windy and cold night, the four retreated, Steck downclimbing all the way, fast, while the others followed more sedately, with some rappels. Only one route, the British Route, has been completed to the main summit of Nuptse from the south, and this still remains unrepeated. 🗎

– RODOLPHE POPIER, *FRANCE*

AMA DABLAM, LAGUNAK RIDGE, FIRST ALPINE-STYLE ASCENT

Climbing as two pairs—Fanny Schmutz and Damien Tomasi, and Fleur Fouque and Sébastien Rougegré—four French guides from the Chamonix Valley made the first alpine-style ascent (fifth overall) of the Lagunak Ridge (south ridge) of Ama Dablam (6,814m). This ridge, first climbed in 1985 by Hooman Aprin, Randy Harrington (USA), and Martin Zabaleta (Spain), finishes up the southwest ridge (normal route). The final crest, forming the left edge of the east face, remains unclimbed.

The four French left advanced base at 5,600m at 2 a.m. on October 22 and bivouacked at 6,000m and then again at 6,600m (on the normal route), before reaching the summit on the 25th at 10:20 a.m. The first day's leading was done by the women, the second day by the men. The four descended the normal route on the 25th. They found the route a little harder than the Brown-Patey on the Pic Sans Nom in the Mont Blanc Range, and they graded the 1,200m ascent TD+ F5 AI5 M4 90°. 📷

– RODOLPHE POPIER, *FRANCE*

PEAK 6,420M, NORTH-NORTHEAST RIDGE

Jorge Martinez and I flew to Lukla and then, using no porters, carried all our gear to Pangboche over two days. From there we went up the Mingbo Valley (Nare Glacier on the HGM-Finn map), south of Ama Dablam, to a camp at 4,800m. Subsequently we moved to a base camp at 5,300m near a dry lake in extensive moraine. This was toward the southwest face of Ombigaichang, our original objective, which we found to be in a dangerous condition. We then walked four hours from camp to reach the glacier and reconnoiter Peak 6,420m, which lies in the southeast corner of the glacial cirque, on the ridge east of Melanphulan.

On October 25 we left camp at 1 a.m. and crossed the glacier toward Peak 6,420m. There was fresh snow hiding crevasses, and the traverse was long and dangerous. We began climbing on the north face at about 5,700m, below enormous seracs, then headed up over windslab to the north-northeast ridge. It was cold and windy here, and although the difficulties were not great (snow, sometimes deep, to 70°), protection was sparse. We reached the short summit ridge and followed it pleasantly to the highest point, arriving at 11 a.m. We went back down the north-northeast ridge, with rappels from snow mushrooms, and continued toward Peak 5,985m so that we could rappel its rocky western flanks (three rappels). As we had no food left in base camp, we decided to continue down, taking a wrong turn and finally, at 9 p.m., arriving at the standard Ama Dablam base camp, where we spent the rest of the night. We then made the two-day descent to Lukla, again without help from porters.

[*Editor's note: Given the location of this peak, it seems unlikely that it has not been climbed in the past, probably from the south. The Spanish route on the north side may well be new. They have proposed the name Boltana, after Salamanca's hometown.*]

— ANGEL SALAMANCA, *SPAIN*

PEAK 41 (6,648M), NORTH FACE, ATTEMPT

IN OCTOBER 2014, Choi Ji-won, Kim Jeong-yeop, Ku Eun-su, and Wang Jun-ho attempted Peak 41, starting up the left-hand couloir on the north face, a little to the right of the line tried by Jack Geldard and Rob Greenwood in 2012 (*AAJ 2013*). On October 6 the four Koreans left base camp at 5,300m. They bivouacked four times in the couloir, including one rest day, and on day five they climbed to a shoulder on the east ridge at 6,140m. The next day they only managed one pitch before being forced back to the bivouac site by heavy snowfall. They sat out two more nights at this spot before an improvement allowed an eight-hour rappel descent and return to base camp.

Editor's note: Partway up the couloir, the Koreans moved right on a line noted by Geldard and Greenwood. This appears to be harder than the continuation of the couloir, but it leads to a much higher exit onto the east ridge, thereby avoiding a loose section that defeated the British pair. 📷

— OH YOUNG-HOON, *KOREA*

MALAHANGUR HIMAL / BARUN SECTION

CHAMLANG, WEST-SOUTHWEST RIDGE, FIRST ALPINE-STYLE ASCENT

THE TRIED AND TESTED Basque team of Alberto Iñurrategi, Juan Vallejo, and Mikel Zabalza hoped to make the first ascent of the north face of Chamlang (7,321m). The team acclimatized on Hongu (Hongku Chuli West, 6,764m) and spent two weeks checking conditions on Chamlang's north face. On their one attempt, toward the east side, they reached 6,000m on a hanging glacier, where they were stopped by bad weather and snow conditions. The western part of the face appeared to have long sections of difficult climbing and no real tent sites.

Instead, they decided to make an alpine-style attempt on the west-southwest ridge, first climbed in October 1986 by a large Japanese team, operating in siege style. Starting from base camp on October 17, the Basques reached 6,100m on the lower ridge without difficulty, but the next day found the crest narrow and exposed. After a bivouac with poor weather at 6,600m, they started at 8 a.m. on the 19th and overcame several steep pitches to reach the summit at 12:30 p.m. This was the second ascent of the complete ridge and sixth overall of Chamlang's main summit. In 1990, Germans Bernd Eberle and Stefan Kohler climbed Chamlang in alpine style by the right side of the northwest face and the upper west-southwest ridge. 📷

— RODOLPHE POPIER, *FRANCE*

Chamlang (7,321m), with the northeast face to the left of the sharp spur, the north face just right of the spur (in shadow), the northwest face (climbed by a German team in 1990) facing the camera, the sharp west-southwest ridge above this face on the right, and the upper section of the south ridge in the right background, in profile. *Andy Houseman*

PEAK 4, SOUTHEAST RIDGE, ATTEMPT

ON APRIL 6 we arrived at Makalu base camp (ca 4,800m), planning to attempt Peak 4 (6,736m), which at the time we believed to be unclimbed. The east face gave few options that were not exposed to serac fall, but the southeast ridge looked like an elegant route to the summit. During our acclimatization toward Makalu, we also checked out lines from the north and found what appeared to be easy access to the northern summit (6,565m). However, from there the long ridge leading to the main summit did not look good.

On April 19 we set off for the southeast ridge, camping that night at 5,100m and then, moving slower than expected because of fresh snow, making an unexpected bivouac at 6,000m. Next day, we gained only 100m per hour because of deep snow on the broad glaciated face that leads to the top. After six hours Tomeu fell into a crevasse. About 150m higher we came to another crevasse that was much wider and too risky to cross. We may have been no more than 150m below the top.

[*Editor's note: Peak 4 was officially opened to climbers in 2003. Earlier, in September 1989, Andy Fanshaw and Ulrich Jessop climbed the southeast ridge with three bivouacs, the third—on the summit—made partly to aid acclimatization for Makalu. Close to the top they had great difficulties turning a large crevasse, which featured 10m of "utterly rotten snow." In 2010 the mountain was attempted by Georgian climbers, possibly via the southwest ridge. They reached 6,400m before heavy snow made conditions too dangerous to continue.*]

— CATI LLADO *AND* TOMEU RUBI, *SPAIN*

Looking up the northwest branch of the Chijima Glacier. (A) Dzanye I. (B) Dzanye II. The route to Dzanye II hugged the left side of the glacier to keep away from the icefalls. (C) Lashar I, climbed in 2005 (Habjan-Stremfelj) by the prominent couloir rising to the left of the summit. *Takanori Mashimo*

JANAK HIMAL

DZANYE II, SOUTH FACE

WE WERE A TEAM of six students gathered from six different universities, celebrating the 110th anniversary of the Japanese Alpine Club, which supported our expedition. In 2013, I had been a member of the expedition that made the first ascent of Janak East (*AAJ 2014*), so in 2015 we decided to look for a nearby unclimbed peak and found Dzanye II (6,318m).

We approached via Lhonak and the Chijima (a.k.a. Tsisima) Glacier, placing our high camp at 5,700m on the northwest branch of the Chijima Glacier. From here we made our attempt. We fixed two ropes to get onto the glacier (removed at the end of the expedition), walked up the flat glacier, avoiding many small crevasses, then moved onto the west side to avoid icefalls. We fixed three more ropes (again removed after the climb) to reach the upper plateau at ca 6,100m, and then climbed directly up the south face of Dzanye II, belaying three pitches. We reached the narrow summit ridge and followed it to the top. All six of us arrived at the summit on October 4. The team was Shinnosuke Ashikari, Kenta Kimura, Shun Kitsui, Kotaro Miyazu (climbing leader), Takehiro Nozawa, and me (expedition leader). 📷

– **TAKANORI MASHIMO**, *JAPAN, SUPPLIED BY* **HIROSHI HAGIWARA**, *JAPAN*

Editor's note: There has been confusion surrounding the names of some of these border peaks, but Dzanye I, climbed in 1949 by the Swiss team of Dittert, Lohner, Partgaetzi-Almer, Sutter, and Wyss-Dunant, is definitely the peak marked 6,581m on the HGM-Finn map. Dzanye II, climbed by the Japanese, is unmarked but registered as 6,318m in the list of more than 100 new peaks brought onto Nepal's permitted list in 2014. This list quotes coordinates of 27°54'08"N, 88°02'28"E (very close to the summit climbed by the Japanese), midway along the frontier ridge between Lashar I (6,842m) and Dzanye I.

TALUNG, NORTH FACE AND NORTH-NORTHWEST PILLAR, ATTEMPT

IN THE SPRING OF 2014, Italians Daniele Bernasconi, Giampaolo Corona, and Mario Panzeri attempted the north face and north-northwest pillar of Talung (7,349m). The three arrived at base camp on April 20 and began a siege-style ascent. They made about a dozen day trips to the face, fixing ropes gradually higher. The weather was unstable through most of the expedition.

Starting at ca 5,600m, they followed the 2013 Holocek-Hruby route, Thumba Party (*AAJ 2014*), to the top of a huge serac, where they installed a camp at ca 6,000m. They then continued up and right on hard ice (up to 90°) to reach a rock band on the north-northwest pillar. On May 16 they fixed a few pitches on the rock band, but, finding no bivouac sites, came back to sleep at their serac camp. The next day they tried to break through the rock band but failed, as they found it very difficult to protect. (On the penultimate pitch the leader climbed 40m without protection.) The difficulty was V A0. They retreated from a height reported to be ca 6,400m, though information from the Ukrainians who succeeded in 2015 on the north-northwest pillar suggests the Italians reached about 6,600m. In total the Italians climbed and fixed 31 pitches, and they were unable to remove all their rope. [*See photo on page 14 for the line of the Italian attempt.*] 🖸

> — LINDSAY GRIFFIN, *WITH INFORMATION FROM* RODOLPHE POPIER, *FRANCE,*
> *AND* GIAMPAOLO CORONA, *ITALY*

Mixed ground on the rock band at ca 6,500m on the north-northwest pillar of Talung, during the Italian attempt in spring of 2014. *Giampaolo Corona*

CHINA

BADA RI ATTEMPT; TA RI, SOUTHWEST RIDGE

BADA RI (6,516M) is the last unclimbed mountain over 6,500m in the western Nyanchen Tanglha (Nyainqentanglha). It lies in the middle of the range, northwest of Yangbajain, and is hidden by other peaks. Our expedition to attempt this peak, celebrating the 100th anniversary of the Kobe University Alpine Club, was jointly organized between Kobe University and the Chinese University of Geosciences, Wuhan. It is believed that no climbers had entered the Bada Qu valley prior to us.

We established base camp at 5,250m, close to the confluence of the two glaciers in the Bada Qu. On October 27, after three days of reconnaissance and ferrying loads to a high camp at 5,700m on the West Bada Glacier, six members made a summit attempt. We first reached the southwest ridge of Bada Ri by a steep ice slope, on which we fixed some rope. We then continued up to the shoulder peak (6,330m GPS). The ridge ahead dropped 20m to a col and then rose in a sharp, snow-covered rocky ridge to the summit. Three climbers tried to climb this ridge, but as the weather had been dry there was insufficient snow cover on the very loose rock, both on the crest and flanks, so the team retreated.

The name Bada Ri comes from Tibetan Pa and Ta, which mean boar and tiger or snow leopard. Pa Ta translates into Chinese Pinyin as Bada. While Ri means mountain, the Tibetans call a snow and ice peak Kangri, so in our opinion this mountain is better named Pata Kangri. Back in base camp local people named our shoulder peak Ta Ri (later ratified by Chinese authorities). Ours was the only expedition to Tibet during the autumn, the CTMA having canceled all others after the Nepal earthquake. 📷 🔍

– TATSUO (TIM) INOUE, *JAPAN*

(A) Bada Ri V (6,396m). (B) Bada Ri IV (6,386m). (C) Ta Ri (6,330m), showing the Japanese route and high point on Bada Ri. (D) Bada Ri (6,516m). *Tatsuo Inoue*

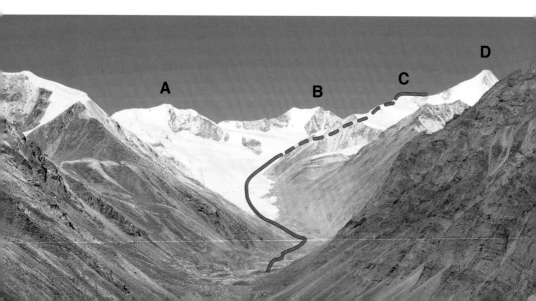

The new route on the north face of Chola II. The X marks the vicinity of the notch where Kyle Dempster was injured during the first attempt. During both ascents, the team rappelled the hidden gully descending left from this point. The 1997 Fowler route took the serac-laden face in left profile. *Bruce Normand*

SICHUAN / CHOLA SHAN

CHOLA II, NORTH FACE

Marcos Costa (Brazil), Kyle Dempster (USA), and I traveled to Sichuan and Yunnan in February in search of more first ascents and new routes above 6,000m in the alpine country of the eastern Himalayan uplift. After an abortive effort to access the north side of the Siguniang Range via the Bipeng Valley, which fell afoul of the park authorities, we continued to the far northwest of Sichuan, where the Ganzi Tibetan Autonomous Region poses few official barriers to alpine activity in the Chola, Shaluli, and Gongkala ranges.

Our target was the north face of Chola II (6,119m), which is accessible directly from 4,000m on the paved road between Ganzi and Dege, and was reached by a hike up a drainage along an amazingly continuous frozen alpine river, gaining 500m over 4km. While Chola I (6,168m) is often ascended by climbing schools and guided parties, Chola II is thought to have been climbed only once, by Charlie Fowler, solo, in May 1997. Fowler's route took the northeast face from the main Chola Glacier; formerly a 50° snow slope, it was now a serac-threatened and dangerous face, unsuitable as an ascent or descent route.

Our first attempt on the north face coincided with a passing weather front, bringing high winds and light snow to accompany the bitterly cold temperatures of the Tibetan winter (well below -20°C all day). We moved quickly on the easiest slopes we could find, stopping to belay only as we approached the summit ridge, where Kyle became dangerously chilled at a notch around 6,000m. As Marcos moved above him, Kyle was hit in the jaw by rockfall, causing an impact and injury serious enough for us to call a retreat. We rappelled a deep gully below the summit, crossing through the icefall low on the face to regain our high camp, and marched out the same day for rest and recovery in Ganzi.

Although all of us had numbness in our toes from the low temperatures, none of us was to be deterred, least of all Kyle. Returning to our high camp two days later, we retraced our steps below the upper northwest ridge and then traversed into the true north face, where Kyle led two absorbing mixed pitches to put us on the summit of Chola II. The face is ca 800m, and all but five pitches were climbed unroped. 🄾

– BRUCE NORMAND, *CHINA*

ASURA PEAK, NORTH FACE

IN LATE OCTOBER, Paul Manson (Scotland), Norihide Yamagishi (Japan), and I (Australia) made the first ascent of the summit at the junction of the western and central massifs of the Gangga Range. It lies at the head of the Niyada Qu river valley, and we named it Asura Peak (31.473447°N, 99.910003°E). Maps give it an altitude of 5,207m, which we were unable to verify. This was the first official ascent of any of the 40 or so peaks in the range above 5,000m; one unauthorized ascent was made in 2013 (*AAJ 2014*).

Once we left the road at 4,200m, without porters or electronic communication devices, we were self-contained for nine days. A three-day approach took us to a cold yet ideally sited camp below the 400m north face of the mountain we eventually called Asura. Nearby peaks and passes afforded good views of the face and chances to acclimate.

Ed Hamman on typical mixed terrain during the first attempt on the north face of Asura Peak. *Paul Manson*

On our first attempt we took a direct line up the center of the face, where we found good snow to 70°, thin ice, and rock of varying quality. There was an obvious ice line, but we found it too thin and instead climbed increasingly difficult mixed terrain beside it. We eventually retreated after Yamagishi took two 6m falls on an overhanging pitch at ca 4,900m and lost an ice tool. Similar long lines cover the face and have great potential.

Our second attempt took a meandering line that linked two tiers of exposed snowfields via pitches of Scottish 5 mixed. These led into the obvious couloir that bisects the face. After

Looking north from Asura Peak into the unexplored lower Niyada Qu valley and the highest peaks of the Gangga Range. From left to right: Peak 5,154m, Gangga II (5,582m), Gangga III (5,525m), and Gangga I (5,688m), all unclimbed. *Paul Manson*

several steep snow pitches in the couloir, we arrived below an overhanging, corniced notch, surrounded by towers and dangerously loose rock; this was ca 60m below what we assumed to be the summit. We retreated down the couloir and returned to camp 13 hours after setting out.

A rest day allowed more discerning reconnaissance and confirmed the true summit would best be reached by crossing the central couloir and making a rising traverse across a series of snowfields at the base of the headwall. Several centimeters of snow fell that night, but the sky had partially cleared by midmorning. With the pressure of an unpredictable weather window, we simul-climbed to the couloir, reaching it in late morning, and then continued to simul-climb across the upper snow and mixed sections. A short, corniced ridge was followed by a traverse to the summit, which we gained at 12:30 p.m. An encroaching cloud base gave only 15 minutes to take photos of the previously unseen southern reaches of the range, as well as the southern aspects of the highest peaks and multiple alpine objectives. We reversed the route to the central couloir, where we used our previous rappel line to descend. The route gave ca 700m of climbing and was Scottish V M5 70° snow.

— ED HANNAM, *JAPAN*

DECHOK PHODRANG, AUSTRIAN-SPANISH CLASSIC & DECHOK DIRECT

INSPIRED BY the published work of Japanese mountaineer Tamotsu Nakamura, an Austrian-Spanish expedition visited the eastern Gangga Massif in the autumn. The expedition comprised mountaineers Gerald Boess, Judith Fall, and Paul Neil, filmmakers Lothar Hofer and Martin Sochor, and Spanish guides Martin and Simon Elias. Even though it was a guided trip, it was a team effort, as the three Austrian mountaineers organized the entire expedition, based on their previous visit to the area. They identified a peak in the middle of the eastern Gangga, east of the Zhuoda Qu valley and Ganbai Road, which local monks called Dechok Phodrang

Dechok Phodrang from the east-northeast. (1) Dechok Direct to the main summit. (2) Austrian-Spanish Classic to the north summit. *Simon Elias Collection*

(Palace of Happiness). This, the main peak of the eastern Gangga, has two summits, and in wintry conditions, with temperatures down to -15°C, the team managed to climb both tops by separate routes.

The group approached via the Zhuoda Qu and then a short tributary valley that branched off southeast. On November 4, after a night in high camp beneath a protective rock wall at 4,740m, where the climbers experienced an earthquake that shook the region, all except Socher followed a traversing line across and then up the east-northeast face to reach the virgin north summit, which they measured at 5,550m. They named the route Austrian-Spanish Classic (800m, D+).

Four days later the same team set off for the main summit. There had been heavy snow the previous night, and they struggled for 12 hours, sometimes breaking trail up to their hips. After climbing a couloir on the left side of the east-northeast face, and then forcing a route through a gully alongside a serac barrier, they followed a ridge to the summit, measured at 5,632m (31.45275°N, 99.99795°E). The route was named Dechok Direct (1,000m, D+). 📷

– **LINDSAY GRIFFIN**, *FROM INFORMATION SUPPLIED BY* **SIMON ELIAS**, *SPAIN*

SICHUAN / DAXUE SHAN – MINYA KONKA RANGE

NYAMBO KONKA, SOUTHEAST FACE AND NORTHEAST RIDGE

ON OCTOBER 28, Koreans Kang Jong-jin, Kim Dong-jin, and Kim Young-yong made the first ascent of Nyambo Konka (6,114m). The nine-member expedition, led by Gang Sung-khu, approached via the Bawang Valley to the south of the mountain. They climbed the southeast flank to reach the crest of the northeast ridge at the 5,596m low point between Nyambo Konka and Peak 6,124m. The ridge above, sharp at first, merges into the broad, glaciated northeast face, which the three summiters followed to the rounded top, arriving at 6 p.m.

Mark Jenkins and Ross Lynn (USA) attempted this side of the mountain in 2005 but failed to reach the northeast ridge. Another attempt, via the central south ridge, was also abandoned. Jenkins returned in 2009 as part of a four-person team and attempted a similar route to the Korean line, but found the northeast ridge too corniced and crevassed to continue safely (*AAJ 2010*).

— LINDSAY GRIFFIN, *WITH INFORMATION FROM* TAMOTSU NAKAMURA, *JAPAN*

LONG SHAN, WEST FLANK AND SOUTH RIDGE ATTEMPT; PEAK 6,124M, NORTHEAST RIDGE

GARRETT BRADLEY, MARCOS COSTA, KYLE DEMPSTER, AND I headed to the Minya Konka Range for our final mountaineering quest of the winter season: one of the unclimbed peaks to the south of 7,556m Minya Konka. In 2014, Marcos, Garrett, and I had found the southern approach to these peaks and climbed Peak ca 6,460m, the western sub-peak of Peak 6,468m. In February we retraced this approach, climbing to the top of the basin west of Long Shan (6,684m) and digging a solid campsite to withstand the extreme winds. As Marcos went down with a stomach bug, Garrett, Kyle, and I made a reconnaissance of Long Shan by climbing the summit to the west of our camp, denoted on the accepted maps of the range as Peak 6,124m. Despite clouds and high winds, we were given views of the south and west faces of the imposing Minya Konka, its approach glacier system, and the summit of Nyambo Konka (6,114m) to the southwest, climbed later in the year by a Korean team (*see report above*).

The next day dawned clear, so Kyle and I made a bid on Long Shan, climbing a hanging glacier system with two vertical bergschrunds. Above, long ice slopes brought us to a shoulder on the south ridge at ca 6,500m. However, the ridge to the summit, still several hundred meters distant, turned into soft, corniced snow, steeply fluted down the eastern (Hailuoguo) side, and with vertical rock on the western side. With night approaching, the cloud deck falling, and the ever-present winter winds rising, we were forced to retreat.

— BRUCE NORMAND, *CHINA*

Looking west from San Lian Southeast. (A) Nyambo Konka (6,114m). (B) Col 5,596m. The 2015 Korean expedition climbed the rocky southeast face of Nyambo Konka to Col 5,596m, and then continued southwest up the snow arête and broad, glaciated face to the summit. (C) Peak 6,124m southwest summit. (D) Peak 6,124m, climbed in 2015 by the northeast ridge (right skyline). *Rafal Zajac*

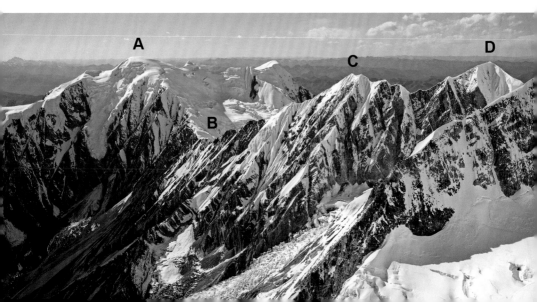

Chu Shan (a.k.a. San Lian group) from the east. (A) San Lian Southeast (ca 6,250m). (B) San Lian Central (ca 6,350m). (C) San Lian Main (6,368m). (1) Hard Camping, 2015. (2) Descent route. *Rafal Zajac*

CHU SHAN, SAN LIAN SOUTHEAST, EAST FACE, HARD CAMPING

ON NOVEMBER 10, after four days of climbing, Marcin Rutkowski, Wojciech Ryczer, and I completed the first ascent of San Lian Southeast (ca 6,250m), one of the three Chu Shan summits to the south of Minya Konka.

We arrived in Chengdu in mid-October and the next day took the bus to Moxi at the entrance to Hailuogou National Park. On the 19th we took the park bus up the valley and then a cable car to ca 3,500m. With porters unable to take our loads to the desired altitude, we spent the next few days establishing base camp (4,150m) and ferrying loads to the rim of the glacier (ca 4,400m) that flows east from the San Lian peaks. We then found a relatively safe route across this glacier to the foot (ca 5,260m) of the east face of San Lian Southeast.

On November 6, Wojciech led the first pitch (M7) and fixed a rope. Next day we jugged this and started up thin, aerated, sun-bleached ice, some sections of which were WI5 R. After dusk we veered left and made one rappel in order to find a place for the night. It took a lot of time and effort to construct a platform big enough for the tent.

On the 8th we regained our line and after a number of ice and mixed pitches, together with a little traversing and one 30m rightward rappel, established ourselves in a steep snow gully. There, we found a ledge big enough for all three of us to sit, so we eagerly chose to stop and settle for the night. Next day we followed the steepening gully to an even steeper rocky arête capped with loose snow. This gave us a hard time: dry-tool bouldering at 6,000m while carrying a pack. The rock was crumbling and the snow offered little more than psychological protection. At one point we decided to abandon the crest for the flanks (M5), but this took so long that we were forced to bivouac again. At around 11 p.m., Wojciech accidentally dropped his sleeping bag, but luckily the temperature was tolerable and there was no wind.

On November 10 we regained the arête via a pitch of M6 and climbed several exposed pitches to the corniced summit ridge. The views were stunning as we quickly traversed north over the top and down to the col between the southeast and central (ca 6,350m) summits. We then rappelled the east-northeast face, mainly from V-threads, and at 1 a.m. reached a large snowfield on the glacier between the southeast and central summits. We began walking down, but in a steeper, crevassed area I took a 15m free fall into a crevasse. Held on the rope, I managed to jug to safety and we decided to make another tent bivouac.

Marcin Rutkowski on the main ridge, with rocky San Lian Central just behind and pointed Peak 6,468m to the left. Long Shan (6,684m) is in the background. *Rafal Zajac*

On the 11th we continued the descent, rappelling between seracs and ice pillars bordering the foot of the east face of San Lian Southeast, until we finally reached a safe section of the glacier and regained the base of our climb that evening. Over the next two days we descended to base camp, and by the 18th we were home in Poland. We felt we had managed a beautiful route on a virgin summit and named it Hard Camping (1,000m, 1,450m of climbing, ED2 WI5 R M7).

Until now, confusing nomenclature (*see editor's note below*) has meant the three summits of the San Lian group have been assigned the altitudes 6,368m (southeast peak), 6,468m (central peak), and 6,684m (northwest peak). On returning home, and in consultation with Grzegorz Glazek, Tamotsu Nakamura, and Bruce Normand, we reassessed the heights of the three San Lian peaks to, respectively, ca 6,250m, ca 6,350m, and 6,368m. We thank the Kukuczka Foundation and the Polish Mountaineering Association for grant aid. 📷 🔍

– RAFAL "WALDORF" ZAJAC, *POLAND*

Editor's note: Recent climbing activity on the peaks constituting the watershed ridge running south from Minya Konka has given rise to some confusion over their nomenclature. The earliest names published in the West date from 1929–1931, when this range was visited by the Swiss geologist Arnold Heim, who at the time was a professor at the Sun

Major peaks south of (A) Minya Konka (Gongga Shan): (B) Long Shan. (C1) Peak 6,460m. (C2) Peak 6,468m. (D1/D2/D3) Chu Shan (the three San Lian peaks). (E) Tai Shan. (F) Peak 6,124m. (G) Nyambo Konka.

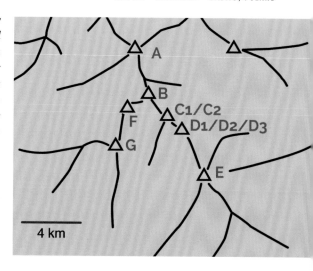

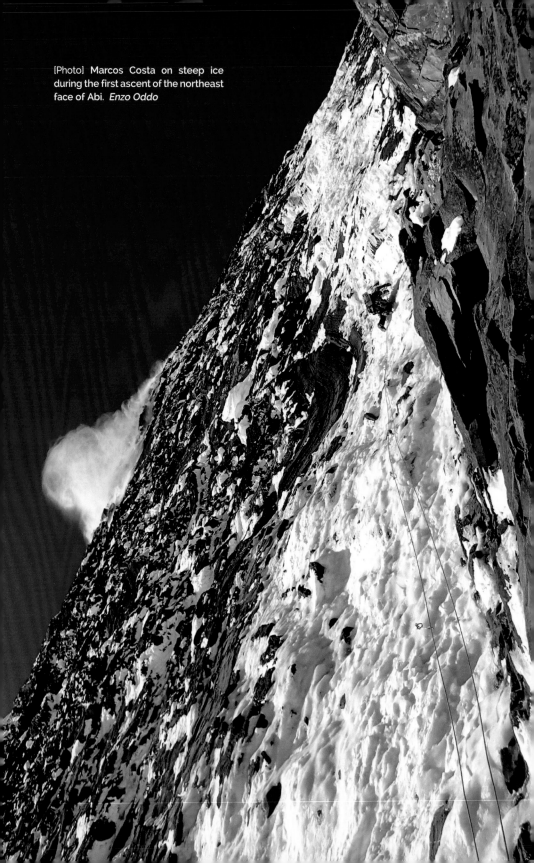

[Photo] Marcos Costa on steep ice during the first ascent of the northeast face of Abi. *Enzo Oddo*

Yat-Sen University in China. In 1930 he was accompanied by Eduard Imhof, a Swiss cartographer, who surveyed the area, made a map, measured the height of Minya Konka, and confirmed the existence of its three principal glaciers.

The most prominent feature visible from the gateway Hailuogou Glacier is the last high peak at the southern end of the ridge, Peak 6,410m. Heim and Imhof gave this mountain the name Mt. Tai (Tai Shan), after Tai Chi–Chao, a member of the university team who accompanied the expedition and, from an organizational perspective, made it possible. This peak has appeared on recent sketch maps with the Chinese name Jinyin Shan (Gold-Silver Mountain).

The other prominent feature when viewed from the lower Hailuogou is a three-peaked mountain, Peak 6,368m, which Heim and Imhof designated Mt. Chu, after Chu Chia-Hua, another university member who accompanied the expedition. This mountain has become known on local Chinese maps as San Lian Feng (Three Connecting Peaks). Additional confusion has been caused by the attribution of the name Mt. Chu (Chu Shan) to surveyed points farther north on the watershed ridge, including Peaks 6,468m and even 6,684m, although these are difficult or impossible to see from the Hailuogou valley.

The 1981 Swiss expedition that made the first ascent of Tai Shan followed the convention of Heim and Imhof, and, if one maintains this nomenclature, then the summits on the main ridge, from south to north, should be referred to as Tai Shan (6,410m), Chu Shan (San Lian Southeast, San Lian Central, and San Lian Main, 6,368m), Peak 6,468m, Peak 6,460m (western top of Peak 6,468m), Long Shan (Dragon Mountain, 6,684m), and Minya Konka (7,556m, a.k.a. Gongga Shan). Point 6,858m, close to Minya Konka and sometimes misidentified as Long Shan, has no prominence and cannot be considered a separate top.

SICHUAN / QIONGLAI SHAN – SIGUNIANG NATIONAL PARK

ABI, NORTHEAST FACE

During the approach to Huang Guan Feng (Crown Peak) in 2014 (*AAJ 2015*), I saw a striking ice line on the northeast face of Abi (5,694m). In late January, Enzo Oddo (France) was around and psyched to make an alpine ascent, and I felt this would be a perfect target for us.

We started from the head of the Shuangqiao Valley at 11 a.m., and by 4 p.m. we were threading through deep snow below the face. We pitched the tent and had time to check out the first couple of pitches, which were technical mixed. By 5 the next morning we were climbing. Enzo climbed the first two mixed pitches in the dark, after which one more mixed pitch led to a snowfield. Above, 300m of simul-climbing brought us to the crux ice and mixed pitches. We managed these quickly, arrived at an amphitheater, and then climbed a couple more technical mixed pitches to the summit ridge, where we found a nice ledge on which to bivouac. Next morning we reached the summit, descended to our tent, and continued to the valley floor. The route is one of the most complete, technical, and beautiful I have done in this area.

– MARCOS COSTA, *CHINA*

SEERDENGPU, WEST FACE, ATTEMPT

In January, Marcos Costa (China) and Enzo Oddo (France) attempted the 900m west face of Seerdengpu (5,592m) via the same gully line that Costa had tried with American Pat Goodman in October 2014 (*AAJ 2015*), retreating because of melting ice and loose rock. This time, Costa found the gully to be in excellent condition, with a couple of overhanging mixed sections, but the pitch above was deemed too dangerous to continue because of loose rock. 📷

– LINDSAY GRIFFIN, *WITH INFORMATION FROM* MARCOS COSTA, *CHINA*

SHUANGQIAO VALLEY: EAGLE PEAK (CA 5,300M), SOUTHWEST FACE, GOLDEN EAGLE; NEW DRY-TOOLING ROUTES

MY MAIN GOAL for the 2014-'15 winter was to complete the Great Wall of China Project, a link-up of the three most iconic peaks of the Shuangqiao Valley. This would involve making the first ascent of Queen's Peak (Nuwang Shan, 5,404m), the second ascent of Seerdengpu (5,592m), and then finishing on Putala Shan (Potala, 5,428m), before descending to Baihaizi Lake. Visiting Frenchman Enzo Oddo and I were not expecting the cold to be so severe. After difficult climbing in a deep, narrow couloir, we reached the col on Queen's Peak's northeast ridge but then retreated, both of us nearly frostbitten. This plan remains in the forefront of my mind.

Eagle Peak has one of the most striking granite walls in the Shuangqiao Valley: completely overhanging for 300m, covered in beautiful golden streaks, and in sun almost all day—a perfect winter big-wall location. Enzo and I took six days to complete a line to the left of my own route Invisible Hand Sit Start (*AAJ 2014*), sleeping in a portaledge. Most pitches were A2+ to A3+, and the cracks were grassy, making progress slow. The last pitch had 15 beak, Pecker, and micro-nut placements in a row. We named the route Golden Eagle (300m, A3+)

Enzo and I also opened about 25 new pitches of mixed climbing or dry-tooling in the Shuangqiao. The two areas on which we mostly focused were Xianxiandong, a new area developed specifically for the Kailash Dry Tooling event, and the Bar, the next cliff up-valley. Grades range from M3 to M11/12. 📷

– MARCOS COSTA, *CHINA*

EAGLE PEAK EAST, SECRET MOON CAKE

I FIRST SAW Eagle Peak East (5,300m) in the fall of 2013, after completing the first ascent of Dayantianwo in the Shuangqiao Valley (*AAJ 2014*). While enjoying the spectacular view from the summit, my wife, Szu-ting Yi, and I noticed a large shark's tooth spire just to the north. We later learned this mountain was part of the Eagle Rock group, a prominent

Dave Anderson on pitch five (5.9 R) of Secret Moon Cake, southeast face of Eagle Peak East. *Szu-ting Yi*

Eagle Peak East from the south. (1) Kyousai (2007). (2) Secret Moon Cake (2015). *Dave Anderson*

trio of rock towers that rise above Baihaizi Lake.

Eagle Peak East had only one published ascent, in August 2007, by a Japanese team that followed the lower-angled southwest face. Toshio Hirayama, Keiichi Nagatomo, Naoki Ouchi (also spelled Ohuchi), Kazuko Ouchi, and Yoshiaki Senoh also referred to the peak as Wagrusei (Warglesei in *AAJ 2015*). They completed their 680m route, Kyousai, in 16 pitches at 5.10c A1.

On September 12 we returned to the Shuangqiao Valley and established a base camp at the foot of Eagle Peak East. The weather was unsettled—we experienced rain and snow almost every day. We initially attempted a route up the south face following a central chimney and crack system. The line turned out to be the main drainage for the upper section of the peak, which made for challenging, wet climbing. In addition, we found numerous bolts and pitons on the first two pitches from an unknown attempt.

Not wanting to follow someone else's route in a waterspout, we rappelled and looked for other options. We eventually settled on a route up the southeast face, fixed four ropes, and waited for a break in the weather. On September 23 we jugged our ropes and continued up sparsely protected steep slabs. At a large ledge system we traversed to the east ridge and followed featured granite to the summit. We rappelled our route, arriving back at base camp after 18 hours of effort. No bolts or pins were placed during the ascent or descent. We called the route Secret Moon Cake (760m 5.10 R), after the delicious pastries people in China enjoy during the mid-autumn festival.

– DAVE ANDERSON, *USA*

KAWAGEBO RANGE: FIRST SUMMIT SUCCESS

BY BRUCE NORMAND

In February, after making the first ascent of Chola II in northwestern Sichuan (*see report earlier in this section*), Marcos Costa, Kyle Dempster, and I headed to the Kawagebo Range, following up on a reconnaissance that Marcos and I had made in 2014. This range, also referred to as Meili Xueshan or Kang Karpo, lies in the far northwest corner of Yunnan province, forming the border with the Tibet Autonomous Region, and is most famous for the beautifully fluted, triangular peak of Mianzimu (6,054m).

This area's highest summit, unclimbed Kawagebo (6,740m), is the second-most sacred mountain in the pantheon of Tibetan Buddhism, after Kailas, and in 1991 was the scene of an infamous episode in the history of mountaineering and Sino-Tibetan relations. The Chinese authorities granted climbing permission to a joint Chinese-Japanese expedition, over the strenuous objections of the Tibetan community. The matter was resolved only when an avalanche took the lives of all 17 of the members, and the peak has been closed for the past 15 years.

Hidden far to the north end of the chain is the second-highest peak, Cogar Lapka (6,516m GPS; attempted twice by Americans, *AAJ 1993 and 1994*). Joined by Garrett Bradley (USA), we began our approach from 2,100m, near the Mekong River—not for nothing is this known as the Deep Gorge Country. We spent our first morning in discussion with the villagers and local police at the last settlement, where Garrett's excellent Mandarin and skillful diplomacy saw us through. We then hiked steep and little-used trails through thick, mixed forests of bamboo and conifers, camping for the first night by the river. On the second day we moved above treeline, crossing summer yak pastures and unused settlements, and sleeping high on a small, icy glacier.

The third day of approach involved soloing up loose snow and ice gullies to 50°, with significant stonefall threat, to gain a 5,500m col between Nairi Denka (6,379m) to the southeast and Peak 6,260m (estimate from Google Earth) to the north. From there we gained a further 200m by climbing north along the ridge toward Peak 6,260m, but then had to downclimb and rappel 150m to the glacier below the east face of Cogar Lapka, finally placing a camp at approximately 5,650m.

The following morning was clear. We moved rapidly to climb the northern edge of the glacier basin to the col between Peak 6,260m and Cogar Lapka, with a view to climbing the upper east ridge. (None of the possible east face routes was remotely safe.) Getting to this col (ca 6,050m) required climbing ice to 60°, and we were greeted on top by howling winds and a descending whiteout, which drove us back to camp.

The next morning was again clear, but since Garrett was too tired and Kyle was too tired of the constant objective dangers, only Marcos and I left camp. We regained our high point and continued up the minor cornices and occasional crevasses of the east ridge. The dramatic views to Peak 6,260m and over the Kawagebo Range soon were blotted out by incoming clouds, which denied us the hoped-for views into southeastern Tibet.

The terrain pushed us to the north side of the ridge and into deeper snow, where Marcos opted to cross a bergschrund with an extremely athletic move through an overhanging ice bulge, and was then left trying to haul my sorry carcass up this feature while anchored only by his legs sunk into the snow (causing him to contemplate the value of the belay knife). This turned out to be the last difficulty, beyond which a final slog up a low-angle ridge brought us to the summit crest, which we mapped out by braille in the whiteout, recording 6,516m by GPS. To our knowledge this is the first summit climbed in the entire Kawagebo Range.

The descent was uneventful, a snow stake taking the teeth out of the overhanging bulge. The storm abated above the col, giving us evening views of Peak 6,260m, and night fell as we were V-threading down the ice face below the col in renewed snowfall. Kyle and Garrett shone some light to guide us in. The next morning was wildly windy as we climbed back out of the glacier basin and descended the stonefall-threatened face to the glacier. We slept that night in the yak pastures at 4,000m, walked out the next day, and thawed out with a few days of spring rock climbing in the valley floors.

SUMMARY: *First ascent of Cogar Lakpa (6,516m GPS), second-highest peak of the Kawagebo Range in northwestern Yunnan province, by the upper east ridge, Marcos Costa and Bruce Normand, February 2015.* 📷

[Previous page] **Bruce Normand** battles the wind on the upper east ridge of Cogar Lapka, with the summit almost in sight. *Marcos Costa* [Right] Unclimbed Peak 6,260m, seen from the east ridge of Cogar Lapka. *Marcos Costa*

Wei Guangguang on pitch four (5.10+ offwidth) during the first ascent of High Tide or Low Tide. *Griff*

JIDEGE SHAN EXPLORATION

THE INDIAN CLIMBER Anindya Mukherjee explored a group of peaks northeast of Yulong Xueshan (a.k.a. Jade Dragon Snow Mountain, 5,596m) and Haba Xueshan (5,396m), which he called Jidege Shan after a small village of this name below the west side of the southern end of the range. In mid-April, Mukherjee climbed two small peaks (coordinates in online report) and photographed unclimbed rocky summits in the group (ca 4,000–4,500m). 📷 📄

– LINDSAY GRIFFIN, *WITH INFORMATION FROM* ANINDYA MUKHERJEE, *INDIA*

HUA SHAN SOUTH PEAK, SOUTH FACE, HIGH TIDE OR LOW TIDE

IN OCTOBER, Gu Qizhi, Wei Guangguang, Wang Zhiming, and I established a new route on the south face of Landing Goose Summit, high point of the south peak of Hua Shan, left of the 2014 route Never Give Up (*AAJ 2015*). We expected clear, dry days, but in fact encountered several unexpected early winter storms during our 13-day capsule-style ascent.

On October 24, after we had fixed rope on the first two pitches, the first rainstorm arrived and we hid in a cave 20m above the ground until the 27th, when the weather finally cleared. That day we climbed 160m, ending at midnight. Next day it was drizzling and we took a rest day. Progress over the following two days was slow due to wide cracks and heavy vegetation. Just after we established our second portaledge camp on the 30th, it began to snow. This lasted 24 hours and we had a cold and wet Halloween. On November 2 we reached a headwall where the crack system we had been following stopped. We began aid climbing and had to make a few pendulums to connect cracks. That night the wind howled and punched our portaledges, preventing anyone from getting any sleep. Fortunately, once the sun rose the wind died down, and beautiful granite cracks made us forget our fatigue.

More bad weather was coming, but on the 4th, after some slow chimney climbing, the angle of the face diminished. After fighting heavy vegetation for another four pitches, we reached the top in the dark and rain. We all felt a bit weightless back on solid ground. Rain quickly turned to snow, and it was not until three days later that we could retrieve all our gear. We named the route High Tide or Low Tide (690m, 18 pitches, VI 5.11 C2), due to the rain, snow, and wind we endured on the wall. 📷 📄

– GRIFF, *CHINA*

HUA SHAN SOUTH PEAK, CLIMB LIKE YOU ARE DYING

IN JULY, He Chuan soloed a new route on the south side of Hua Shan's South Peak. He spent eight days on the route, which he called Climb Like You Are Dying (580m, 20 pitches, VI 5.10+ R A3). In 2014, He Chuan and Zhu Xiaofei climbed the first route up the south face of Landing Goose Summit on South Peak: Never Give Up (VI 5.10+ R C2+, *AAJ 2015*). [*The online versions of these Hua Shan reports has a new photo showing all three routes on the south face.*] 📷

NEW ZEALAND

NEW ROUTES IN SUMMER AND WINTER

The bulk of the new-route activity in New Zealand has been focused in and around the Darran Mountains, both in summer and winter.

A sustained period of fine weather in February brought a flurry of activity. On the upper tier of the south face of Barrier Peak (2,039m), Daniel Joll and Pete Harris established a nine-pitch route directly to the summit: Peaking Pete (440m, 20/5.10c A2). On the same day, Jaz Morris and Michael Eatson climbed a rib on the left side of the face to a point high on the south ridge: Jaz Hands (240m, 17/5.9).

During the same period, Zac Orme and Troy Mattingly climbed five new pitches on the Mighty Dur, a small subpeak below Mt. Taiaroa (2,154m). The climb, Yeah, Nah, Dur (24/5.11d), follows a striking line up a steep, golden shield of rock on the east face, above the Te Puoho basin.

In the true depths of the central Darrans, three stalwart pioneers of development in the area, Rich Turner, Richard Thomson, and Dave Vass, along with James Spears, climbed a trio of new routes. Turner and Spears established Katabatic Gravity Well (300m, 23/5.11c) on the Statue Wall, below the north ridge of Karetai Peak (2,206m), and also Kilroy Wuz Ere (250m, 21/5.11a) on the west face of Nga Mokopuna (2,073m), an outlier peak on the ridge between Karetai Peak and Mt. Te Wera (2,309m). On the same wall, Turner, Thomson, and Vass climbed Brothers In Arms (325m, 22/5.11b).

In March, Kyle Dempster and Jewell Lund (both USA) climbed a new 300m line on the

Ben Dare high on Tramadol Dreams (460m, V, 5), upper south face of Mt. Crosscut. *Steve Fortune*

[Left] Steve Fortune on the new route Ether (III, 5+) in the McPherson Cirque. *Ben Dare* [Right] Ben Dare leads the crux WI5+ pillar of Crystal Ship (IV, 7), a new route in the McPherson Cirque. *Steve Fortune*

east face of Karetai Peak: Tabula Rasa (5.11b, 7 pitches), right of the Thomson-Vass route (2012).

Moving into the winter season, some of the best ice conditions in recent years were seen at the annual Darrans Winter Climbing Meet, in July, allowing for a number of great climbs to be completed. Steve Fortune and I found two new routes in the McPherson Cirque. The first, Crystal Ship (IV, 7), climbs a striking, freestanding ice pillar (WI5+) through the center of the upper tier. The second, Ether (III, 5+), follows a thinly iced groove angling up through the lower tier between Rabbit Run (Perry, 1981) and Stirling Moss (Alder-Evrard-Fearnley, 1992) for five pitches.

Shortly after the winter meet, I ventured into Cirque Creek to climb a new four-pitch ice line, parallel to Squealing (Rogers-Vass, 1993), called Tempest (200m, IV, 6+, WI5- R). Meanwhile, Lionel Clay and Allan Uren made the first ascent of Bill's Way (120m, WI6), at the head of Eyre Creek in the Eyre Mountains.

To close out the ice season, two more multi-pitch routes were added on the upper south face of Mt. Crosscut (2,263m). In late September, Milo Gilmour and Allan Uren climbed a series of iced-up ramps and corners to the East Peak, directly right of Hotel Caribbean (Cradock-Perry, 1982), to claim the first ascent of Up Cirque Creek Without a Shovel (400m, VI, 6, WI4). Two weeks later, Steve Fortune and I climbed a line to the left of this, between White Knight (McLeod-Widdowson, 1987) and Heart of Gold (Perry-Ritchie, 1981). Tramadol Dreams (460m, V, 5 (WI4) starts up steep, thinly iced slabs before traversing left into a deep gully leading to the summit of the Middle Peak (2,250m). 🗎 📷 🔍

– BEN DARE, *NEW ZEALAND*

BOOK REVIEWS

EDITED BY **DAVID STEVENSON**

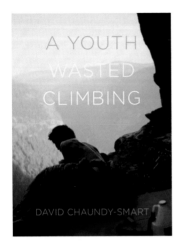

A YOUTH WASTED CLIMBING

David Chaundy-Smart. Rocky Mountain Books (Canada), 2015. 247 pages. Paperback, $20.

IN 1972 A BOY stared out the back window of his parents' car, straining for a last glimpse of his family's sold-off farm before it vanished in a cloud of late-summer dust. To David Chaundy-Smart and his brother, Reg, the recollection of a nearby limestone escarpment fringed with trees and moss turned into an emblem of a lost paradise, the beginnings of a deep attachment to place. By the time they were young men, climbing had become a means to recapture some of that initial wonder, to find an inner wild on cliffs just beyond the edges of Toronto suburbs. As Chic Scott later wrote in his history of Canadian mountaineering, *Pushing the Limits* (2000), David represented "one of the first Ontario climbers who considered the local crags to be an end in themselves and not just training for bigger routes elsewhere."

David Chaundy-Smart went on to become the founding editor of the Canadian climbing magazine *Gripped*, to publish five guidebooks, and to complete hundreds of first ascents. But his memoir, *A Youth Wasted Climbing*, is not a typical climbing autobiography preoccupied with the progression to ever-harder routes. Instead, it's something both quieter and more ambitious: an examination of what it means to climb and live, as Chaundy-Smart puts it, "by the authority of…[the] imagination." Scene by scene, his prose captures impressions of intense beauty and awe concentrated into small moments: how the afterimage of an adventure on a brushy, shale cliff can linger in a schoolchild's mind; how even short ascents can seem to offer access to some hidden, luminous existence; the ways that fantasies and realities elide each other; the layers of stories from books and magazines that form a youthful alpine mythology; the split longings for stone lines and human love; the passage of light through a canopy of leaves and across a face; the persistent belief that there's always "something wonderful that's just a little more climbing away."

In the now-classic 1990 book *Flow*, the psychologist Mihaly Csikszentmihalyi quoted a climber and a poet: "The mystique of rock climbing is climbing; you get to the top of a rock glad it's over but really wish it could go on forever…. The act of writing justifies poetry. Climbing is the same: recognizing that you are a flow. The purpose of the flow is to keep on flowing, not looking for a peak or utopia but staying in the flow." Reading Chaundy-Smart's memoir, you get the sense that this writer is, indeed, as deeply immersed in the rhythm of creating sentences as he is in movement over stone. The result is a book that unfolds a series of unexpected wonders, like glowing vistas along a forest path. During an age when not only the climbing world but also much of mainstream society has become engrossed with quantifiable data, technology, and profit, *A Youth Wasted Climbing* makes a strong, implicit argument for the recovery of lost arts of unfettered daydreaming and backyard wandering—a reawakening to the wildness and mystery of both the extraordinary and the ordinary world.

– KATIE IVES

ALPINE WARRIORS

Bernadette McDonald. Rocky Mountain Books (Canada), 2015. 335 pages. Hardcover, $30.

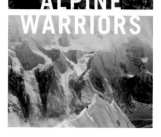

ANY FOLLOWER OF MODERN CLIMBING in the Himalaya will know of the exploits—bold, inspirational, occasionally shameful—of Slovenian climbers. The names Štremfelj, Česen, Humar, and Prezelj have filled magazines and Internet reports for decades. But it's likely only the cognoscenti will recall the importance of the earlier Slovenian greats: Stane Belak, Viki Grošelj, Aleš Kunaver, Marjan Manfreda, and others. In the 1970s, these climbers in the former Yugoslavia were at the forefront of Himalayan climbing, with first ascents like the south face of Makalu and the direct west ridge of Everest. In *Alpine Warriors*, Bernadette McDonald tells the full story of these climbers and the country that shaped them—a country riven by war and privation, but also one unified by a mountain, Triglav, which every citizen aspires to climb.

Of all the climbers in the years before Sloevnia won independence in a 10-day war in 1991, one man had outsized influence: Nejc Zaplotnik, who died in an avalanche on Manaslu in 1983, at age 31. Zaplotnik not only was a key figure in several great Himalayan climbs, he also wrote a slim book in 1981 that profoundly influenced Slovenian climbers. *Pot*, meaning "the Path" or "the Way," is a philosophical work on life and climbing, and when McDonald discovered how much Slovenian climbers treasure the book, she arranged to have it translated. *Alpine Warriors* is peppered with quotes from Zaplotnik's work, as here, reflecting on his dull day job in a bank:

> *"Day after day I sit at the window in a smoky office. Darkness falls quietly on the bustling city streets, only the mountains still glow scarlet. Their blinding light falls directly onto my miserable window.... My coworkers are beautifully adjusted to me, so perfectly that they never even notice me. How I would like to share with them at least some of the yearnings and hopes and blue horizons within me."*

McDonald's tale does not end with the 1970s and '80s climbs on the 8,000-meter giants, but extends to modern arenas and characters, including scandals (Tomo Česen) and antics (Tomaž Humar) that McDonald covers thoroughly and objectively. In its unveiling of lives and climbs previously hidden by the curtains of politics and language, *Alpine Warriors* serves like a sequel to McDonald's much-lauded previous book, *Freedom Climbers* (2011), which covered Polish climbers before and after the fall of communism. Both books perform an essential service, ensuring the stories of those bold and deadly years in the Himalaya are preserved, while the surviors are still around to tell them. With its colorful characters and the fascinating thread of *Pot* running throughout, plus a lighter, more agile touch in her writing, *Alpine Warriors* is McDonald's best book yet. Now, who will tackle the great untold story of Soviet and Russian climbing?

– DOUGALD MACDONALD

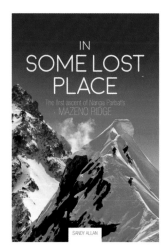

IN SOME LOST PLACE: THE FIRST ASCENT OF NANGA PARBAT'S MAZENO RIDGE

Sandy Allan. Vertebrate Publishing (U.K.), 2015. 185 Pages. Hardcover, £24.

THIS BOOK IS A COMPELLING and straightforward account of the epic, 18-day first ascent of the Mazeno Ridge on Nanga Parbat (*AAJ 2013*). The 10-kilometer ridgeline was one of the great unclimbed features on an 8,000-meter peak and had been attempted in the 1990s by several expeditions that included experienced climbers such as Doug Scott, Voytek Kurtyka, and Erhard Loretan. Sandy Allan, along with his partner Rick Allen, participated in one of Scott's attempts, in 1995, and as Sandy writes, "It was then that the Mazeno first got under my skin." In 2004, Doug Chabot and I made the first ascent of the ridge from Mazeno Pass to the Mazeno Gap, where it intersects the Schell Route, but we didn't climb the rest of that 1976 route to the summit, because I was sick and the weather was poor. This was a route with a lot of history.

Sandy does a nice job explaining how he and Rick learned from the previous attempts to develop a strategy for the ridge in 2012. They decided to go with a larger team and more supplies, so they could stay on the route longer. To help provide horsepower for this approach, they invited three Sherpa friends to be part of the team. Sandy's description of how modern Sherpas can be equal partners on a difficult new route is enlightening to those who might view them primarily as load carriers on commercial mountains. The team used fixed ropes to get to 6,400 meters for acclimatization, but this ended up being such a small part of the overall effort that I don't believe it detracts from their alpine-style ascent. I enjoyed reading how they developed a plan that honored the spirit of the previous attempts but also worked for them.

Sandy expresses a level of comfort and even joy while spending a long time at extreme altitude on a route where it would be easy to get trapped by bad weather or snow conditions. His state of mind is in sharp contrast to that of many Himalayan climbers who believe that safety and success while climbing alpine style only comes from going light and fast. Reading Sandy's book made me wonder whether, if Doug and I had been more like Sandy and took an extra day at the Mazeno Gap to think about it, we might have been able to keep going. It reminds me there isn't a single formula for practicing our craft.

After the team completed the ridge, most of them made a summit attempt to around 7,900 meters, and then they all returned to high camp. Sandy and Rick decided to try again for the top while everyone else descended the Schell Route. Their experience in reaching the summit of Nanga Parbat and getting back down took them very close to the edge. It's a dangerous place to go, but maybe those are the kinds of experiences we seek.

– STEVE SWENSON

CLIMBING TO FREEDOM: CLIMBS, CLIMBERS AND THE CLIMBING LIFE

Dick Dorworth. Western Eye Press, 2015. 242 pages. Paperback, $15.95.

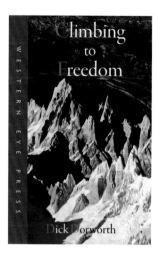

DICK DORWORTH'S BOOK starts in the year 1972 with the title story, "Climbing to Freedom." He's freshly estranged from his wife and year-old son, living in a 1965 VW, traveling between rocks and mountains in the western United States. Chuck Pratt walks up to his camper and gives Dorworth his first guiding job, a week in the Wind Rivers with Elizabeth. She's in her mid-40s, a mother of two, happily married, and she's hired a guide every summer to climb in a different mountain range. She's a model client—never complains, doesn't fight with the stone, shows an appreciation of the experience.

On a dark night, over a noodle feast, he asks Elizabeth how she got into climbing. Born an Austrian Jew in the late 1920s, at 14 she fled to France and was one of the fortunate few smuggled through the Pyrenees to Spain. A Basque from a small village guided the refugees in a dangerous nonstop journey through ice and snow over two days. Fifteen years later she returned to the Pyrenees, found the Basque guide, and hired him to retrace her journey. They took time to smell the roses and laze in meadows. Each year afterward she climbs for a week or two to be reminded what, exactly, her new life and freedom mean. The story ends with the author thanking Elizabeth for her example of not dwelling on the past, not dreaming of the future, but concentrating on the present moment, the only one that exists.

Dorworth writes about what matters. He climbs big rock faces, gets real cold, and has troubles at altitude, but rarely does this book linger on the route or the doldrums of climbing. Often he philosophizes, and there's some preaching too. He has his heroes and he writes them up, but he never gives them a free ride. He has no mercy on himself either.

In his late 60s, Dorworth climbs Gallatin Tower with 84-year-old Fred Beckey. The story screams with respect and admiration for the "King of Dirtbags." Fred keeps asking him if he should go to Mt. Assinboine or climb Lucky Streaks in Tuolumne. The author tells us: Beckey at 84 is not going to lead 5.10d or a climb of Assiniboine, but also points out that no one else that age is even thinking about it.

This book made me feel at home. I know many of the characters, and he got them right. The stories were easy to read again and again. Dorworth's meditations on skiing, climbing, the country, and the characters are the gospel of us mountain folk.

— JAMES SWEENEY

YOSEMITE IN THE FIFTIES: THE IRON AGE

Edited by Dean Fidelman and John Long. Patagonia Books, 2015. 176 pages. Hardcover, $60.

LAVISHLY ARRANGED AND EDITED by Valley legends Dean Fidelman and John Long, *Yosemite in the Fifties* is a heady blend of source photographs, pristinely documented archival objects—never have rusty pitons looked so polished—and short essays, many of which are trip reports

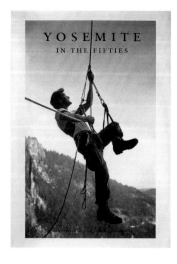

culled from the pages of the *Sierra Club Bulletin*. It's hard to imagine how a climber's coffee table could do better.

As the title makes plain, the focus here is the so-called "Iron Age" of Yosemite Valley climbing. This period, roughly bookended by the first ascents of Lost Arrow Spire in 1946 and the Nose in 1958, marked the birth of big-wall climbing in the United States. As Long puts it in his introduction, it was "that critical span of years found in any adventure or exploratory pursuit…where technology is a limiting factor." Steve Grossman's "The Tool Users," one of the more compelling essays, explains how John Salathé's improved 40/60 carbon vanadium steel pitons, along with his introduction of expansion bolts and prusik ascension, radically altered the scope of possible ascents on Sierra granite. These advancements, Grossman argues, were as much the creation of the place itself as they were of Salathé—purpose-built for local endeavors.

Being more a compendium than a history, the writing is mixed, both in source and in quality. Some climbers report their ascents briefly, some go on for pages. Some focus on the variety of gear utilized, others on how damn thirsty they were, with the cool, flowing waters of the Merced far below a frequent lament. Ranging from Ax Nelson's moralizing over the "false stimulus of alcohol" in the late '40s to Wayne Merry's wry appreciation of Warren Harding— "He trained on red jug wine for every climb that I can remember"—the collection also displays the wide range of beliefs and sentiments that drove some climbers up these cliffs, and, perhaps more often, the ideas they used as justification when they came back down.

In its photographic exhibition the book is meticulous and detailed, demonstrative of not only the full range of climbing technology of the time, but also the humane capabilities of documentary photography. Robbins' scrupulousness stands out in small details. Homemade shoulder pads for unthinkably petrifying rappel techniques. Hand-forged angles and knifeblades and D-rings. A gallon can of Dau's Good Styletone paint—for hauling water? Rubber soles nailed onto military surplus boots. For these wild explorers, such objects were both cutting-edge and normal, their everyday companions. For us, they're out of this world.

– ISAAC ZIZMAN

EXTREME EIGER: THE RACE TO CLIMB THE DIRECT ROUTE UP THE NORTH FACE OF THE EIGER

Peter and Leni Gillman. Simon & Schuster (U.K.), 2015. 394 pages. Paperback, $21.95.

Arguably, the U.K.'s most significant climbing never occurred on British soil. The southwest and east faces of Everest come to mind, as does the south face of Annapurna and many others. But the single most significant "U.K." ascent, in terms of everything that goes into a good story about climbing—the personalities, the equipment, the public misconceptions, the media circus—might just be the 1966 Eiger Direct route. Peter Gillman covered the climb for his newspaper, the *Daily Telegraph*. Chris Bonington took the photographs, and Gillman and Dougal Haston produced a book on the climb, *Eiger Direct*. Now, Gillman, with help from his

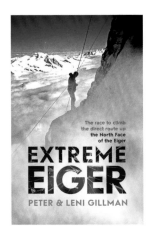

wife, Leni, has produced a more complete version of the story, *Extreme Eiger*.

The Gillmans' goal was to marry the separately crafted stories of the British-American team and the Germans—that is, to tell the entire story. The result is a fascinating investigation into what we know about the 1966 climb and what we thought we knew, plus a whole bunch of stuff we never would have guessed. Gillman brings decades of his own reflection about the ascent to this version of the story, explaining everything from the backgrounds of both teams' members to their spaghetti-like relationships on the mountain to their post-climb lives, deaths, and legacies.

This is not reporting in the "he-said, she-said" style. Rather, *Extreme Eiger* is proper narrative, a result of Gillman putting in the hours on the ground and deploying the care and consideration that accurate storytelling requires. In Switzerland, Gillman actually became part of the British-American team, simply because no one else was available as a base manager. For the new book, he interviewed all five German survivors of the climb, assisted by the writer and researcher Jochen Hemmleb.

Extreme Eiger is filled with anecdotes that cast the shadow of humanity across the story. It's almost as if the entire cast knew the play was going to be a monumental tragedy, but still they beavered on together. It is also an exploration of how stories change over time. "Our story also became an inquiry into the nature of human memory and how it influences narratives. Some of the stories we unearthed contradict the earlier published accounts—and sometimes each other," the couple writes. "We have presented these for the insights they offer into the nature of human experience as mediated by memory."

Any reader with the slightest interest in the Eiger, European climbing, the "stars" involved, British-American and German relationships, and the nature of mountain journalism will find *Extreme Eiger* the kind of story you can't put down. Bravo to Peter and Leni.

— CAMERON M. BURNS

TOO CLOSE TO GOD: SELECTED MOUNTAIN TALES

Jeff Long. Imaginary Mountain Surveyors (Canada), 2015. 290 pages. Paperback, $19.95.

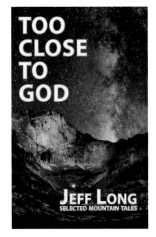

FOR FOUR DECADES Jeff Long has been on lead, moving climbing fiction from stock genres to serious and deep explorations into the human condition. This collection is a lens through which readers can view the growing maturity of climbing literature; the stories and excerpts arc from Long's seminal "The Soloist's Diary" (1974) to an excerpt, "When God Throws Angels Down," from his novel *The Wall* (2006).

Beyond the scope of history that this collection encompasses is the impressive diversity of the stories. "The

Virgins of Imst" is a realist's vision of the closed world of a remote valley in the Alps and of the intrusion of outsiders, while the excerpt from Long's novel *The Descent* hearkens to the madness found in *Heart of Darkness*. My favorite here is "In Gentle Combat with the Cold Wind," an honest recount of a climber picking up an old man hitchhiking on a wintry Halloween night. I love how this story hints at hauntings within the soul of alpine climbing.

These stories are firmly forged by Long's hands—hands that know cracks and cold. Descriptions of moves in high, remote places resonate exceptionally true. In this collection death also figures large. Without question death factors in climbing, in adventure, in life. It must. However, I must add a suggestion: Don't plow through Long's work in a mad dash. Jam these stories together and you will muddy their singular luminosities and finish feeling dark, missing the light the stories shine. The final excerpt, taken from *Angels of Light*, is particularly satisfying in the hope of its final lines.

Jeff Long writes in his introduction that he hopes his stories will serve as ink for future writers of mountain fiction. This echoes of Walt Whitman in "Poets to Come": "But you, a new brood, native, athletic…greater than before known, Arouse! Arouse, for you must justify me, you must answer." As Whitman shaped modern American poetry, so does Long shape modern climbing fiction. He calls to be read. And he calls for new young writers to explore, to go to the regions his stories and novels have mapped.

– MARK RODELL

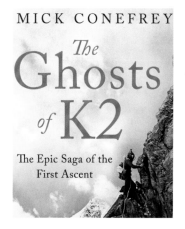

MICK CONEFREY

The Ghosts *of* K2

The Epic Saga of the First Ascent

THE GHOSTS OF K2: THE EPIC SAGA OF THE FIRST ASCENT

Mick Conefrey. One World Publications (U.K.), 2015. 336 pages. Hardcover, £20.

ACCOUNTS OF THE EARLY ATTEMPTS on K2 take up about two-thirds of this book. Then follows a skimpy narrative of the first ascent in 1954 by Achille Compagnoni and Lino Lacedelli, followed by 15 tedious pages on post-expeditionary squabbles about money and film credits. Finally, somewhat weary in the legs, the reader will come to the book's claim to be a revisionist account of this climb as it is now understood. Conefrey starts with Walter Bonatti's struggle to set the record straight and demolish the narrative advanced by expedition leader Ardito Desio (nicknamed Little Duce by the climbers) and Compagnoni, which lasted for more than 40 years as the official truth. To most of the world this epic brouhaha came to a close in 2004, when a three-man commission appointed by the Club Alpino Italiano trashed Desio/Compagnoni's misrepresentations and accepted in toto the scenario of the deeply aggrieved Bonatti.

Conefrey concedes there's zero appetite for opening up the debate today, but he believes that his insight and reconstructions are clever enough to be an excuse for yet another K2 book. Of these I've picked two items that are central to his project. First he tries to undermine the Australian Robert Marshall, Bonatti's paladin. In 1992 Marshall stumbled across a summit photograph in *Mountain World* (1953) that showed Compagnoni with an oxygen mask and Lacedelli with a ring of ice that indicated he'd just taken his off. The photo, which had not appeared in Desio's official story, strongly supported Bonatti's insistence that the oxygen he and the porter Mahdi had carried up to 26,000 feet was used all the way to the top. It marked a turning point in Bonatti's campaign of vindication. Conefrey makes a fuss about his discovery that this was not the first publication of the photo, as Marshall likely believed, but had appeared in Italian newspapers in the weeks following the ascent. This is a pretty feeble "aha!"

Second, Conefrey believes the extent of the summit duo's oxygen cylinder malfunction has been under-reported, which would substantiate Compagnoni's tale of running out of gas well before the summit. His aha! moment here is a "discovery" from photographs that one of the summit cylinders was an Italian make, not the superior German Dräger. But the discussion that follows cites no experts in oxygen technology and instead treats us to airy speculations from the Conefrey brain.

The book claims to be based on exclusive interviews with surviving team members and access to letters and diaries never before seen. But this is true where it matters least: the pre-1954 attempts. His Italian narrative fails to reflect deep contact with local sources. (I recall only one quote from his talk with Lacedelli.) Finally, there's the book's woeful graphics: a handful of half-page pencil sketches and no diagrams, maps or photographs.

— JOHN THACKRAY

ALONE ON THE WALL

Alex Honnold with David Roberts. W.W. Norton, 2015. 248 pages. Hardcover, $26.95.

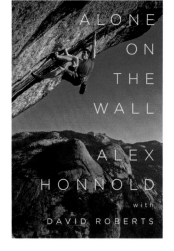

UNLESS YOU'VE BEEN LIVING under a rock for the last eight years, you've seen video evidence of Alex Honnold's perhaps otherwise unbelievable free soloing feats. Video is great medium for exhibiting his climbs. The language in a statement like, "Honnold free soloed Sendero Luminoso in two hours," reads like an abstraction, even if you know the route has 11 pitches of 5.12 and four of 5.11. But seeing the six-minute film is a visceral, mind-blowing experience. So if you've seen a Honnold film or two and read the list of his climbs, how much more is there to learn?

Quite a bit, as it turns out, in Honnold's somewhat reluctant autobiography, overseen by the sure eye of David Roberts. The book is constructed so it's always clear who is speaking, with Roberts' sections providing context and fleshing out the details, though Roberts obviously had a strong hand in Honnold's passages as well. Honnold is, as we might expect, as economical and precise in his descriptions of climbing as he is moving over stone.

Interestingly, Honnold has "a hard time remembering the details" of his childhood. It's almost as if he emerged from the shadows of a rock gym, fully formed as the badass who free soloed Moonlight Buttress when he was 22 years old. It takes alpine climbing to put some fear into him. On Mt. Dickey, Honnold, along with Freddie Wilkinson and Renan Ozturk, makes the fourth ascent of the route Roberts himself put up in 1974 with Ed Ward and Galen Rowell. "I guess I was surprised by how much shit—rock and snow and ice—is constantly falling down the faces," Honnold says. "Alpine climbing is dangerous."

One of the central tensions of Honnold's life is between his apparent contentedness to be alone and what he refers to repeatedly as "the gong show," which essentially means "other people." Participation in the gong show is how he makes a living: endorsements, sponsorships, and the media blitz, none of which appears to come naturally to him. He finds all this generates too much money and so he gives it away through his Honnold Foundation. He continues to live out of his van. I would hesitate to use the term "dirtbag" to describe his lifestyle—he's more of a climbing ascetic.

At some point I lost the sense of reading about someone whose ropelessness may eventually lead to his death and was reading instead about a super-motivated, extremely gifted climber who was doing very interesting things on big walls and in the mountains. I concur with Tommy Caldwell: "I really like Alex. I don't want him to die."

Roberts is the author of 24 books, most on mountaineering and exploration. He also has collaborated with Krakauer, Anker, Viesturs, and now Honnold. If there were a Nobel Prize for American Mountaineering Literature, Roberts would have it. The title of his Brad Washburn biography, *The Last of His Kind*, serves well as a self-descriptor: We're not likely see another writer of Roberts' literary talents and drive. In his collaboration with Honnold, the two writers have hitched their wagons to each other's brilliant stars.

– DAVID STEVENSON

SNOWBLIND: STORIES OF ALPINE OBSESSION

Daniel Arnold. Counterpoint, 2015. 296 pages. Paperback, $15.95.

FIRST-CENTURY ROMANS reminisced about the empire's expansion by watching gladiators in the Coliseum. Early 20th-century Americans relived their frontier on horseback and at Wild West shows. Similarly, at the start of the Industrial Revolution, Europeans climbed the Alps to satisfy a nostalgia for the challenges of wild nature. Climbing's come a long way since Whymper, but its perpetual risk still enforces a certain intellectualization of the sport revealed as literature. No other adventure activity offers such a diversity of creative nonfiction, novels, novellas, and collections of short stories.

Daniel Arnold's *Snowblind* is the best collection of short stories about alpinism I have read. It reads like a sort of choss fiction, not because it's bad, but because it's good—good in the way that early pulp generated today's media. I flew through its pages as I kept up with the protagonists racing up the alpine faces, ridges, walls, and couloirs of the world.

There are a lucky eight stories. From the Alps to Yosemite Valley, Alaska, Canada, the Karakoram, and the Andes, Arnold expends few words describing the views. Rather, he masterfully describes the colorful, twisted, archetypal characters most of us have roped ourselves to or maybe just watched as they climbed past.

Each tale is cast among a fistful of themes common to our ambition but freshly delivered. The responsibilities among partners that extend beyond a belay. The perpetual risk of death and harm. The nearly animate wind, cold, altitude, and falling debris. The suffering. The bad anchors and cramped bivouacs. The low-angle approach and retreat—both physical and emotional—as challenging as the vertical, technical climb. The drug-like addiction. The simple fact that "climbing is best when it's done." Our pervasive superstition. A useless glory none but ourselves can bestow.

If there is any complaint, it would be that while each chapter spins a different and engaging plot, the author's voice and style come through thickly, with each chapter reading as variant on the last. But isn't that alpine climbing anyway?

— ROMAN DIAL

DRAWN: THE ART OF ASCENT

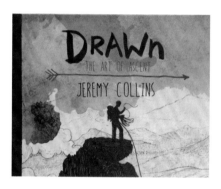

Jeremy Collins. Mountaineers Books, 2015. 176 pages. Hardcover, $24.95.

ON A CLIMB IN COLORADO, Jeremy Collins told his friend and mentor Jonny Copp about his dream "...to go in the four cardinal directions from home—West, East, South, North—to climb something spectacular and fill my sketchbooks with the experiences, the stories, the visions." Jonny slapped him on the back and said, "When do we get started?" Then Copp died in China, caught in an avalanche on Mt. Edgar with Micah Dash and Wade Johnson. So Collins did the only thing he could: took his notebook and a tiny bag of Copp's ashes, called the people he trusted, and got after it.

The result is a memoir-slash-climbing-story-slash-collection-of-art, the companion to a 42-minute film Collins wrote and directed. In words, drawings, and photos, he documents the places he goes to climb: Yosemite, the Yukon, Venezuela, and the Keketuohai Valley in Xinjiang, China. There are photos of remote villages, diary-like reflections, and quotes from John Muir, René Daumal, Cormac McCarthy, Simon Garfield. There's even Jonny Copp's last poem, written the night before he died. In the back of the book are tear-out postcards of Collins' art. It's an exploration of the journey, a meditation on art, a celebration of the challenge. It's an acknowledgment of the value of travel and the value of coming home.

At the end, Collins is humble. "I received no higher knowledge at the summit of those mountains, no cloth-diapered yogi squatting on a hemp carpet with nuggets of wisdom awaited curiosity.... There was only rock, water, air, and the way back down. There was, however, perspective—I promise you that. The only way to see from the summit is to go there. And in between the summits, we live and gain strength. In between summits, life happens."

— CHARLOTTE AUSTIN

EAST OF THE HIMALAYA: MOUNTAIN PEAK MAPS

Editor's note: Just before going to press we received a copy of East of the Himalaya, the extraordinary "life work" of Japanese explorer Tamotsu Nakamura. This 334-page, large-format hardcover details the little-climbed peaks of eastern Tibet, Sichuan, and Yunnan, China, in hundreds of photographs and maps, making it an indispensable reference. U.S. readers can order the book at Kinokuniya. com/us for $140, including shipping, or write to ibd@kinokuniya.co.jp for other options.

IN MEMORIAM

EDITED BY JAMES BENOIT

These articles have been edited for length. The complete tributes may be found at the AAJ website: publications.americanalpineclub.org. Online readers also will find an In Memoriam tribute to the late ski mountaineer and guide Peter Inglis.

TEX BOSSIER, 1943–2015

FLOYD ALLEN "TEX" BOSSIER, a key figure in Colorado climbing's "golden age," died in Saint-Joriez, France, on September 6, at the age of 71.

Tex was born far from the mountains in the oil town of Port Arthur, Texas, the youngest of four. When he was nine, his father, a pipefitter in a refinery, died of emphysema. The family had little money, but Tex was bright, curious, and unconventional. At Thomas Jefferson High School, the misfits tended to join the slide-rule club, whose members included Tex and and fellow student Janis Joplin.

After his freshman year, Tex's mother married a stonemason who did not like to stay long in one place. By the late 1950s the family was living in Colorado, where Tex learned to climb and earned a reputation for high-quality ascents in Rocky Mountain National Park, the Tetons, and elsewhere. His regular partners in the early 1960s included Bob Culp, Layton Kor, and Jim McCarthy. In 1961, at the age of 17, Tex and Culp established the route that is now considered the best climb on Hallett Peak: the Culp-Bossier. In desperate weather, he and Kor pioneered the Diagonal Direct on Longs Peak; together, they established several other new routes on Longs in the summer of 1963. Tex also took part in the 1979 Ama Dablam expedition led by Tom Frost.

In 1973, after a stint as an employment counselor for the state of California, Tex came to work for us in Ventura, first as manager of our retail store, then as one of the first sales reps for Chouinard Equipment and Patagonia (touring five states in a battered yellow Corolla), and eventually working as national sales manager. In 1987 he moved to Chamonix to help set up our business in Europe, and he lived the rest of his life in France.

We will remember Tex for his gifts as a climber and as a loyal and valuable colleague who helped build our company, but also for his capacity for friendship. He was a wonderful companion on the road or at dinner—his humor was wry, and he never told a bad story. Those of us lucky enough to be his friend will be forever grateful to have the cadence of Tex's voice, and several of his stories, carried within us like a tune, and will forever miss the chance to hear something new to add to the repertoire.

Some of the qualities that made Tex such a good salesman and friend—equanimity, psychological insight, patience—also made him a first-rate teacher. For a decade, while managing the store and repping for Patagonia, he also taught climbing in Santa Barbara and then in the unlikely places of Wichita and Tulsa, at the invitation of dealers there. Hundreds of his "graduates," including Phil Powers, CEO of the AAC, count Tex as one who taught them something to be valued. So does his son, Jack Miller, who survives him. So do we.

— YVON AND MALINDA CHOUINARD

ROBERT CRAIG, 1924–2015

In 1953, when Bob Craig joined the famed Anglo-American expedition to K2, most mountaineers in the United States were amateurs. Climbing mountains was a seasoning that complemented another life, in which they pursued their big dreams and goals. Bob exemplified this juxtaposition in spades.

Robert W. Craig was born in California in 1924. As he entered his teens, his family moved to Seattle, where, as a Boy Scout, Bob discovered mountains. He and a fellow student at Garfield High School, Fred Beckey, pulled off first ascents in the North Cascades, including classics like Nooksack Tower and the north face of Shuksan. A crowning achievement, in 1946, was their journey to the Stikine Icecap in Alaska, along with Cliff Schmidtke, to make first ascents of Kates Needle and Devils Thumb.

Bob garnered combined bachelor's degrees in biology and philosophy from the University of Washington, initial hints at the wide range of his intellectual curiosity. With the onset of World War II, Bob followed in his father's footsteps in the U.S. Navy, participating in the Pacific War. Once the radiation had cleared, he was among the first to view the total devastation of the Hiroshima bomb crater. This experience left a lasting imprint, influencing his later concerns about the use of nuclear energy. Following the war, Bob was completing a Ph.D. in philosophy at Columbia when the Korean War diverted him to the Army's Mountain and Cold Weather Command as a civilian adviser.

In the early 1950s, Bob landed in Aspen as #009 in the Colorado Professional Ski Instructors Association. Shortly before Bob and his teammates left for K2 in the summer of 1953, Walter Paepcke, the visionary behind the modern Aspen incarnation, said to him something to the effect of, "If you come back, let me know. I may have a job for you."

Beyond the climbing done by Bob and his K2 teammates, they will be best remembered as members of a unique band, "the brotherhood of the rope," as Charlie Houston described them. Charlie and Bob wrote a classic book, *K2: The Savage Mountain*, that tells the story of their epic retreat from K2 in full.

Bob Craig did come home from K2, and Paepcke got his man: Craig became the first director of the Aspen Institute. Over the next decade, he built the institute into a think tank where executives and others in leadership roles gathered to learn and exchange ideas. His proudest accomplishment was creating with physicists George Stranahan and Michael Cohen the Aspen Center for Physics. Bob married Carol Gallun and soon became a father of three: Kathleen, Jennifer, and Michael. He bought land in the valley north of Aspen with fantasies of becoming a gentleman rancher.

Bob and Carol separated in 1969 and divorced not long afterward. In 1974 mountains were back in his life. Bob and Pete Schoening led a contingent of young American climbers to participate in an international gathering of teams in the Soviet Pamirs. The title of Bob's book, *Storm and Sorrow in the High Pamirs*, captures the essence of this endeavor.

In 1975, Bob's friend Bob Maynard, then head of Keystone Resort, lured him out of the ranching/designer phase in his life to create the Keystone Center, which Craig ran until 1996, along the way creating the Keystone Symposia and the Keystone Science School. In 1983, Galen Rowell asked him to lead a team of top American climbers in an attempt to climb the true west ridge of Everest without the use of supplemental oxygen or Sherpa support. Though they did not succeed in summiting with this bold endeavor, I like to imagine that in the aftermath he was finally ripe for the most precious adventure of his life, a more than 30-year love affair with Terry McGrath, who became his wife in 1999. Witnessing the patience, caring, humor, and love of their relationship has been a special gift for many.

I never shared more than a metaphorical rope with Bob, but our friendship really blossomed during the Terry era, as we shared dreams and meddlesome fantasies, not least as members of the board of the Altitude Research Center Foundation at the University of Colorado Medical School—this was a precious opportunity for me to see the old pro in action and to take note. Bob Craig was a visionary. He also had the wisdom to take chewable bites of big challenges. He exemplified Harry Truman's statement, "You can accomplish anything in life, provided that you do not mind who gets the credit."

When missing Bob becomes too hard, in my mind's eye I conjure up one image that remained so precious a gift, even in his final days. That is, his smile. It starts with a captivating grin that is complemented by twinkling eyes and a slightly quixotic gaze, then it moves right to the top of his head as a feast of furrows, extending from ear to ear beneath thinning hair, magnifying what the mouth began. It's an unforgettable, whole-body experience.

– TOM HORNBEIN

JUSTIN GRIFFIN, 1980–2015

JUSTIN TYLER GRIFFIN wore many hats. He was an above-average athlete, a husband, a father, a son, a brother, and by profession a builder. He grew up in Kentucky and graduated college in South Carolina, and then spent a few years traveling around the globe, climbing, and perfecting his skills as a carpenter. In 2003, Justin moved west and landed in Pinedale, Wyoming, where he met his wife to be, Laura Love, a.k.a. Fats. After living in northern California and Sun Valley, Idaho, the two moved to Bozeman, Montana, in 2006, and I had the privilege of becoming Justin's friend.

I was immediately drawn to his voracious appetite for climbing and endless energy. He frequently climbed in Clarks Fork Canyon, repeating many of the hardest rock routes while contributing a handful of his own. Justin was most fulfilled by huge days that leave one haggard for a week afterward. One of his ideas was to link three of Clarks Fork's long free routes in a day, adding up to about 3,000 feet of climbing and rappelling. As soon as we had finished, on our second attempt, Justin was already talking about adding another climb to the enchainment.

In 2009, Justin and Fats were married on the western slope of the Bridger Mountains in Bozeman. Going back to school at Montana State University, he completed four years of the architecture program and received a drafting degree in 2010. He started his own design/build construction company called Griffin Creations. Three of the many building projects he completed were awarded beautification awards by the city of Bozeman.

After many seasons of ice climbing in Hyalite Canyon, Justin became increasingly interested in alpine climbing. It was in his nature to constantly push his boundaries as a climber. He connected with Kyle Dempster, and the two of them forged a strong climbing friendship. On one trip to Alaska they made two separate ascents of the north buttress of Mt. Hunter, one via French Route and the second by Wall of Shadows. In December 2014, Kyle and Justin climbed Wild Thing on Mt. Chephren in the Canadian Rockies in 17 hours and 25 minutes, car to car.

For Justin, 2014 and 2015 were big years. Most exciting was the birth of his baby girl, Alice Maple Griffin—a girl with a smile and energy just like her dad's. Soon after this, Justin and Fats bought a horse farm called Tri-H Stables, where Fats could expand her business of training horses. Justin had plans to build a shop on the property. In 2015, he and Skiy DeTray won two AAC grants for an expedition to Nepal. In the fall, after two weeks of volunteer work, helping to rebuild the Khumbu Climbing Center, the two climbed a new line up the northeast buttress of Tawoche (*see Climbs and Expeditions*). Toward the end of the descent from this difficult climb, unroped, Justin lost his footing on a section of ice and fell.

Justin didn't go to Nepal to die—he had lots to live for and he knew it. He went on that expedition because that's how he was wired. He needed to squeeze every drop out of the life he was living. Fats saw that and loved him for it. We all loved him for it. Justin Griffin was an inspiration. Those of us who knew him are thankful for what he has left us with.

– WHIT MAGRO

DEAN POTTER, 1972–2015

DEAN POTTER is one of the few people in sports history to have pushed the limits in multiple, widely disparate disciplines. Yet he saw his pursuits as arts and not as sport—himself as an artist not an athlete. He was a climber before the gym era, drawn to climbing by a love of the outdoors and a pursuit of adventure. It wasn't about the physical act, and certainly not about the ratings or any other metrics applied to climbing. It seemed to be an inward journey or, as he often described it, a journey toward his fears.

We shared many of the same experiences, but they seemed to originate from wildly different motivations. When Dean soloed he was right on the edge and seemed to thrive there. A video of Dean free soloing Heaven (5.12d in Yosemite Valley) strikingly reveals that

raw emotion: barely contained fear, or maybe just intense focus, or who knows what, really, as he sits at the base preparing. And then uncontainable joy when he tops out. Only he knows what he experienced for the 16 or so moves he made up that wildly overhanging crack.

And that's probably the essence of Dean: doing things that no one else considered possible, experiencing things that no one had before and may never again. Dean authored extremely difficult crack climbs across the Utah desert and highball boulder problems in the Valley like the Wizard, an insane-looking jump start that never really gets attempted because it's just too daunting. At the same time he was doing some of the longest wing-suit flights in the world and walking outrageous highlines, sometimes free solo, sometimes with a BASE rig, but always in the most beautiful places.

This speaks toward his motivations: Dean was willing to take risks and pursue seemingly crazy goals because they were beautiful. He was the one who thought up the *Moonwalk*, an incredible short film by Reel Water Productions and Mikey Schaefer of Dean free soloing a highline on the summit of Cathedral Peak with an enormous full moon as his backdrop. The physical beauty of the places he performed inspired him to push further.

And yet he was also spurred by competition or a desire to be first—the same mundane things that motivate most people. He spoke often of trying to overcome his ego, yet it clearly was at play as he tried to break speed records or do first ascents. That competitive side seemed to come out a lot around Hans Florine, who he compared to an annoying dog humping his leg in the film *Race for the Nose*. They traded speed records on the Nose several times, and when Dean heard that Hans was aiming to be the first person to link up Half Dome and the Nose, he flew back to Yosemite and started the night before, so he could finish the enchainment first.

Dean was the first person to link the three biggest walls in Yosemite, and at various times held many of the most coveted speed records in the Valley. But his exploits in Patagonia make the Yosemite climbs look small, including soloing the Compressor Route on Cerro Torre and a new link-up on Fitz Roy in a single season. Last May, less than two weeks before his unfortunate death in a wing-suit flying accident in Yosemite, he set the car-to-car speed record for running up Half Dome. It's worth remarking how impressive it is for a 43-year-old alpinist/aerialist/highliner to set a trail-running record on an objective as high-profile as this.

Dean's biggest contribution to his arts might be the way he helped to subtly rewrite what's considered normal. Speed climbing, simul-climbing, daisy soloing, even the big Yosemite link-ups are now much more common, partially as a result of his influence. Movies like *Masters of Stone 5* and *Fly or Die* exposed people to ways of climbing that would have seemed insane if they weren't seeing them happen before their eyes.

Dean learned from the climbing community and owed a lot to those who came before him. And then he climbed toward his fears and changed the perception of what was possible.

– ALEX HONNOLD

ALEXANDER RUCHKIN, 1963–2015

ALEXANDER "SASHA" RUCHKIN, along with his climbing partner, Vyacheslav Ivanov, died while attempting a new route on the south face of Huandoy Sur (6,160m) in Peru. Sasha was born in Kazakhstan, grew up and studied in Ukraine, and later lived in Kazakhstan and Russia. Fusing the best traditions of Soviet mountaineering and contemporary trends, he was a leader not only of Russian mountaineering but also world climbing.

Over the years he climbed classic routes in the Pamir, Tien Shan, Alps, and Patagonia, including new routes up the north faces of Ak-Su North and Svobodnaya Korea (Free Korea) in Kyrgyzstan, the Troll Wall in Norway, Great Sail Peak on Baffin Island, and in the Minya Konka range in China. One of his most important achievements undoubtedly was the first ascent of the north face of Jannu in Nepal (*AAJ 2005*). Although Jannu and other ascents were completed with large teams, in recent years Alexander's true calling card became his two-person first ascents. These included such climbs as Kusum Kanguru in Nepal, Gongga North in China, and the Shark's Tooth in Greenland. At 51, he continued going to the mountains with youthful enthusiasm and passion.

I was very fortunate not only to know Alexander but also to participate in trips and expeditions, to climb with him and just talk. He was very positive, easy-going, an absolutely agreeable friend, and at the same time a very reliable partner. Sasha is survived by his wife, son, and daughter. It is so painful to see how they endure this tragedy.

– VALERY ROZOV

ROBERT SCHALLER JR., 1934–2014

ROBERT T. SCHALLER JR., M.D., died of pneumonia on December 7, 2014, surrounded by family. He was a leading pediatric surgeon in the Seattle area until arthritis forced him to give up operating, but he continued to teach.

Jane Green and Rob Schaller met and married at Harvard Medical School in 1958. That fall, Jane took Rob on his first mountain trip, to the White Mountains, where Jane had climbed as a camp counselor. In 1960 they chose Seattle for their internships, to go where the big mountains were. They enrolled in the climbing course at the University of Washington led by Pete Schoening, including a climb of Mt. Rainier. Rob was a miler, a marathoner, had captained the Yale track team, and was set for the challenges of mountaineering.

I first climbed with him in May 1968. Dee Molenaar and Lee Nelson had organized the first early season climb of Liberty Ridge. The climb was a delight, save for a storm and unplanned bivouac on Columbia Crest. A clear dawn and downhill run to Camp Schurman restored our spirits. That year, Rob was in the final stretch of his residency in general surgery and I was completing my thesis at the university. When conditions were good and he had his 12

hours off, I would come by at 6 a.m. and we would climb nearby peaks. We often carried a rope but seldom used it, pleased to find enjoyable ways to the summits. Once, early in the season on Forbidden Peak, the route was snowed up and there weren't any anchor points. Two-thirds of the way to the north ridge, we looked at each other and turned back. Why risk spoiling such a beautiful day? Rob was the perfect companion—whether going up, pinned down in a storm, or turning back.

In 1965, Rob was recruited by the CIA as a climbing doctor for a joint U.S.–Indian effort to place a listening device on an Indian peak with a view toward missile tests in China. The monsoon forced retreat and the device was left high on Nanda Devi. The 1966 recovery team included Rob, Barry Corbet, and Tom Frost, and Rob made the first solo ascent of the peak—part of a then-secret operation. Climber and lawyer Jim McCarthy said this "might well have been the singular [climbing] achievement of the '60s, if it had been known."

Rob joined the 1975 and 1978 expeditions to the northwest ridge of K2, and after Jim Wickwire bivouacked at 27,700 feet while descending from the summit, he survived thanks to exceptional care by Rob. Accounts of these expeditions tell of the care Rob provided to villagers, porters, and climbers. They also speak of his ironing out differences between team members to hold the expeditions together.

In 1996, Norm Breslow organized a trek to Mera Peak in Nepal, and I called to see if Rob might join us. Four of us made a 23-day trek early in the post-monsoon season. There were few other trekkers, and high on Mera we were wading through virgin snow. I was reminded of trips with Rob in the Cascades—everything was fresh and delightful. There was no better person with whom to share a pleasant day or to shiver alongside through a cold bivouac or to pull you through in a desperate spot. Those with whom Rob shared his gifts will count themselves lucky and remember him for the rest of their lives.

– PETER RENZ

LEON RUSSELL "PETE" SINCLAIR, 1935–2015

PETE SINCLAIR passed away due to complications of Alzheimer's disease in Olympia, Washington, on November 28, 2015. In Pete's passing we lost an important participant in and chronicler of the American mountaineering scene. Pete was introduced to climbing in his early undergraduate years at Dartmouth College, where he was a contemporary of Barry Corbet and Jake Breitenbach. In 1959 he made the breakthrough first ascent of the West Rib of the south face of Denali with Corbet, Breitenbach, and Bill Buckingham. Upon returning to Wyoming, he became a seasonal ranger in Grand Teton National Park and then ran the Jenny Lake mountain rescue team, one of the country's finest, from 1960 to 1967. Pete's pioneering climbs in the Tetons included first ascents of the northwest face of Thor Peak and the north face of Mt. Moran, as well as a new variation on the north face of the Grand Teton.

In 1962, Pete enrolled at the University of Wyoming, where he earned a B.A. in English and philosophy; a few years later he earned a Ph.D. in English from the University of Washington. He held faculty positions at the University of Wyoming from 1969 to 1971, and at Evergreen State College in Olympia from 1971 to 1998.

During summers at Jenny Lake, Pete supervised a number of dramatic rescues, which later formed the backbone of his first book, *We Aspired: The Last Innocent Americans* (1993). The book was short-listed for the Boardman Tasker Prize for mountaineering literature. One chapter became the basis for the film *The Grand Rescue*, about a gripping 1967 rescue on the north face of the Grand Teton, for which the rescue team received the Department of Interior's Valor Award.

In his second book, *Thinking Out Loud Through the American West* (1999), Pete reflected on what it meant to live in the West and the values of wilderness. In addition to climbing, Pete was an avid sailor and sea kayaker, and some of his nautical adventures are chronicled in a third book, *Somewhat Troubled Waters* (2002).

In 1968, Pete partnered with Barry Corbet to form Jackson Hole Mountain Guides, where he served as chief guide for the first two years of operation. Pete was always searching for new and unique methods for the teaching of literature, writing, and climbing. In the final two decades of his life, Pete enjoyed old friends, easy climbs in the Tetons and Bighorns, and canyon adventures in the Cedar Mesa area of Utah.

— RAY JACQUOT, RICK REESE, AND BOB IRVINE

DOUG TOMPKINS, 1943–2015

DOUG TOMPKINS was my friend for almost 60 years. We first met while climbing in the Shawangunks of New York. He was only 15 and had either dropped out or been kicked out of school. In any case, he probably thought the teachers had nothing important to teach him. If you want to understand the entrepreneur, study the juvenile delinquent. That was Doug.

Over the years, I taught him to surf. He taught me to kayak. We learned to climb mountains together. We boldly broke the rules of business and made it work. Doug didn't like anyone telling him what to do, but he didn't hesitate in lecturing others.

Doug was good at many "do" sports: skiing, fencing, tennis, squash and, of course, climbing. Together we did an early ascent of the Salathé Wall of El Capitan, which, at the time, was considered one of the most difficult rock climbs in the world. We climbed in Canada, Scotland in winter, the Karakoram, Bhutan, Antarctica, and, of course, Patagonia, where we climbed Fitz Roy. We fell in love with the area, and later I built a company around that mysterious name and Doug spent a fortune to protect its natural beauty.

From so many days living among mountains and rivers, we expanded our love of

nature to include the whole of this lovely planet. Doug was especially influenced by the Norwegian climber Arne Næss and his philosophy of Deep Ecology. Early on, we recognized that we humans were destroying our home planet, and that each of us, in our own way, was responsible to protect and restore the wild nature that we loved.

We were always looking for an adventure, but there is no possibility of adventure without risk. Sometimes you have to purposely leave a crack open in the door—for the opportunity of a good fight or possible serendipity. We loved life and were not afraid of death, but did not wish to die. On a Do-Boys kayaking trip to the Russian Far East, our only maps went flying out the window of the helicopter. We all exchanged high-fives. We were on our way to an adventure!

Another time we made the first descent of the Maipo River outside of Santiago. We eddied out before a blind turn and Doug got out to scout. Two soldiers came up from behind, with guns pointed, and demanded to see his papers. Basically, he told them to "Get stuffed!" ran down the hill, jumped into his boat, and took off around the bend. Later we found out the river flowed through the dictator Augusto Pinochet's summer grounds.

On our fateful trip last December, I was a little shocked to see how frail the old fig looked. But then he probably thought the same of me. Doug was dressed in his signature pressed chinos, his Brooks Brothers shirt, a light wool sweater, and a light rain jacket. This was the same outfit he wore to climb the last mountain we did together, Cerro Kristine, named for his wife. On the lake we ran into a perfect trap: a 40-knot wind at our back and an equally strong wind from the side, making for large, confused waves. We could not miss even one paddle stroke for fear of going over. The boys made a valiant effort, but we lost Doug. We lost the Chief.

By his actions, Doug became the teacher we all needed—and he still is.

– YVON CHOUINARD

ANDY TYSON, 1968–2015

IN 2006, on a climbing expedition to China, Andy Tyson and his team found themselves on the wrong side of a raging river 80 miles from their objective. Not trusting their driver, who insisted the team needed to ford the river, Andy's expedition mates convinced him to get behind the wheel. They didn't pick Andy for his driving skills, but because they believed there was no better person to overcome any problem or challenge, regardless of what it might be. And Andy proved them right. He found a bridge upstream.

Andrew David Tyson, 46, died in a small-plane crash on April 10 in central Idaho. Tyson had flown into the area with a team from Creative Energies, a renewable energy company that he co-founded in 2001, to begin work at a remote ranch. Two other Creative Energies employees, Rusty Cheney and AJ Linnell, and the pilot, John Short, also were killed.

Born in Mercersburg, Pennsylvania, Andy loved the outdoors from an early age. In high school Andy joined the outing club and began boating, climbing, and hiking. After college, an extended trip to Australia, and crewing on a sailing voyage across the Atlantic, Andy went west in 1992. He attended an instructors' course with the National Outdoor Leadership School in Lander and soon began leading rock climbing, mountaineering, sailing, hiking, and caving courses throughout North America and in India and Patagonia. During his time at NOLS, Andy met his beloved wife, Molly Loomis Tyson, who became his partner in adventure. The pair would leave their home and dog, Kali, in Teton Valley, Idaho, to travel the world—climbing, boating, skiing, exploring, and writing about their experiences.

In addition to working for NOLS, Andy spent 25 years guiding for Exum, Alpine Ascents International (where he worked as expedition manager), and Antarctic Logistics and Expeditions. Recent personal expeditions included a trip to the Genyen Massif in China, where he and Molly completed first ascents of several peaks, and to Myanmar, in 2013, when he led an American-Burmese team that did the first ascent of Gamlang Razi, possibly Southeast Asia's highest peak. He is the author of two how-to books on climbing and mountaineering: *Climbing Self Rescue* (with Molly Loomis) and *Glacier Mountaineering* (with Mike Clelland).

Andy was known for his physical strength, stamina, grit, and determination, but more importantly to his friends and family, he was loved for his kindness, curiosity, energy, and willingness to try whatever was thrown at him. He could jump off the couch and run 20-plus miles through the mountains, float a singletrack, make a difficult climb look easy, ski a steep couloir, longboard twisty roads, and build or fix just about anything. Yet he carried himself with humility and relished in others' successes. He loved his family, community, and dog tremendously, and often spoke of how lucky he was to live in such a place among such people.

– MOLLY ABSOLON

BELA GABOR VADASZ, 1953–2015

MOUNTAIN GUIDE Bela Vadasz, of Truckee, California, passed away on September 15 at age 62. He is survived by Mimi Maki Vadasz, co-founder and director of Alpine Skills International, and his grown sons Tobin and Logan. Bela escaped the communist takeover of Hungary with his parents in 1956 and emigrated to the United States, ultimately settling in San Francisco. His mountain-loving parents introduced him to the Sierra Nevada in all seasons at a young age. Bela met Mimi while studying outdoor education at San Francisco State University. The couple climbed and skied together, married, and in 1979 formed Alpine Skills International

(ASI). They converted a dilapidated building on Donner Pass into the European hut–inspired Donner Spitz Hütte, from which ASI operated for 25 years.

Among his personal climbing and skiing achievements, Bela made the first free-heel descents of Denali and the V-Notch couloir in the Palisades. With Mimi, he made the first American ascent of the long and complex Peuterey Integrale on Mont Blanc in 1988. In 1990, Bela skied from 22,000 feet on Makalu in the Nepal Himalaya. He also was an avid surfer and musician his entire life.

It was guiding and teaching, however, that meant the most to Bela. In his foreword to Lou Dawson's *Wild Snow*, Bela remembered how, as a boy, he kept the great mountaineering guidebooks and manuals by his bedside and read himself to sleep with stories of first ascents and descents. "As my eyes grew heavy, I would begin to dream myself into those pictures and stories, and beyond, into the adventures I hoped I would someday lead." Bela taught thousands of climbers and skiers not only to be competent mountaineers but also to love the mountains and carry that spirit with them in all aspects of their lives.

Bela was among the leaders of the American Mountain Guides Association (AMGA), pushing for and designing a training program for international guide certification. In 1997, he was among the first American guides to earn the international IFMGA pin. In 2008, Bela received the AMGA's Lifetime Achievement Award for his vast contributions to the guiding profession. He also posthumously received the AMGA President's Award. Under his direction, ASI taught mountaineering skills to Marine Corps and special operations forces for over 20 years. For all his mountain prowess, Bela will be most remembered for his spirit and his passion, and for sharing both with others.

– DAVID RIGGS

DOUG WALKER, 1950–2015

AAC President Doug Walker was killed on December 31, 2015, by an avalanche on Granite Mountain in the Cascades. He was a climber, entrepreneur, philanthropist, devoted husband, and father. His death leaves a huge hole in many hearts.

Doug was born in South Carolina, and he learned his deep love for wild places at his family's mountain cabin. He and his wife, Maggie, came to Seattle in 1972, where he attended graduate school in mathematics and the Cascades fueled his interest in climbing.

In 1981, Doug and his partners started the computer software company Walker, Richer & Quinn (WRQ). Over 25 years it grew to more than 600 employees. Doug was proud of creating a company that many former employees still call "the best place I ever worked."

After retiring from the software business, Doug threw himself into philanthropy and nonprofit leadership. He was board president of the AAC, a past chair of the REI board and the

Wilderness Society governing council, and served on the Sierra Club Foundation Board. In Seattle he co-founded Social Venture Partners and was former board chair of the Fred Hutchinson Cancer Research Center.

Doug strongly believed that to ensure protection of our wild lands the conservation movement needed to attract younger, more diverse members. His personal crusade to get everyone he met outdoors meant not just youngsters from the climbing gym but also new employees at his company, fellow board members from his philanthropic endeavors, and his daughter Kina. He had an uncanny ability to pick a climb that was a stretch for his partners and challenge them to step up to their next level.

Doug volunteered for the Seattle YMCA's Bold & Gold program to teach rock climbing and soon discovered that permit issues on federal lands made it impossible for the Y to take inner-city kids to local crags, whereas private school programs were able to do so. This issue of access and equity became Doug's major focus, and he worked tirelessly on this problem for many years. One result was announced at the AAC's national banquet, just two months after his death, when Doug's good friend, Secretary of the Interior Sally Jewell, announced the "Walker Permit." This order expedites the permit process to allow disadvantaged and under-resourced youth to access America's public lands and waters. The web of people and organizations that Doug inspired carry on his access work.

Doug climbed iconic mountains around the world, such as the Matterhorn and Ama Dablam, and he loved road trips to the Bugaboos and the Winds, where he could move quickly and competently over mixed terrain. After retiring he worked hard on his rock climbing skills, both in and out of the gym. It pleased him to find that even in his late 50s he could improve. Yet he was more driven by a sense of adventure than by a desire to do ever more difficult climbs. Just as he loved enlisting people in his business and philanthropic projects, he truly loved introducing people to the mountains.

– CRAIG MCKIBBEN

NECROLOGY

In addition to those covered above, AAC members who passed away in 2015 included:

RICHARD D. BASS	MARISA GIRAWONG	RODNEY KORICH
ANDREW BOWER	DAVID HULTING	ARTHUR G. MAKI JR.
MATTHEW DAVIS	PETER INGLIS	JOSEPH E. MURPHY JR.
RUSSELL FAURE-BRAC	JON Z. INSKEEP	BILLY ROOS
KAYAH GAYDISH	RYAN JENNINGS	THOMAS TAPLIN

INDEX

COMPILED BY **RALPH FERRARA & EVE TALLMAN**

Mountains are listed by their official names. Ranges, geographic locations, and maps are also indexed. Unnamed peaks (eg. Peak 2,340) are listed under P. Abbreviations are used for the following: Cordillera: C.; Mountains: Mts.; National Park: Nat'l Park; Obituary: obit. Main personnel and expedition leaders are listed for major articles and for Climbs & Expeditions. Indexed photographs are listed in bold type.

the AMERICAN ALPINE club

AAJ

INTERNATIONAL GRADE COMPARISON CHART

SERIOUSNESS RATING:

These often modify technical grades when protection is difficult

R: Poor protection with potential for a long fall and some injury

X: A fall would likely result in serious injury or death

YDS=Yosemite Decimal System
UIAA=Union Internationale des Associations D'Alpinisme
FR=France/Sport
AUS=Australia
Sax=Saxony
CIS=Commonwealth of Independent States/Russia
SCA=Scandinavia
BRA=Brazil
UK=United Kingdom

Note: *All conversions are approximate. Search "International Grade Comparison Chart" at the AAJ website for further explanation of commitment grades and waterfall Ice/ mixed grades.*

YDS	UIAA	FR	AUS	SAX	CIS	SCA	BRA	UK (tech)	UK (adj)
5.2	II	1	10	II	III	3			D
5.3	III	2	11	III	III+	3+			D
5.4	IV- / IV	3	12		IV-	4			VD
5.5	IV+		13		IV	4+			S
5.6	V-	4	14		IV+	5-		4a	HS
5.7	V / V+		15	VIIa		5		4b	VS
5.8	VI-	5a	16	VIIb	V-	5+	4 / 4+	4c	HVS
5.9	VI	5b	17	VIIc		6-	5 / 5+	5a	E1
5.10a	VI+	5c	18	VIIIa	V	6	6a	5b	E2
5.10b		6a							
5.10c	VII-	6a+	19	VIIIb		6+	6b		
5.10d	VII	6b		VIIIc	V+	7-	6c		E3
5.11a	VII+	6b+	20	IXa			7a	5c	
5.11b	VIII-	6c	21	IXb		7	7b		
5.11c		6c+	22		VI-	7+	7c		E4
5.11d	VIII	7a	23	IXc				6a	
5.12a	VIII+	7a+	24			8-	8a		E5
5.12b		7b	25	Xa	VI	8	8b		
5.12c	IX-	7b+	26	Xb		8+	8c		
5.12d	IX	7c	27				9a	6b	E6
5.13a	IX+	7c+	28	Xc		9-	9b		
5.13b		8a	29				9c		
5.13c	X-	8a+	30	XIa		9	10a	6c	E7
5.13d	X	8b	31		VI+		10b		
5.14a		8b+	32	XIb			10c	7a	E8
5.14b	X+	8c	33			9+	11a		
5.14c	XI-	8c+	34	XIc			11b		E9
5.14d	XI	9a	35				11c	7b	
5.15a	XI+	9a+	36	XIIa		10	12a		E10
5.15b	XII-	9b	37		VII		12b		E11
5.15c	XII	9b+	38	XIIb			12c		